エスカフローネ

ESCAFLOWNE

3

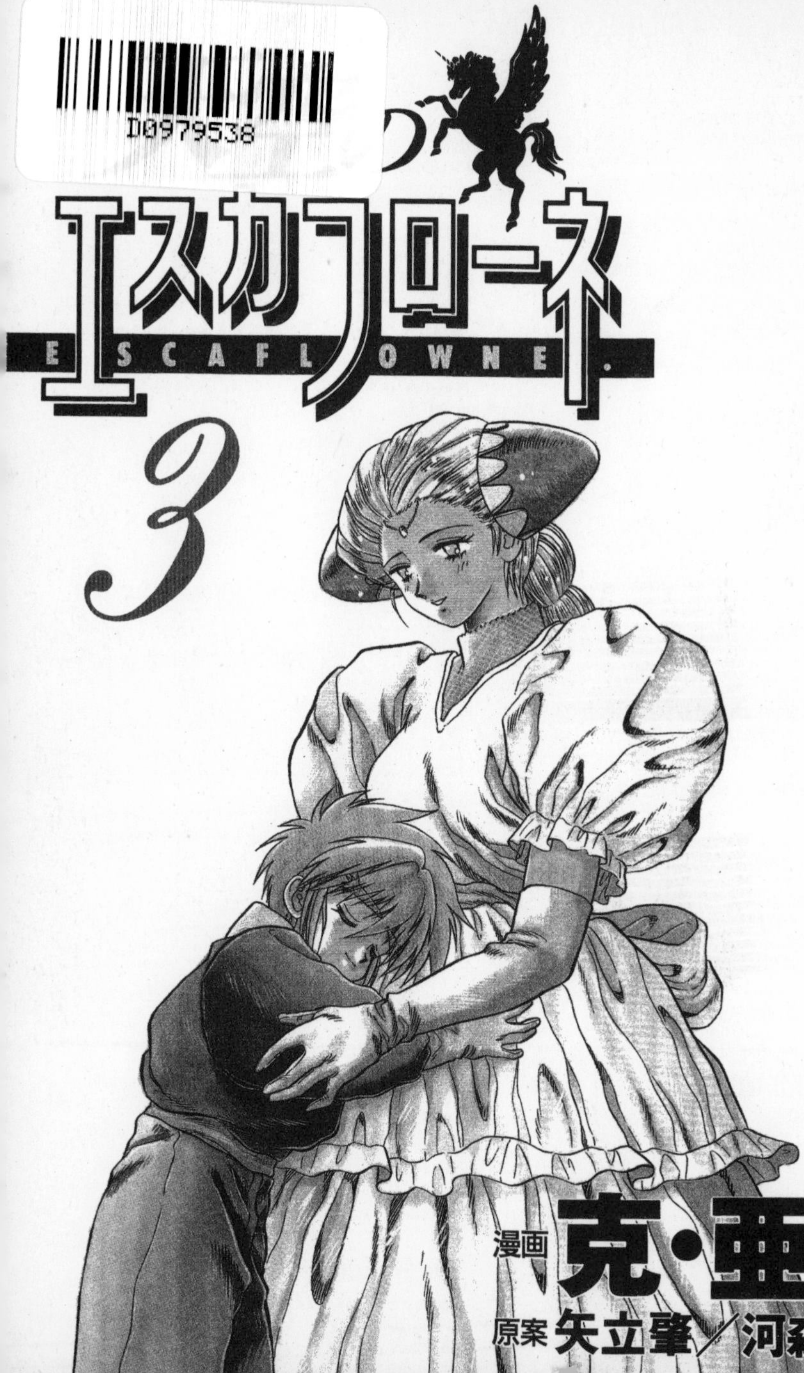

漫画 克・亜樹

原案 矢立肇／河森正

(スタジオ

ALSO AVAILABLE FROM TOKYOPOP

THE · VISION · OF
ESCAFLOWNE

Volume 3

By

KATSU AKI

Original concept
by
HAJIME YATATE
SHOJI KAWAMORI
(STUDIO NUE)

LOS ANGELES · TOKYO · LONDON

Translator - Jeremiah Bourque
English Adaptation - Lianne Sentar
Associate Editor - Tim Beedle
Copy Editor - Bryce P. Coleman
Retouch and Lettering - Eric Botero
Cover Layout - Raymond Makowski

Editor - Rob Tokar
Managing Editor - Jill Freshney
Production Coordinator - Antonio DePietro
Production Manager - Jennifer Miller
Art Director - Matt Alford
Editorial Director - Jeremy Ross
VP of Production - Ron Klamert
President & C.O.O. - John Parker
Publisher & C.E.O. - Stuart Levy

Email: editor@TOKYOPOP.com
Come visit us online at www.TOKYOPOP.com

A  Manga

TOKYOPOP Inc.
5900 Wilshire Blvd. Suite 2000
Los Angeles, CA 90036

THE VISION OF ESCAFLOWNE VOLUME 3

THE VISION OF ESCAFLOWNE volume 3 © SUNRISE•TV TOKYO ©KATSU AKI 1995.
First published in Japan in 1995 by KADOKAWA SHOTEN PUBLISHING, CO., LTD., Tokyo.
English translation rights arranged with KADOKAWA SHOTEN PUBLISHING CO., LTD., Tokyo
through TUTTLE-MORI AGENCY, INC., Tokyo.
English text copyright ©2003 TOKYOPOP Inc.

ISBN: 1-59182-368-4

First TOKYOPOP printing: November 2003

10 9 8 7 6 5 4 3 2 1
Printed in the USA

THE · VISION · OF
ESCAFLOWNE

INTRODUCTION

"Escaflowne" began as a story in the minds of Hajime Yadate and Shoji Kawamori, two brilliant creators who planned Hitomi's epic tale to appear as an animated television series. Whereas most anime series begin as manga, Escaflowne's two manga series were built off the ideas for the anime: a shojo, or "girls" manga consisting of two volumes, and a shonen, or "boys" manga, the longer of the two series and the one you are currently reading. This version of the Escaflowne tale is quite different from the anime, featuring more action, tweaked character designs, and an altered story. The appeal of Escaflowne has always crossed gender lines, and even this "boys" version of the manga has elements that will appeal to everyone, but it will be difficult to compare this comic to the television series--it's quite different. That being said, please sit back, relax, and enjoy the tale of Escaflowne like you've never seen it before.

Special thanks to Egan Loo and his Escaflowne Compendium (http://www.anime.net/escaflowne/).

ESCAFLOWNE VOL. 3
CONTENTS

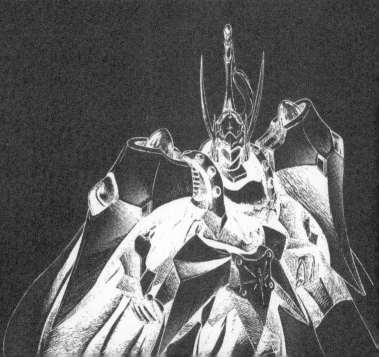

The Story Thus Far

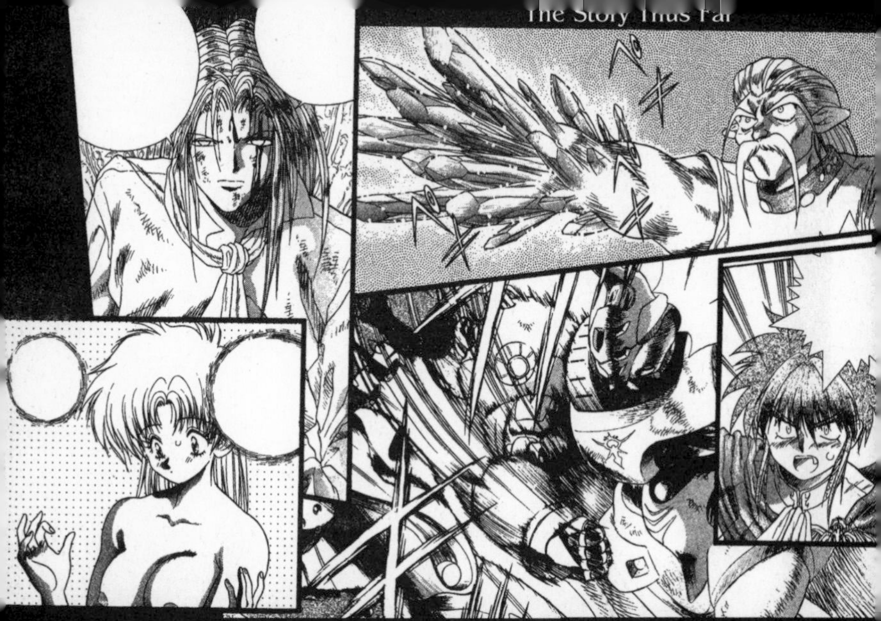

Hitomi Hoshino's interest in fortune-telling was both simple and innocent--until she started having strange, recurring visions of a prince and a jewel. During a routine reading, Hitomi's soul was snatched from her body and she found herself in the land of Gaea—the place she had seen in her visions—and in a strange body that looks like her own but is formed from the mysterious crystal known as Energist.

The prince from her dreams turned out to be a rash, hot-headed, and rather short teenager named Van. The magic of his country (Fanelia) selected Hitomi to be the Energist power of their mechanical god Escaflowne. As Van tried to push Hitomi into her new role as robot fuel, Fanelia was attacked by the aggressive Zaibach Empire. Hitomi managed to power Escaflowne to save her life an Van's, but the Zaibach warrior Dilandau flattened Fanelia, killed Captain Balgus, and kidnapped Queen Escalina.

During some dangerous run-ins with Zaibach and Dilandau, Hitomi and Van gained the aid of th Asturian knight Allen Schezar. Allen accompanied them on a dangerous journey to the Holy Spring Ubdo where Elder Lagusu taught Hitomi more about her abilities. After returning to Asturia, Hitomi was kidnapped by Shian, a Fanelian survivor who blamed Van for their country's fate. Agreeing to join forces, Van, Shian, and Hitomi took Escaflowne underwater to infiltrate Zaibach through one of its waste disposal pipes. Unfortunately, the pipes close much more quickly than they expected...

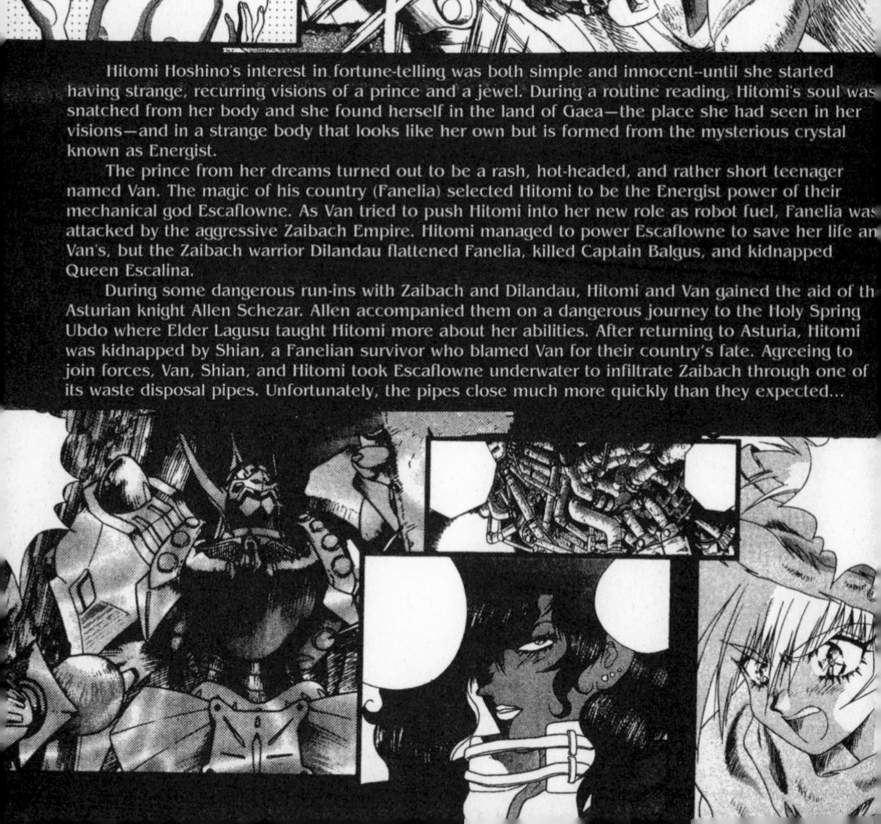

CHARACTER INTRODUCTIONS

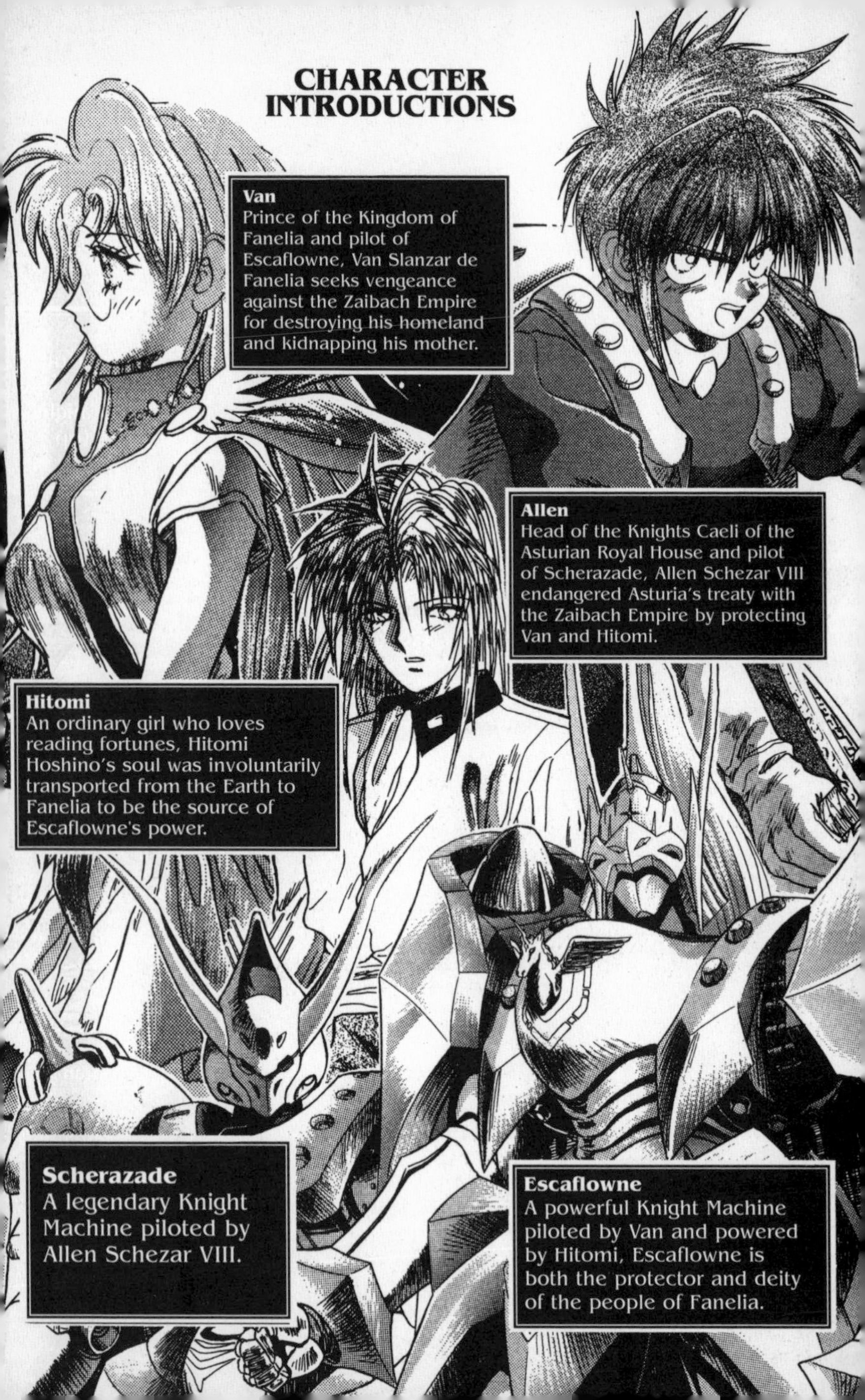
Van
Prince of the Kingdom of Fanelia and pilot of Escaflowne, Van Slanzar de Fanelia seeks vengeance against the Zaibach Empire for destroying his homeland and kidnapping his mother.
Allen
Head of the Knights Caeli of the Asturian Royal House and pilot of Scherazade, Allen Schezar VIII endangered Asturia's treaty with the Zaibach Empire by protecting Van and Hitomi.
Hitomi
An ordinary girl who loves reading fortunes, Hitomi Hoshino's soul was involuntarily transported from the Earth to Fanelia to be the source of Escaflowne's power.
Scherazade
A legendary Knight Machine piloted by Allen Schezar VIII.
Escaflowne
A powerful Knight Machine piloted by Van and powered by Hitomi, Escaflowne is both the protector and deity of the people of Fanelia.

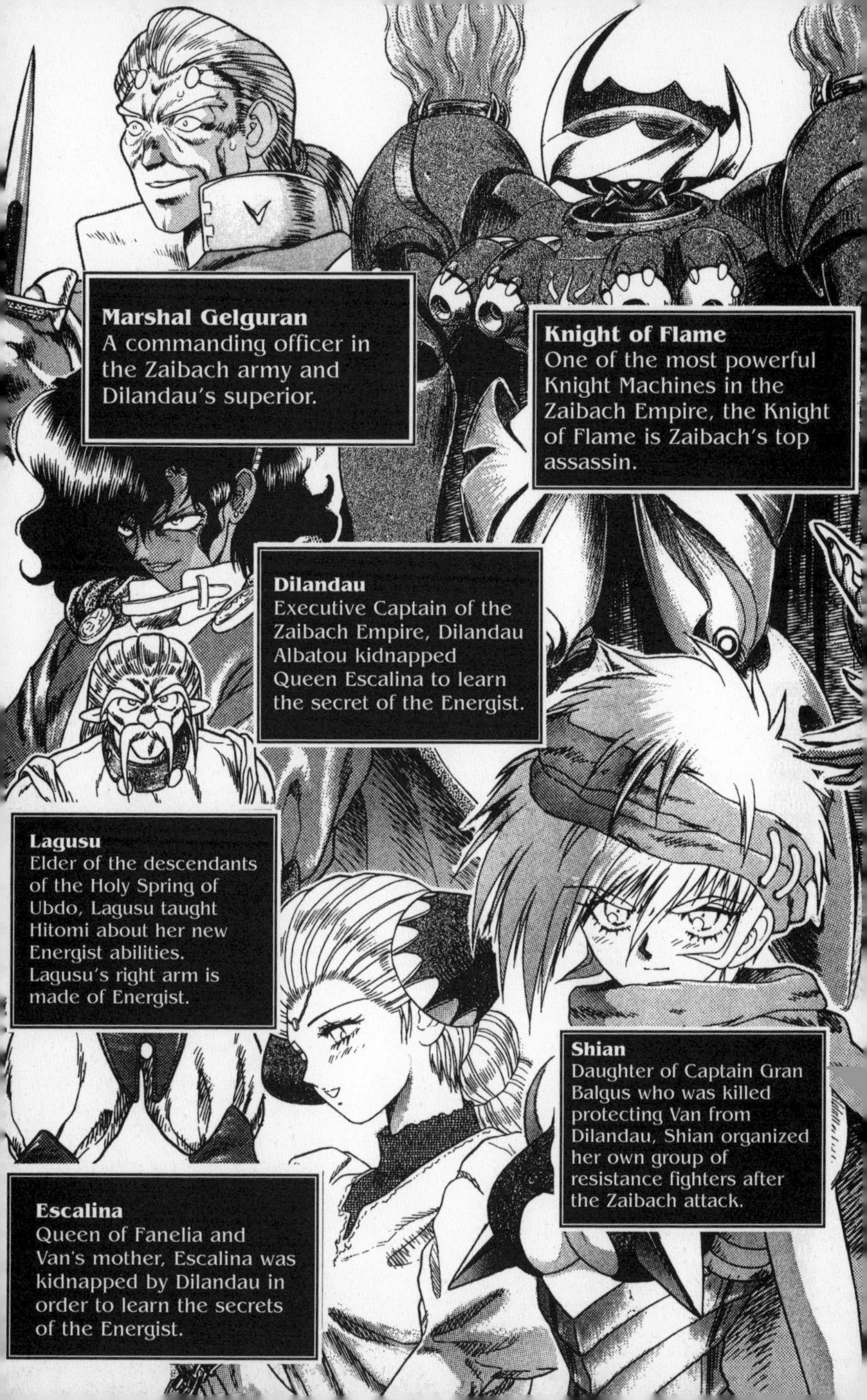
Marshal Gelguran
A commanding officer in the Zaibach army and Dilandau's superior.
Knight of Flame
One of the most powerful Knight Machines in the Zaibach Empire, the Knight of Flame is Zaibach's top assassin.
Dilandau
Executive Captain of the Zaibach Empire, Dilandau Albatou kidnapped Queen Escalina to learn the secret of the Energist.
Lagusu
Elder of the descendants of the Holy Spring of Ubdo, Lagusu taught Hitomi about her new Energist abilities. Lagusu's right arm is made of Energist.
Shian
Daughter of Captain Gran Balgus who was killed protecting Van from Dilandau, Shian organized her own group of resistance fighters after the Zaibach attack.
Escalina
Queen of Fanelia and Van's mother, Escalina was kidnapped by Dilandau in order to learn the secrets of the Energist.

VISION 10:
CONSPIRACY

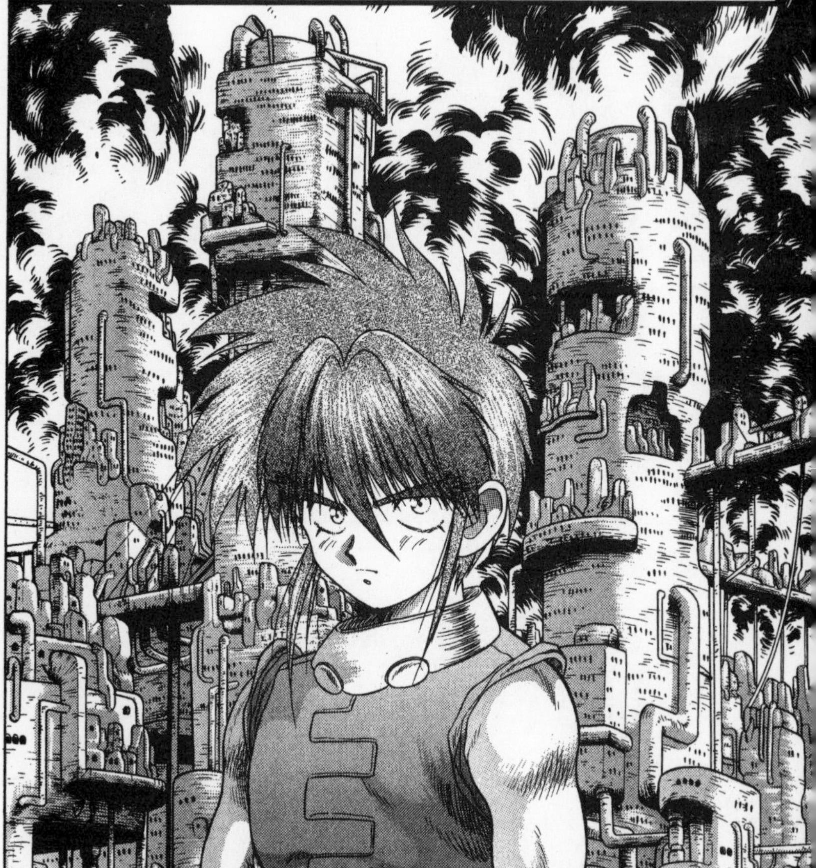

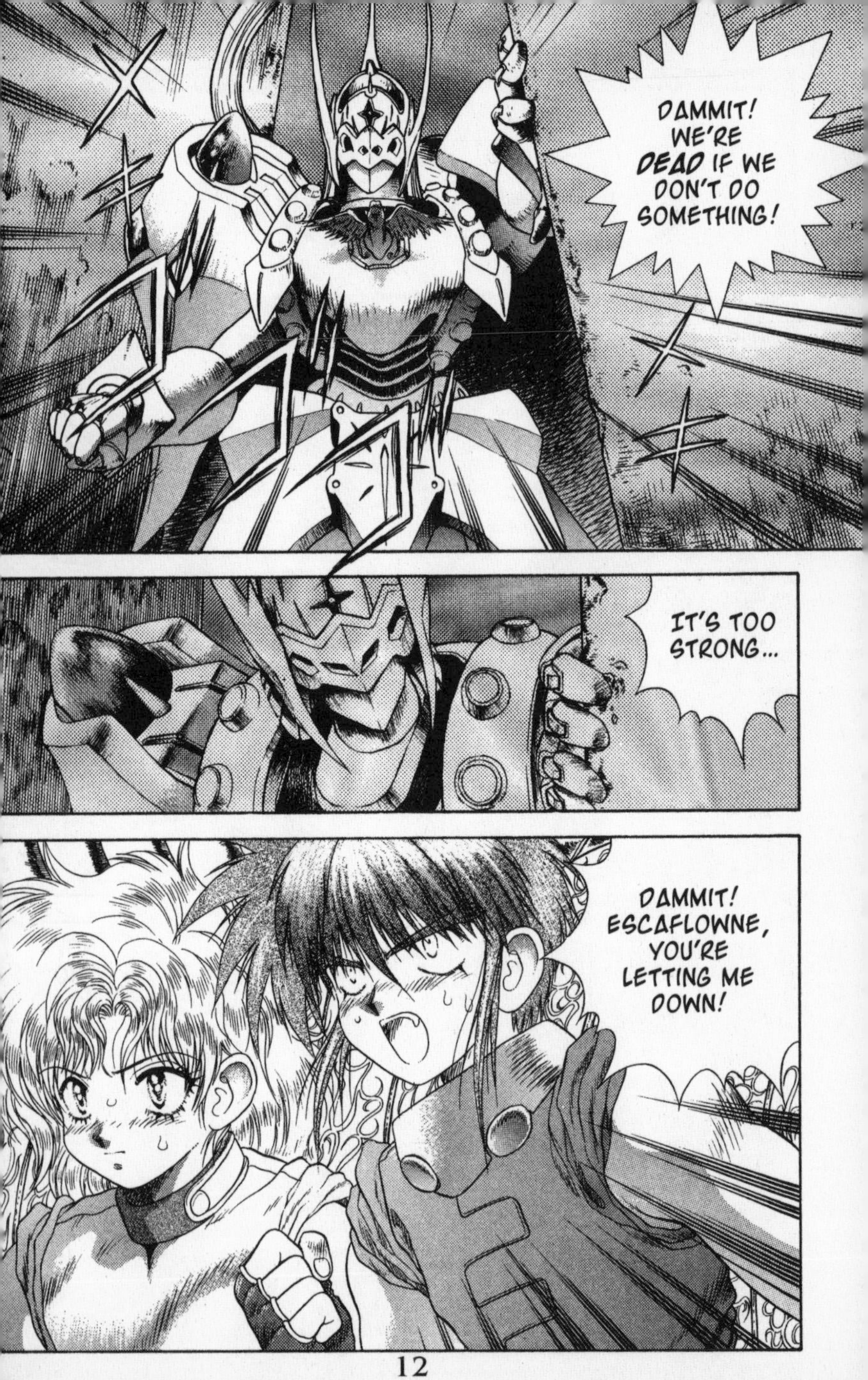
DAMMIT! WE'RE **DEAD** IF WE DON'T DO SOMETHING!
IT'S TOO STRONG...
DAMMIT! ESCAFLOWNE, YOU'RE LETTING ME DOWN!

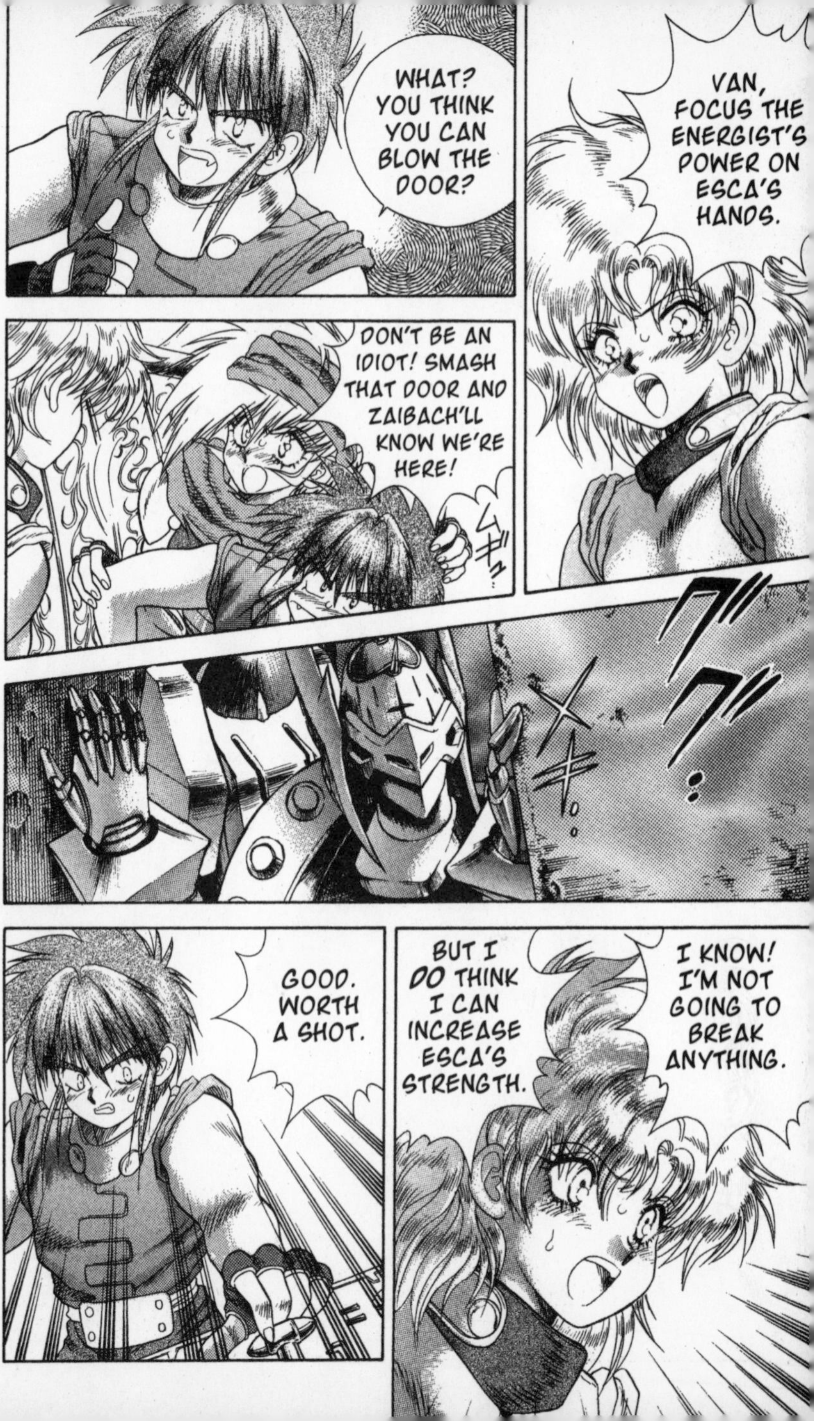
VAN, FOCUS THE ENERGIST'S POWER ON ESCA'S HANDS.
WHAT? YOU THINK YOU CAN BLOW THE DOOR?
DON'T BE AN IDIOT! SMASH THAT DOOR AND ZAIBACH'LL KNOW WE'RE HERE!
ムギュ
I KNOW! I'M NOT GOING TO BREAK ANYTHING.
BUT I *DO* THINK I CAN INCREASE ESCA'S STRENGTH.
GOOD. WORTH A SHOT.

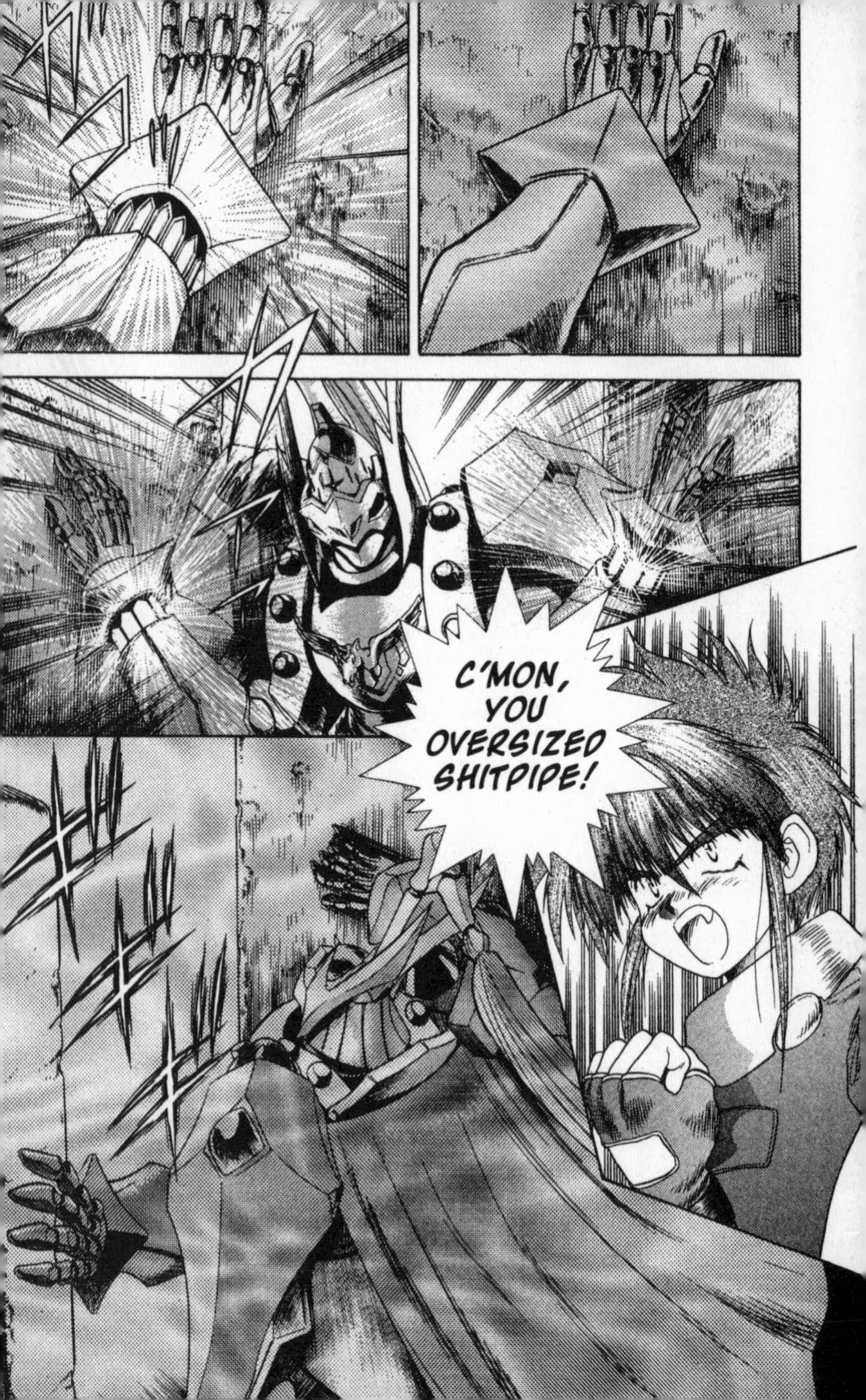
C'MON, YOU OVERSIZED SHITPIPE!

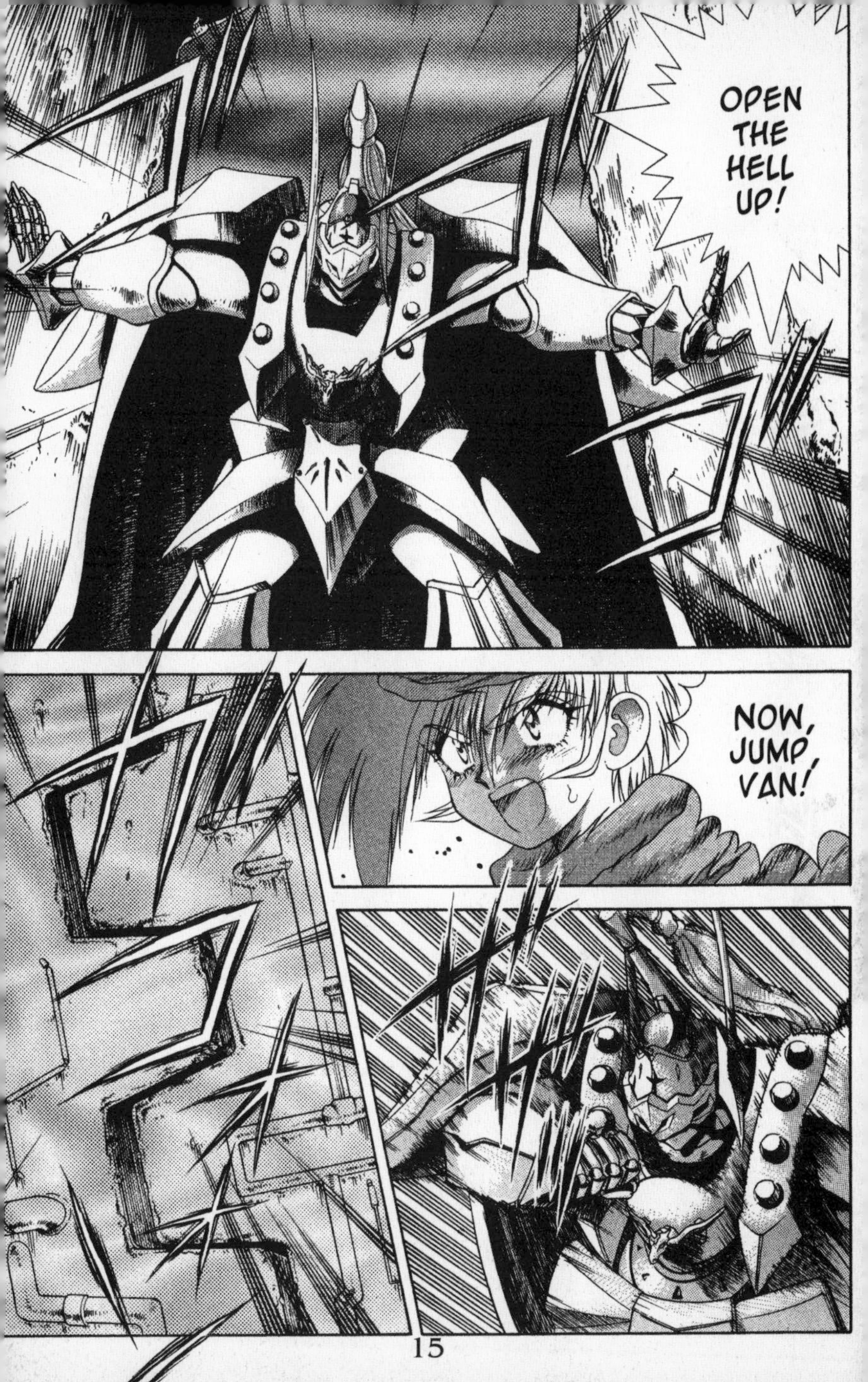
OPEN THE HELL UP!
NOW, JUMP VAN!

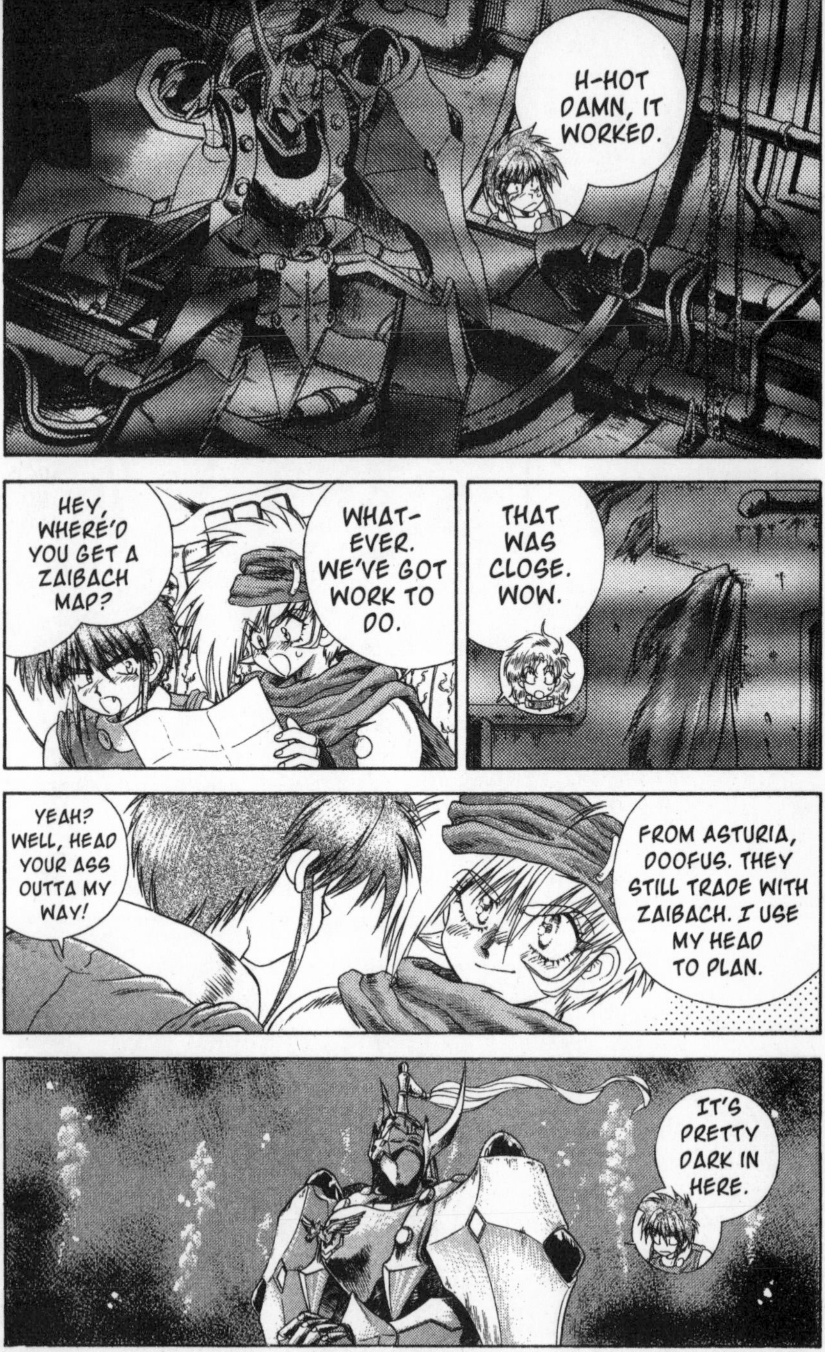
H-HOT DAMN, IT WORKED.
THAT WAS CLOSE. WOW.
WHAT-EVER. WE'VE GOT WORK TO DO.
HEY, WHERE'D YOU GET A ZAIBACH MAP?
FROM ASTURIA, DOOFUS. THEY STILL TRADE WITH ZAIBACH. I USE MY HEAD TO PLAN.
YEAH? WELL, HEAD YOUR ASS OUTTA MY WAY!
IT'S PRETTY DARK IN HERE.

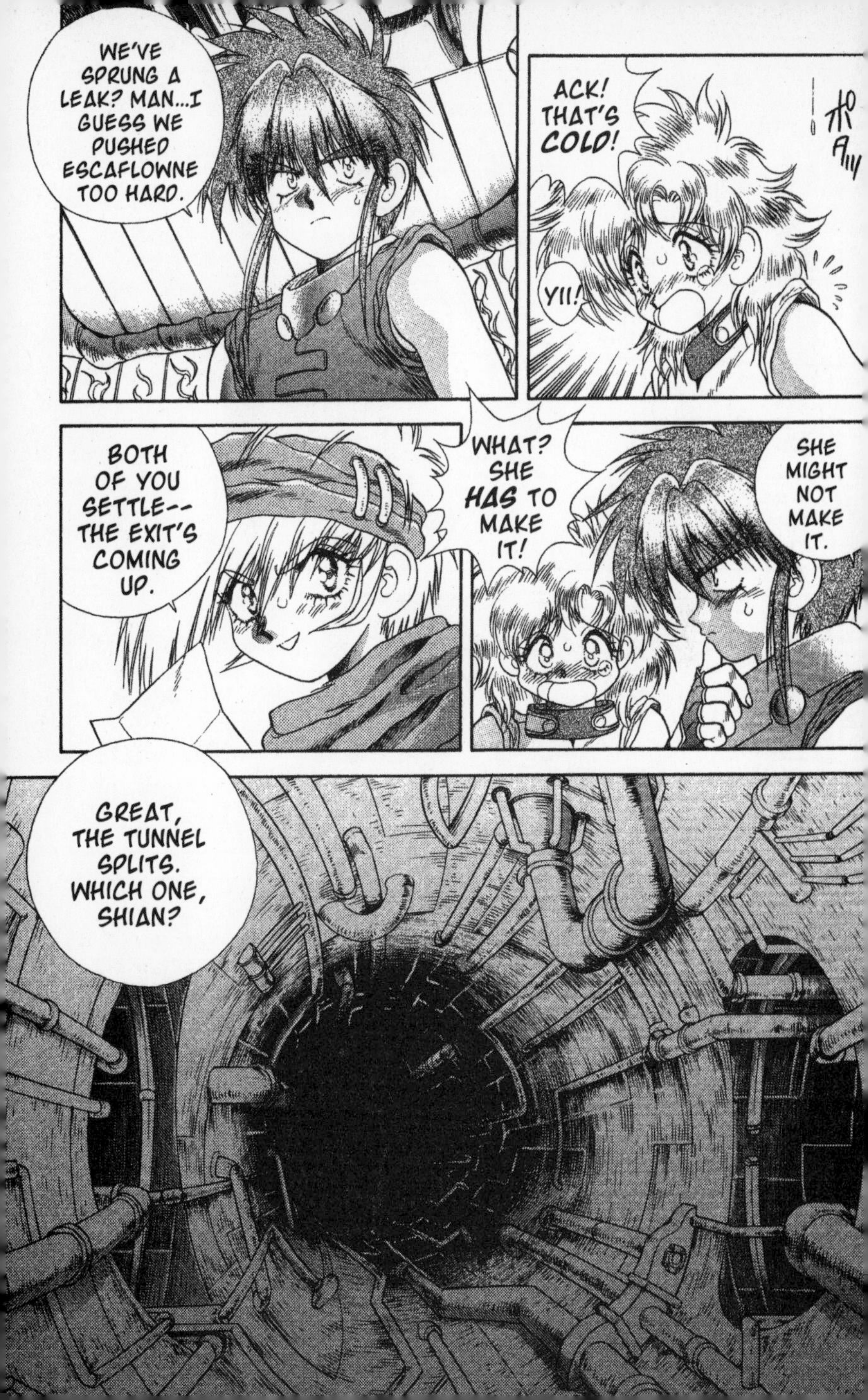
ACK! THAT'S COLD!
ポタ
YII!
WE'VE SPRUNG A LEAK? MAN...I GUESS WE PUSHED ESCAFLOWNE TOO HARD.
SHE MIGHT NOT MAKE IT.
WHAT? SHE HAS TO MAKE IT!
BOTH OF YOU SETTLE--THE EXIT'S COMING UP.
GREAT, THE TUNNEL SPLITS. WHICH ONE, SHIAN?

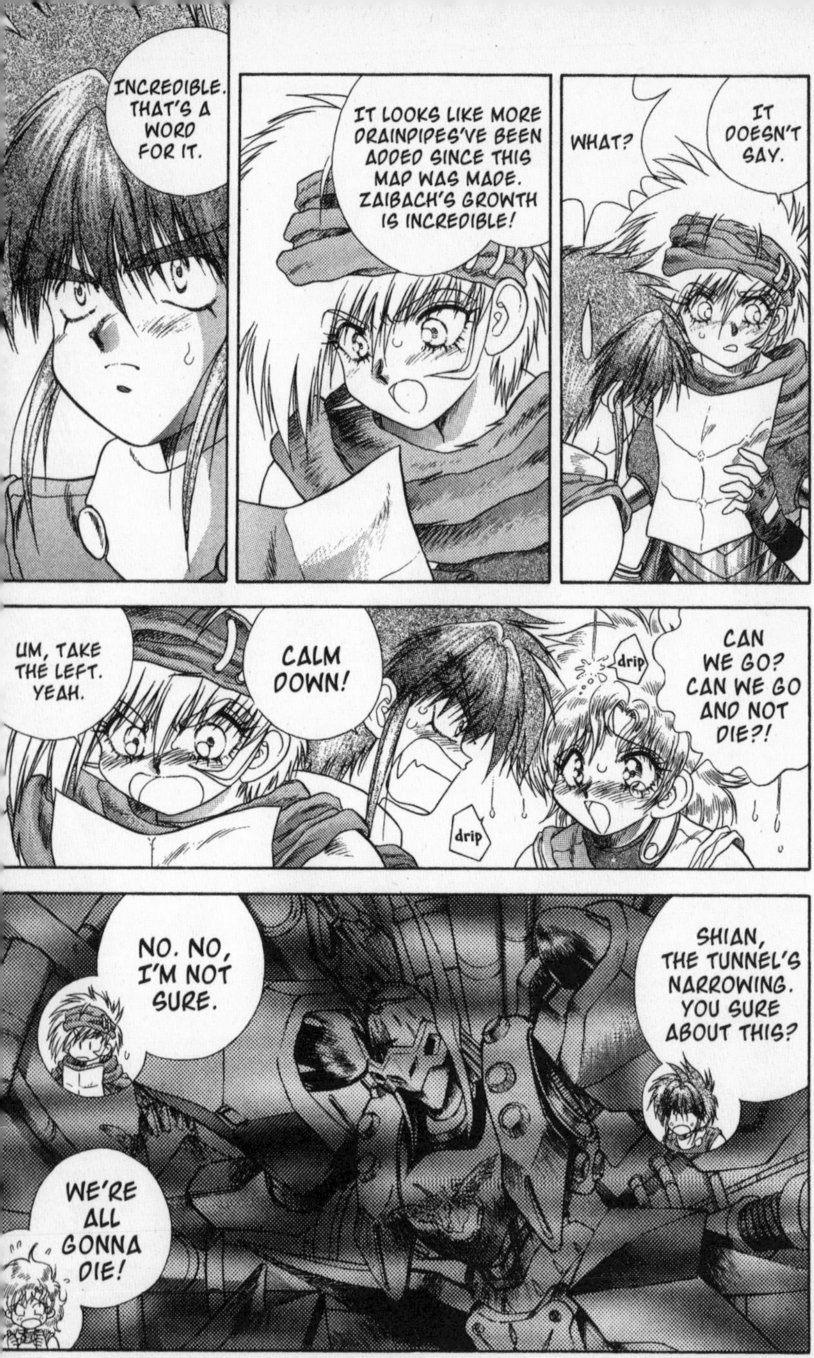
IT DOESN'T SAY.
WHAT?
IT LOOKS LIKE MORE DRAINPIPES'VE BEEN ADDED SINCE THIS MAP WAS MADE. ZAIBACH'S GROWTH IS INCREDIBLE!
INCREDIBLE. THAT'S A WORD FOR IT.
CAN WE GO? CAN WE GO AND NOT DIE?!
drip
CALM DOWN!
UM, TAKE THE LEFT. YEAH.
drip
SHIAN, THE TUNNEL'S NARROWING. YOU SURE ABOUT THIS?
NO. NO, I'M NOT SURE.
WE'RE ALL GONNA DIE!

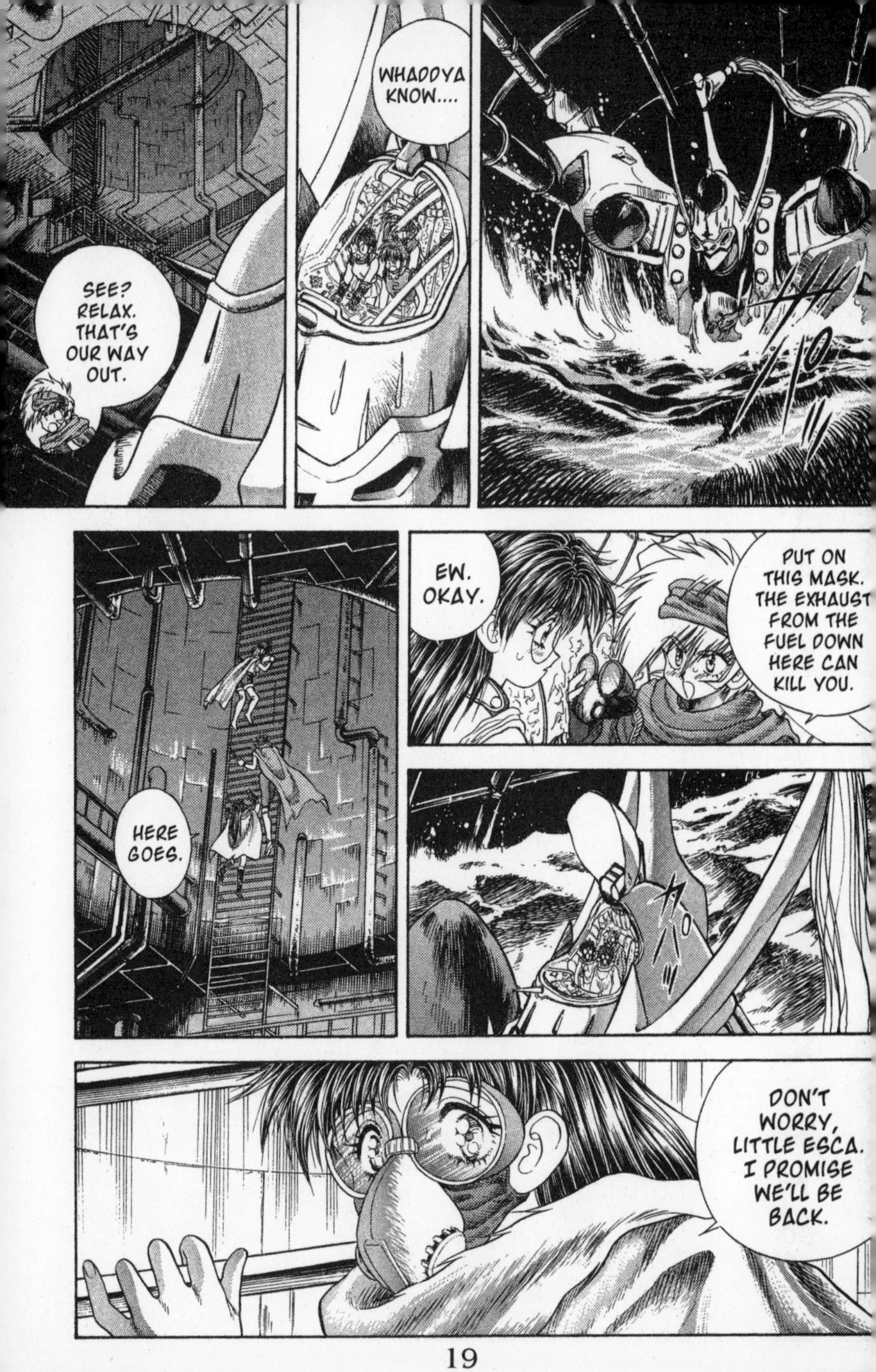
WHADDYA KNOW....
SEE? RELAX. THAT'S OUR WAY OUT.
PUT ON THIS MASK. THE EXHAUST FROM THE FUEL DOWN HERE CAN KILL YOU.
EW. OKAY.
HERE GOES.
DON'T WORRY, LITTLE ESCA. I PROMISE WE'LL BE BACK.

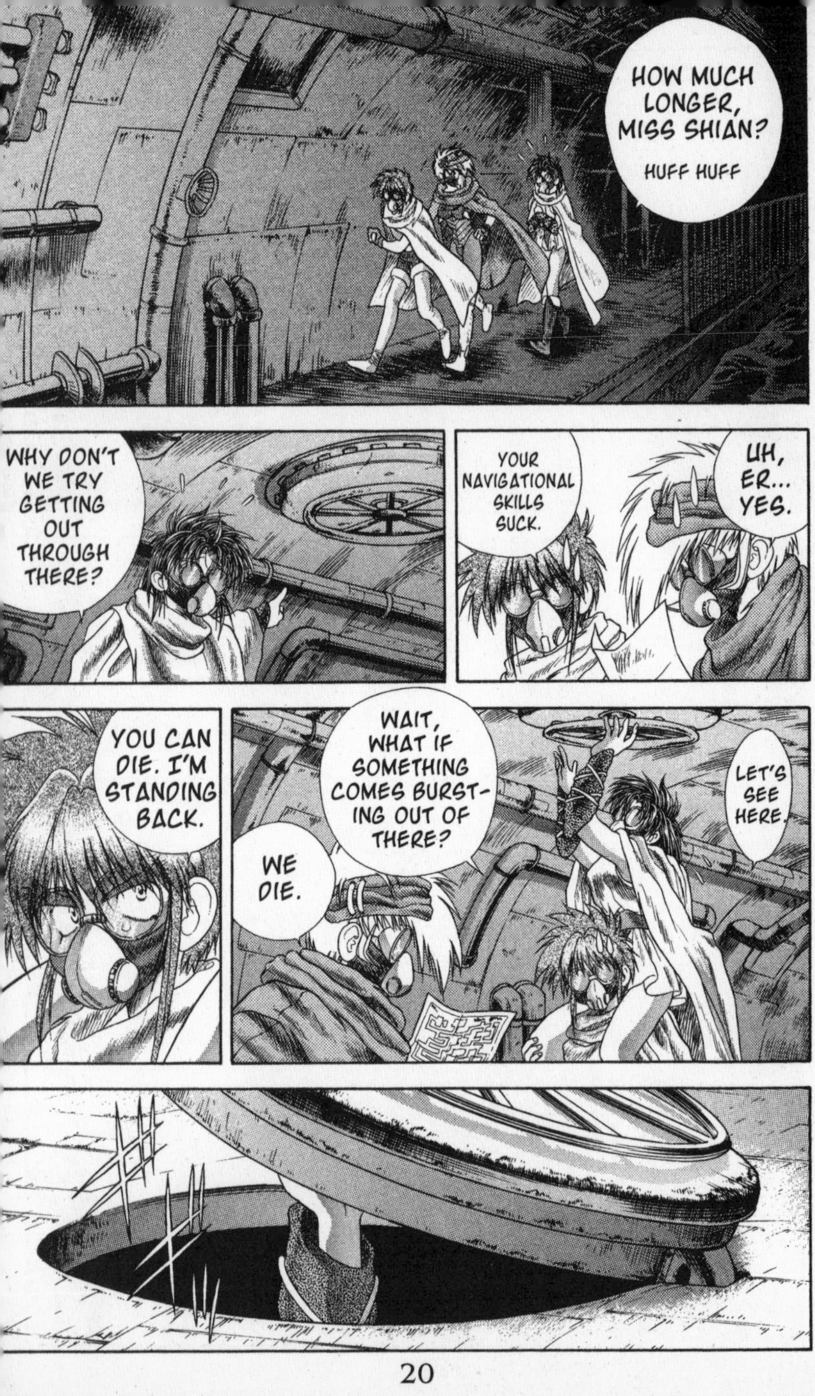
HOW MUCH LONGER, MISS SHIAN?
HUFF HUFF
UH, ER... YES.
YOUR NAVIGATIONAL SKILLS SUCK.
WHY DON'T WE TRY GETTING OUT THROUGH THERE?
LET'S SEE HERE.
WAIT, WHAT IF SOMETHING COMES BURST-ING OUT OF THERE?
WE DIE.
YOU CAN DIE. I'M STANDING BACK.

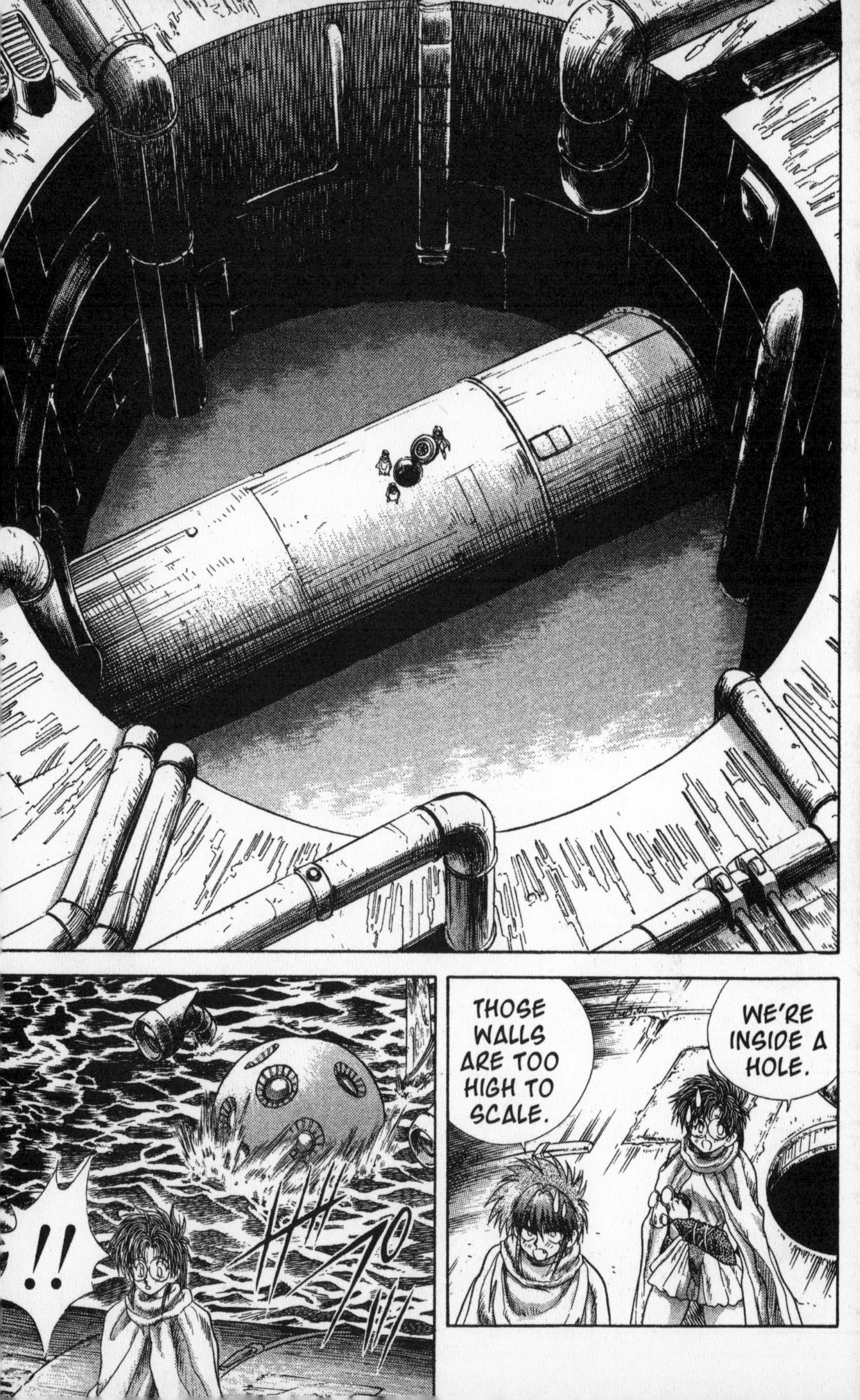

WE'RE INSIDE A HOLE.
THOSE WALLS ARE TOO HIGH TO SCALE.
!!

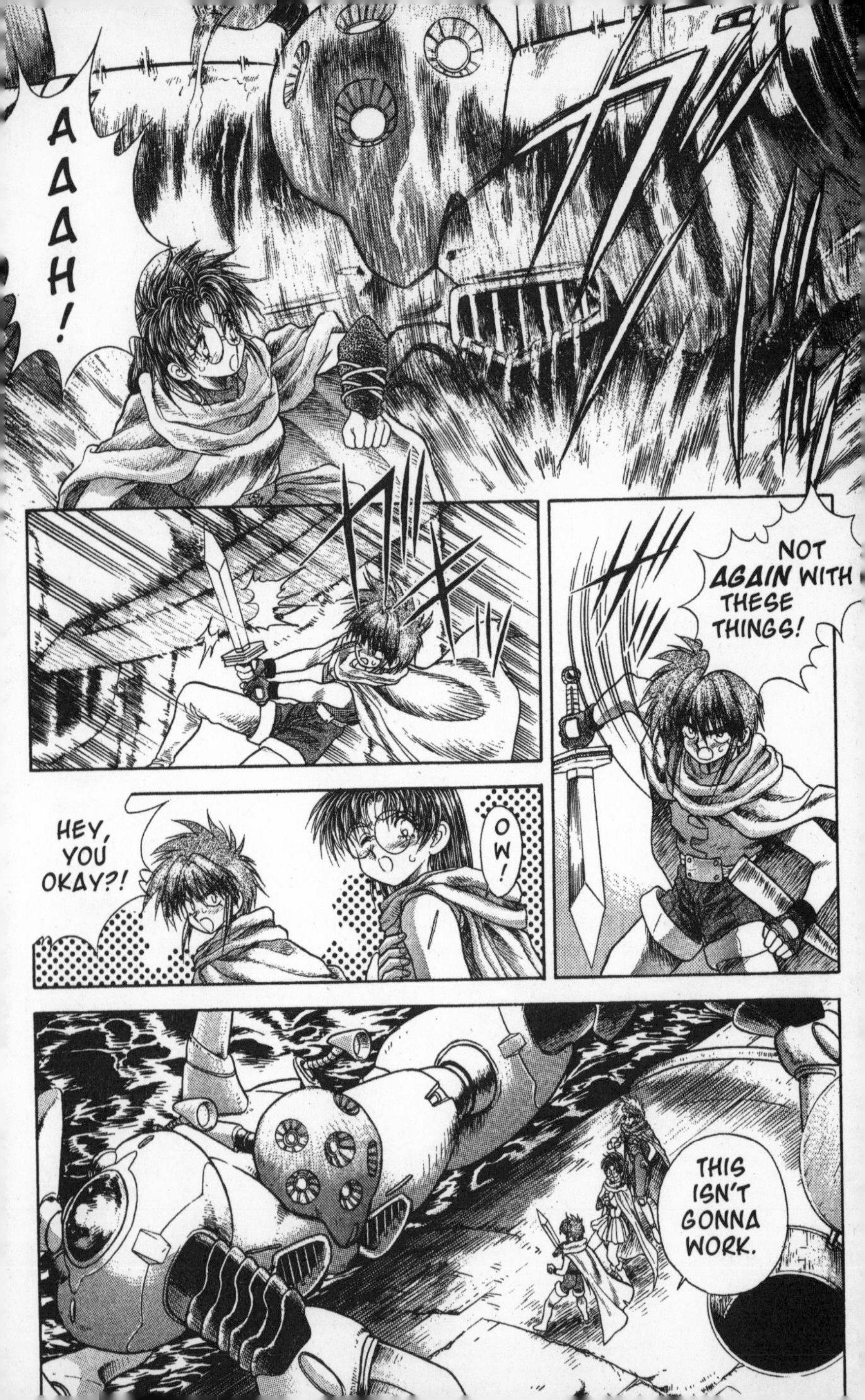
AAAAH!
NOT AGAIN WITH THESE THINGS!
OW!
HEY, YOU OKAY?!
THIS ISN'T GONNA WORK.

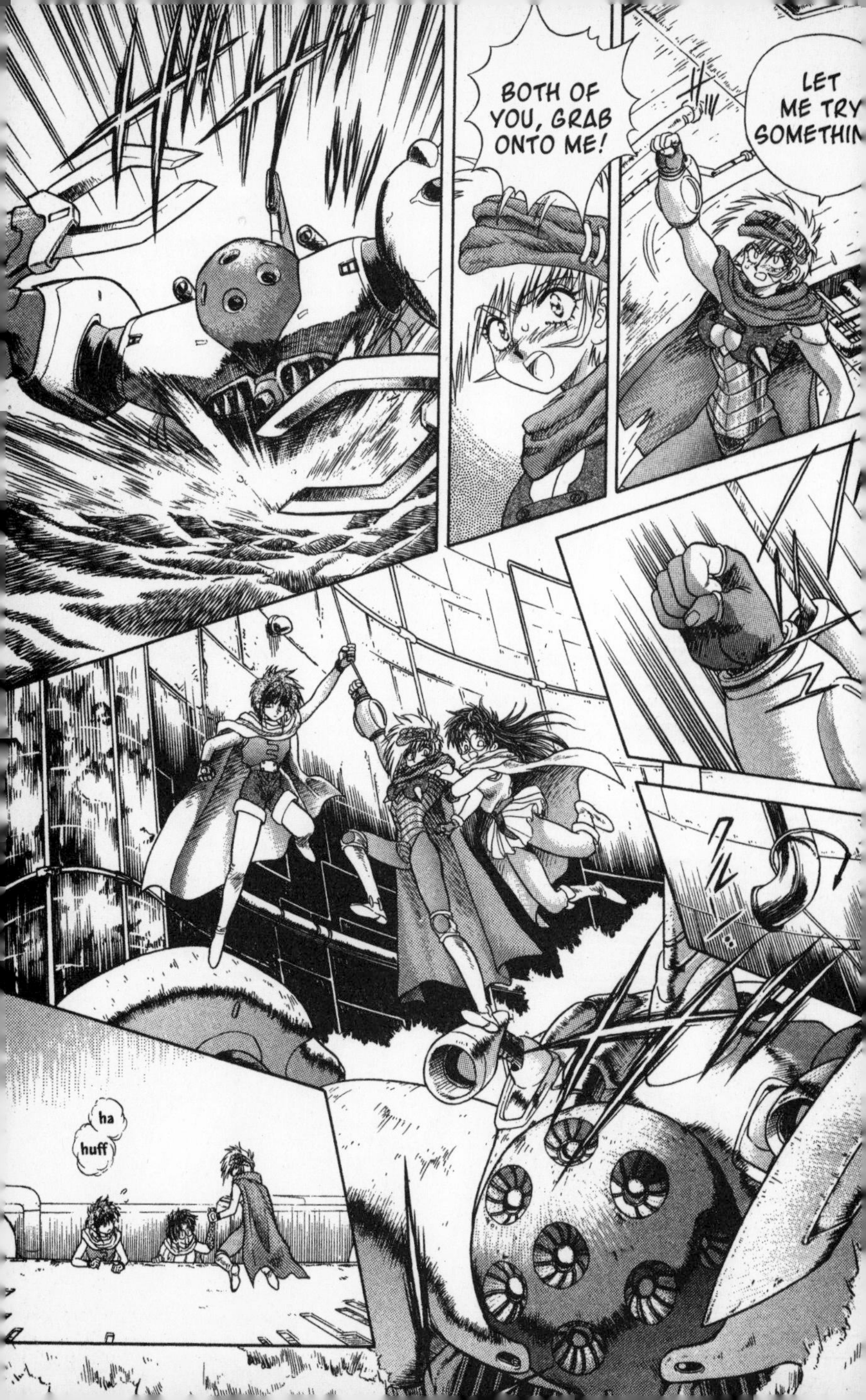
LET ME TRY SOMETHIN
BOTH OF YOU, GRAB ONTO ME!
ha
huff

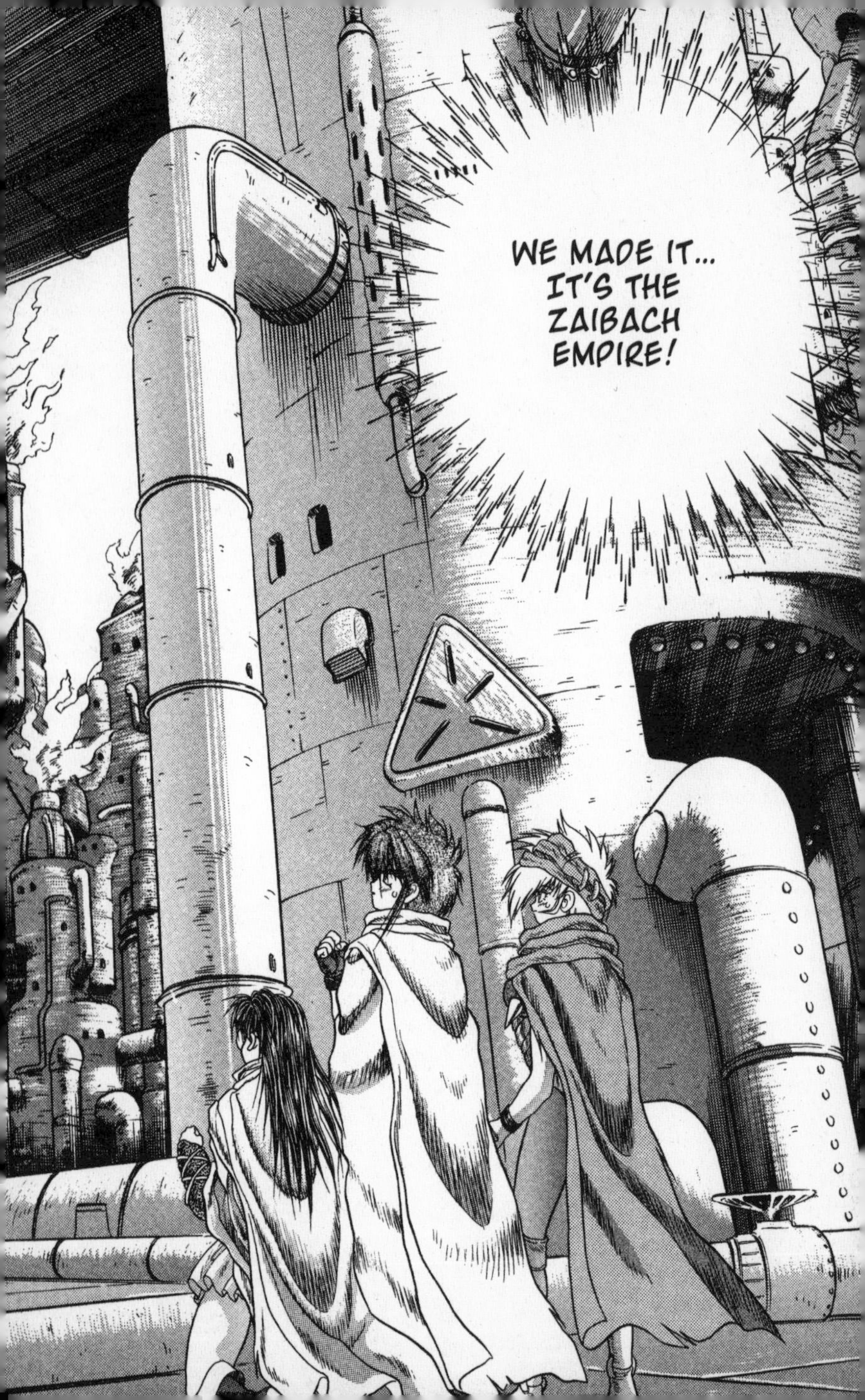
WE MADE IT... IT'S THE ZAIBACH EMPIRE!

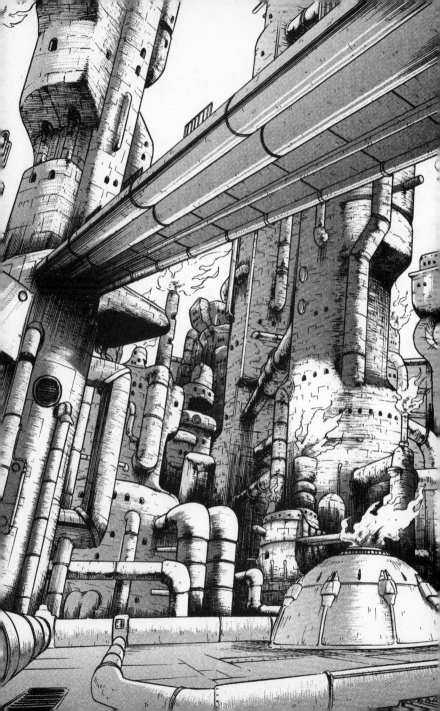

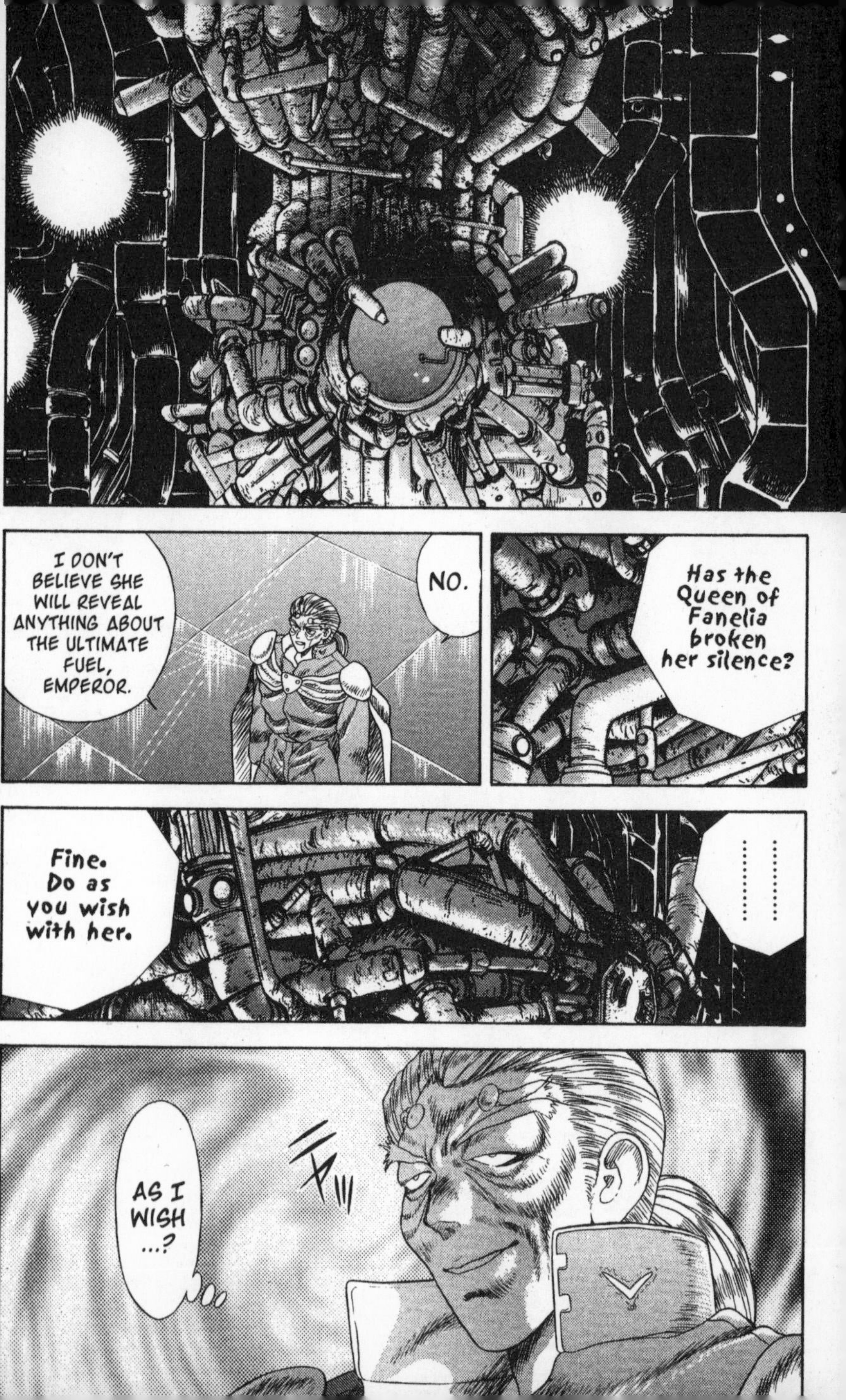
Has the Queen of Fanelia broken her silence?
NO.
I DON'T BELIEVE SHE WILL REVEAL ANYTHING ABOUT THE ULTIMATE FUEL, EMPEROR.
......
Fine. Do as you wish with her.
ニヤ
AS I WISH ...?

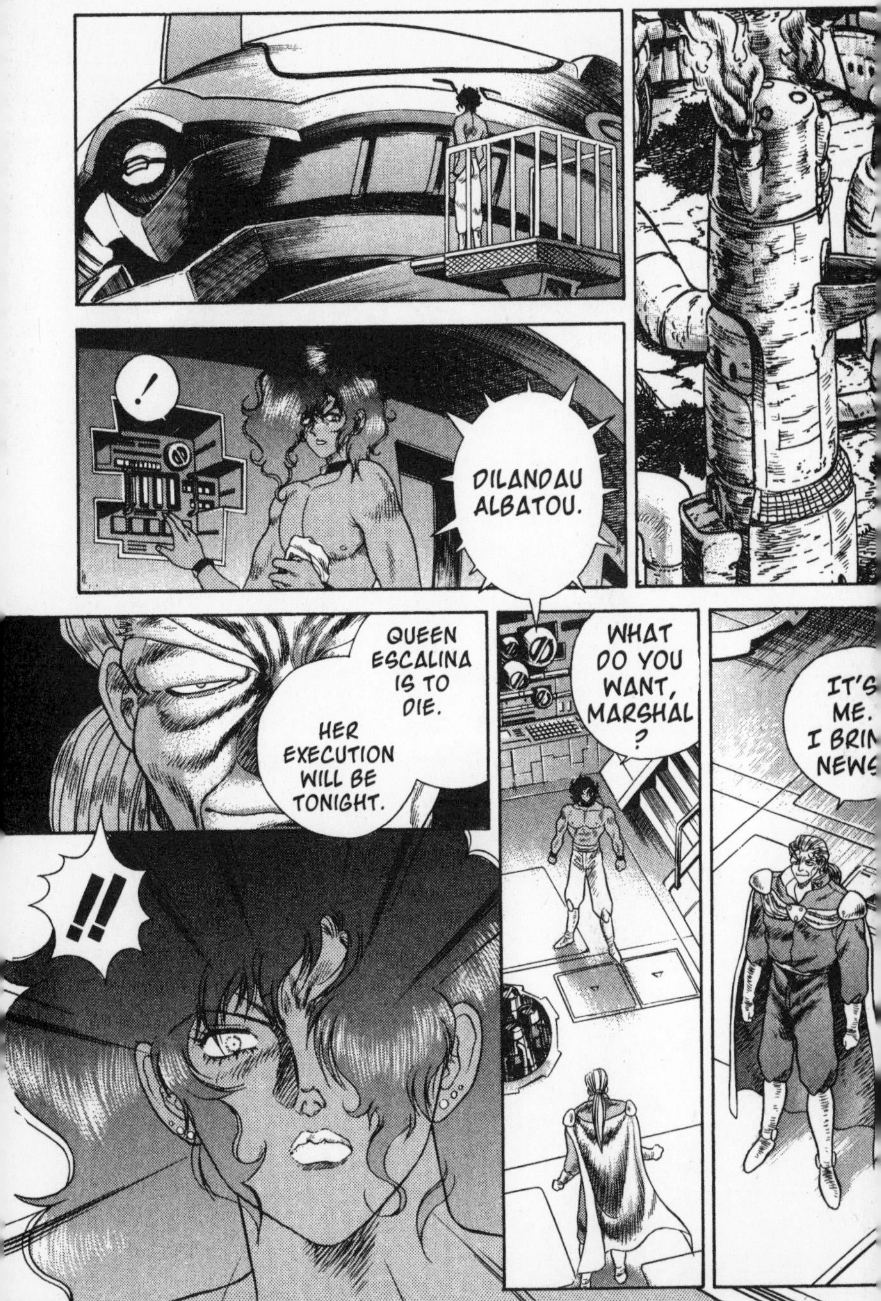

!
DILANDAU ALBATOU.
IT'S ME. I BRIN NEWS
WHAT DO YOU WANT, MARSHAL?
QUEEN ESCALINA IS TO DIE.
HER EXECUTION WILL BE TONIGHT.
!!

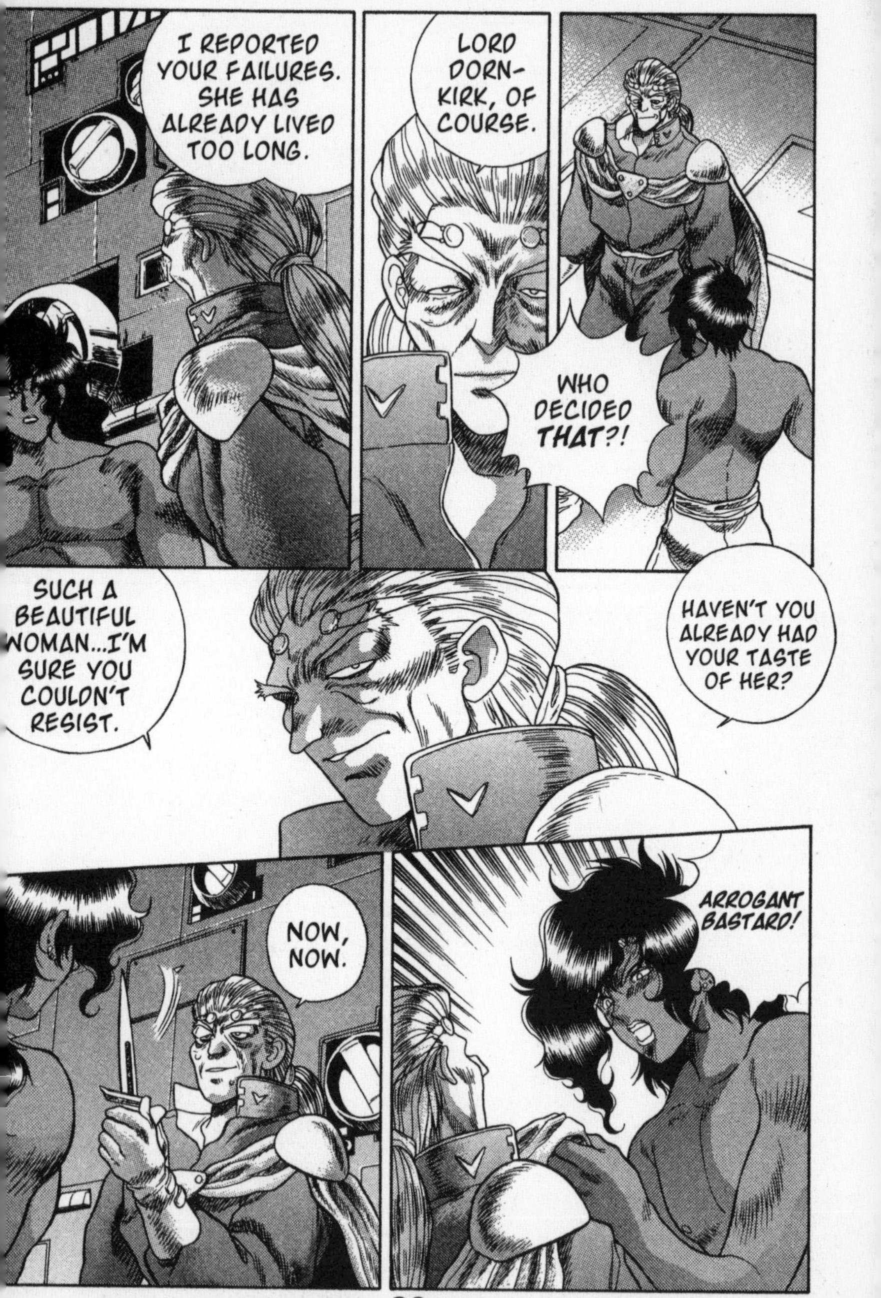
WHO DECIDED **THAT**?!
LORD DORN-KIRK, OF COURSE.
I REPORTED YOUR FAILURES. SHE HAS ALREADY LIVED TOO LONG.
HAVEN'T YOU ALREADY HAD YOUR TASTE OF HER?
SUCH A BEAUTIFUL WOMAN...I'M SURE YOU COULDN'T RESIST.
ARROGANT BASTARD!
NOW, NOW.

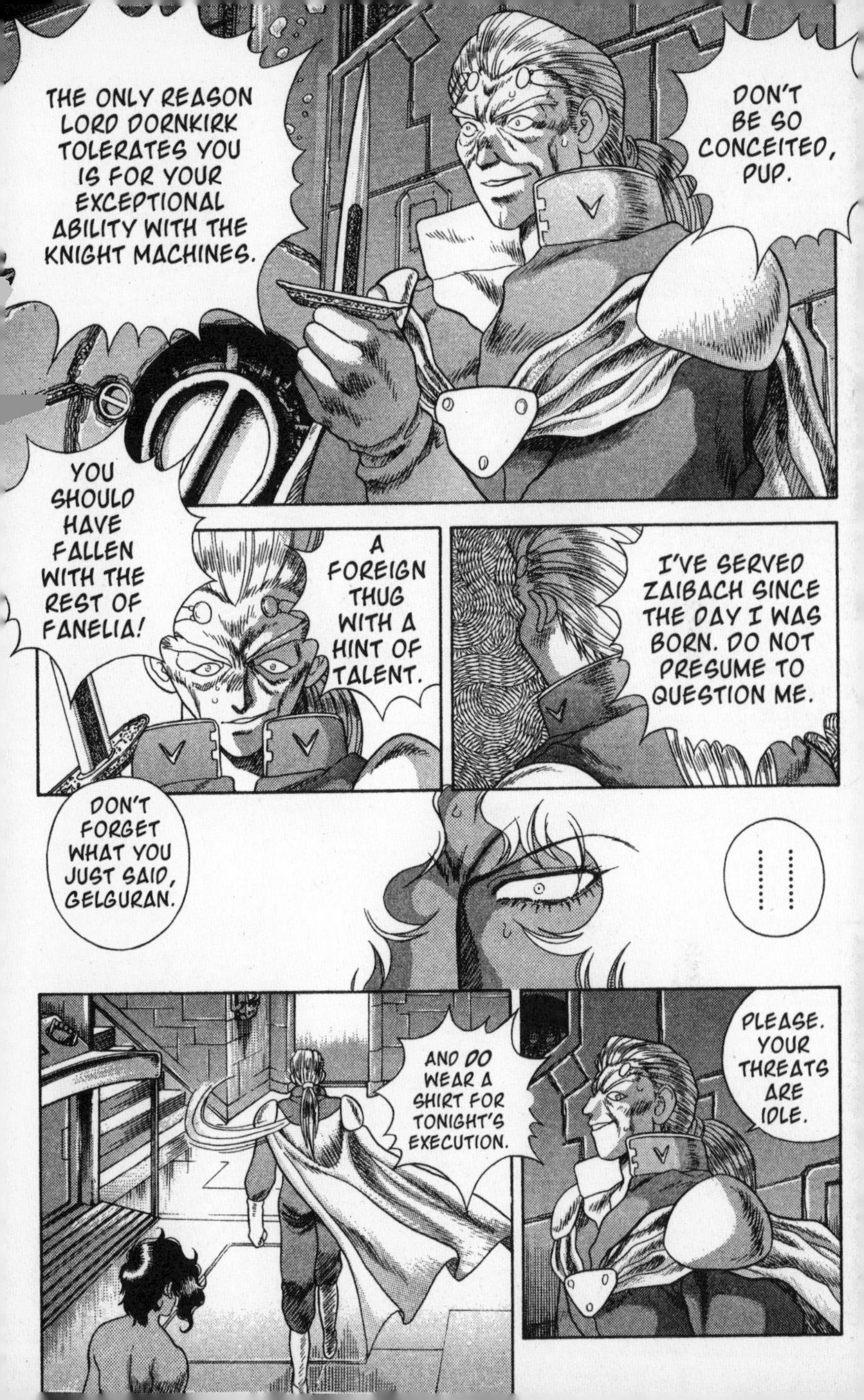
DON'T BE SO CONCEITED, PUP.
THE ONLY REASON LORD DORNKIRK TOLERATES YOU IS FOR YOUR EXCEPTIONAL ABILITY WITH THE KNIGHT MACHINES.
I'VE SERVED ZAIBACH SINCE THE DAY I WAS BORN. DO NOT PRESUME TO QUESTION ME.
A FOREIGN THUG WITH A HINT OF TALENT.
YOU SHOULD HAVE FALLEN WITH THE REST OF FANELIA!
......
DON'T FORGET WHAT YOU JUST SAID, GELGURAN.
PLEASE. YOUR THREATS ARE IDLE.
AND DO WEAR A SHIRT FOR TONIGHT'S EXECUTION.

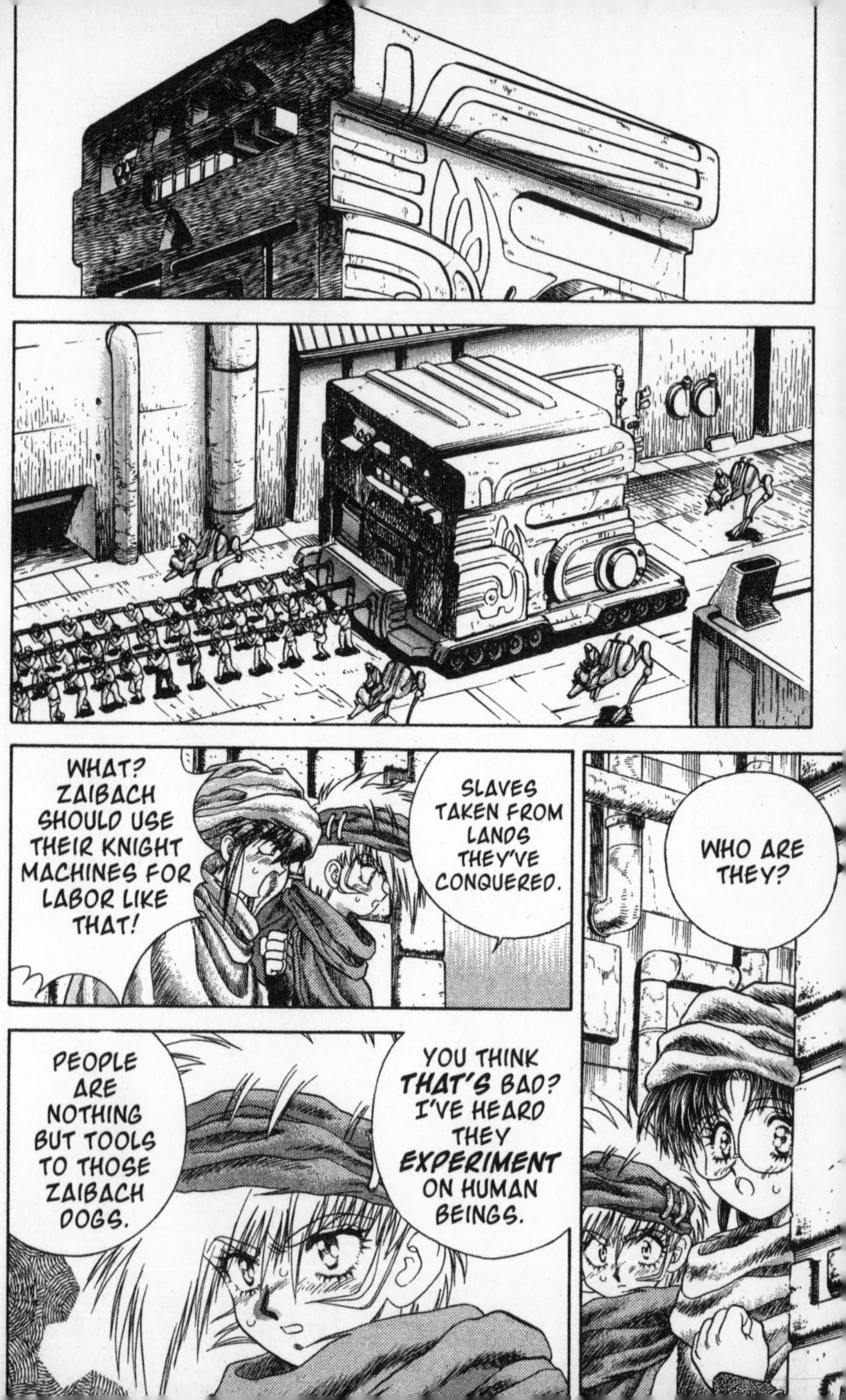
WHO ARE THEY?
SLAVES TAKEN FROM LANDS THEY'VE CONQUERED.
WHAT? ZAIBACH SHOULD USE THEIR KNIGHT MACHINES FOR LABOR LIKE THAT!
YOU THINK *THAT'S* BAD? I'VE HEARD THEY *EXPERIMENT* ON HUMAN BEINGS.
PEOPLE ARE NOTHING BUT TOOLS TO THOSE ZAIBACH DOGS.

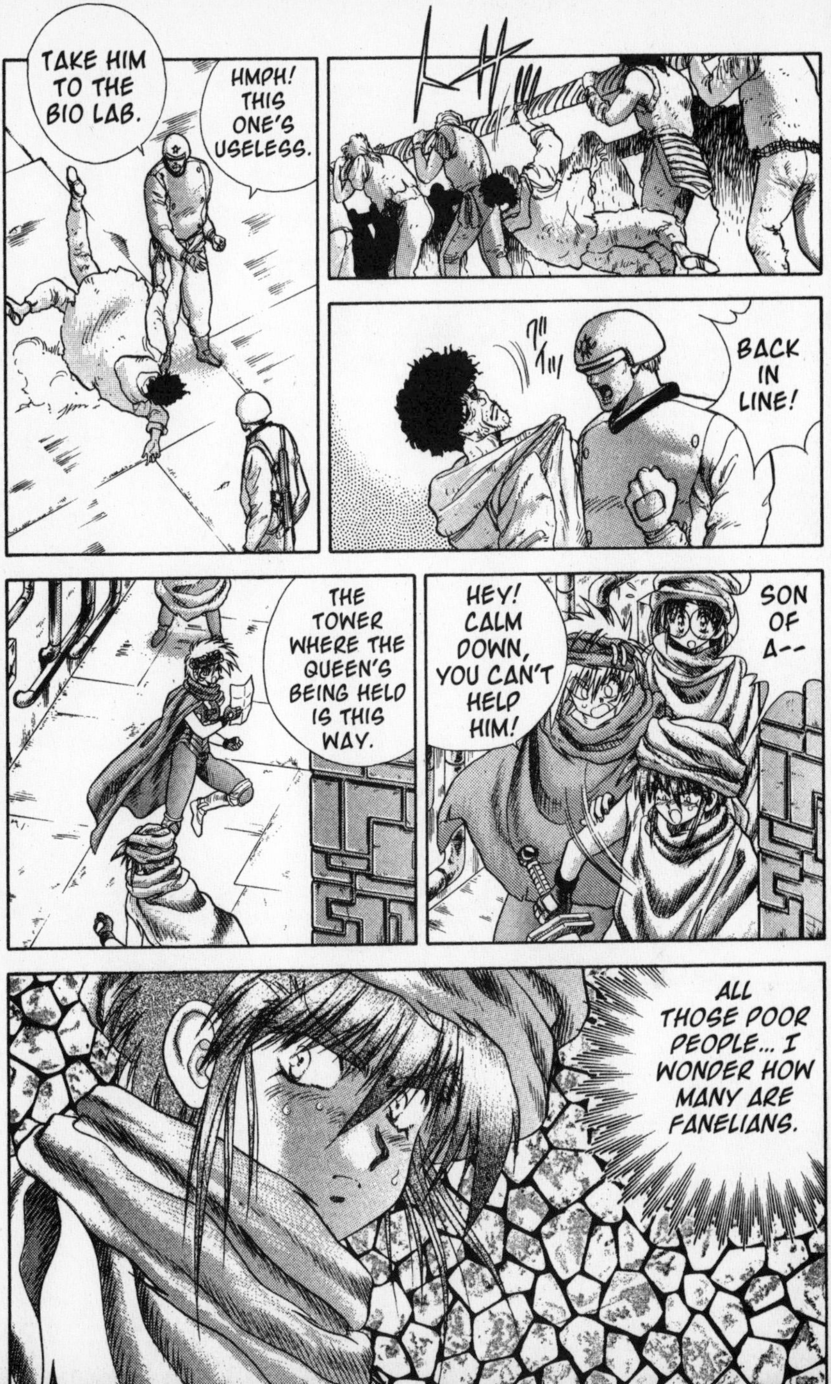
BACK IN LINE!
HMPH! THIS ONE'S USELESS.
TAKE HIM TO THE BIO LAB.
SON OF A--
HEY! CALM DOWN, YOU CAN'T HELP HIM!
THE TOWER WHERE THE QUEEN'S BEING HELD IS THIS WAY.
ALL THOSE POOR PEOPLE... I WONDER HOW MANY ARE FANELIANS.

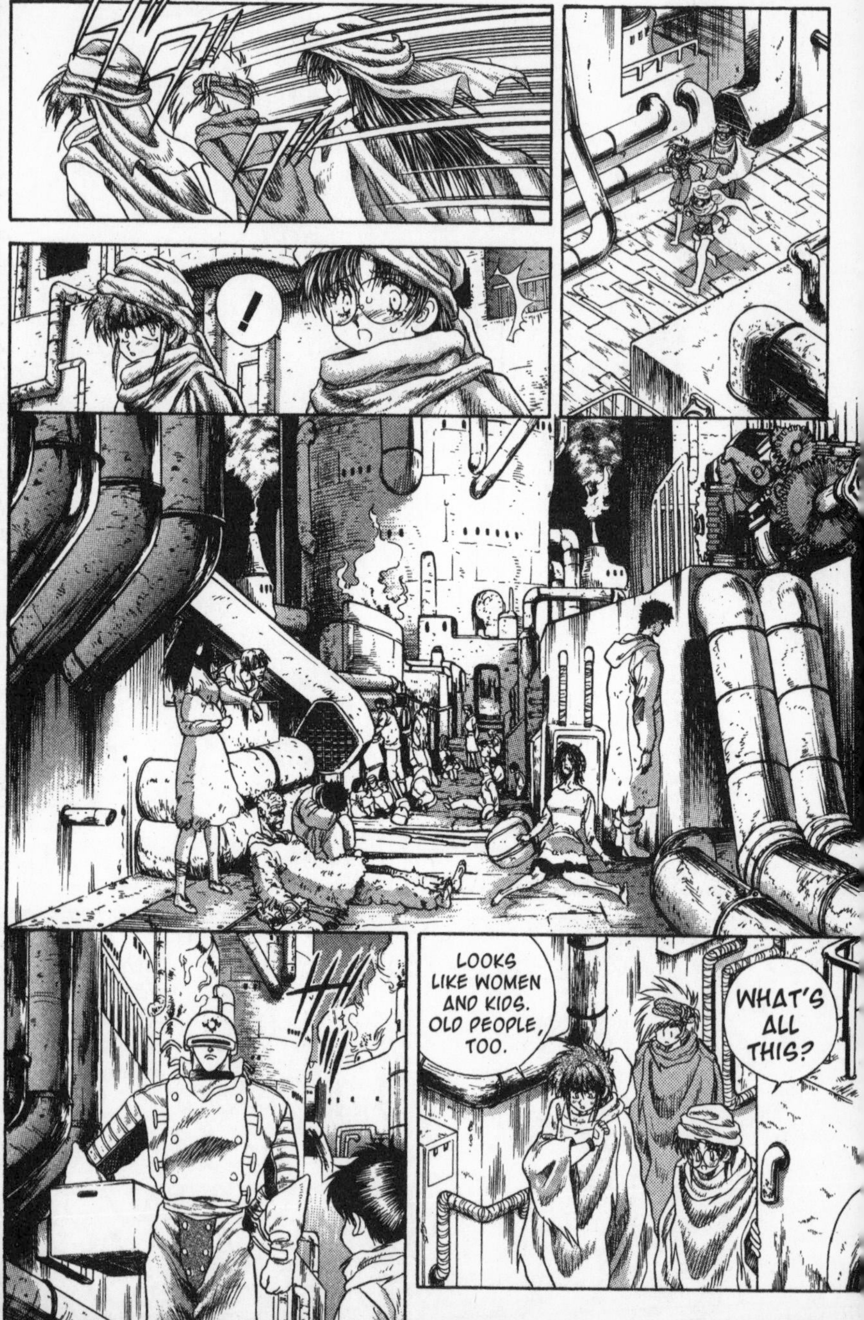
!
WHAT'S ALL THIS?
LOOKS LIKE WOMEN AND KIDS. OLD PEOPLE, TOO.

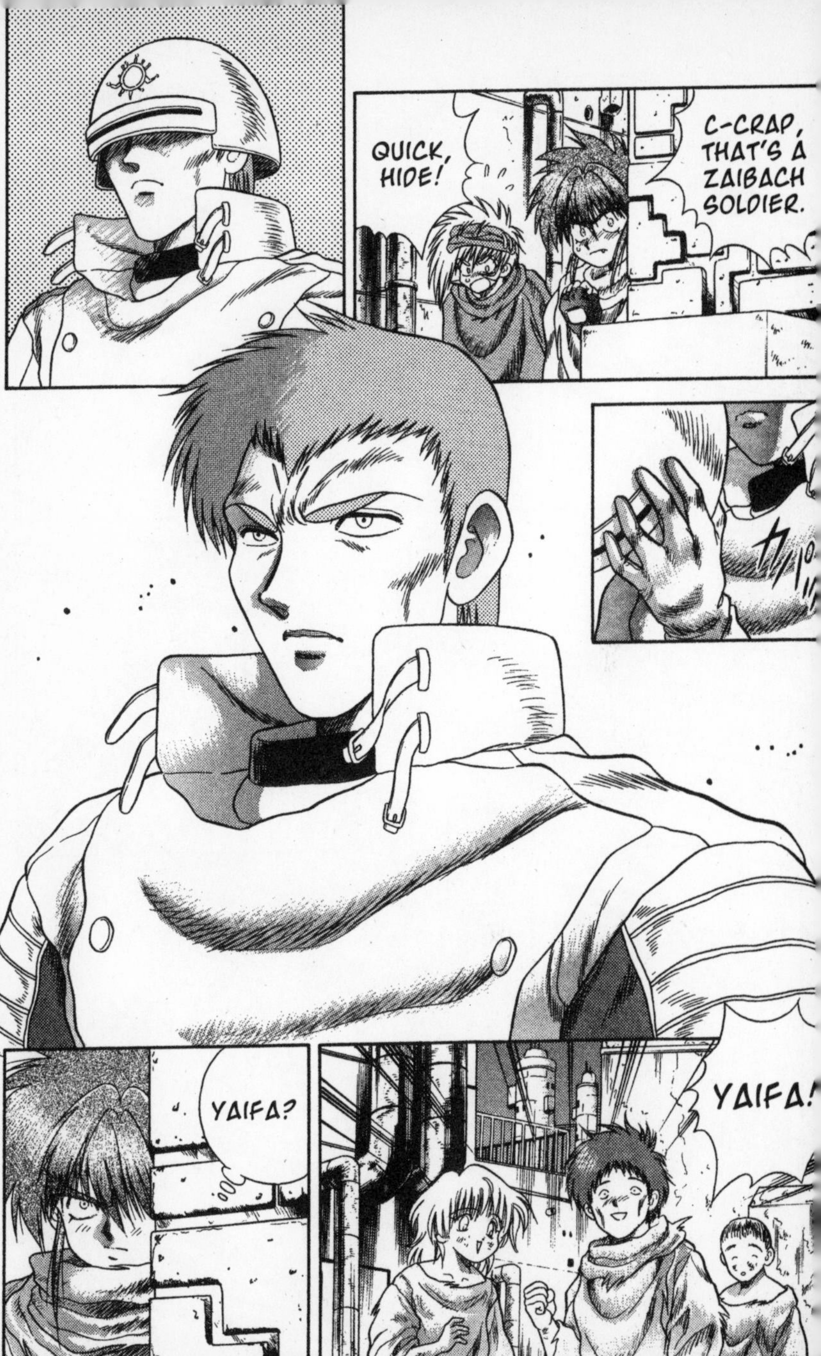
C-CRAP, THAT'S A ZAIBACH SOLDIER.
QUICK, HIDE!
YAIFA!
YAIFA?

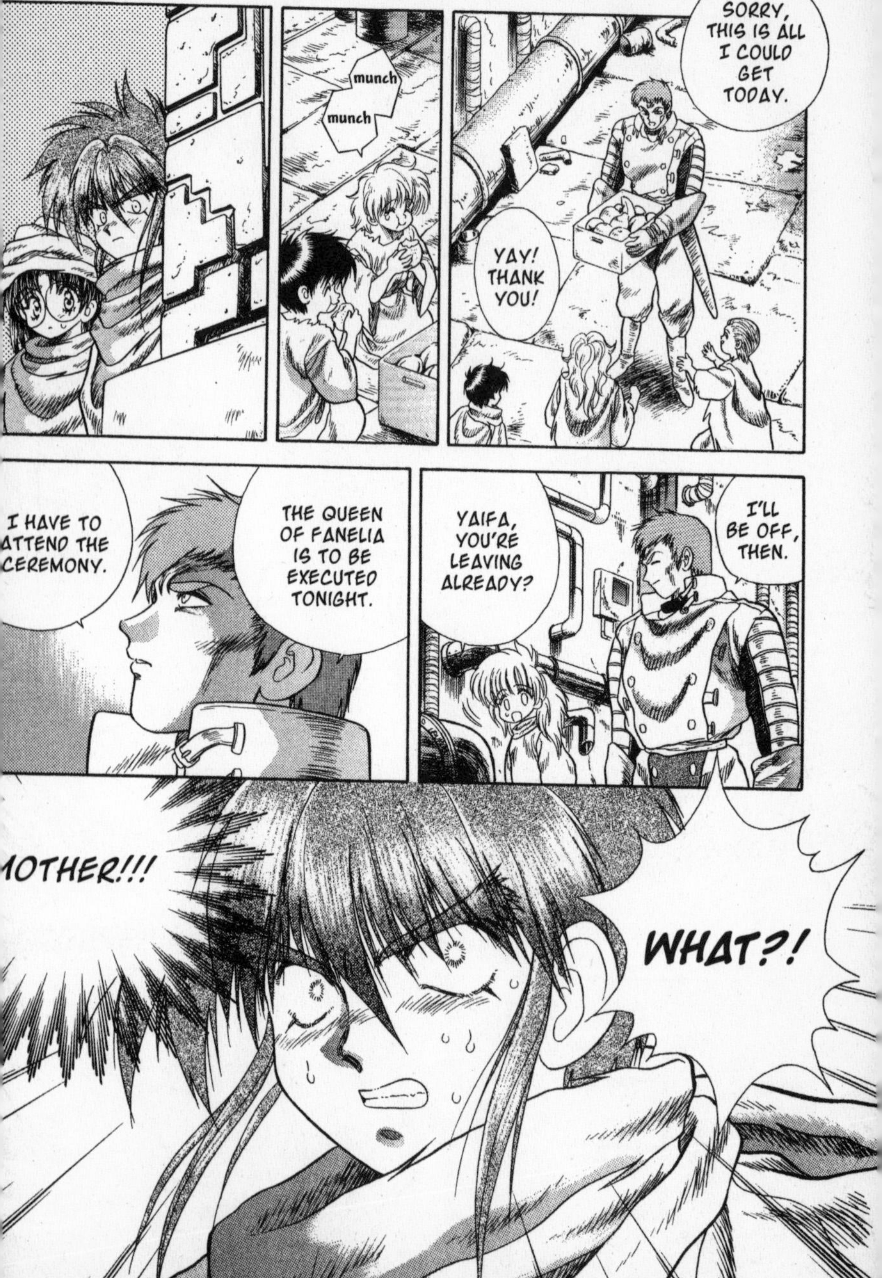
SORRY, THIS IS ALL I COULD GET TODAY.
YAY! THANK YOU!
munch
munch
I'LL BE OFF, THEN.
YAIFA, YOU'RE LEAVING ALREADY?
THE QUEEN OF FANELIA IS TO BE EXECUTED TONIGHT.
I HAVE TO ATTEND THE CEREMONY.
WHAT?!
MOTHER!!!

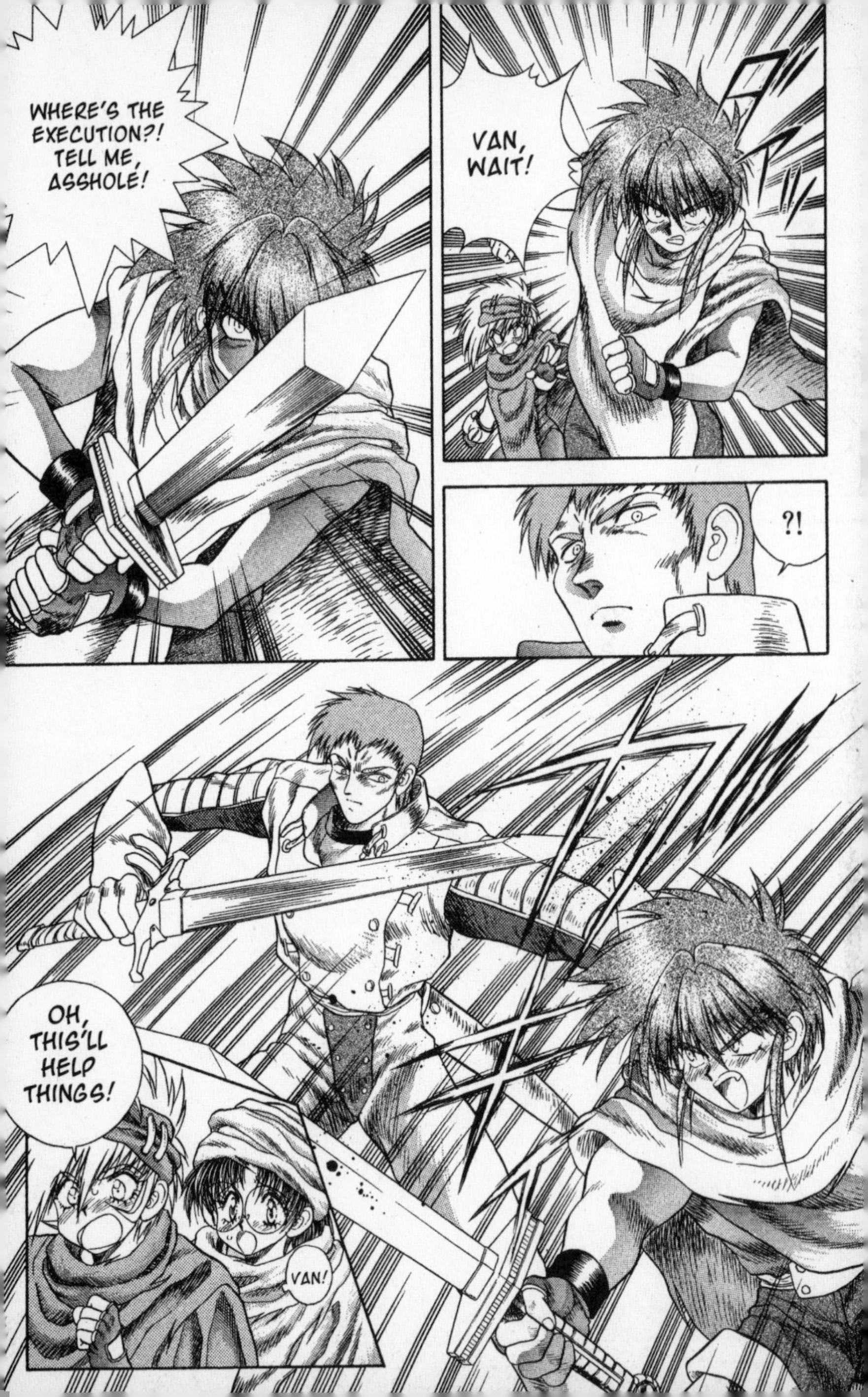
VAN, WAIT!
?!
WHERE'S THE EXECUTION?! TELL ME, ASSHOLE!
OH, THIS'LL HELP THINGS!
VAN!

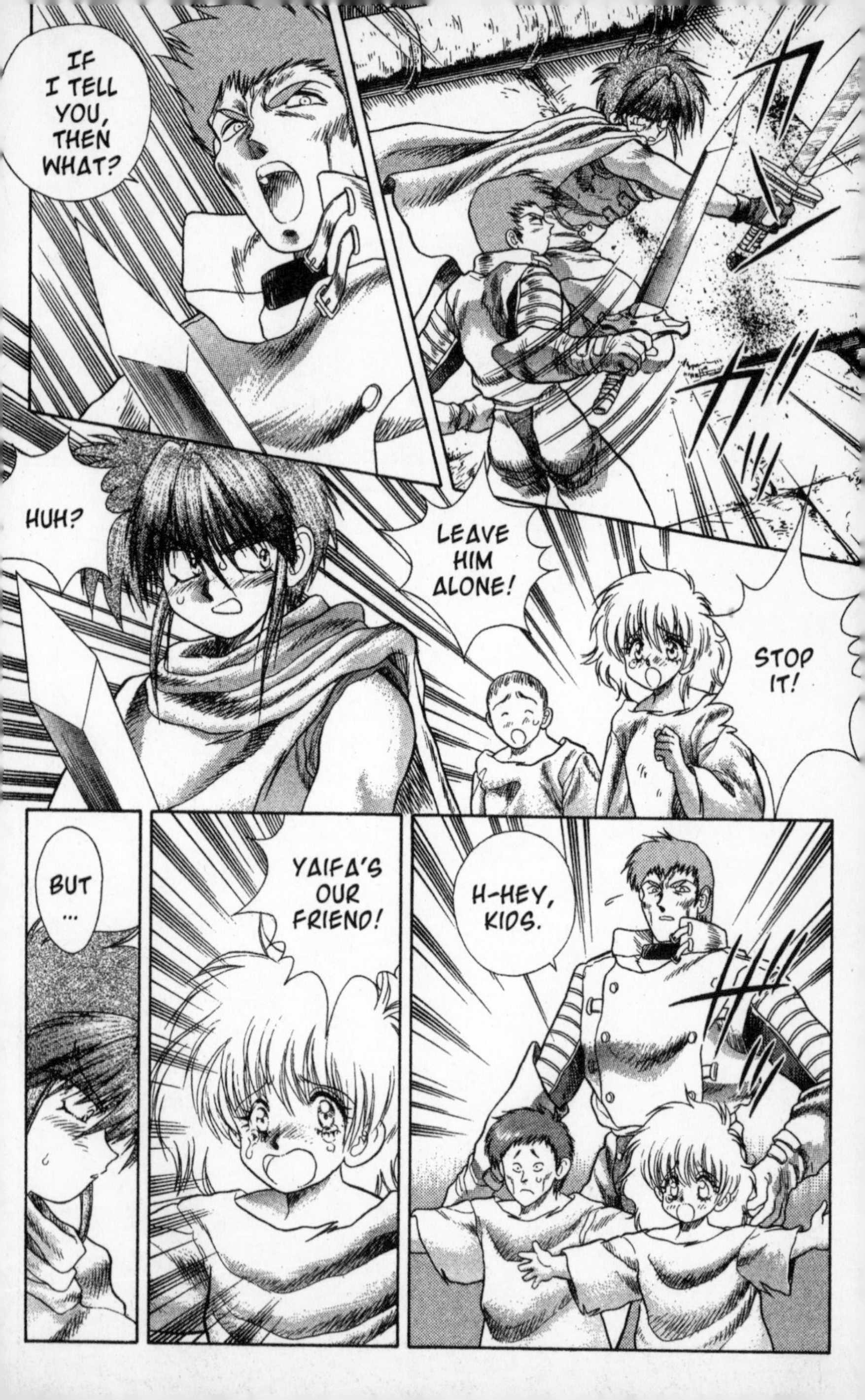
IF I TELL YOU, THEN WHAT?
STOP IT!
LEAVE HIM ALONE!
HUH?
H-HEY, KIDS.
YAIFA'S OUR FRIEND!
BUT ...

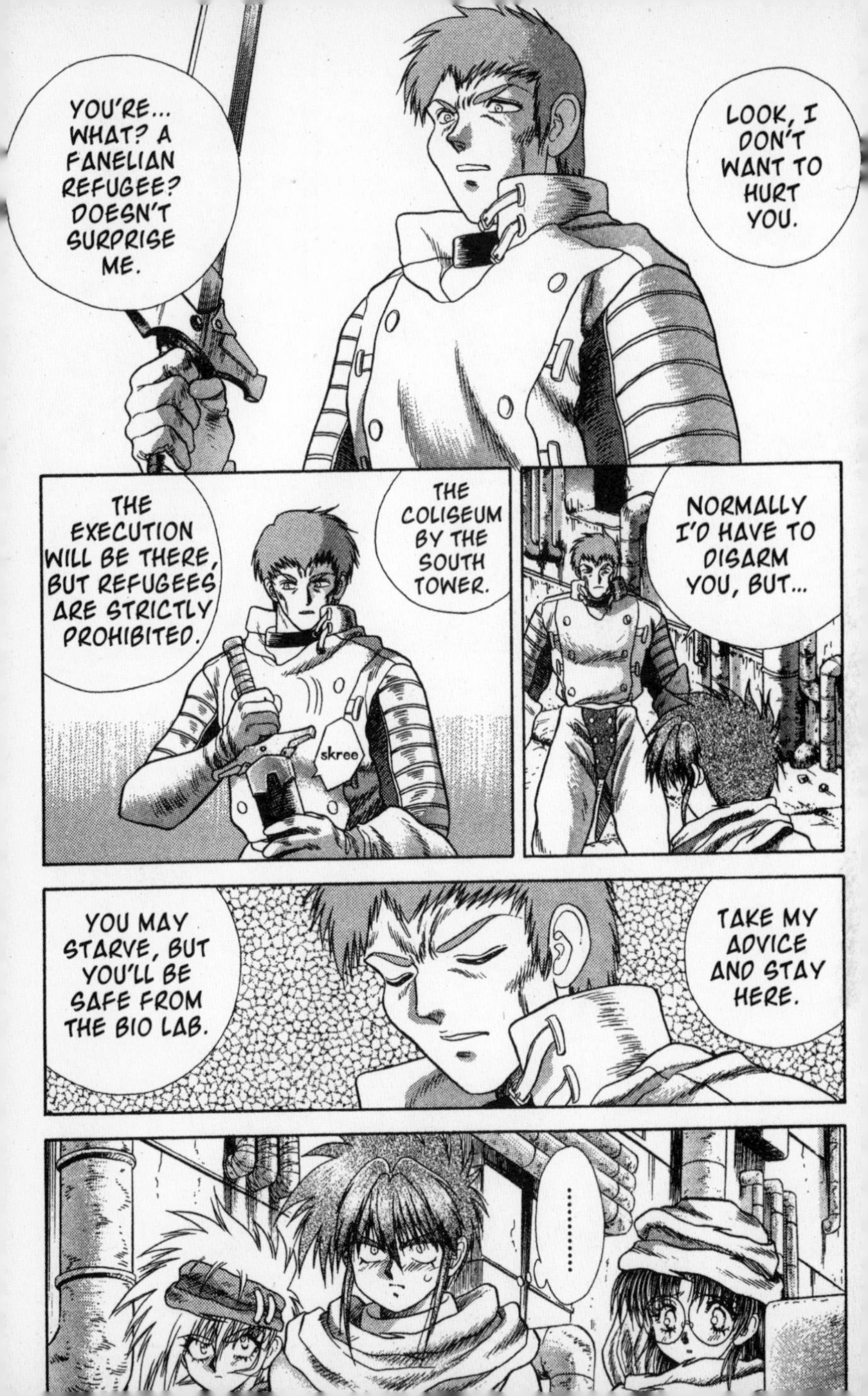
LOOK, I DON'T WANT TO HURT YOU.
YOU'RE... WHAT? A FANELIAN REFUGEE? DOESN'T SURPRISE ME.
NORMALLY I'D HAVE TO DISARM YOU, BUT...
THE COLISEUM BY THE SOUTH TOWER.
THE EXECUTION WILL BE THERE, BUT REFUGEES ARE STRICTLY PROHIBITED.
skree
TAKE MY ADVICE AND STAY HERE.
YOU MAY STARVE, BUT YOU'LL BE SAFE FROM THE BIO LAB.
....

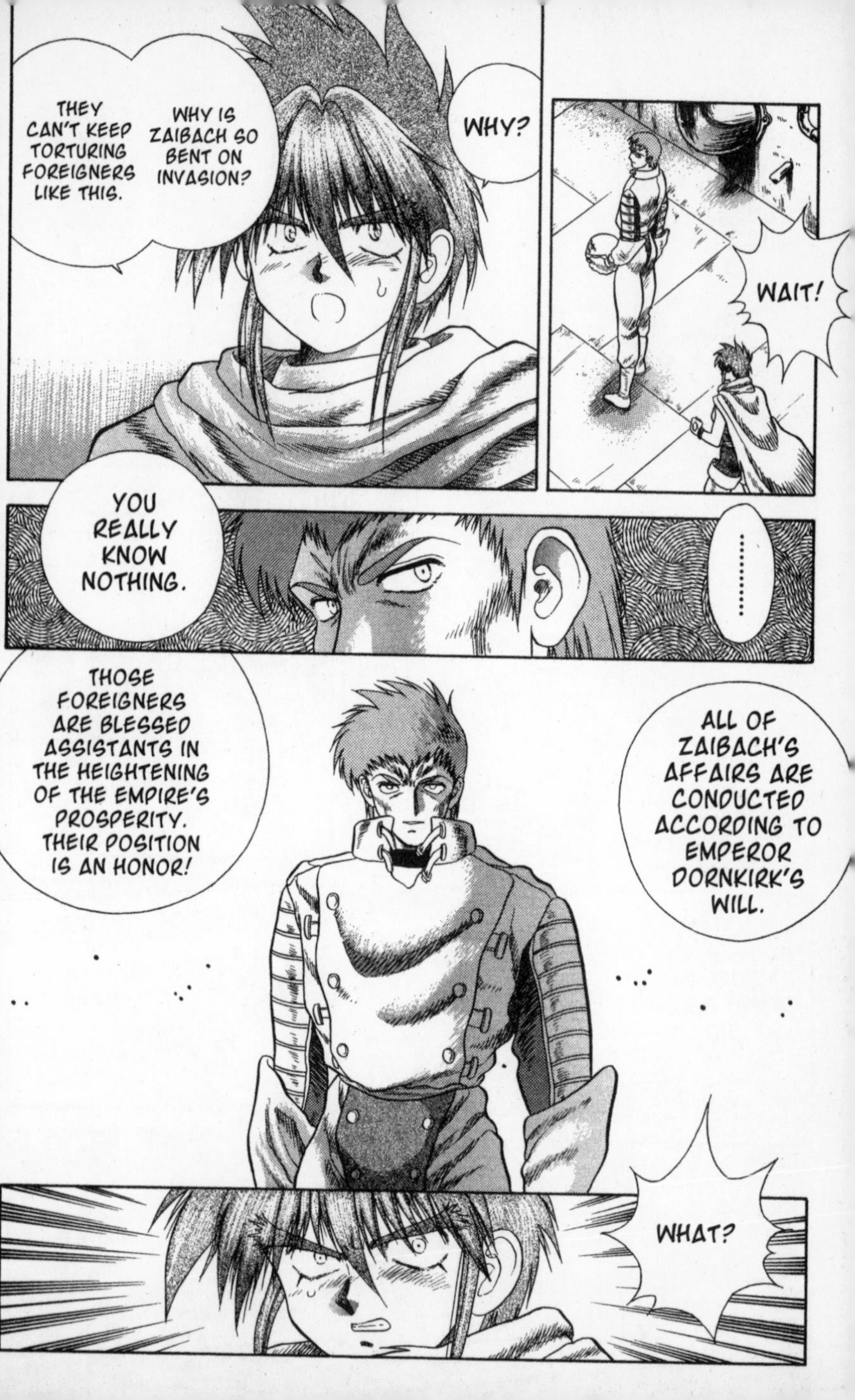
WAIT!
WHY?
WHY IS ZAIBACH SO BENT ON INVASION?
THEY CAN'T KEEP TORTURING FOREIGNERS LIKE THIS.
......
YOU REALLY KNOW NOTHING.
THOSE FOREIGNERS ARE BLESSED ASSISTANTS IN THE HEIGHTENING OF THE EMPIRE'S PROSPERITY. THEIR POSITION IS AN HONOR!
ALL OF ZAIBACH'S AFFAIRS ARE CONDUCTED ACCORDING TO EMPEROR DORNKIRK'S WILL.
WHAT?

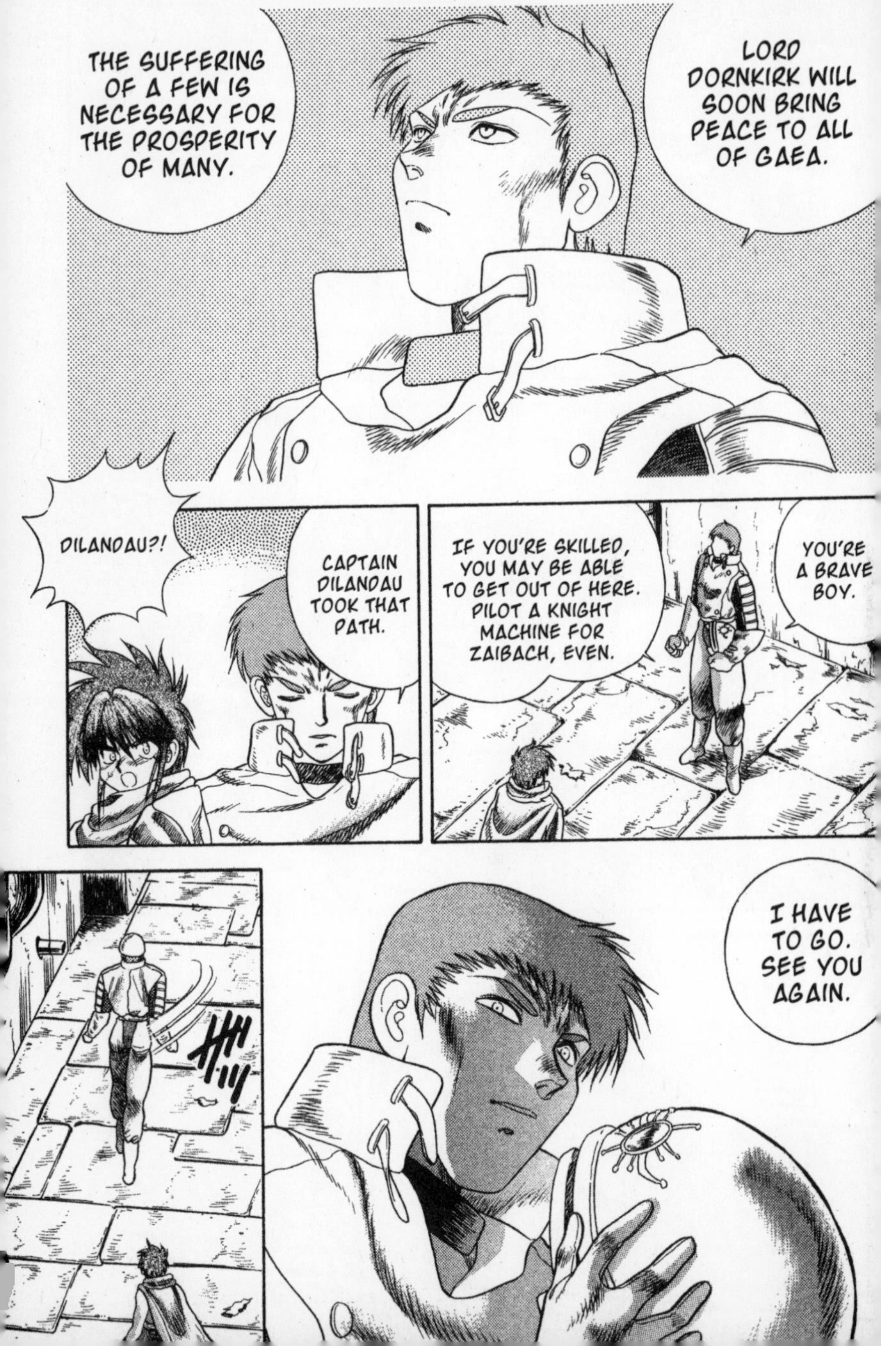
LORD DORNKIRK WILL SOON BRING PEACE TO ALL OF GAEA.
THE SUFFERING OF A FEW IS NECESSARY FOR THE PROSPERITY OF MANY.
YOU'RE A BRAVE BOY.
IF YOU'RE SKILLED, YOU MAY BE ABLE TO GET OUT OF HERE. PILOT A KNIGHT MACHINE FOR ZAIBACH, EVEN.
CAPTAIN DILANDAU TOOK THAT PATH.
DILANDAU?!
I HAVE TO GO. SEE YOU AGAIN.

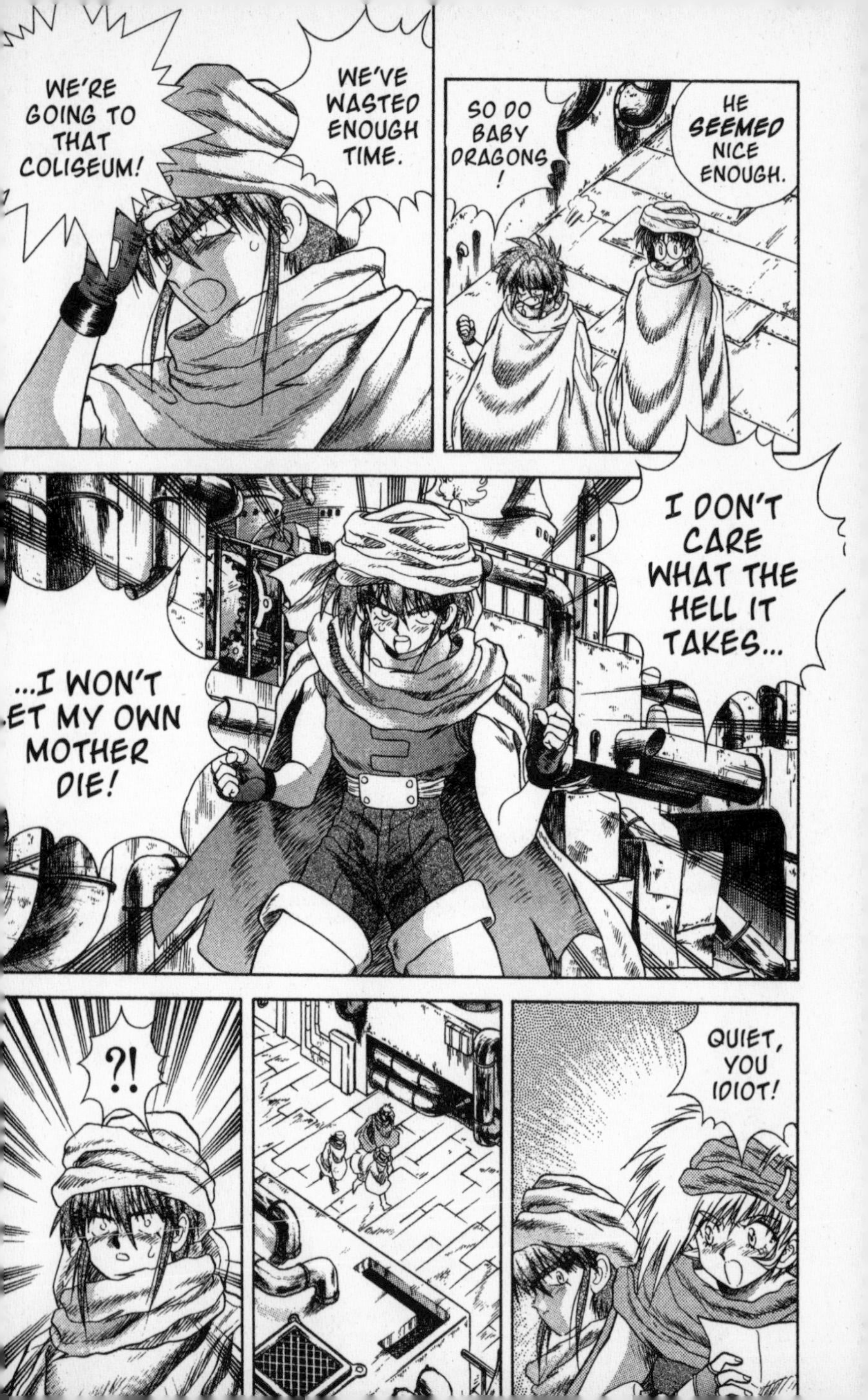
HE SEEMED NICE ENOUGH.
SO DO BABY DRAGONS!
WE'VE WASTED ENOUGH TIME.
WE'RE GOING TO THAT COLISEUM!
I DON'T CARE WHAT THE HELL IT TAKES...
...I WON'T ET MY OWN MOTHER DIE!
QUIET, YOU IDIOT!
?!

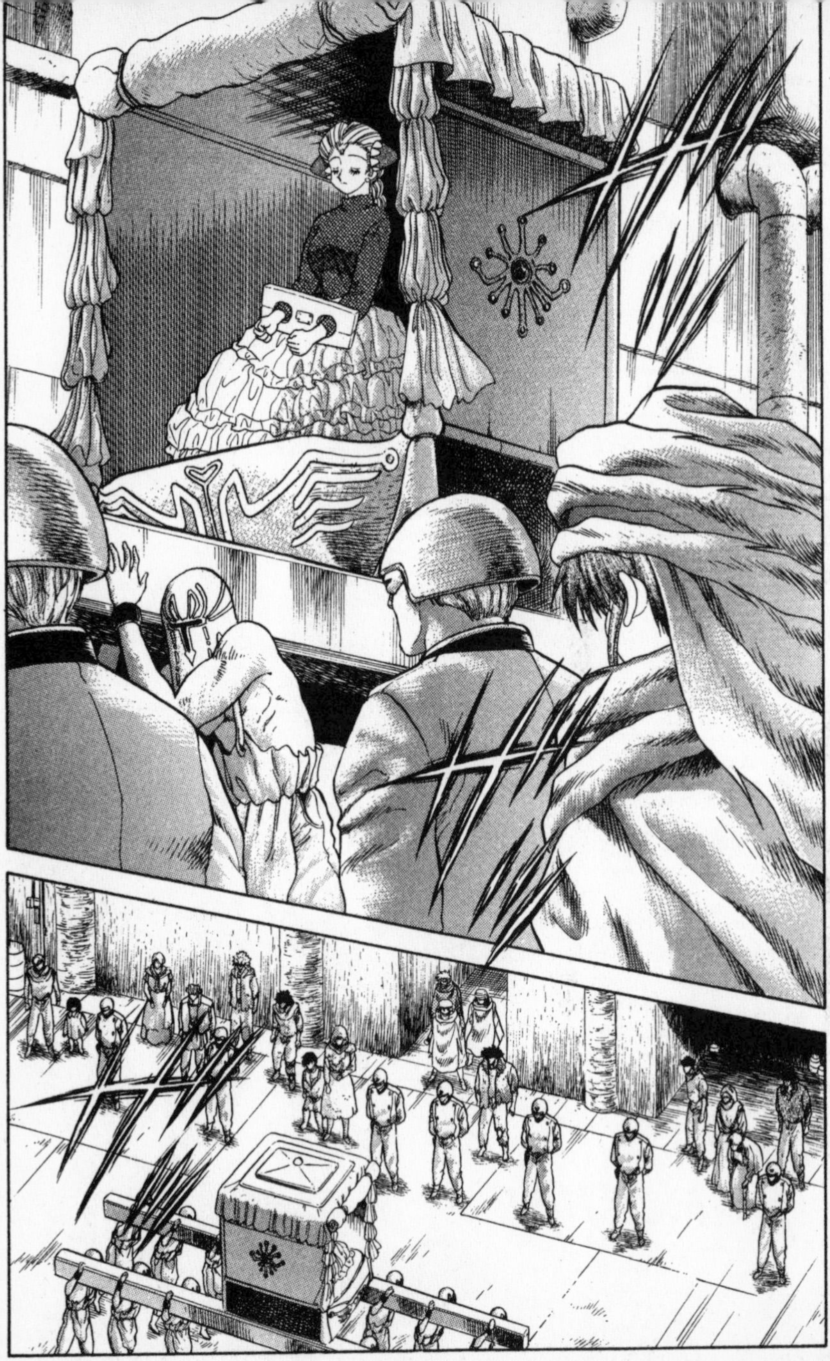

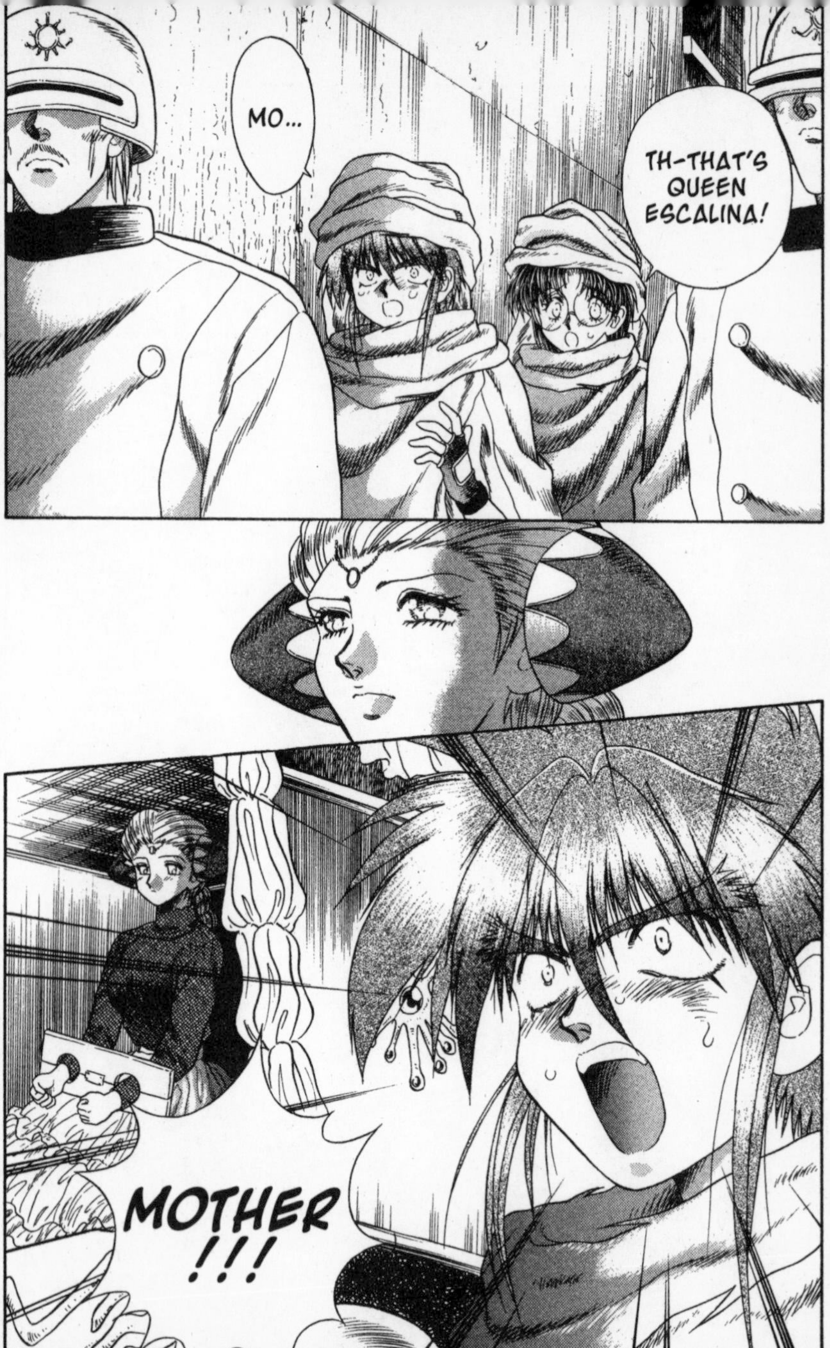
TH-THAT'S QUEEN ESCALINA!
MO...
MOTHER !!!

VISION 11:
DEATH TO THE QUEEN

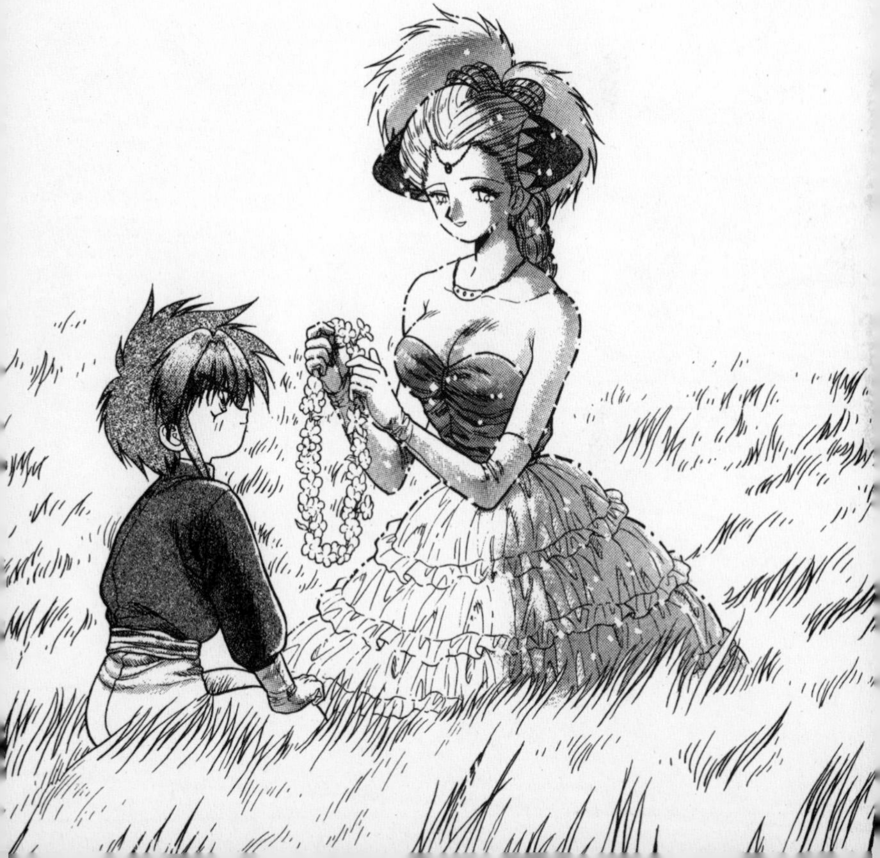

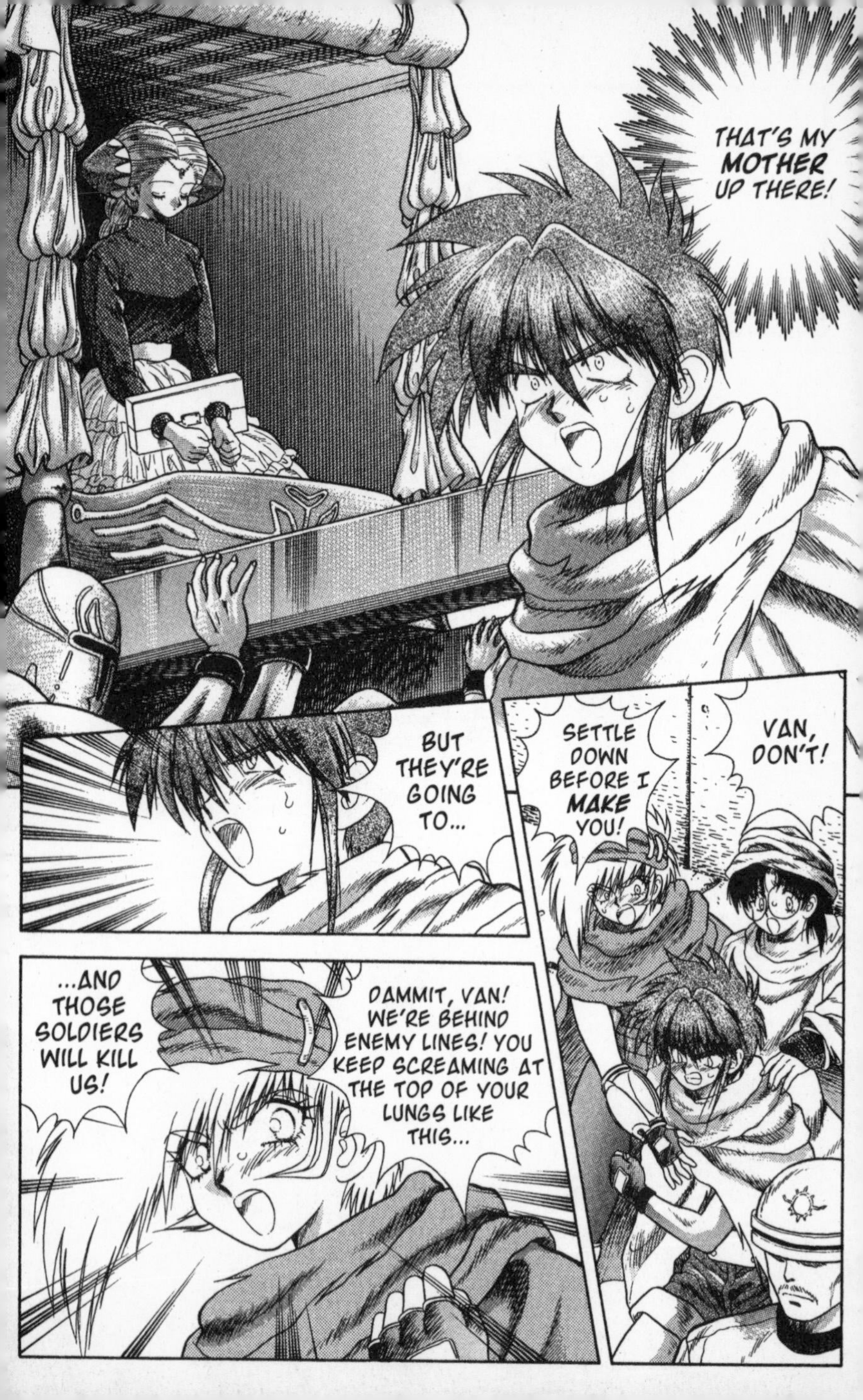
THAT'S MY MOTHER UP THERE!
VAN, DON'T!
SETTLE DOWN BEFORE I MAKE YOU!
BUT THEY'RE GOING TO...
DAMMIT, VAN! WE'RE BEHIND ENEMY LINES! YOU KEEP SCREAMING AT THE TOP OF YOUR LUNGS LIKE THIS...
...AND THOSE SOLDIERS WILL KILL US!

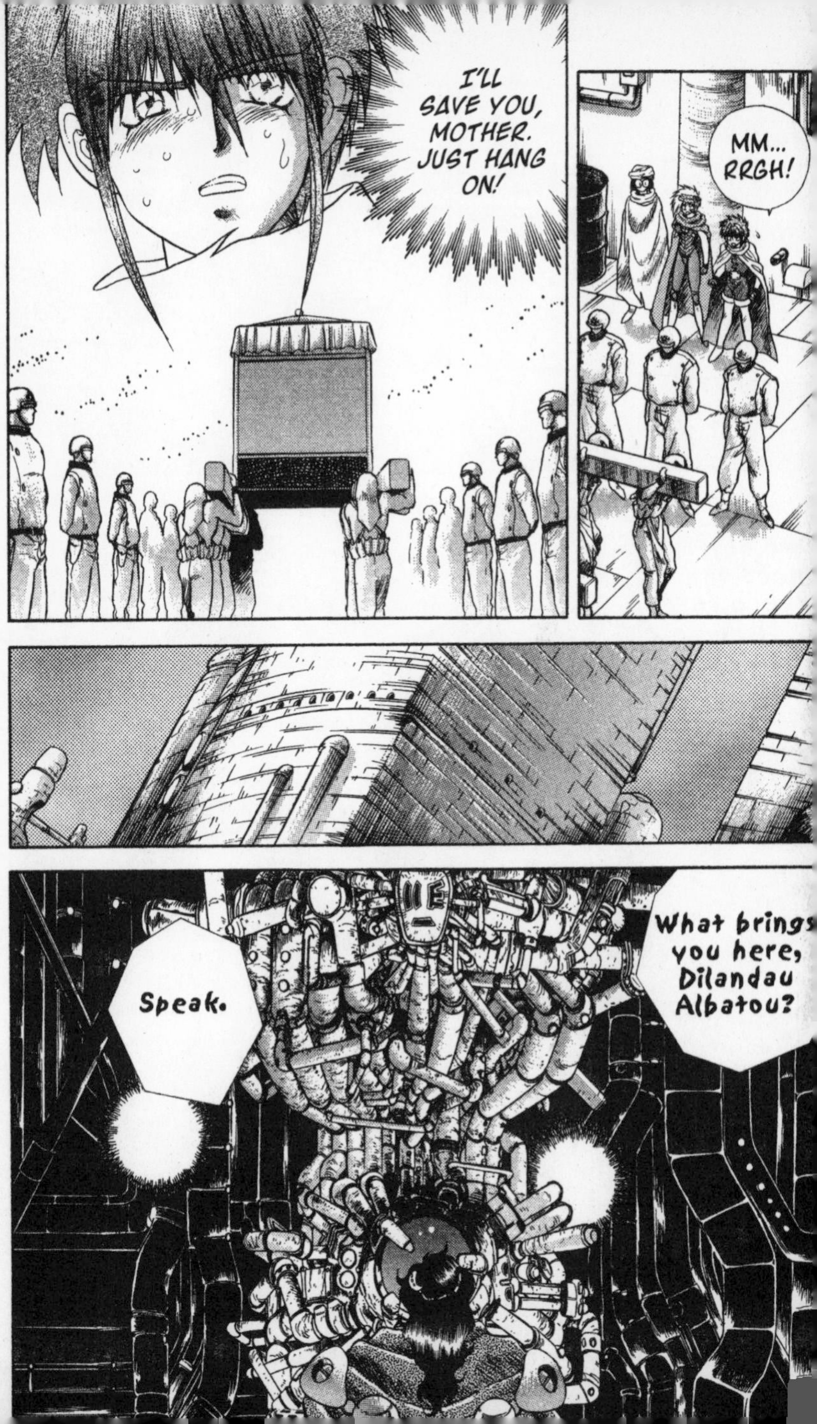
MM... RRGH!
I'LL SAVE YOU, MOTHER. JUST HANG ON!
What brings you here, Dilandau Albatou?
Speak.

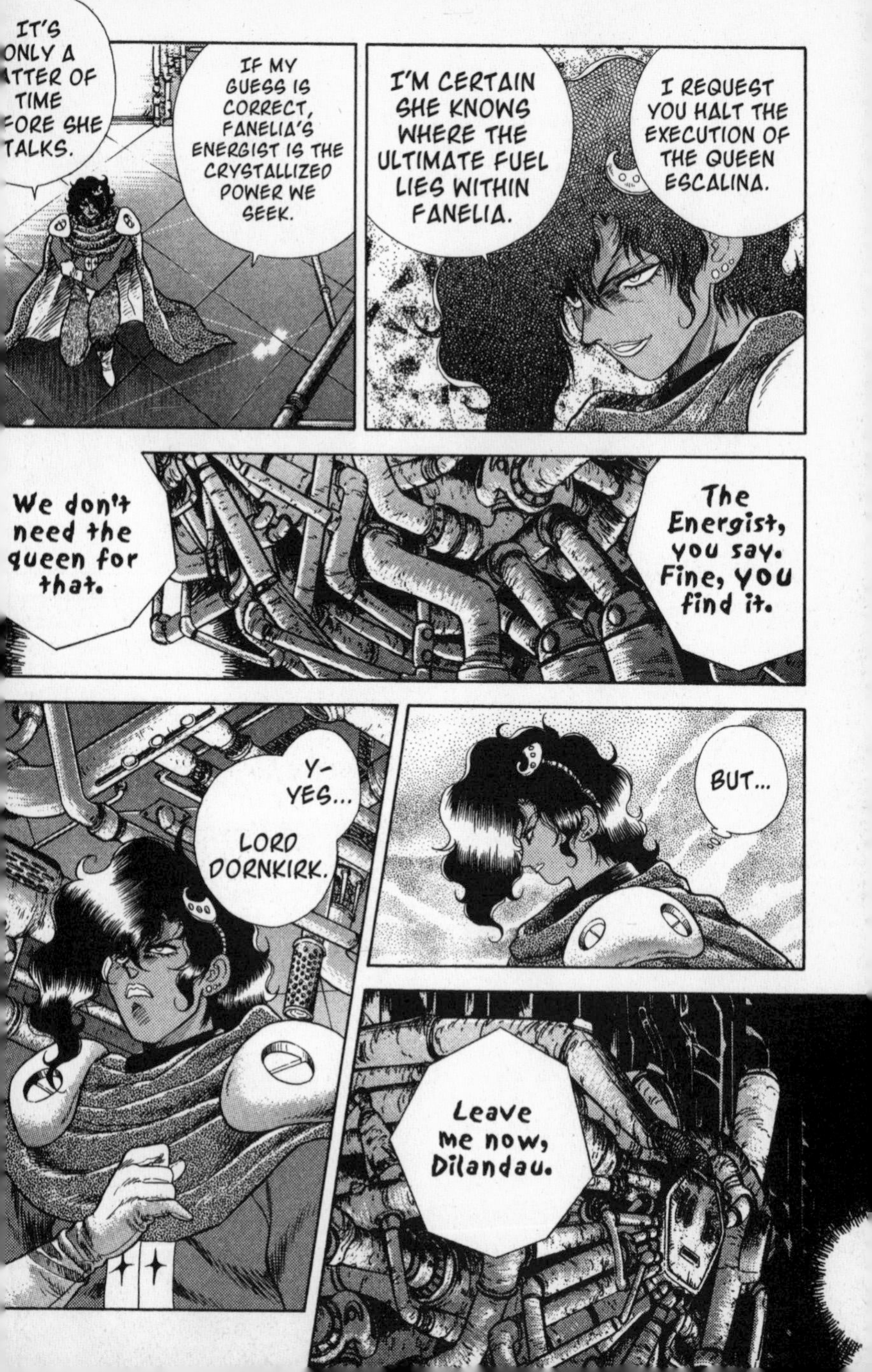
I REQUEST YOU HALT THE EXECUTION OF THE QUEEN ESCALINA.
I'M CERTAIN SHE KNOWS WHERE THE ULTIMATE FUEL LIES WITHIN FANELIA.
IF MY GUESS IS CORRECT, FANELIA'S ENERGIST IS THE CRYSTALLIZED POWER WE SEEK.
IT'S ONLY A ATTER OF TIME FORE SHE TALKS.
The Energist, you say. Fine, YOU find it.
We don't need the queen for that.
BUT...
Leave me now, Dilandau.
Y-YES... LORD DORNKIRK.

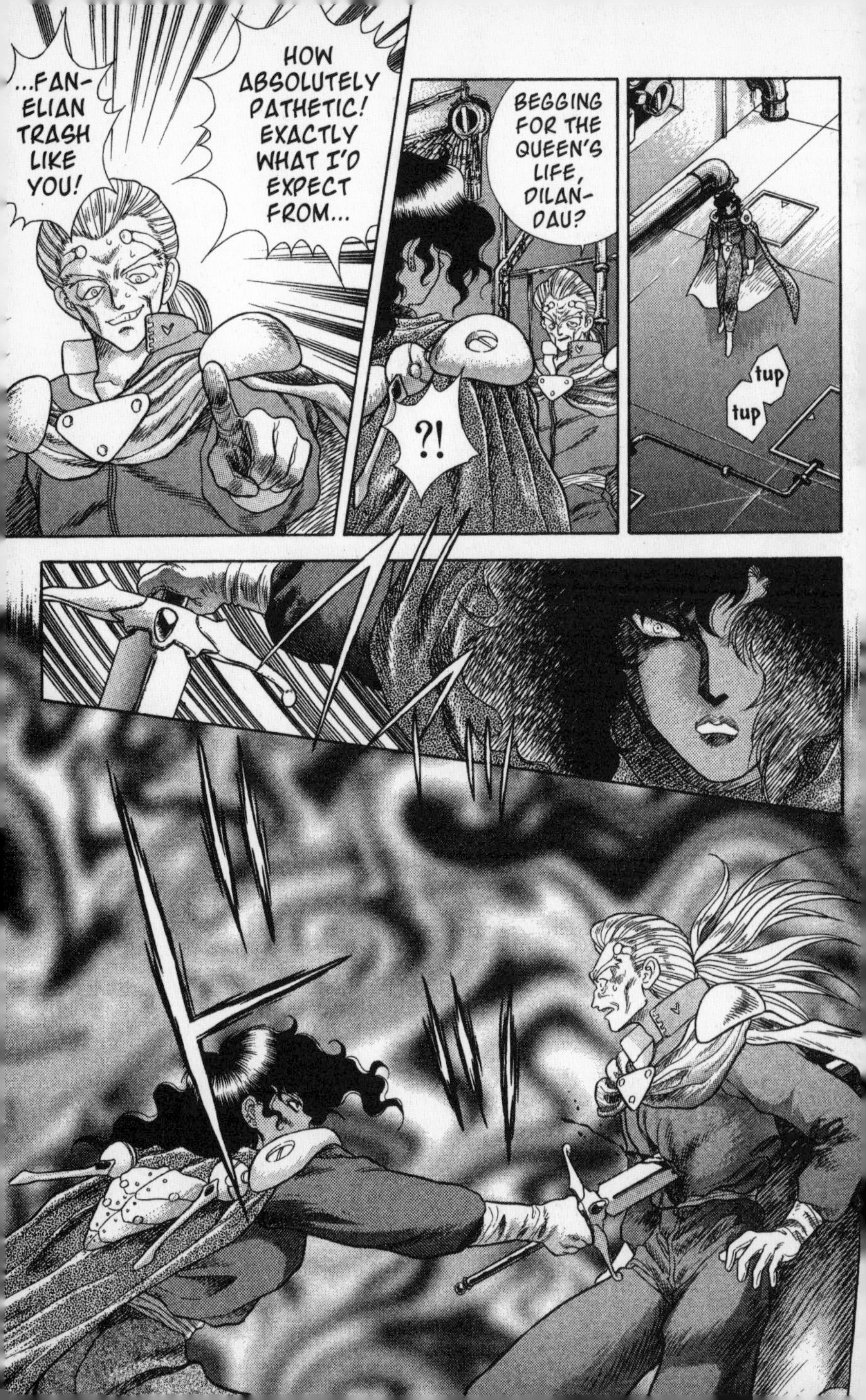
tup
tup
BEGGING FOR THE QUEEN'S LIFE, DILAN-DAU?
?!
HOW ABSOLUTELY PATHETIC! EXACTLY WHAT I'D EXPECT FROM...
...FAN-ELIAN TRASH LIKE YOU!

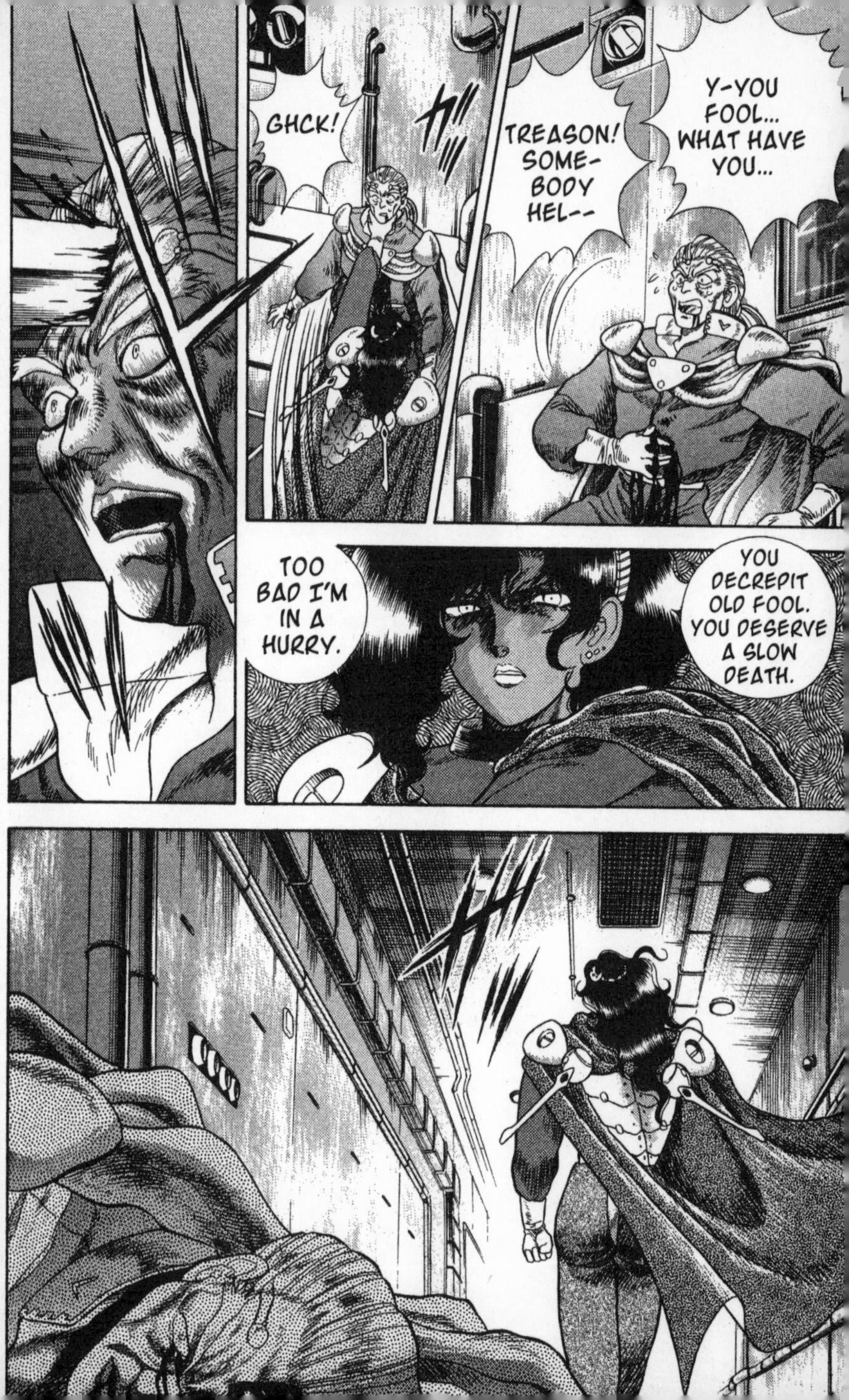
Y-YOU FOOL... WHAT HAVE YOU...
TREASON! SOMEBODY HEL--
GHCK!
YOU DECREPIT OLD FOOL. YOU DESERVE A SLOW DEATH.
TOO BAD I'M IN A HURRY.

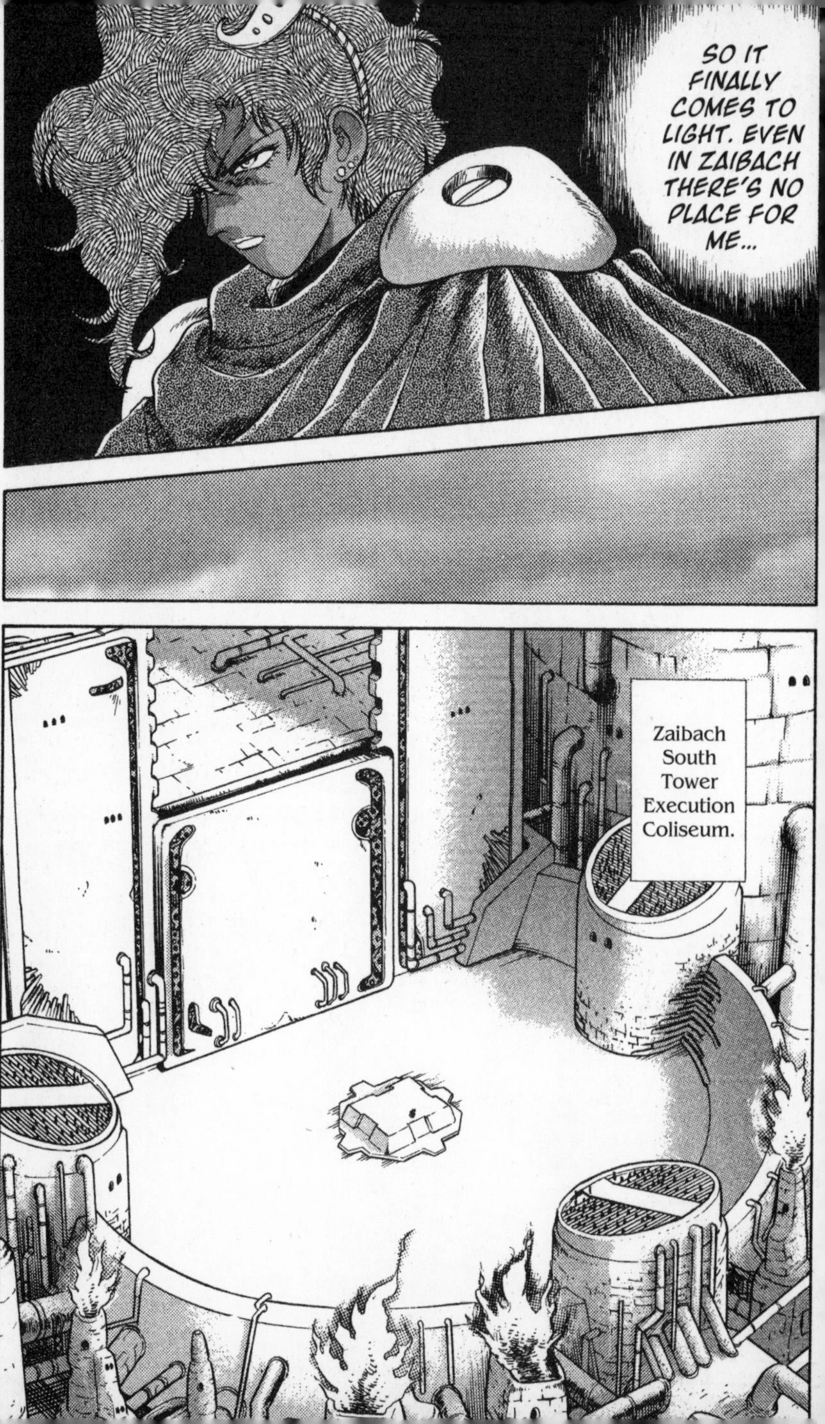
SO IT FINALLY COMES TO LIGHT. EVEN IN ZAIBACH THERE'S NO PLACE FOR ME...
Zaibach South Tower Execution Coliseum.

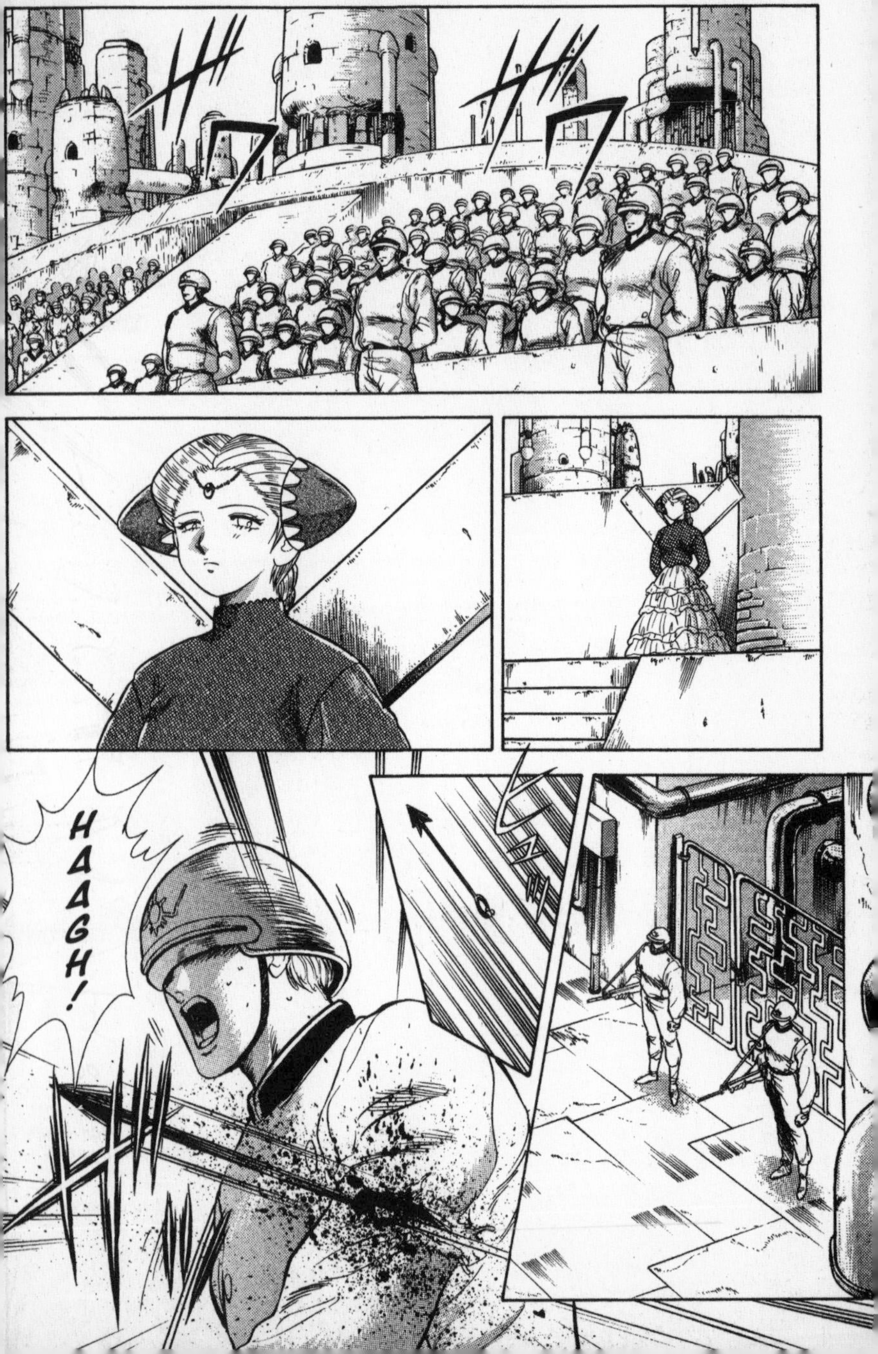
HAAGH!

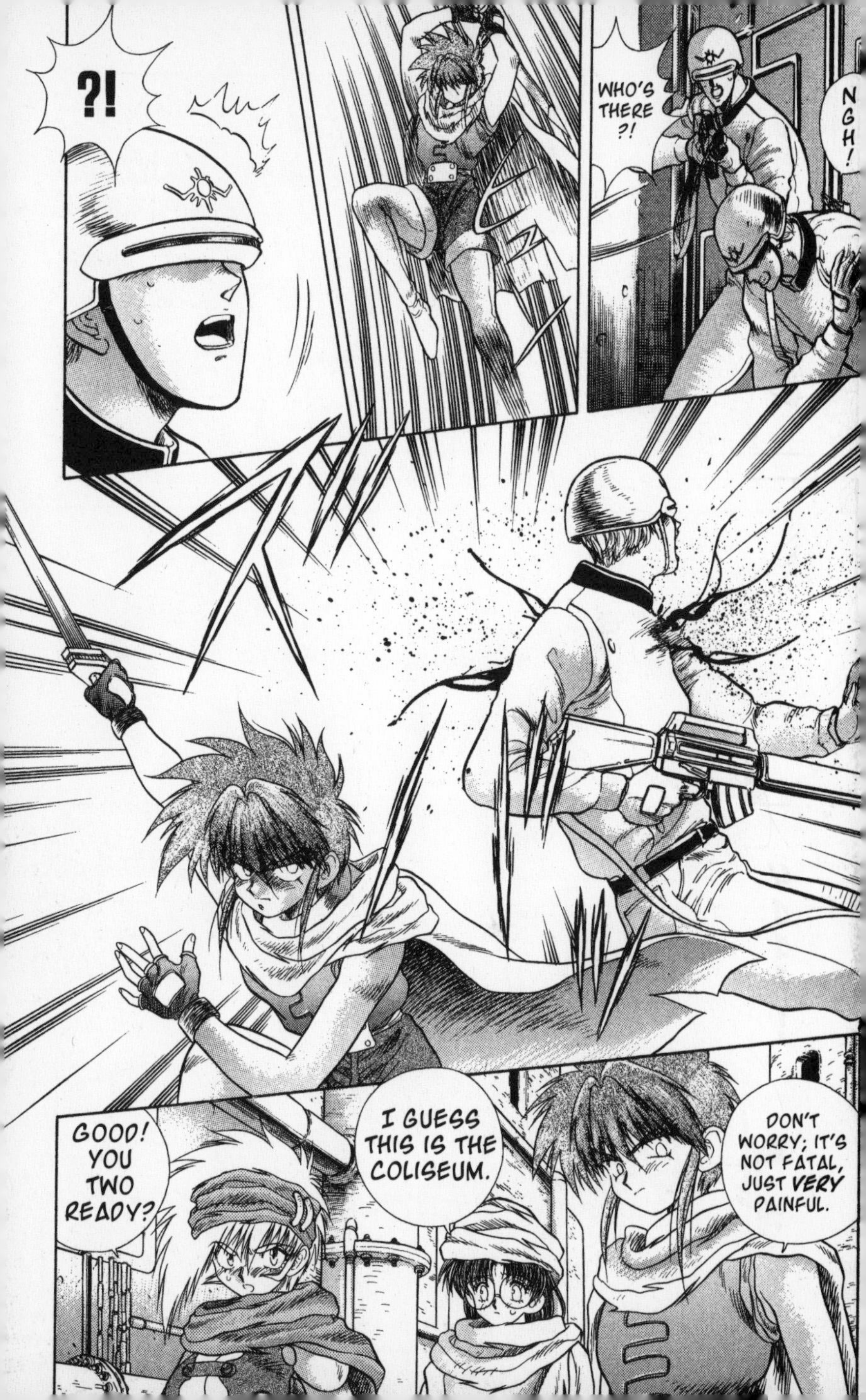
NGH!
WHO'S THERE ?!
?!
DON'T WORRY; IT'S NOT FATAL, JUST VERY PAINFUL.
I GUESS THIS IS THE COLISEUM.
GOOD! YOU TWO READY?

OPEN THE DOOR! RELEASE THE EARTH DRAGON!

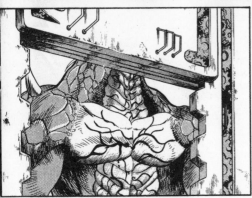

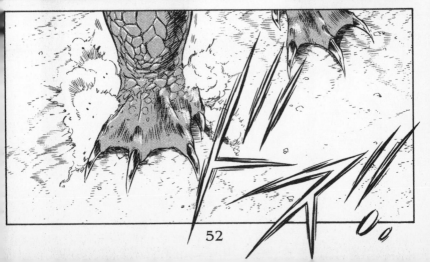

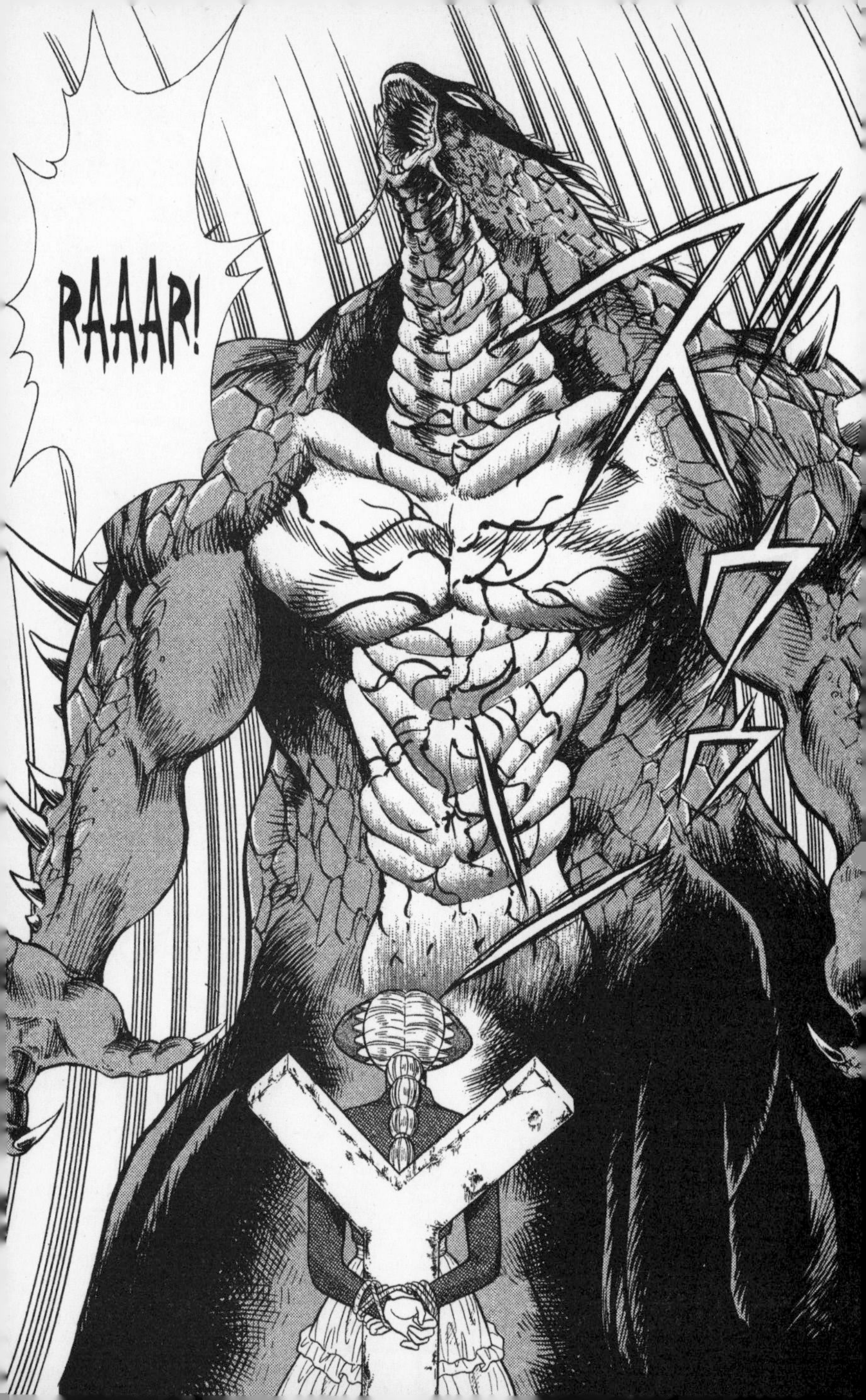
RAAAR!

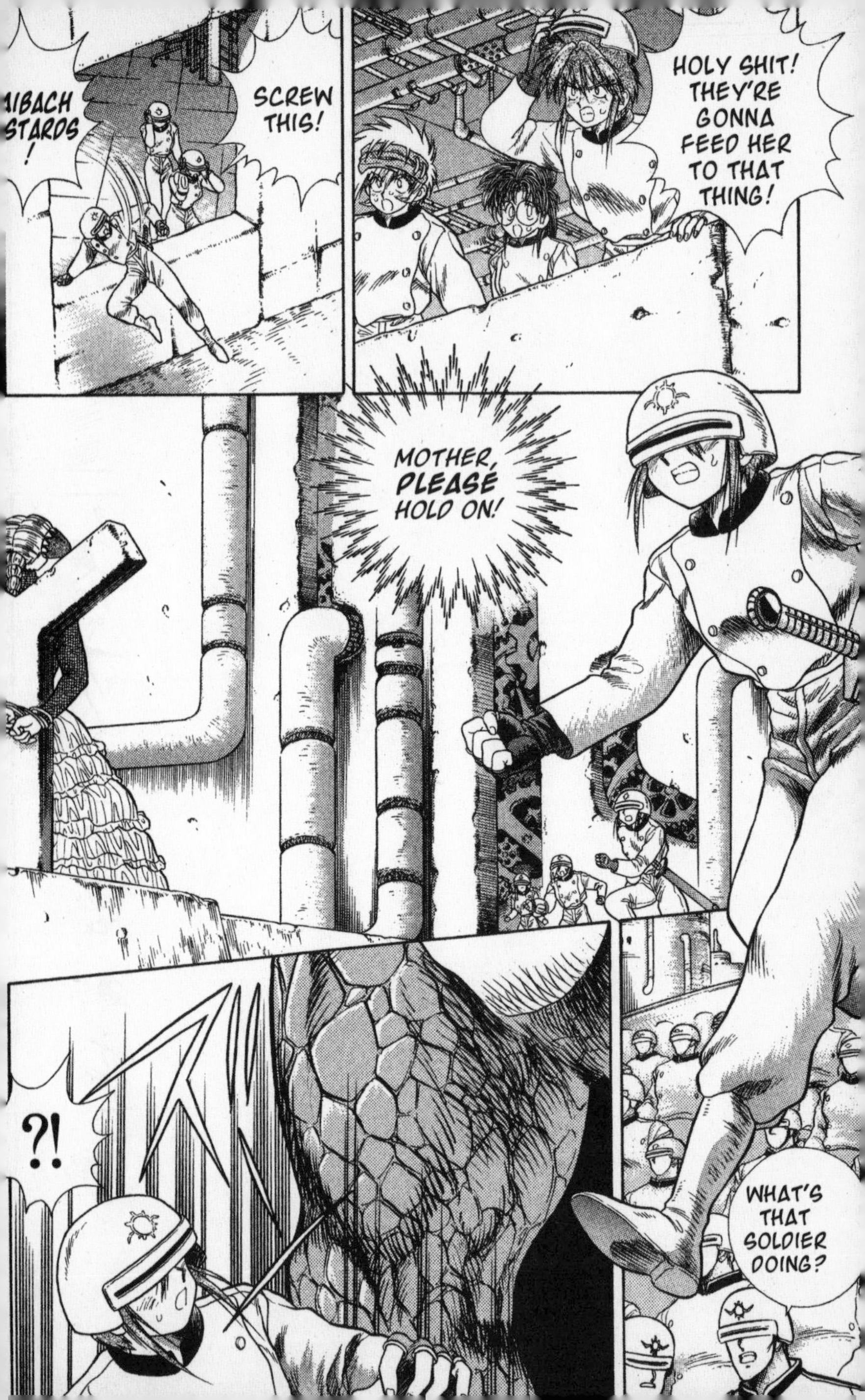
HOLY SHIT! THEY'RE GONNA FEED HER TO THAT THING!
SCREW THIS!
AIBACH STARDS!
MOTHER, **PLEASE** HOLD ON!
WHAT'S THAT SOLDIER DOING?
?!

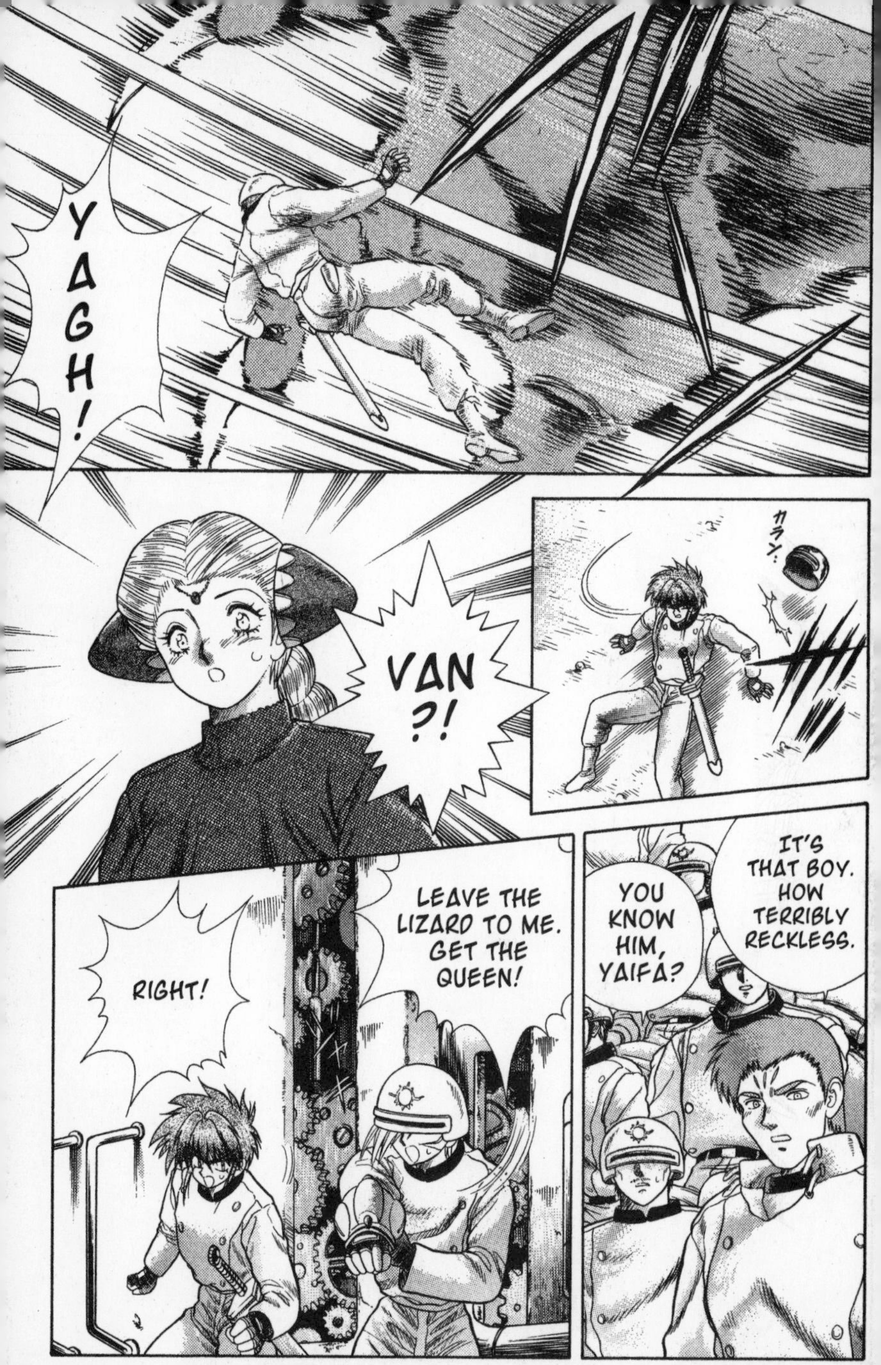
YAGH!
カラン!
VAN ?!
IT'S THAT BOY. HOW TERRIBLY RECKLESS.
YOU KNOW HIM, YAIFA?
LEAVE THE LIZARD TO ME. GET THE QUEEN!
RIGHT!

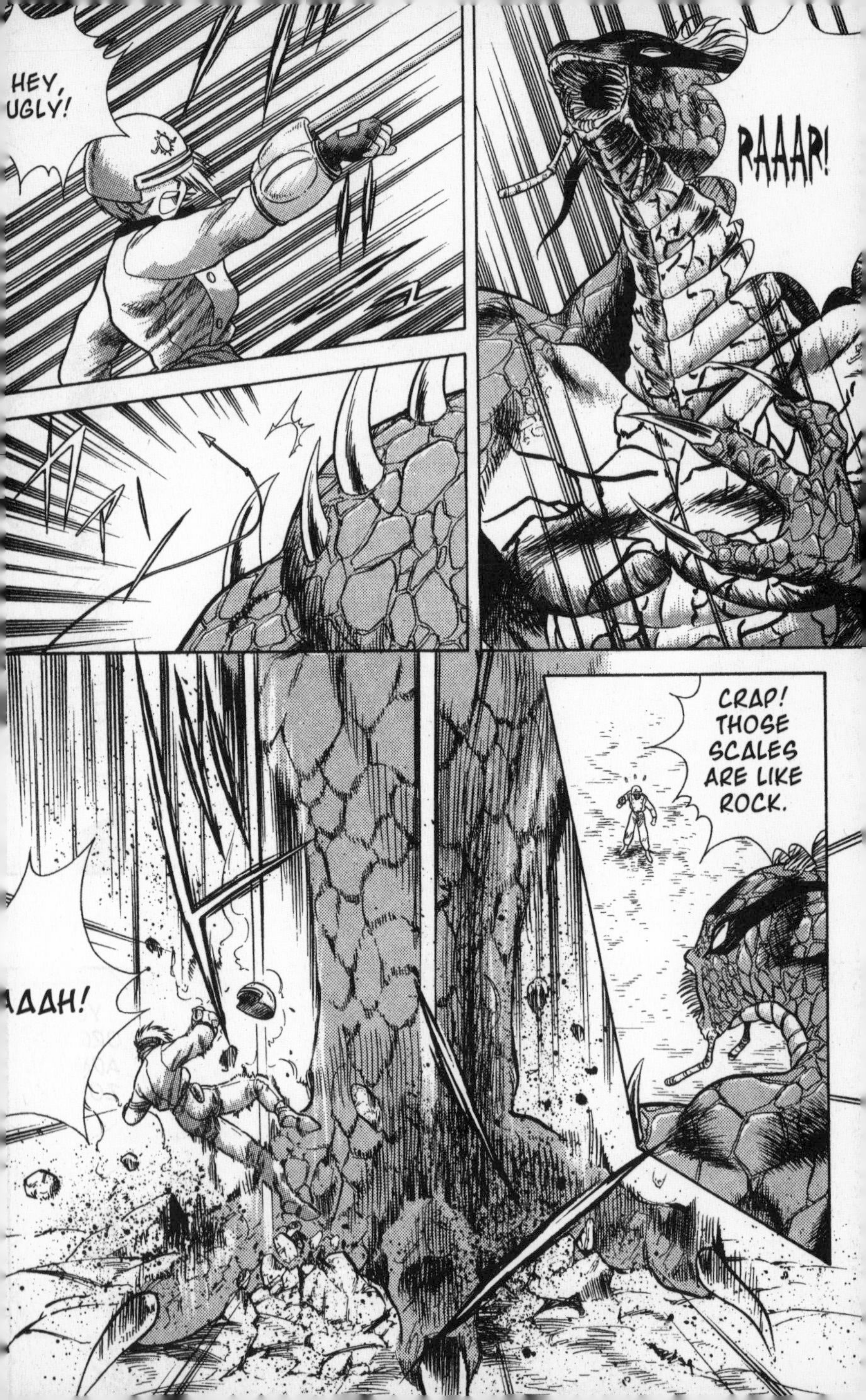
RAAAR!
HEY, UGLY!
CRAP! THOSE SCALES ARE LIKE ROCK.
AAAH!

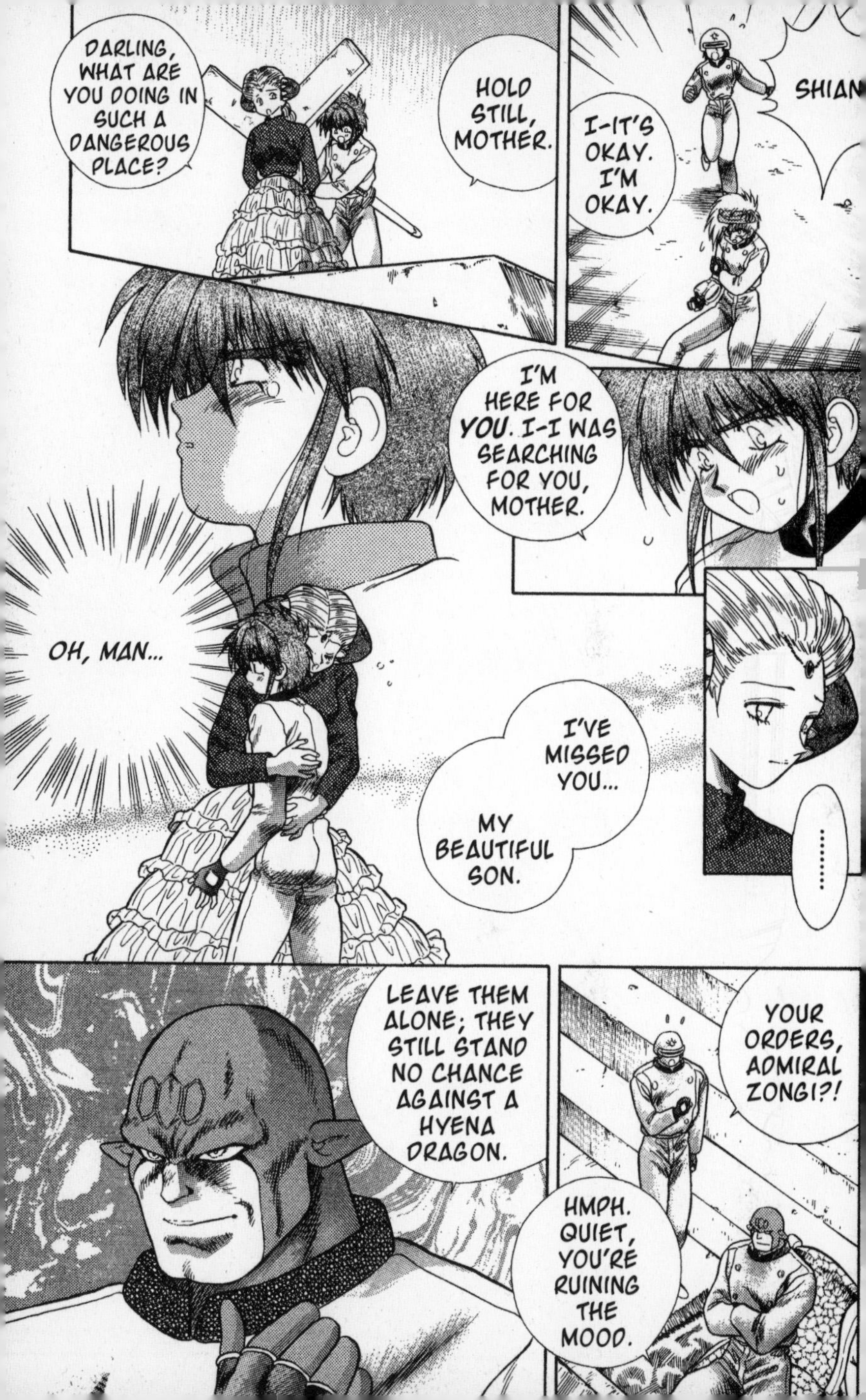
SHIAN
I-IT'S OKAY. I'M OKAY.
DARLING, WHAT ARE YOU DOING IN SUCH A DANGEROUS PLACE?
HOLD STILL, MOTHER.
I'M HERE FOR *YOU*. I-I WAS SEARCHING FOR YOU, MOTHER.
......
I'VE MISSED YOU...
MY BEAUTIFUL SON.
OH, MAN...
YOUR ORDERS, ADMIRAL ZONGI?!
HMPH. QUIET, YOU'RE RUINING THE MOOD.
LEAVE THEM ALONE; THEY STILL STAND NO CHANCE AGAINST A HYENA DRAGON.

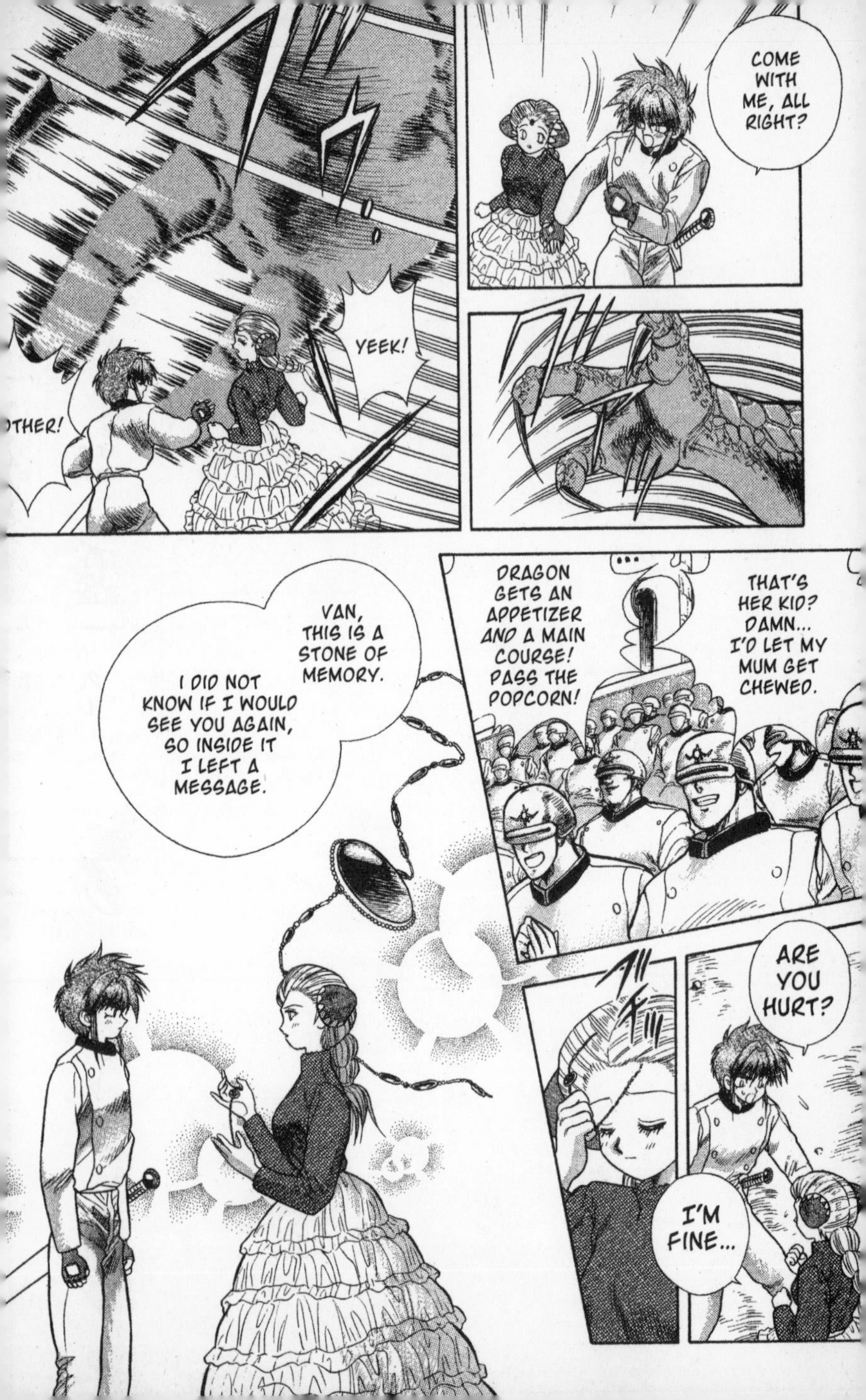
COME WITH ME, ALL RIGHT?
YEEK!
OTHER!
THAT'S HER KID? DAMN... I'D LET MY MUM GET CHEWED.
...
DRAGON GETS AN APPETIZER AND A MAIN COURSE! PASS THE POPCORN!
ARE YOU HURT?
I'M FINE...
VAN, THIS IS A STONE OF MEMORY.
I DID NOT KNOW IF I WOULD SEE YOU AGAIN, SO INSIDE IT I LEFT A MESSAGE.

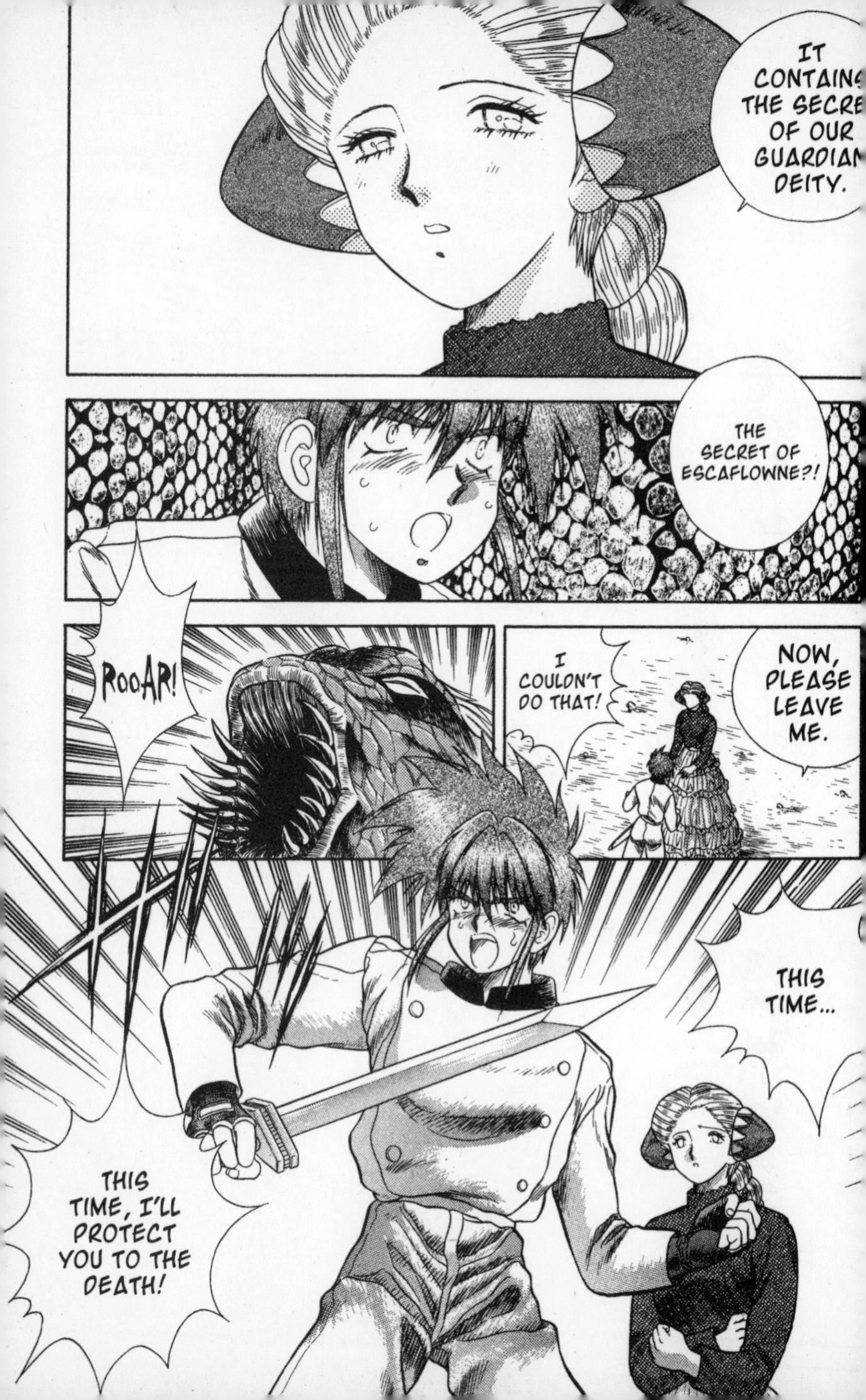
IT CONTAINS THE SECRE OF OUR GUARDIAN DEITY.
THE SECRET OF ESCAFLOWNE?!
NOW, PLEASE LEAVE ME.
I COULDN'T DO THAT!
RooAR!
THIS TIME...
THIS TIME, I'LL PROTECT YOU TO THE DEATH!

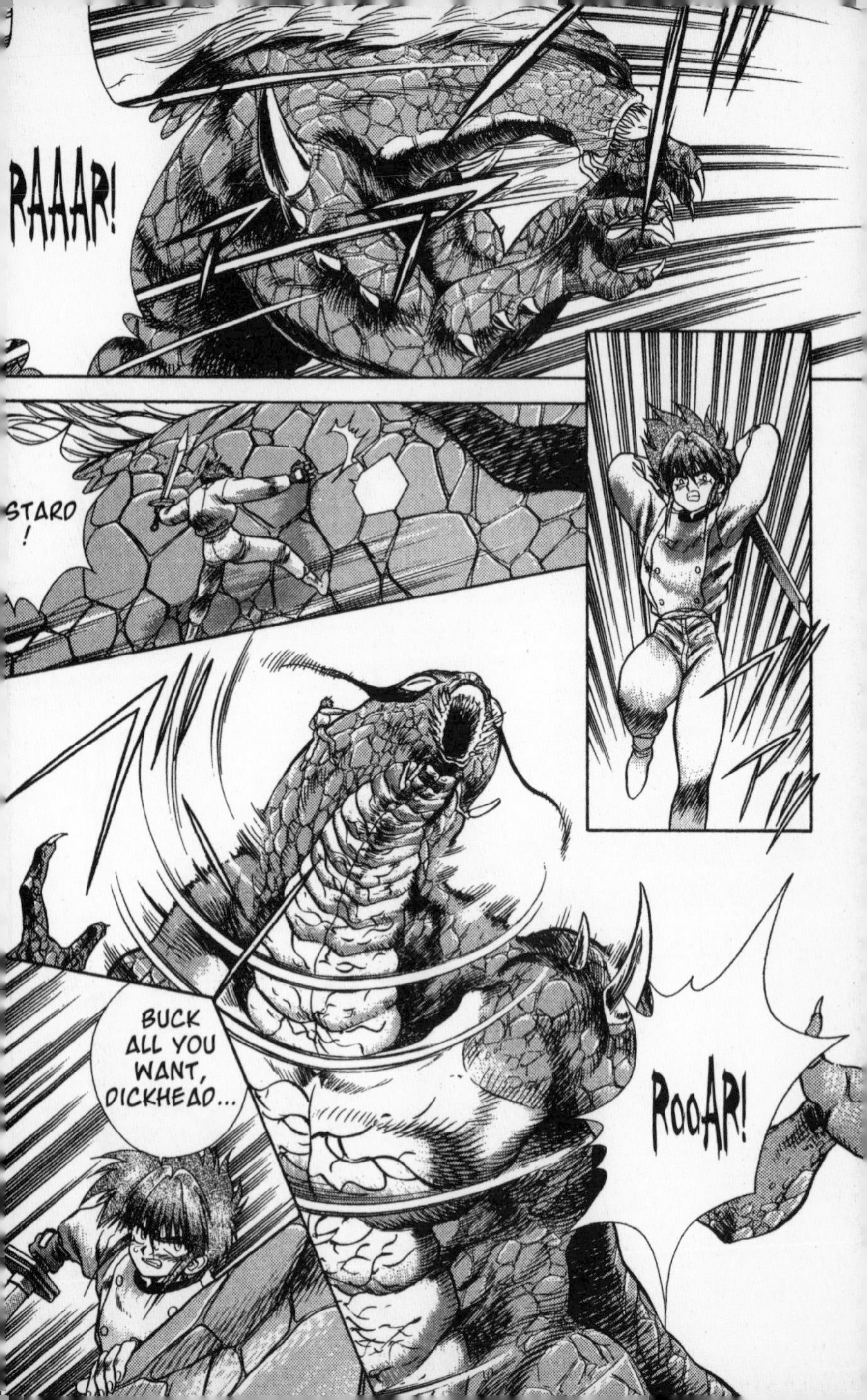
RAAAR!
STARD !
RooAR!
BUCK ALL YOU WANT, DICKHEAD...

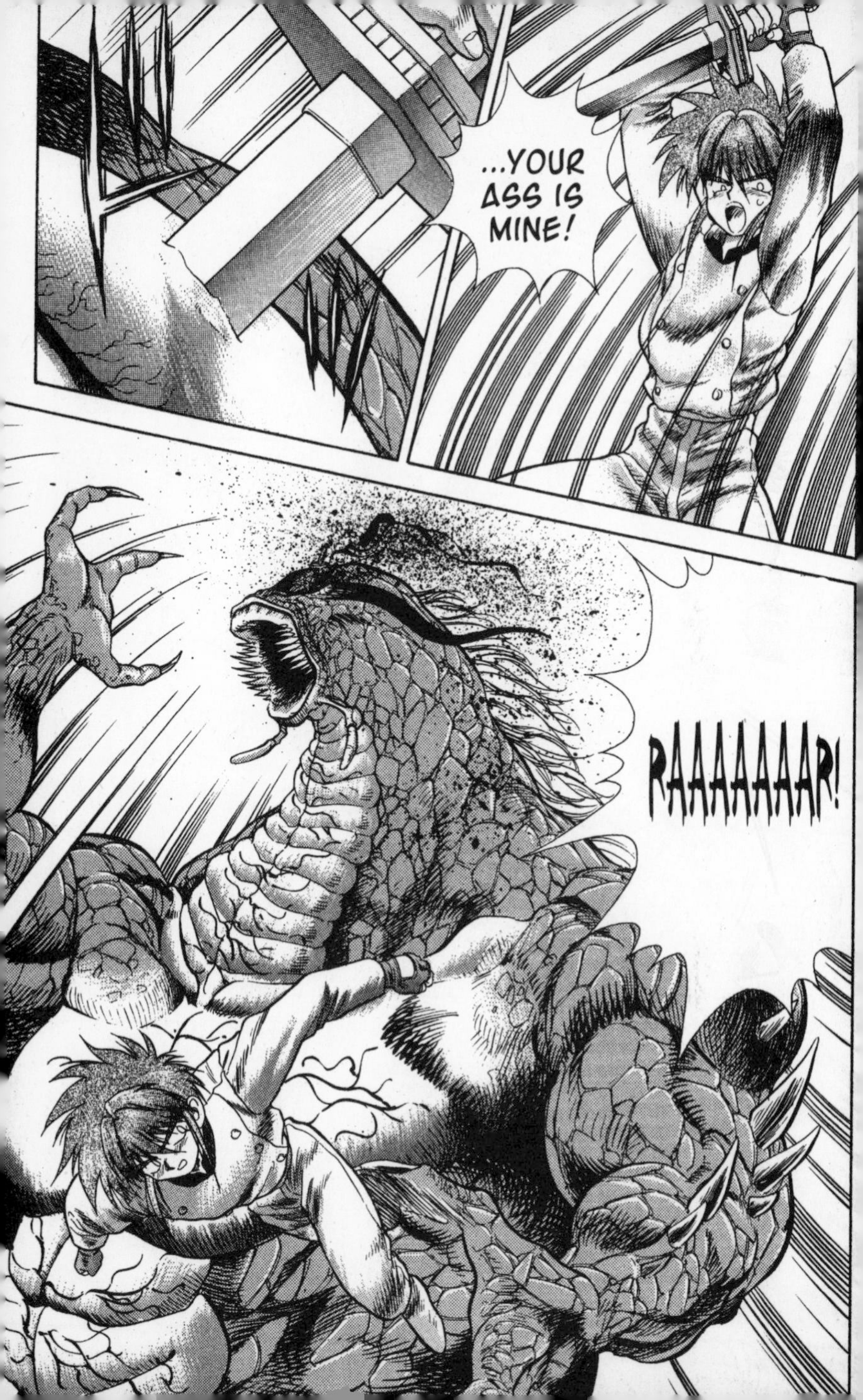
...YOUR ASS IS MINE!
RAAAAAAR!

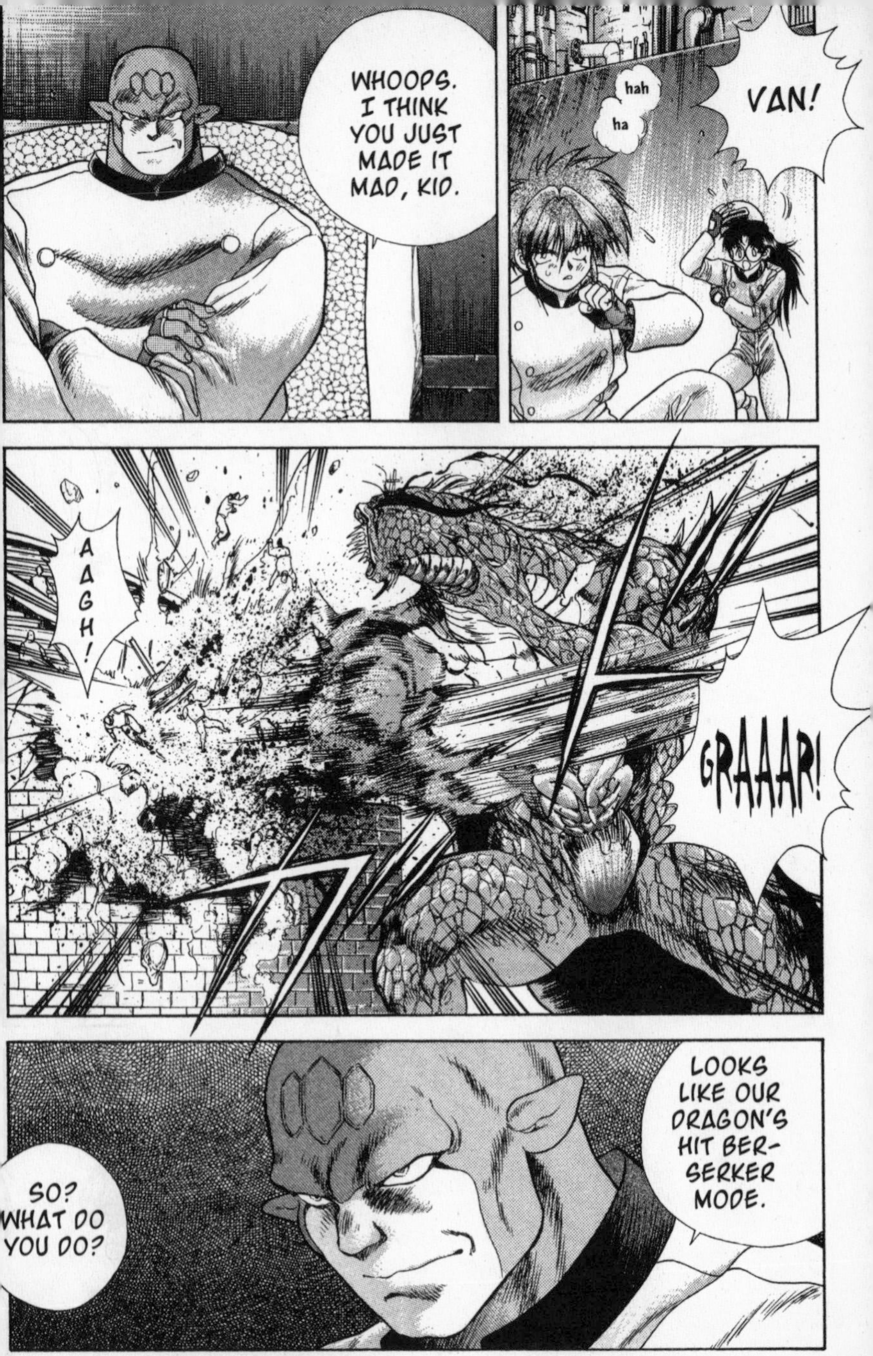
VAN!
hah
ha
WHOOPS. I THINK YOU JUST MADE IT MAD, KID.
GRAAAR!
AAGH!
LOOKS LIKE OUR DRAGON'S HIT BER-SERKER MODE.
SO? WHAT DO YOU DO?

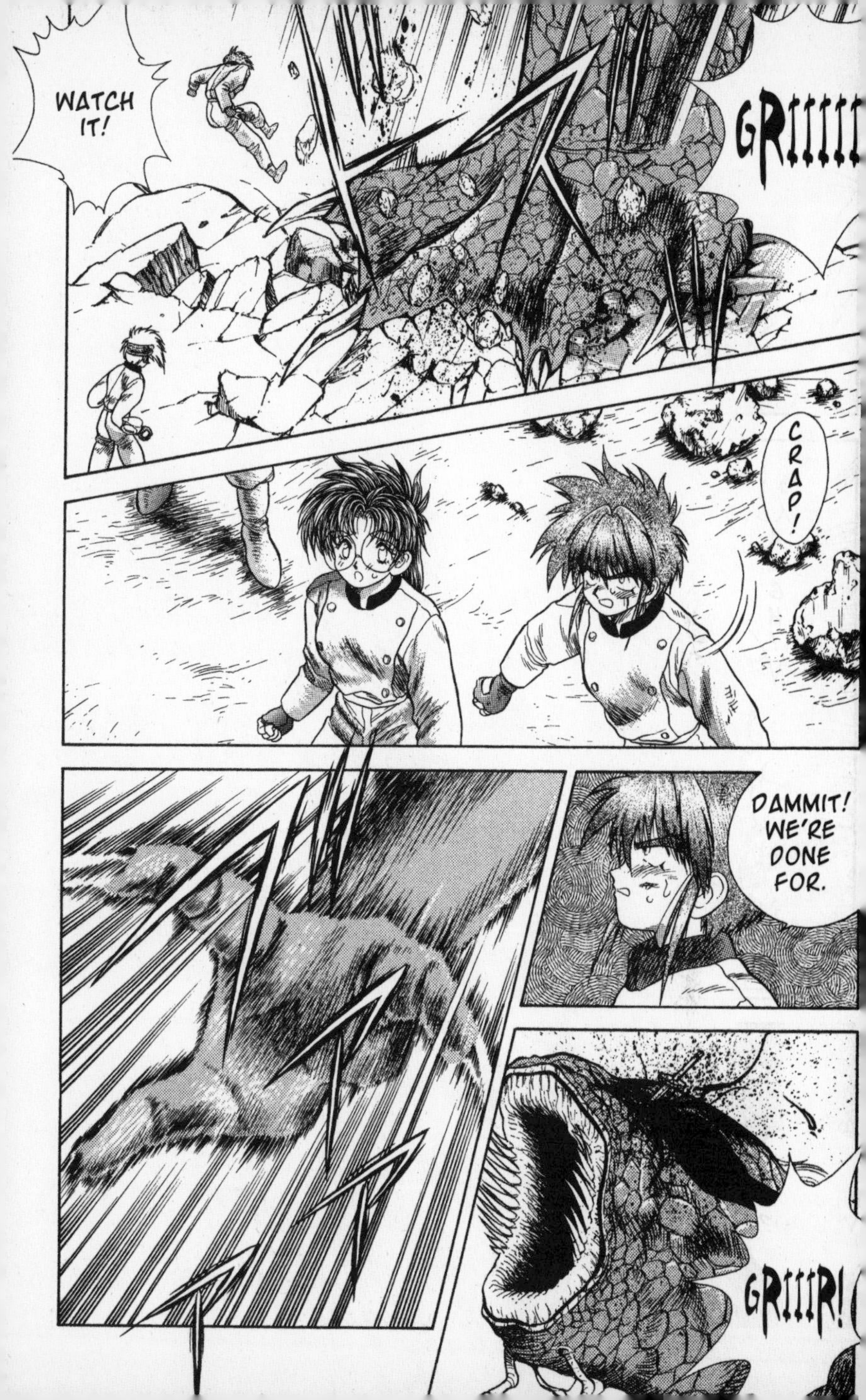
GRIIIII
WATCH IT!
CRAP!
DAMMIT! WE'RE DONE FOR.
GRIIIR!

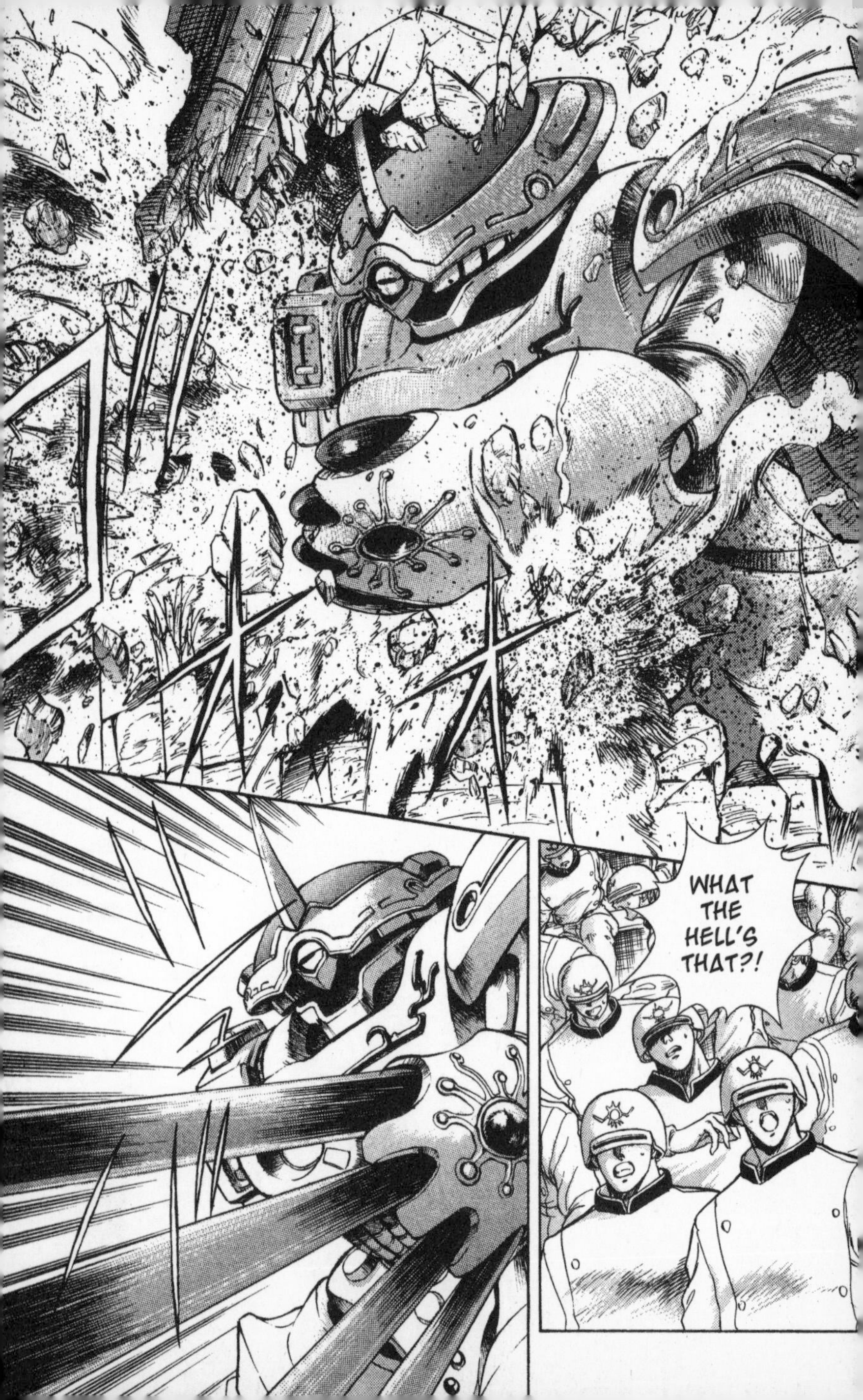
WHAT THE HELL'S THAT?!

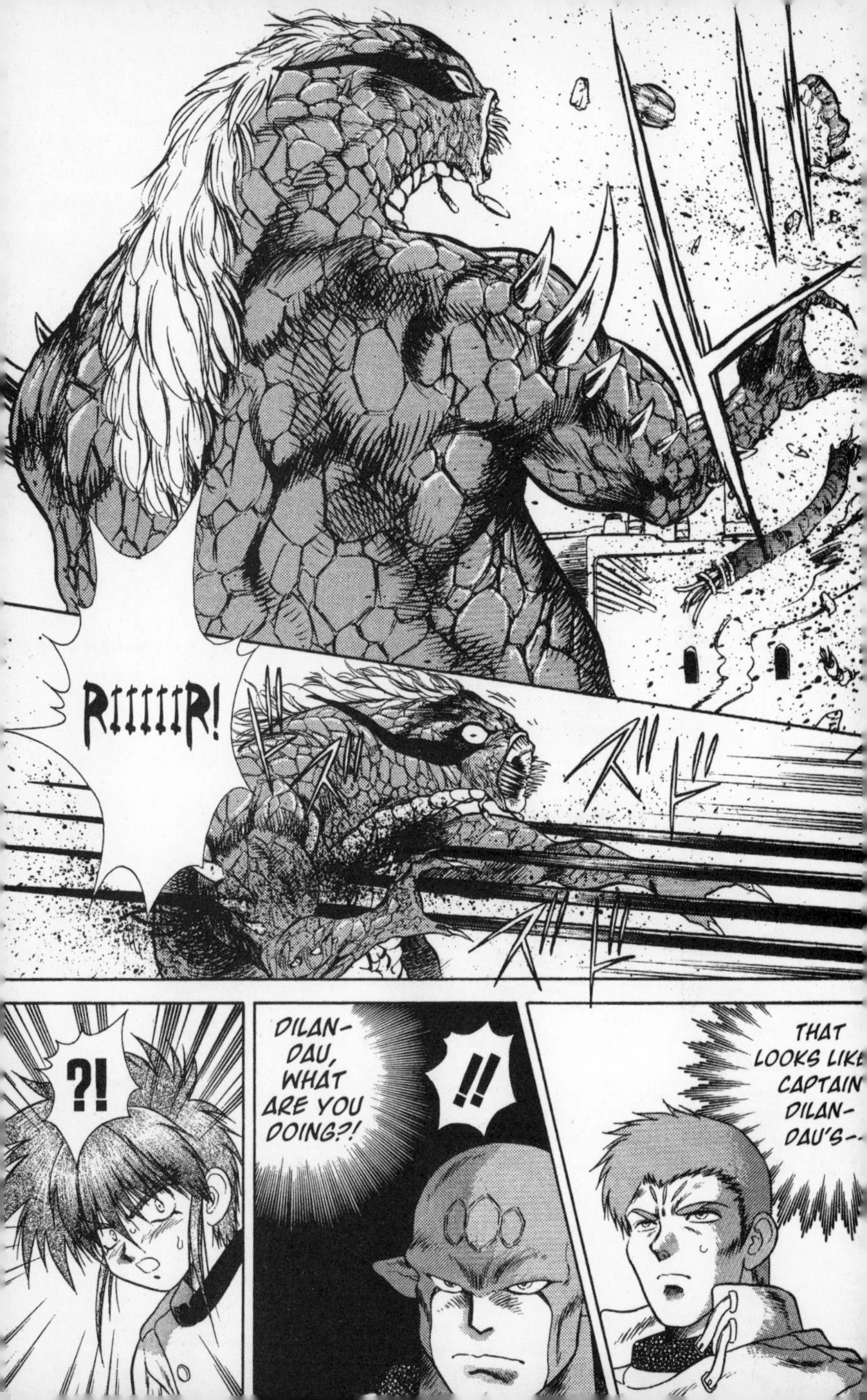
RIIIIIR!
THAT LOOKS LIKE CAPTAIN DILAN-DAU'S--
!!
DILAN-DAU, WHAT ARE YOU DOING?!
?!

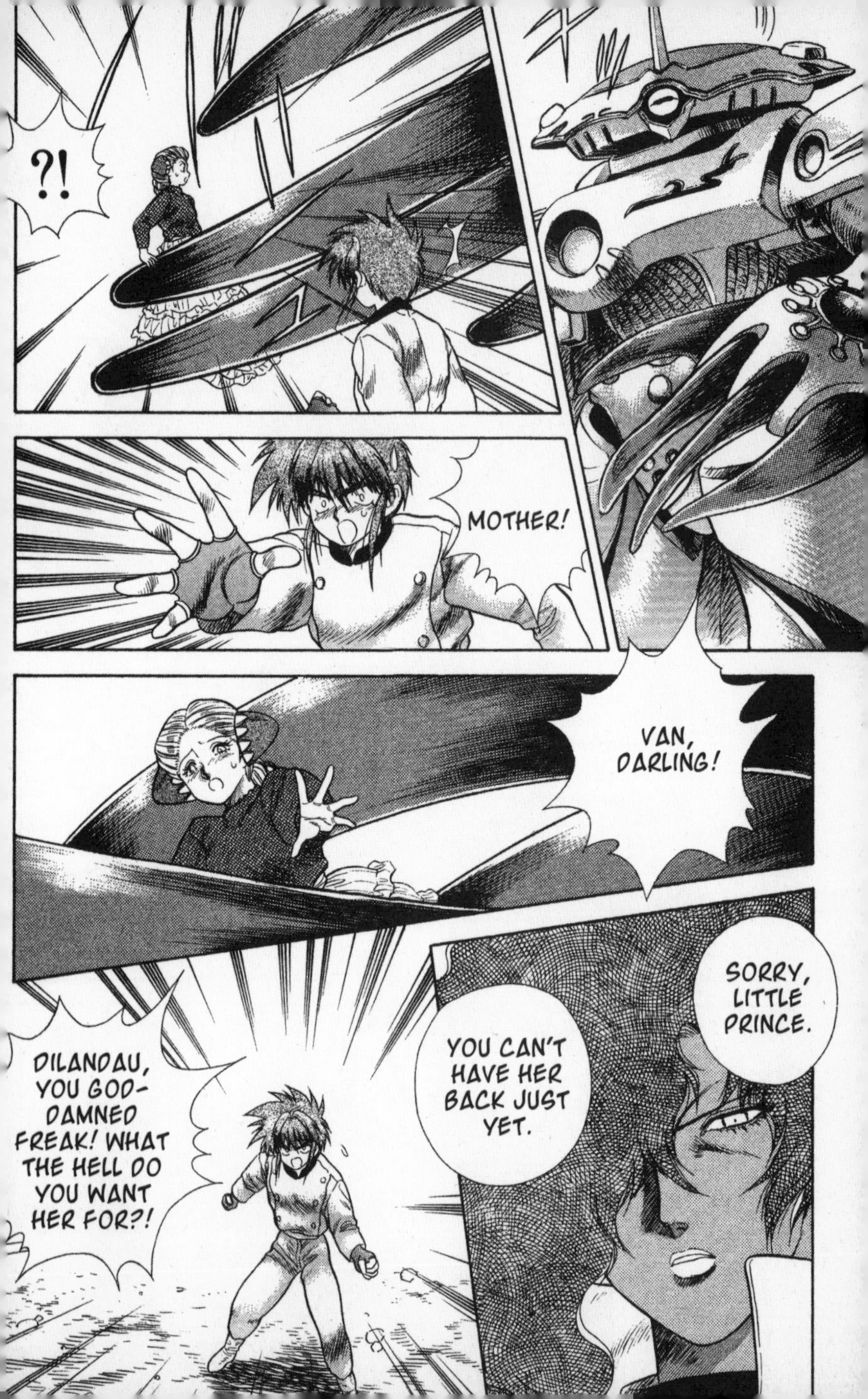
?!
MOTHER!
VAN, DARLING!
SORRY, LITTLE PRINCE.
YOU CAN'T HAVE HER BACK JUST YET.
DILANDAU, YOU GOD-DAMNED FREAK! WHAT THE HELL DO YOU WANT HER FOR?!

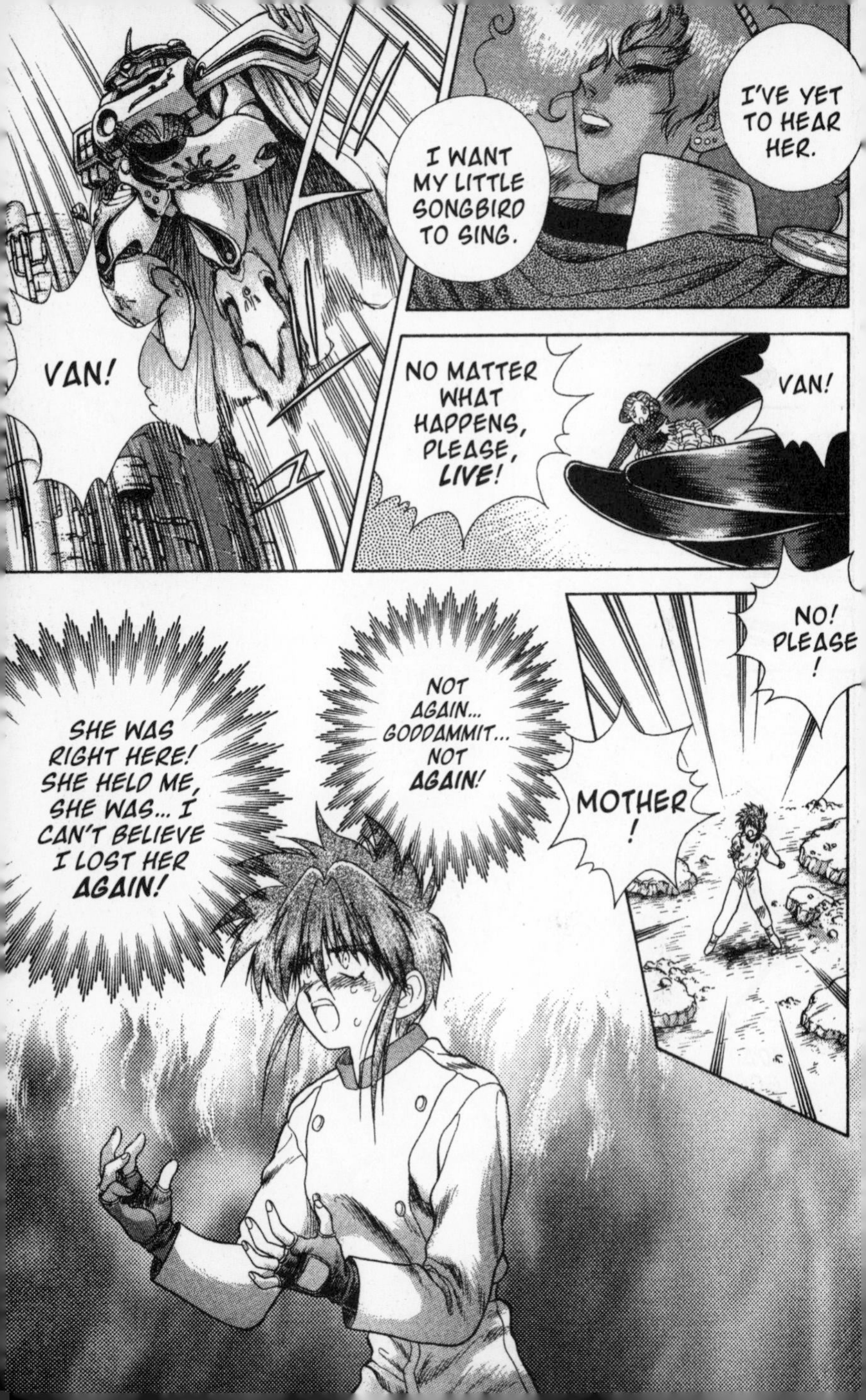
I'VE YET TO HEAR HER.
I WANT MY LITTLE SONGBIRD TO SING.
VAN!
NO MATTER WHAT HAPPENS, PLEASE, LIVE!
VAN!
NO! PLEASE!
MOTHER!
NOT AGAIN... GODDAMMIT... NOT AGAIN!
SHE WAS RIGHT HERE! SHE HELD ME, SHE WAS... I CAN'T BELIEVE I LOST HER AGAIN!

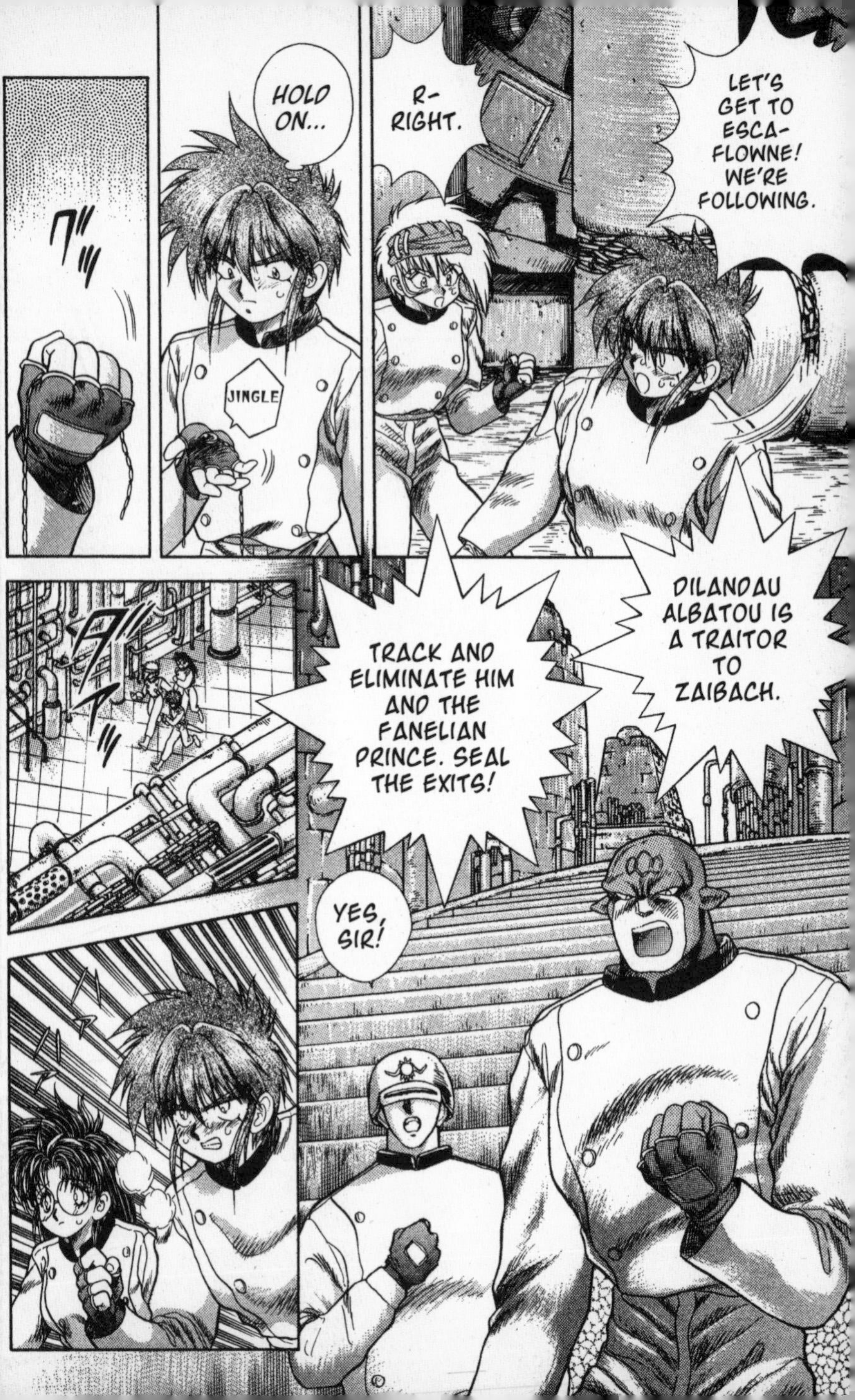
LET'S GET TO ESCA-FLOWNE! WE'RE FOLLOWING.
R-RIGHT.
HOLD ON...
JINGLE
DILANDAU ALBATOU IS A TRAITOR TO ZAIBACH.
TRACK AND ELIMINATE HIM AND THE FANELIAN PRINCE. SEAL THE EXITS!
YES, SIR!

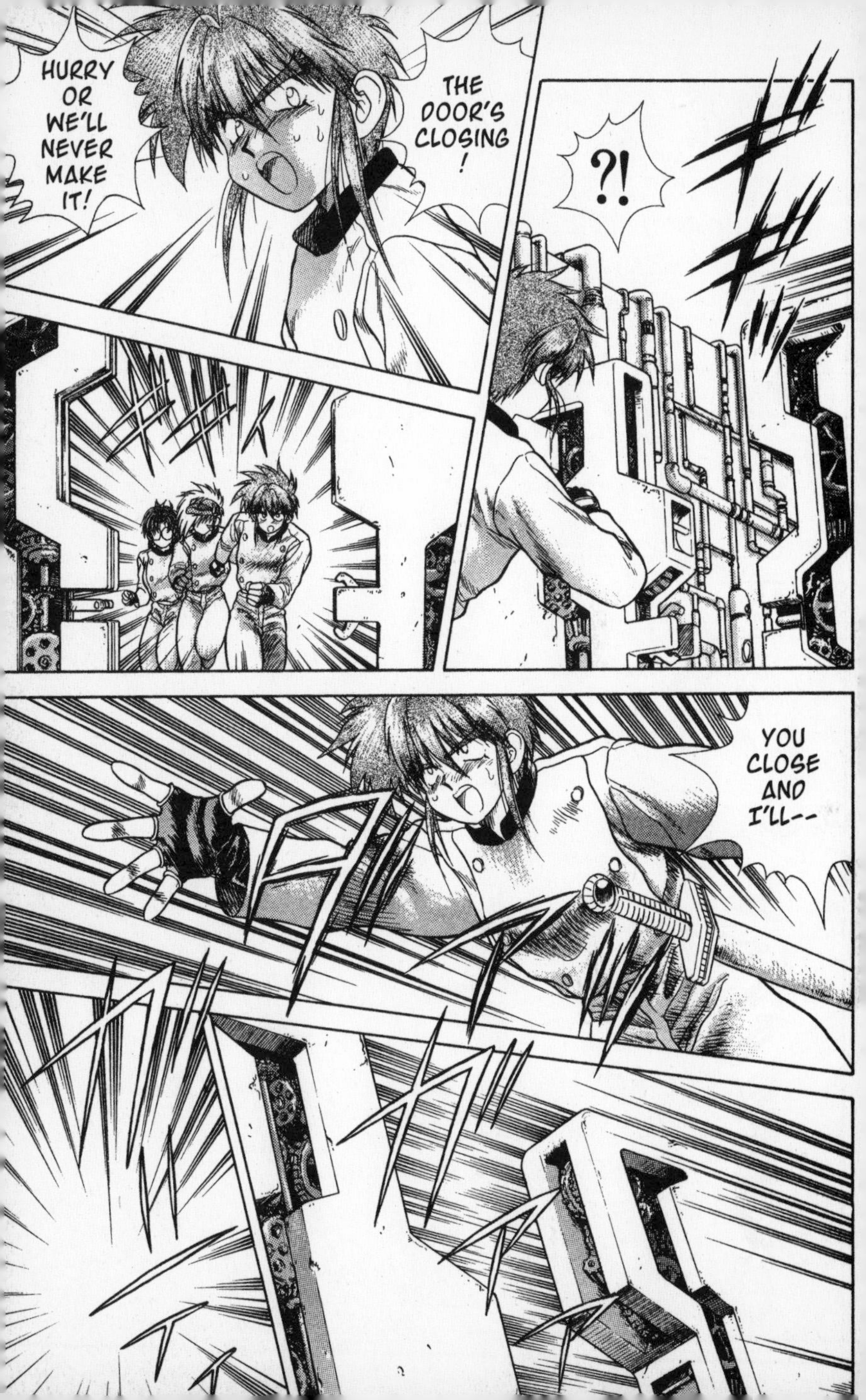
?!
THE DOOR'S CLOSING!
HURRY OR WE'LL NEVER MAKE IT!
YOU CLOSE AND I'LL--

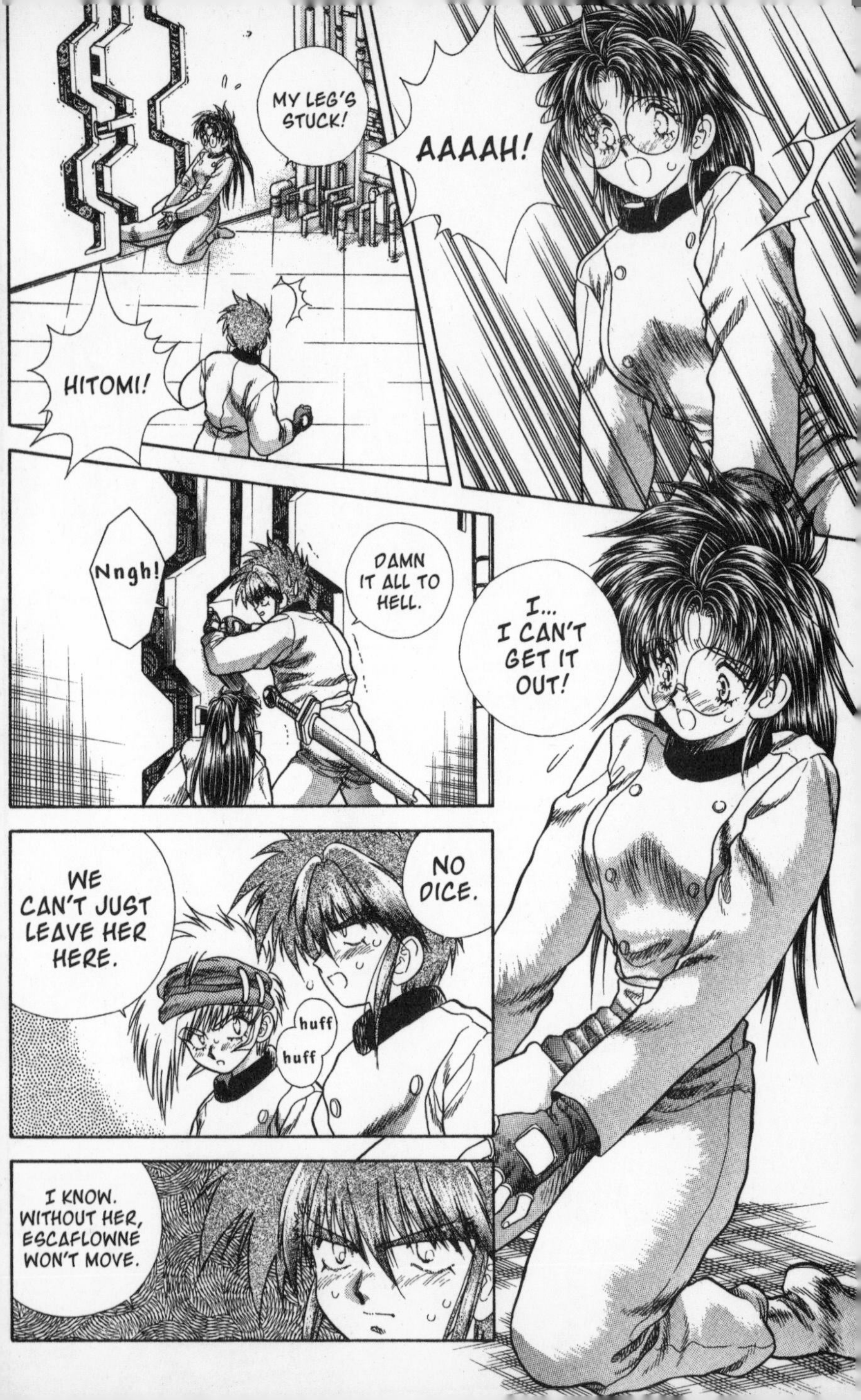
AAAAH!
MY LEG'S STUCK!
HITOMI!
I... I CAN'T GET IT OUT!
DAMN IT ALL TO HELL.
Nngh!
NO DICE.
huff
huff
WE CAN'T JUST LEAVE HER HERE.
I KNOW. WITHOUT HER, ESCAFLOWNE WON'T MOVE.

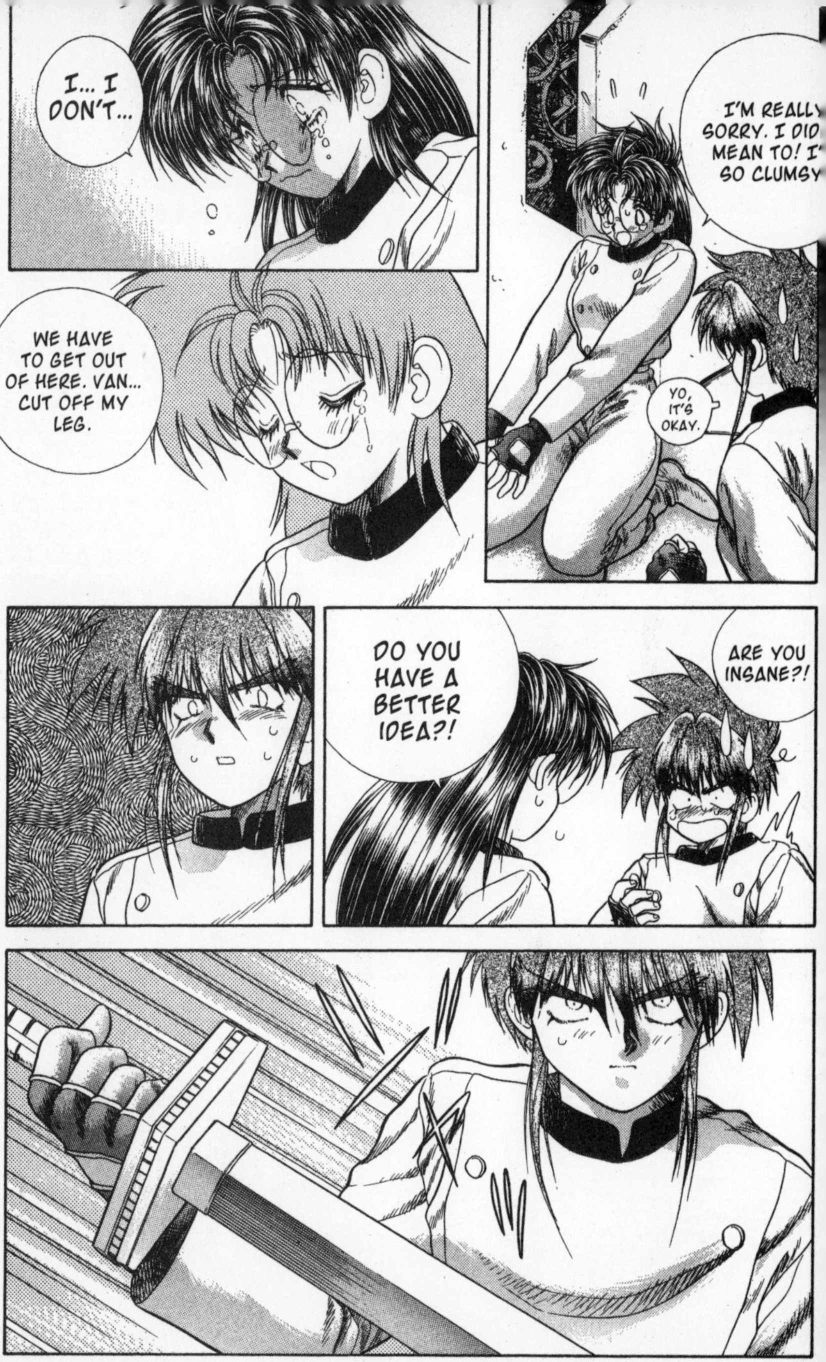
I'M REALLY SORRY. I DID MEAN TO! I' SO CLUMSY
YO, IT'S OKAY.
I... I DON'T...
WE HAVE TO GET OUT OF HERE. VAN... CUT OFF MY LEG.
ARE YOU INSANE?!
DO YOU HAVE A BETTER IDEA?!

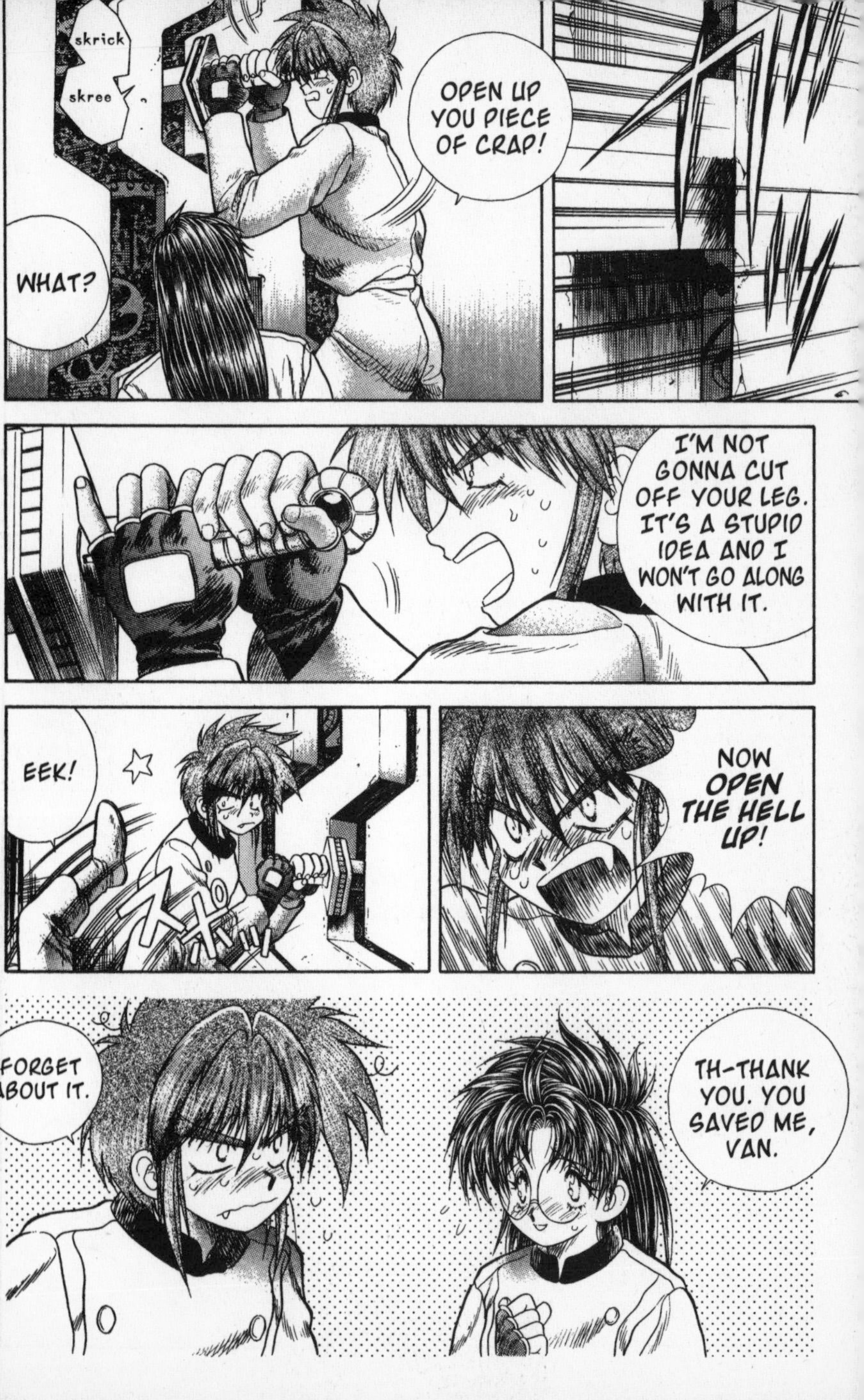
OPEN UP YOU PIECE OF CRAP!
skrick
skree
WHAT?
I'M NOT GONNA CUT OFF YOUR LEG. IT'S A STUPID IDEA AND I WON'T GO ALONG WITH IT.
NOW OPEN THE HELL UP!
EEK!
TH-THANK YOU. YOU SAVED ME, VAN.
FORGET ABOUT IT.

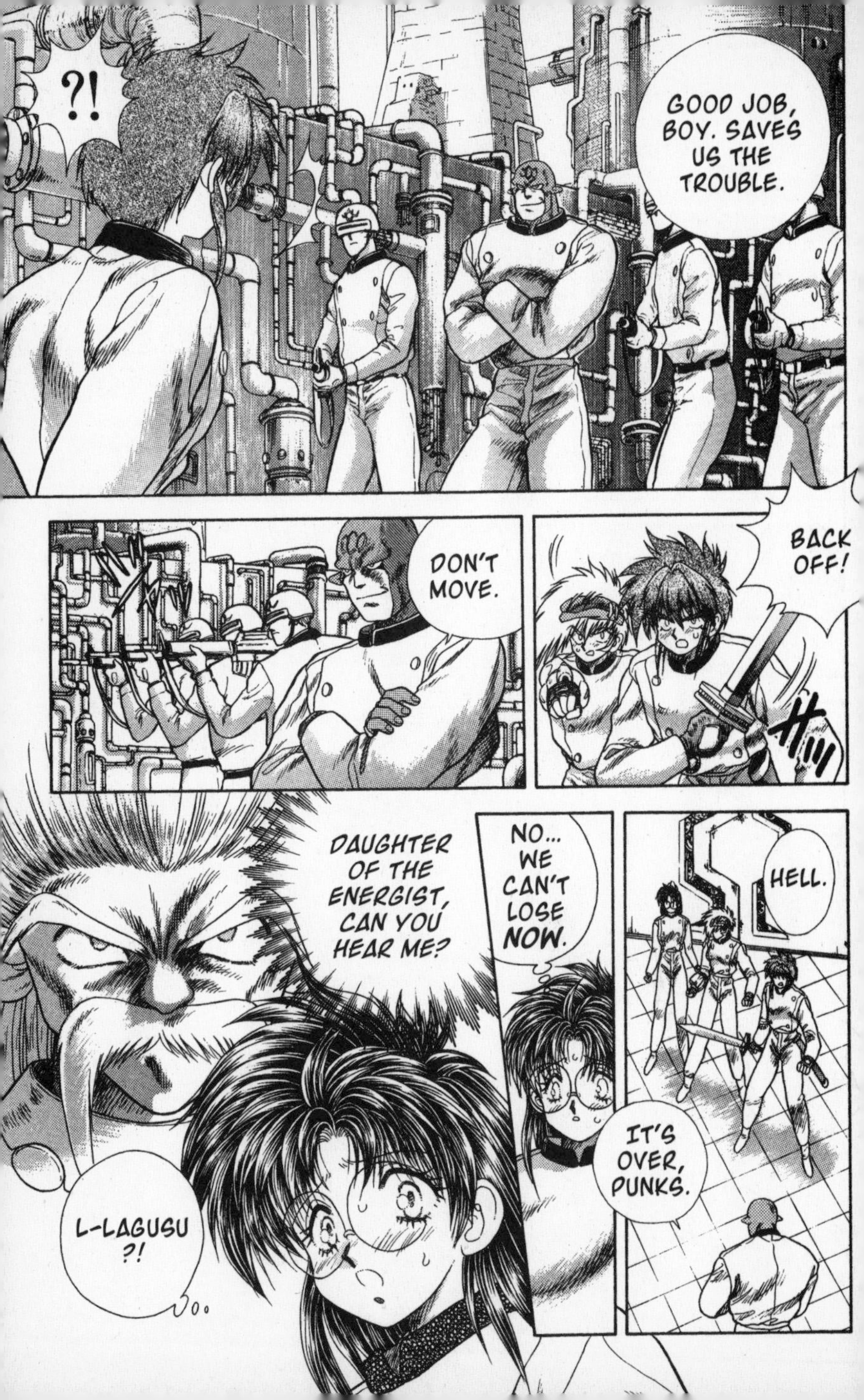
GOOD JOB, BOY. SAVES US THE TROUBLE.
?!
BACK OFF!
DON'T MOVE.
HELL.
IT'S OVER, PUNKS.
NO... WE CAN'T LOSE NOW.
DAUGHTER OF THE ENERGIST, CAN YOU HEAR ME?
L-LAGUSU ?!

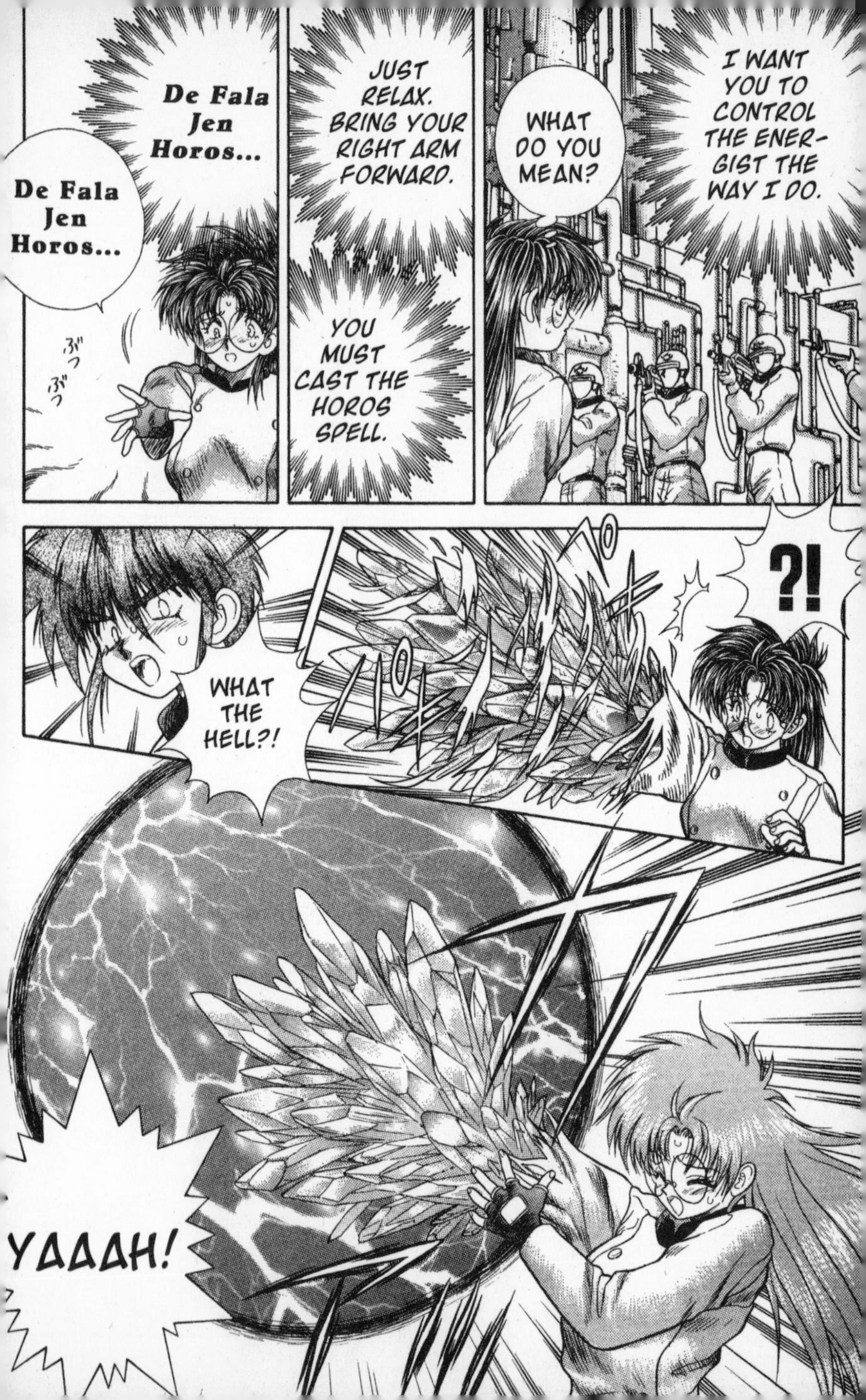
I WANT YOU TO CONTROL THE ENER-GIST THE WAY I DO.
WHAT DO YOU MEAN?
JUST RELAX. BRING YOUR RIGHT ARM FORWARD.
YOU MUST CAST THE HOROS SPELL.
De Fala Jen Horos...
De Fala Jen Horos...
ぶつぶつ
?!
WHAT THE HELL?!
YAAAH!

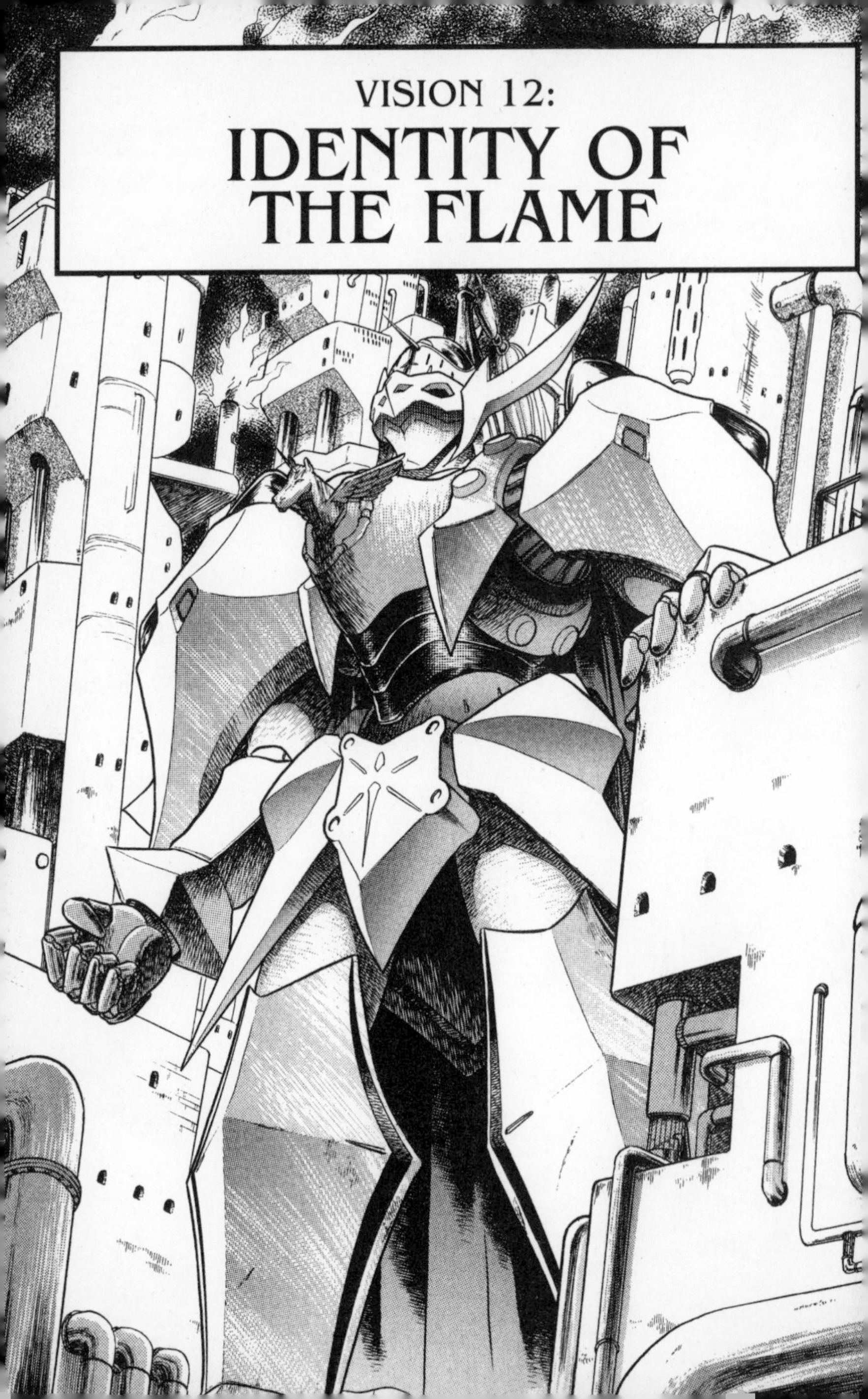
VISION 12:
IDENTITY OF THE FLAME

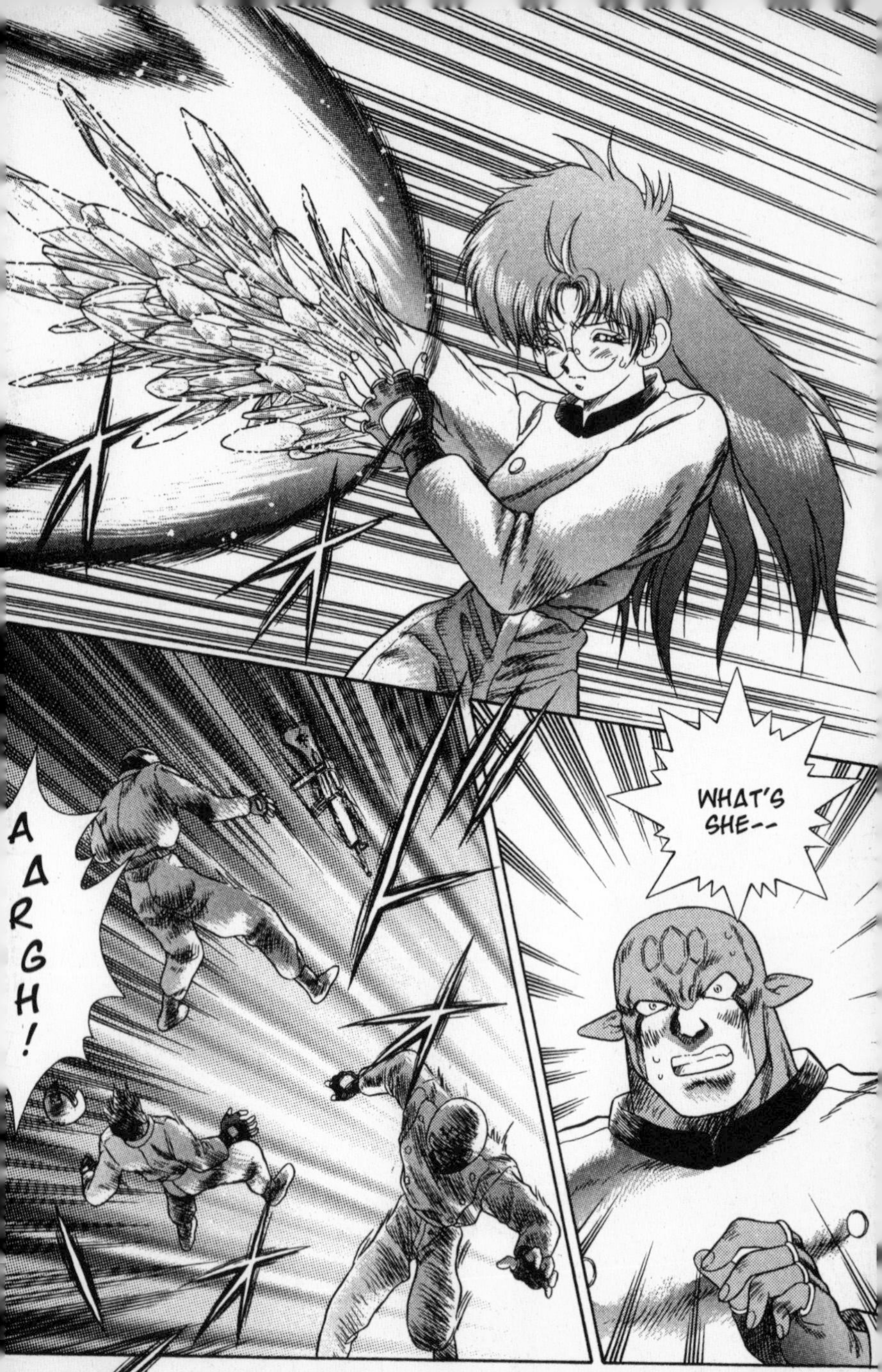
WHAT'S SHE--
AARGH!

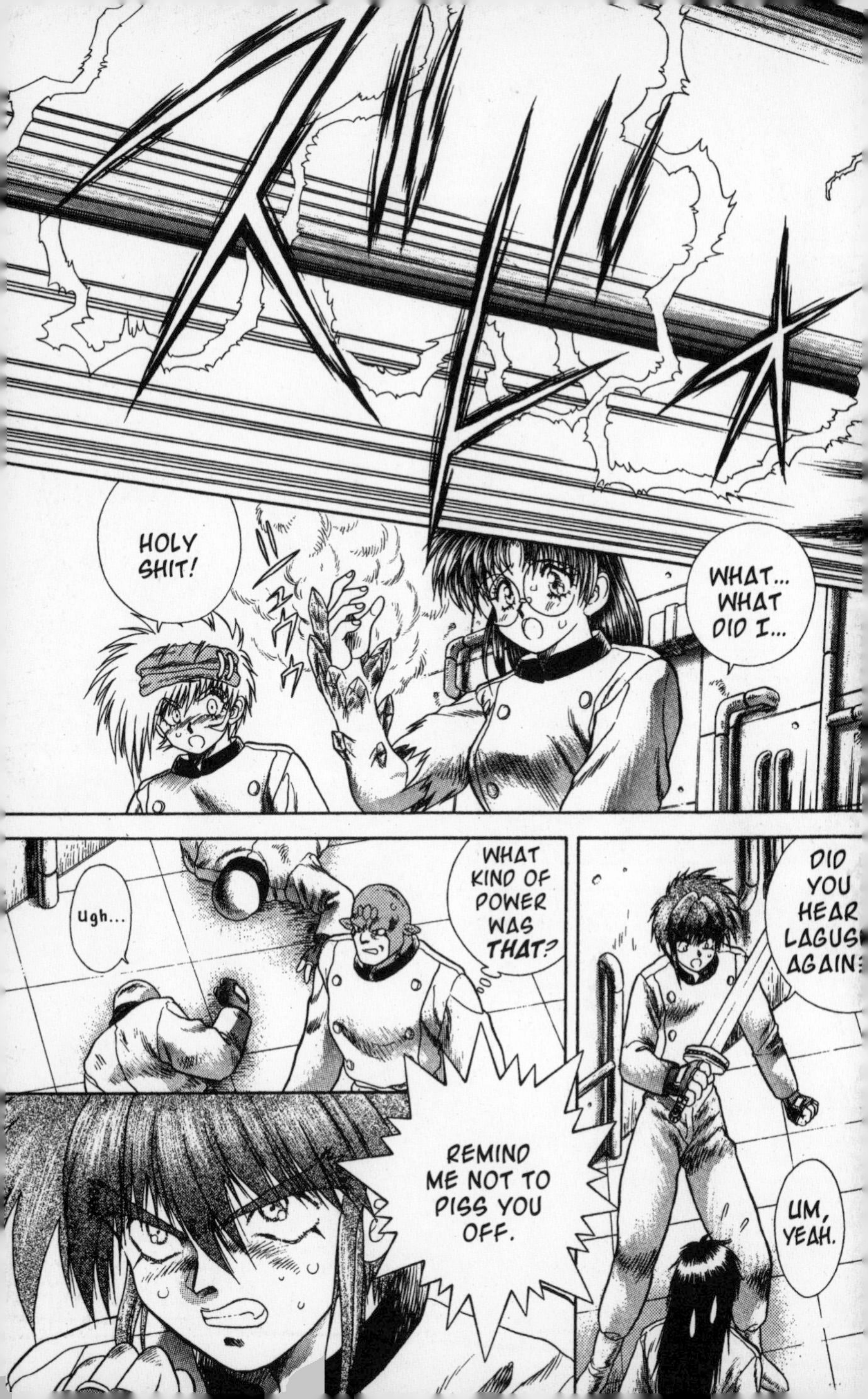
WHAT... WHAT DID I...
HOLY SHIT!
DID YOU HEAR LAGUS AGAIN
UM, YEAH.
WHAT KIND OF POWER WAS THAT?
Ugh...
REMIND ME NOT TO PISS YOU OFF.

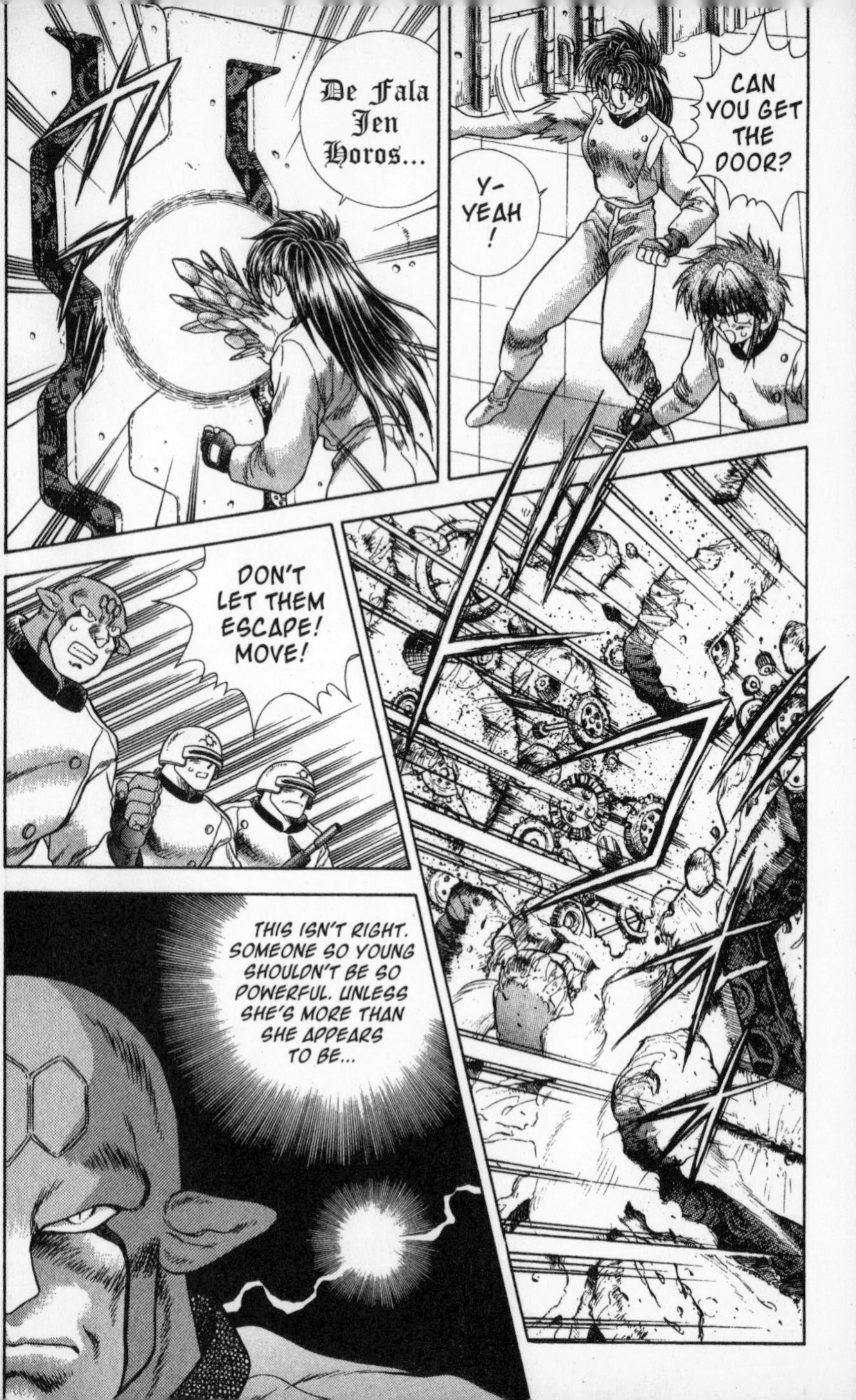
CAN YOU GET THE DOOR?
Y-YEAH!
De Fala Jen Horos...
DON'T LET THEM ESCAPE! MOVE!
THIS ISN'T RIGHT. SOMEONE SO YOUNG SHOULDN'T BE SO POWERFUL. UNLESS SHE'S MORE THAN SHE APPEARS TO BE...

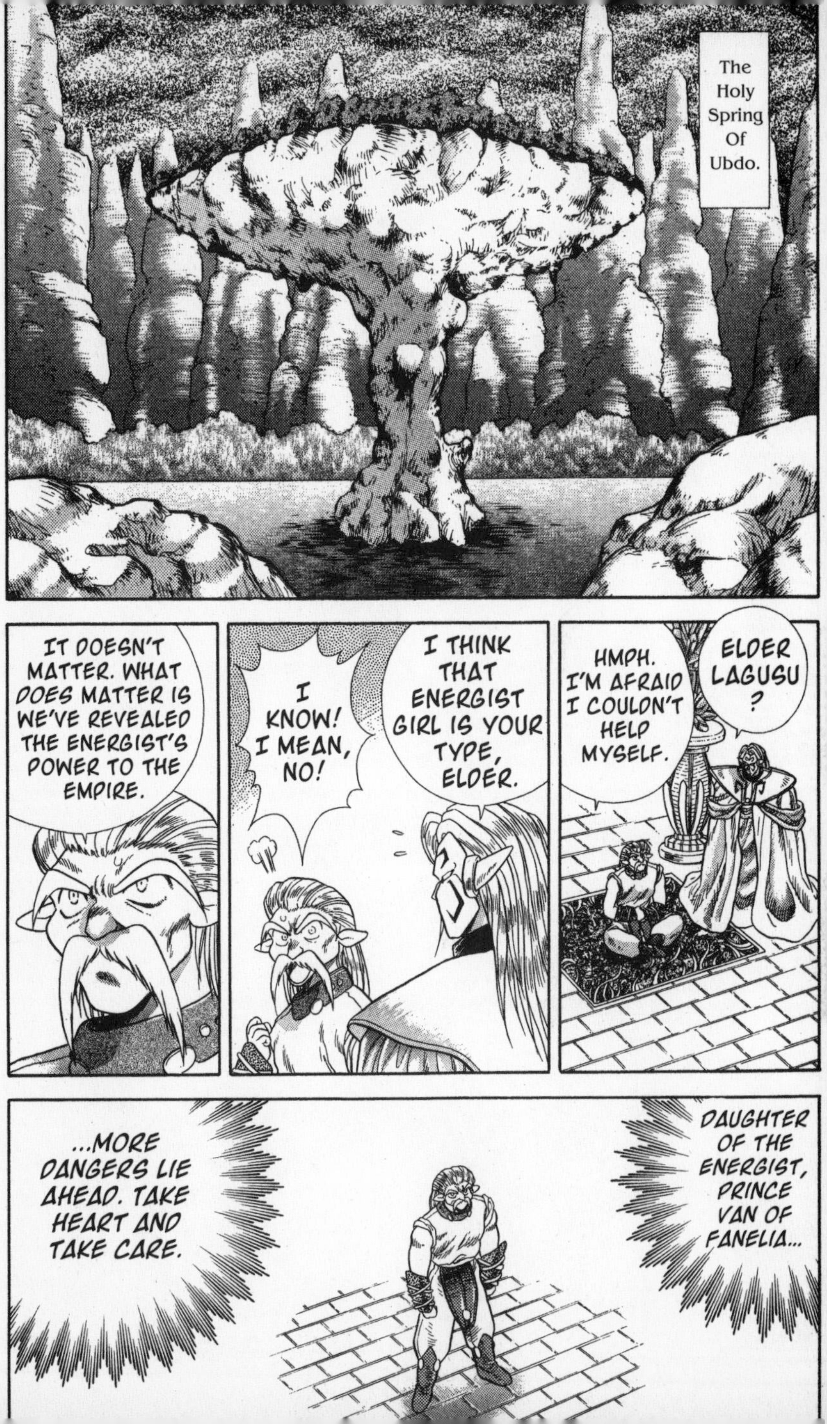
The Holy Spring Of Ubdo.
ELDER LAGUSU?
HMPH. I'M AFRAID I COULDN'T HELP MYSELF.
I THINK THAT ENERGIST GIRL IS YOUR TYPE, ELDER.
I KNOW! I MEAN, NO!
IT DOESN'T MATTER. WHAT DOES MATTER IS WE'VE REVEALED THE ENERGIST'S POWER TO THE EMPIRE.
DAUGHTER OF THE ENERGIST, PRINCE VAN OF FANELIA...
...MORE DANGERS LIE AHEAD. TAKE HEART AND TAKE CARE.

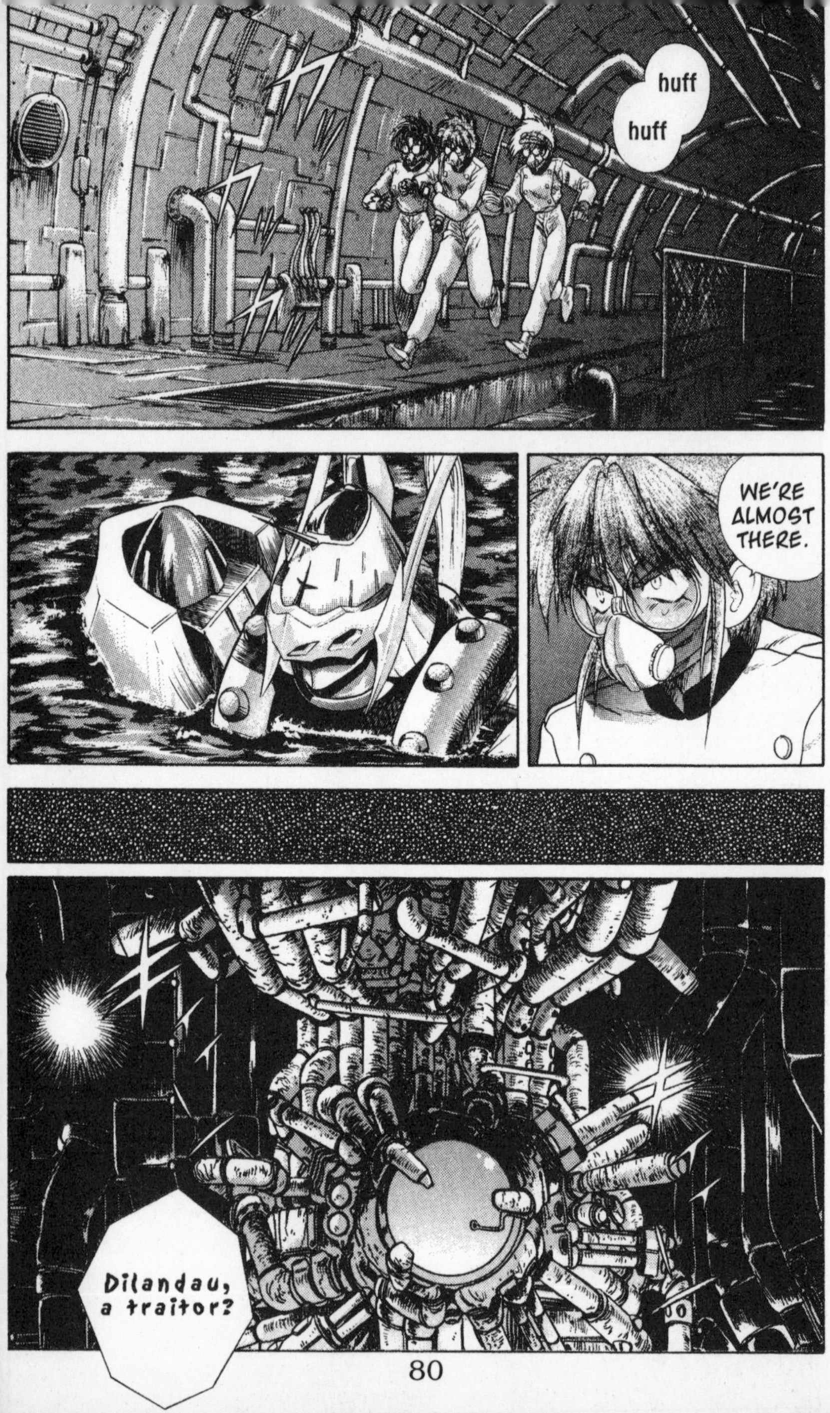
huff
huff
WE'RE ALMOST THERE.
Dilandau, a traitor?

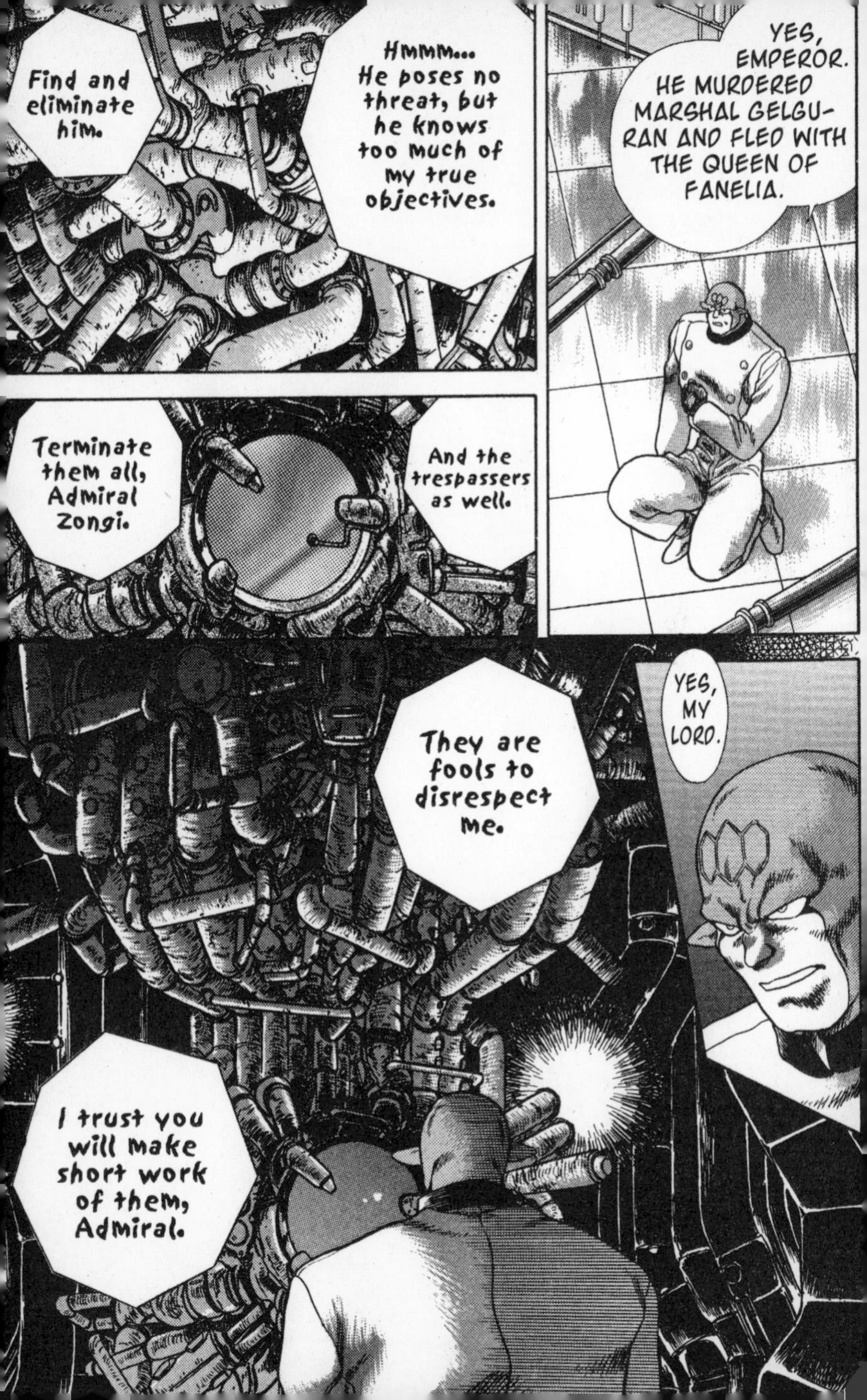
YES, EMPEROR. HE MURDERED MARSHAL GELGURAN AND FLED WITH THE QUEEN OF FANELIA.
Hmmm... He poses no threat, but he knows too much of my true objectives.
Find and eliminate him.
And the trespassers as well.
Terminate them all, Admiral Zongi.
YES, MY LORD.
They are fools to disrespect me.
I trust you will make short work of them, Admiral.

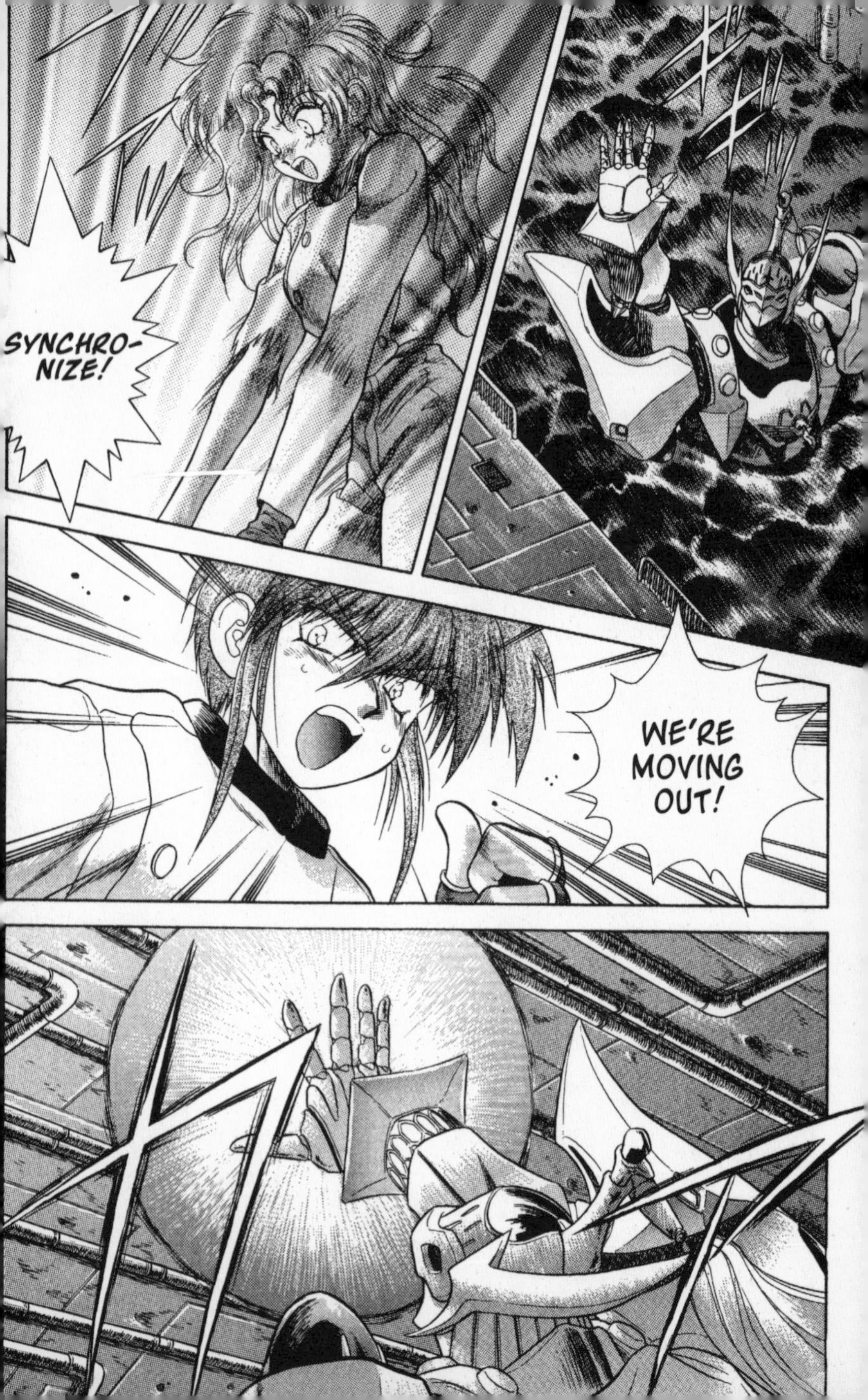
SYNCHRO-NIZE!
WE'RE MOVING OUT!

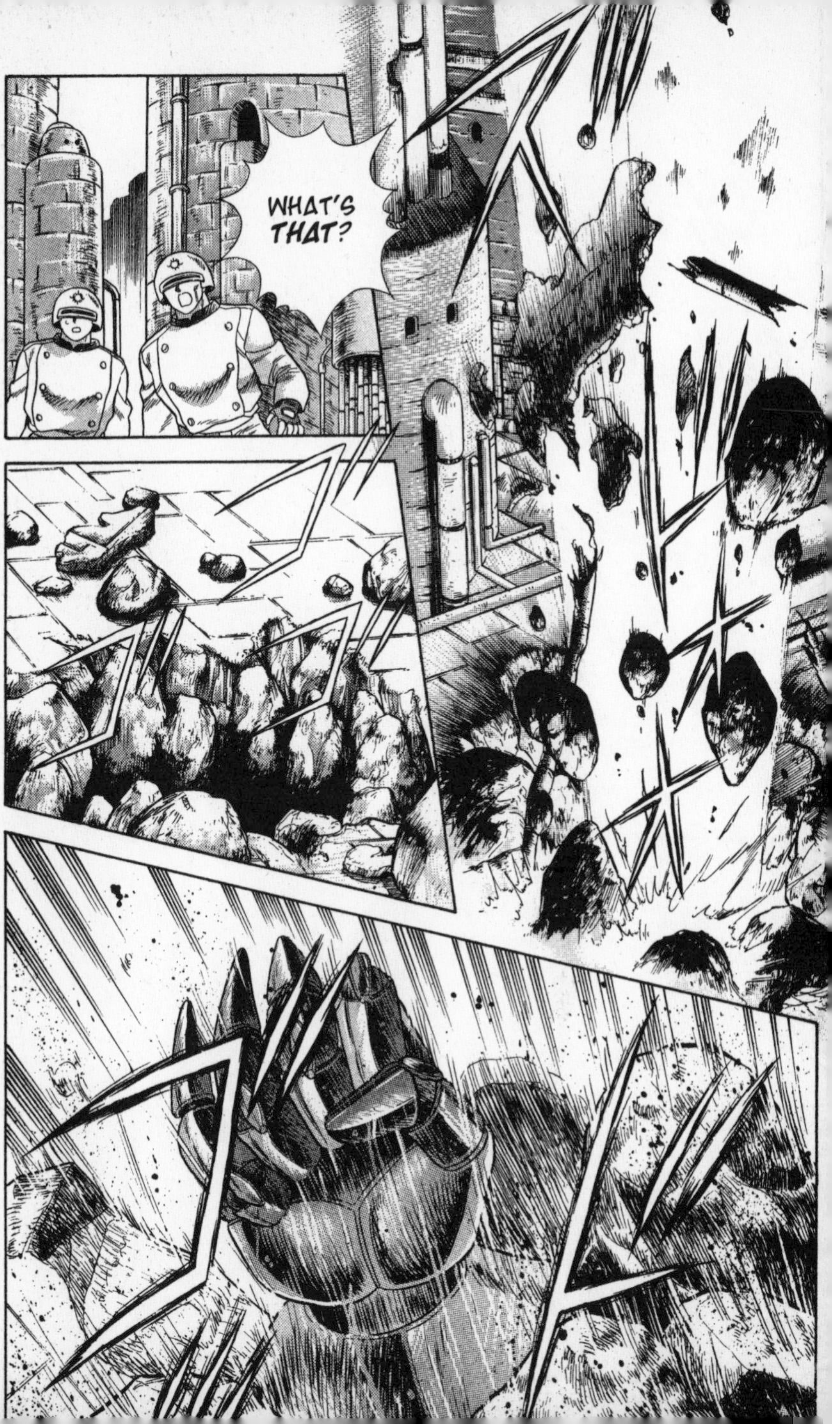
WHAT'S THAT?

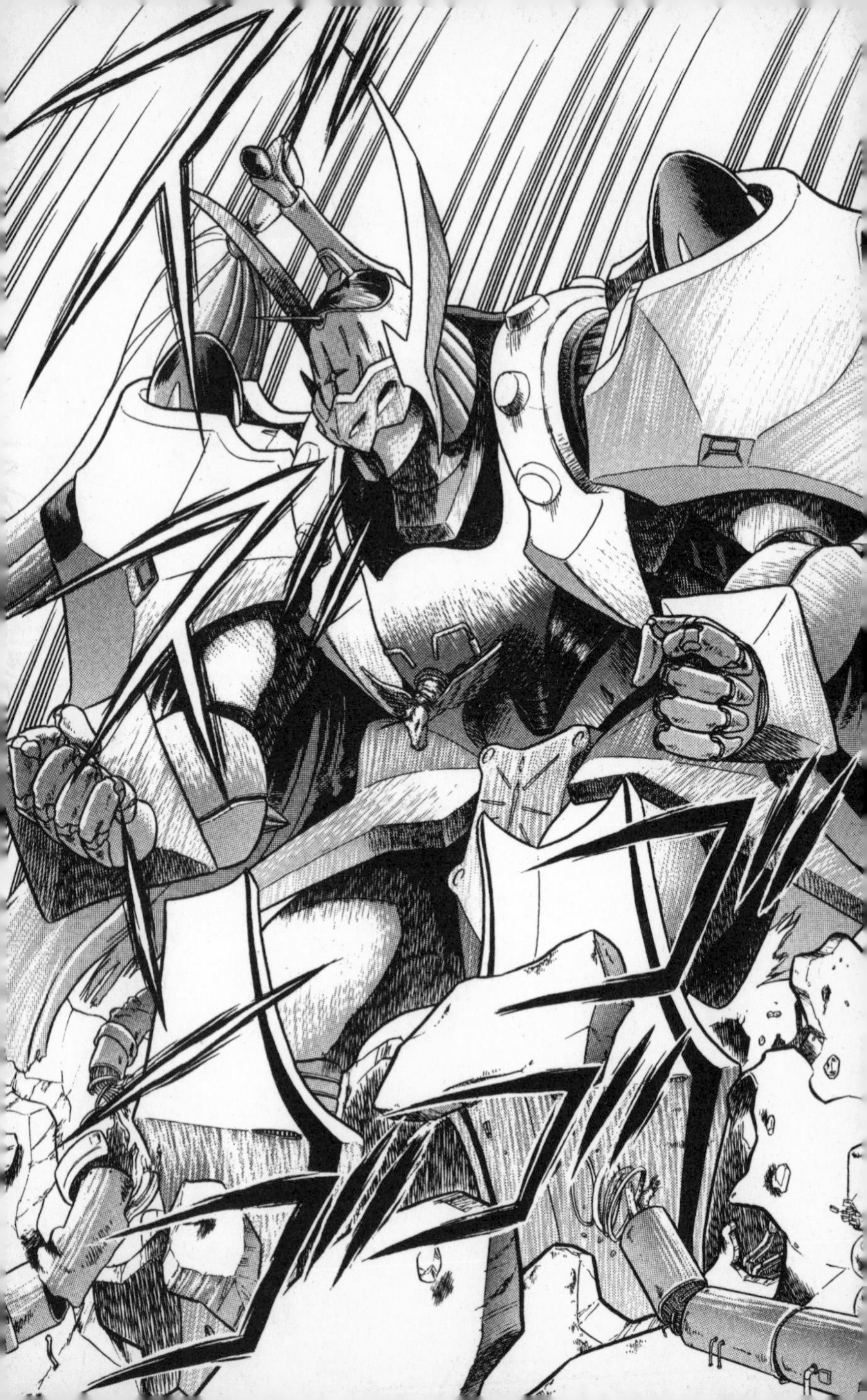

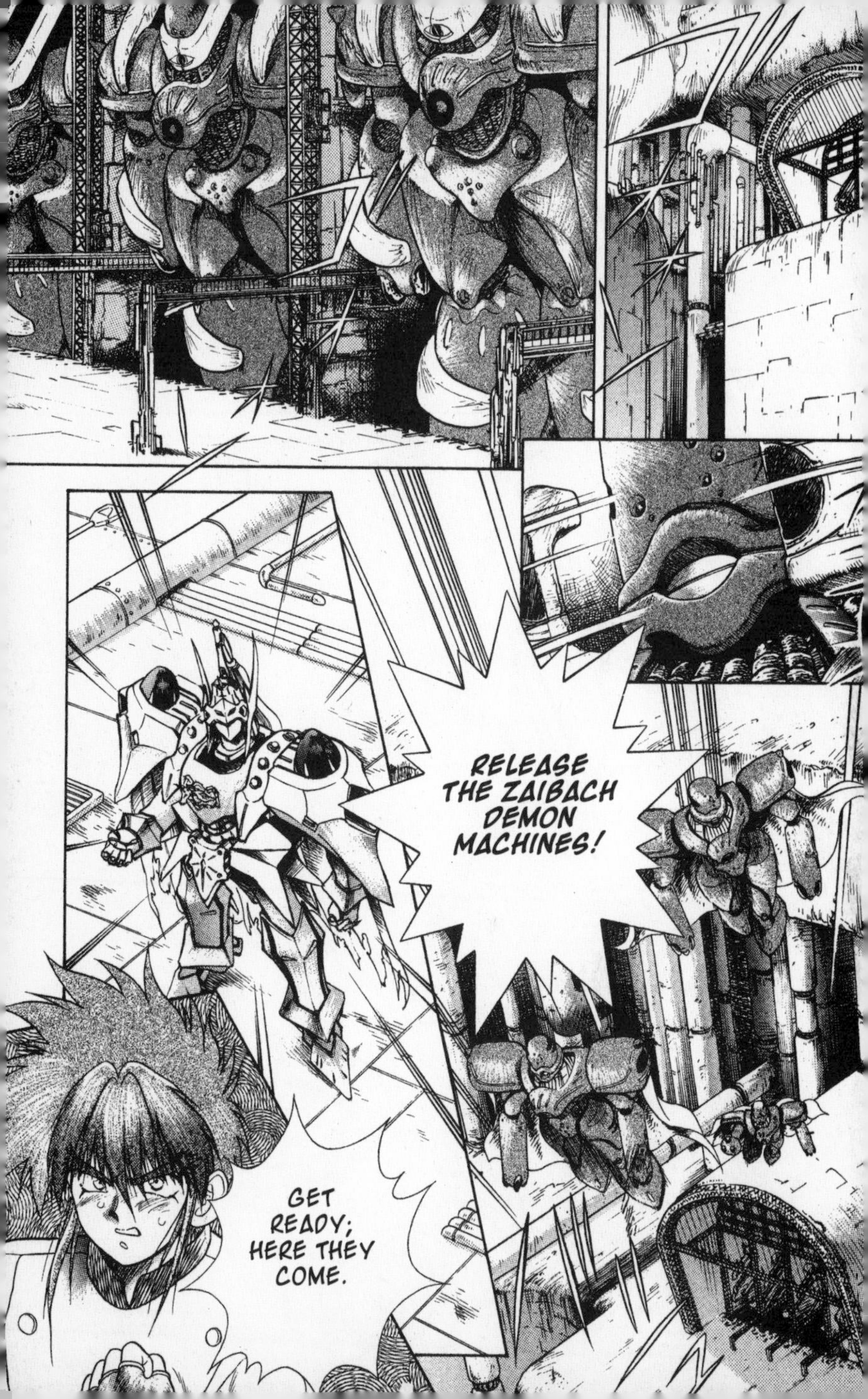
RELEASE THE ZAIBACH DEMON MACHINES!
GET READY; HERE THEY COME.

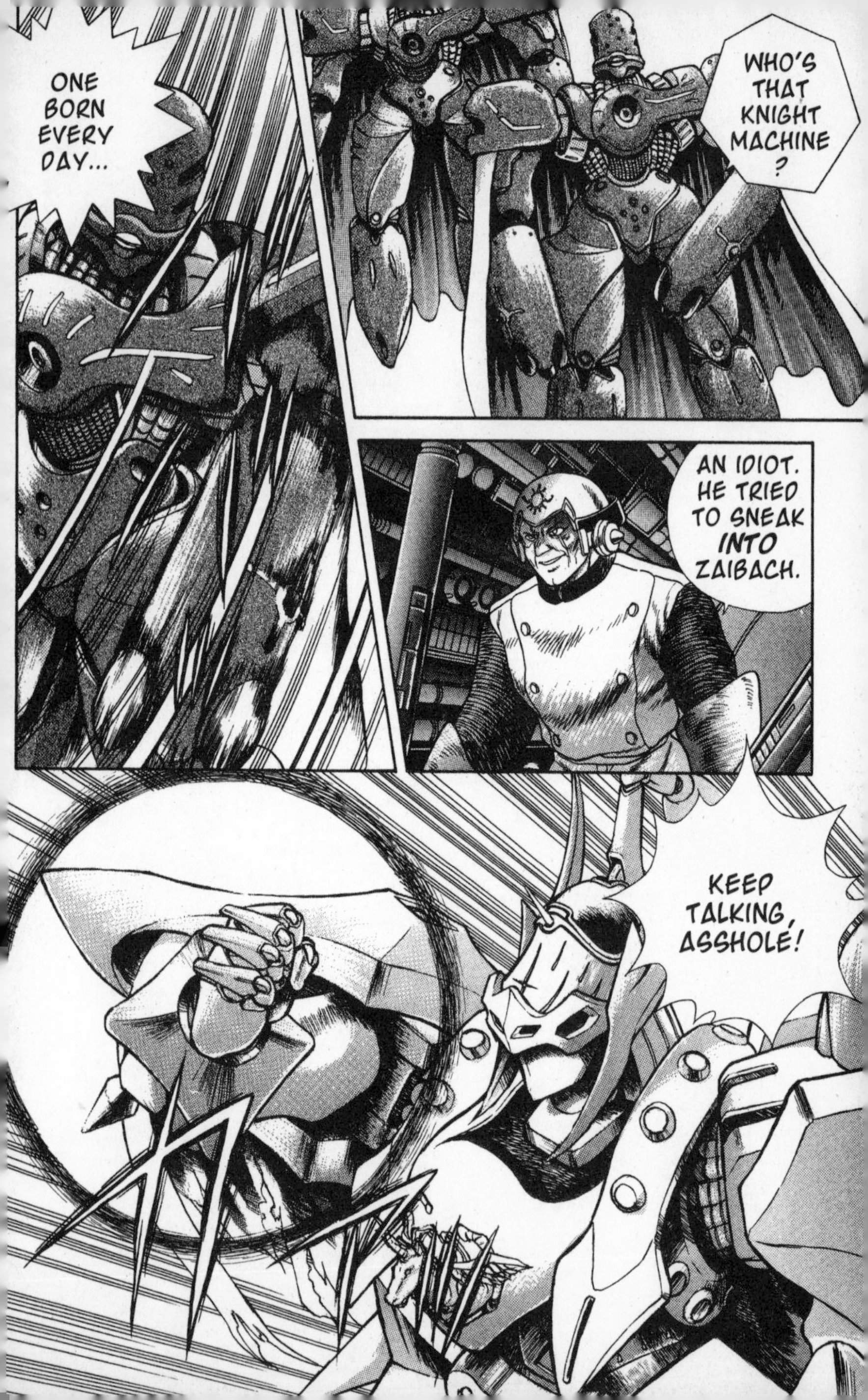
WHO'S THAT KNIGHT MACHINE ?
AN IDIOT. HE TRIED TO SNEAK *INTO* ZAIBACH.
ONE BORN EVERY DAY...
KEEP TALKING, ASSHOLE!

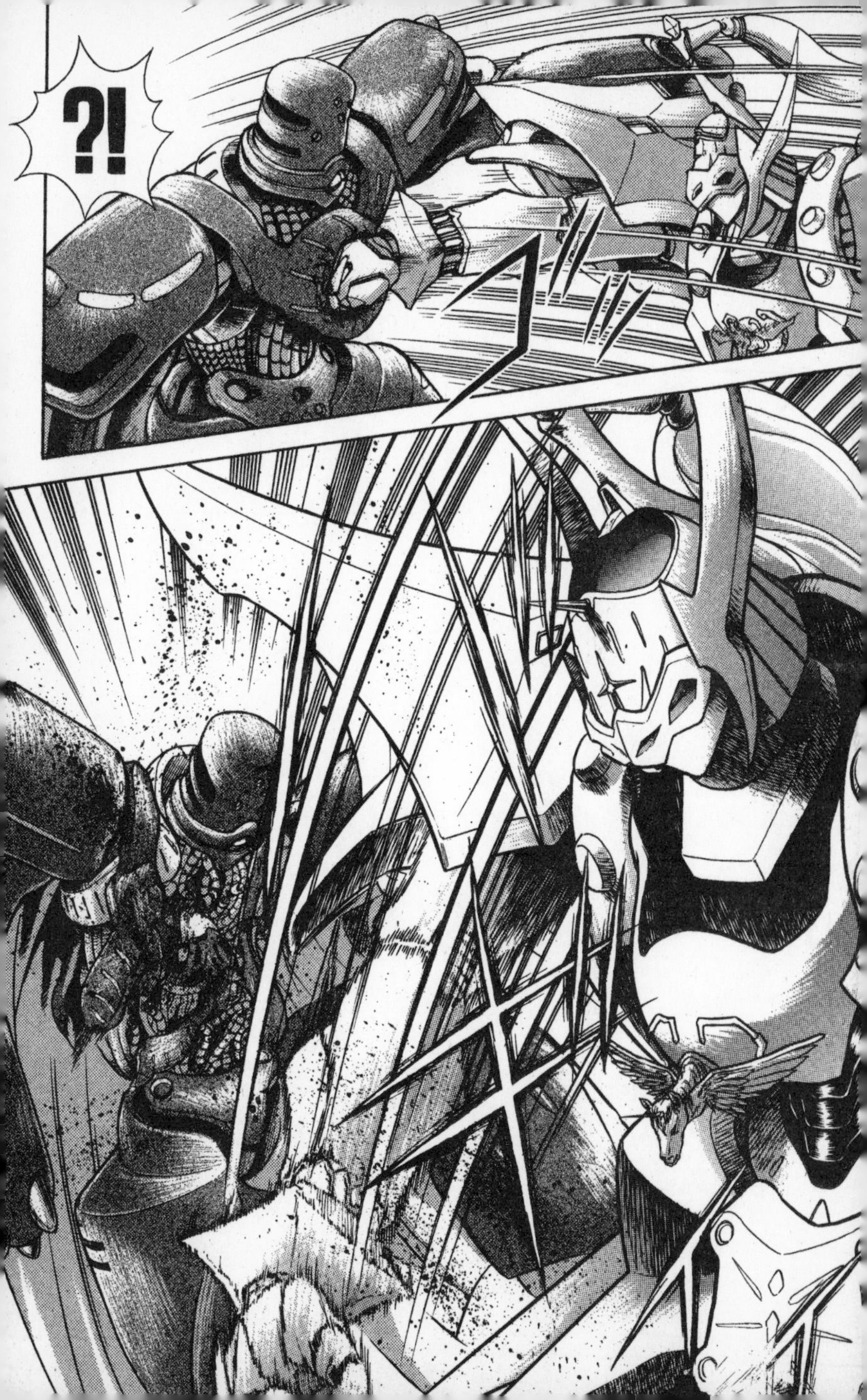
?!

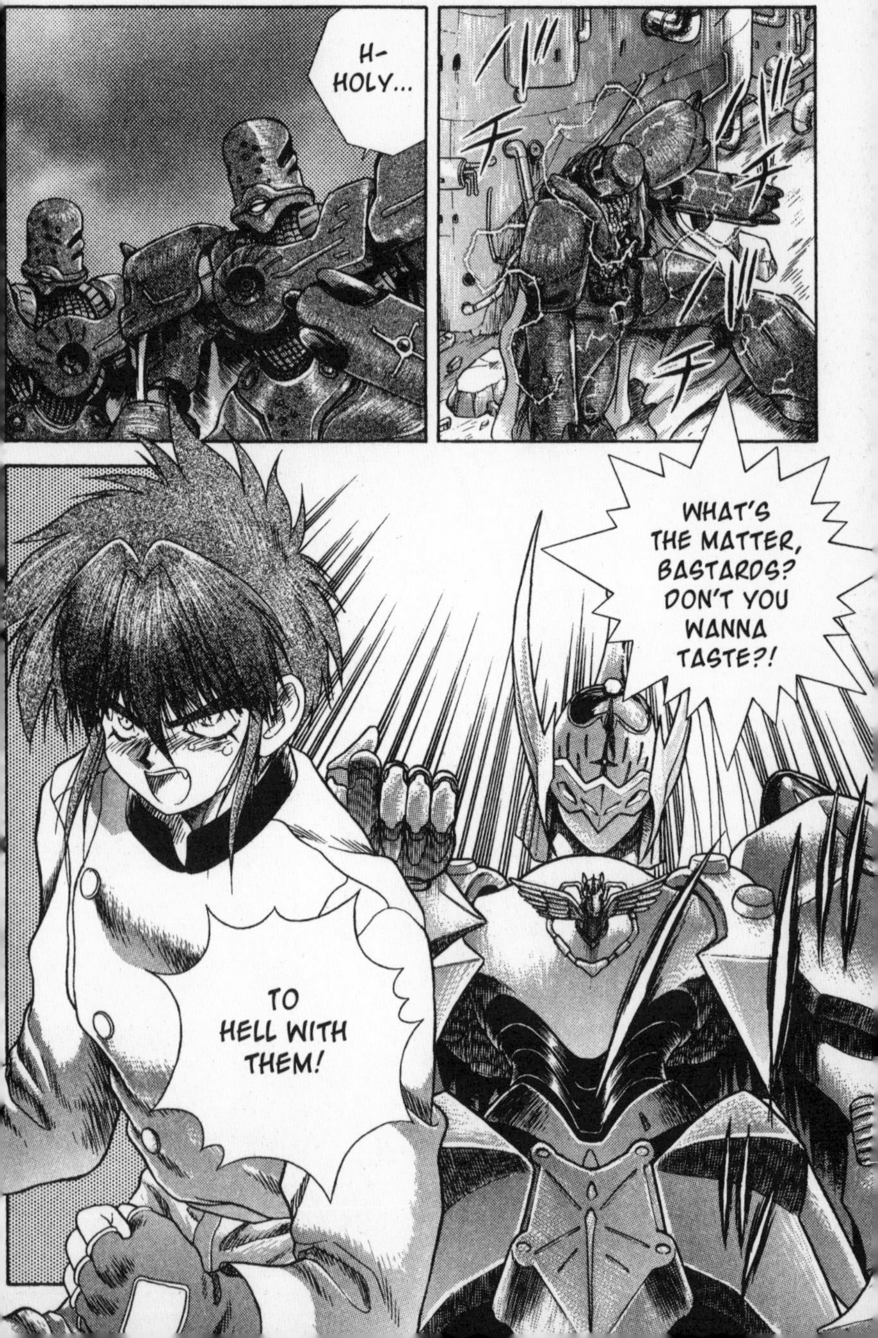
H-HOLY...
WHAT'S THE MATTER, BASTARDS? DON'T YOU WANNA TASTE?!
TO HELL WITH THEM!

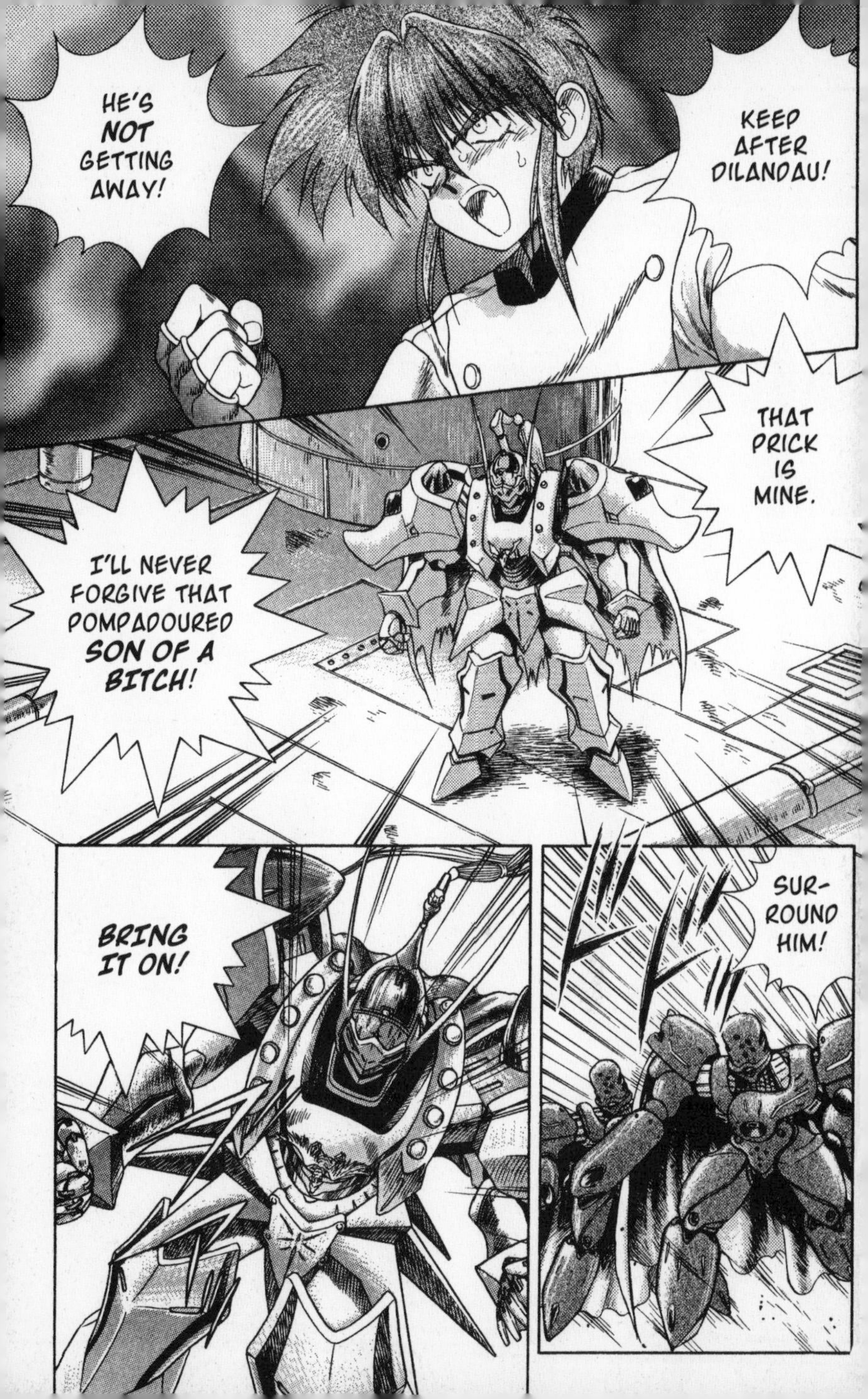
KEEP AFTER DILANDAU!
HE'S NOT GETTING AWAY!
THAT PRICK IS MINE.
I'LL NEVER FORGIVE THAT POMPADOURED SON OF A BITCH!
SUR-ROUND HIM!
BRING IT ON!

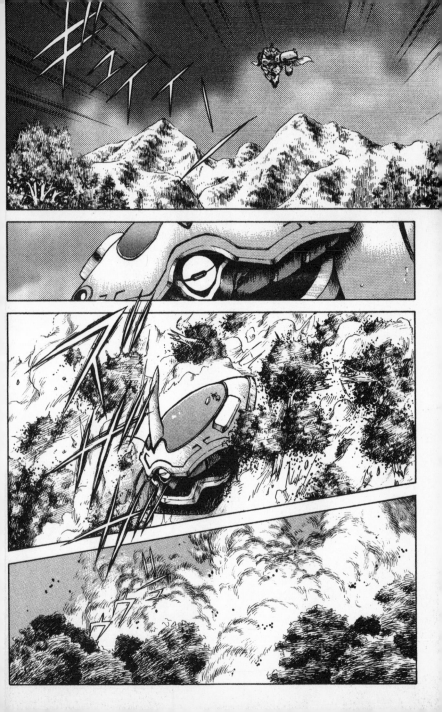

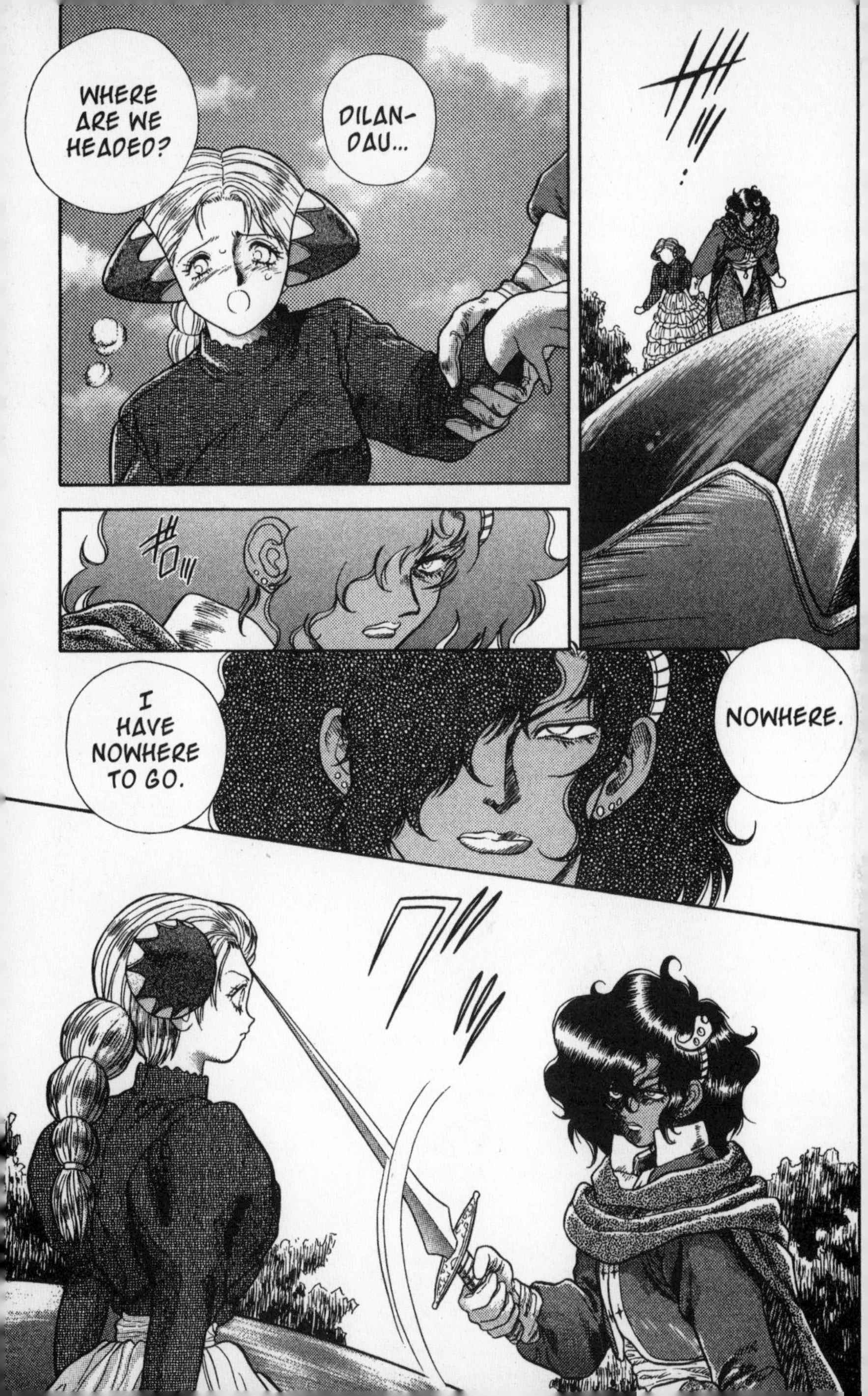
DILAN-DAU...
WHERE ARE WE HEADED?
NOWHERE.
I HAVE NOWHERE TO GO.

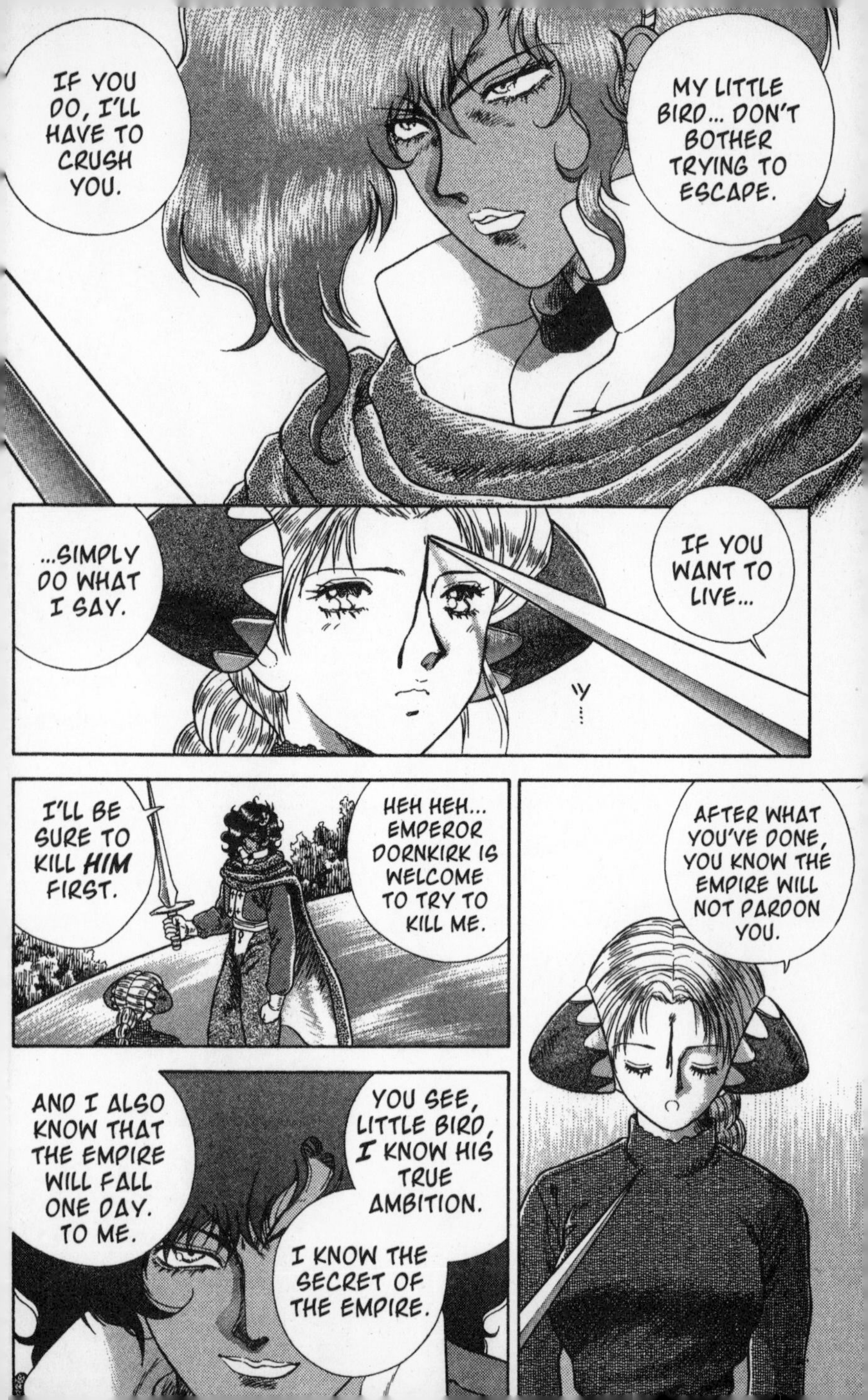
MY LITTLE BIRD... DON'T BOTHER TRYING TO ESCAPE.
IF YOU DO, I'LL HAVE TO CRUSH YOU.
IF YOU WANT TO LIVE...
...SIMPLY DO WHAT I SAY.
AFTER WHAT YOU'VE DONE, YOU KNOW THE EMPIRE WILL NOT PARDON YOU.
HEH HEH... EMPEROR DORNKIRK IS WELCOME TO TRY TO KILL ME.
I'LL BE SURE TO KILL *HIM* FIRST.
YOU SEE, LITTLE BIRD, *I* KNOW HIS TRUE AMBITION.
I KNOW THE SECRET OF THE EMPIRE.
AND I ALSO KNOW THAT THE EMPIRE WILL FALL ONE DAY. TO ME.

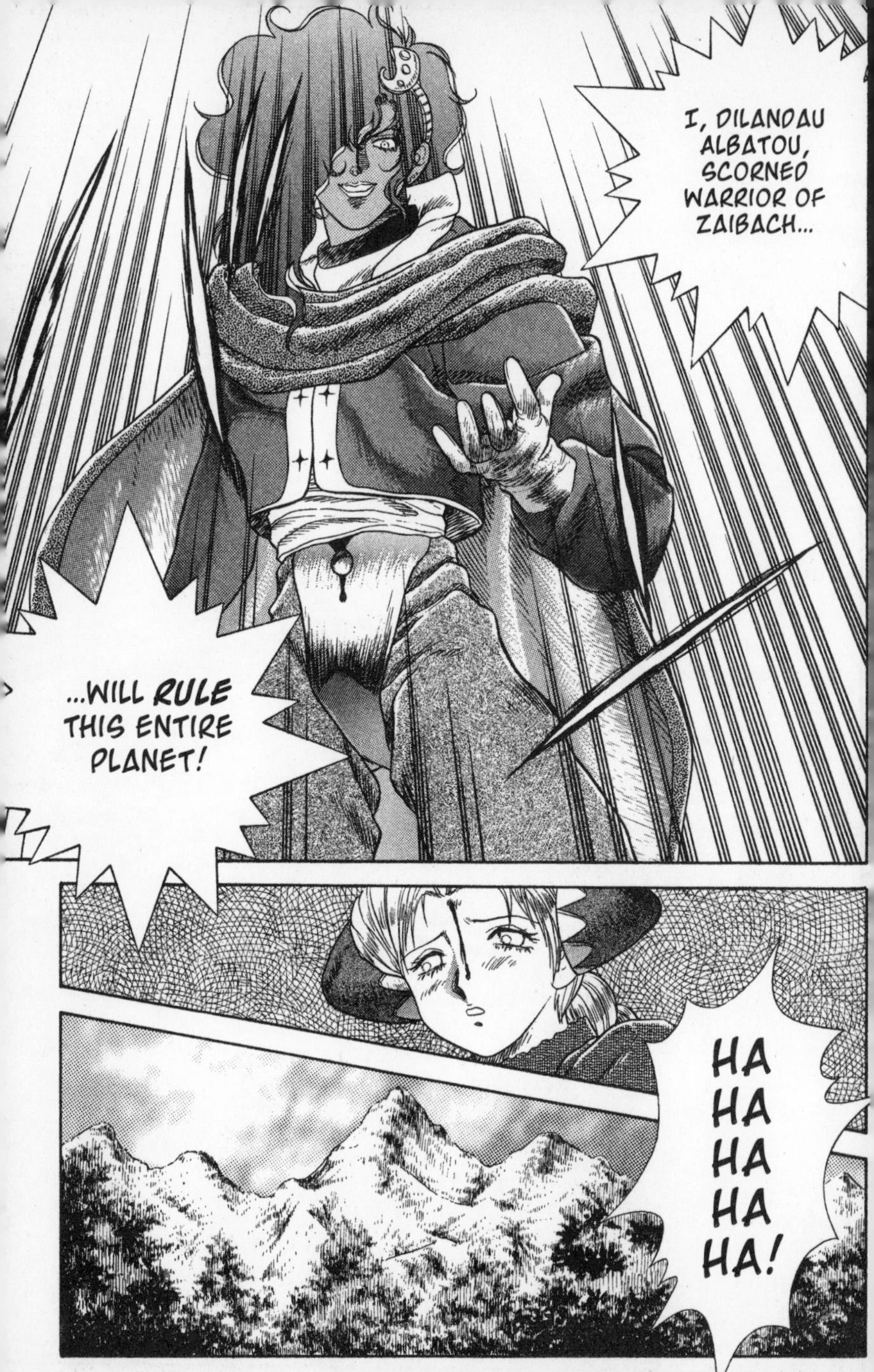
I, DILANDAU ALBATOU, SCORNED WARRIOR OF ZAIBACH...
...WILL *RULE* THIS ENTIRE PLANET!
HA HA HA HA HA!

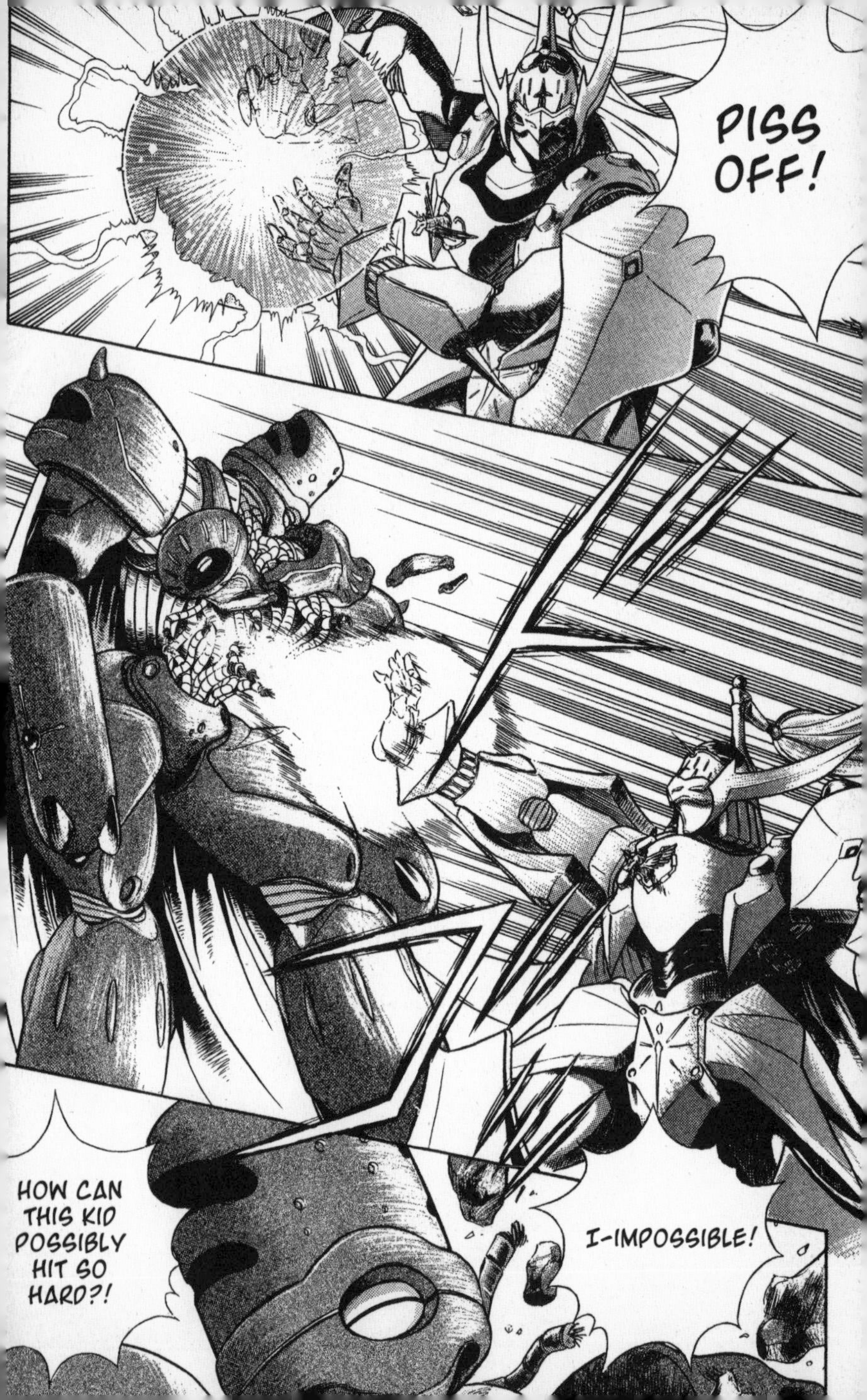
PISS OFF!
I-IMPOSSIBLE!
HOW CAN THIS KID POSSIBLY HIT SO HARD?!

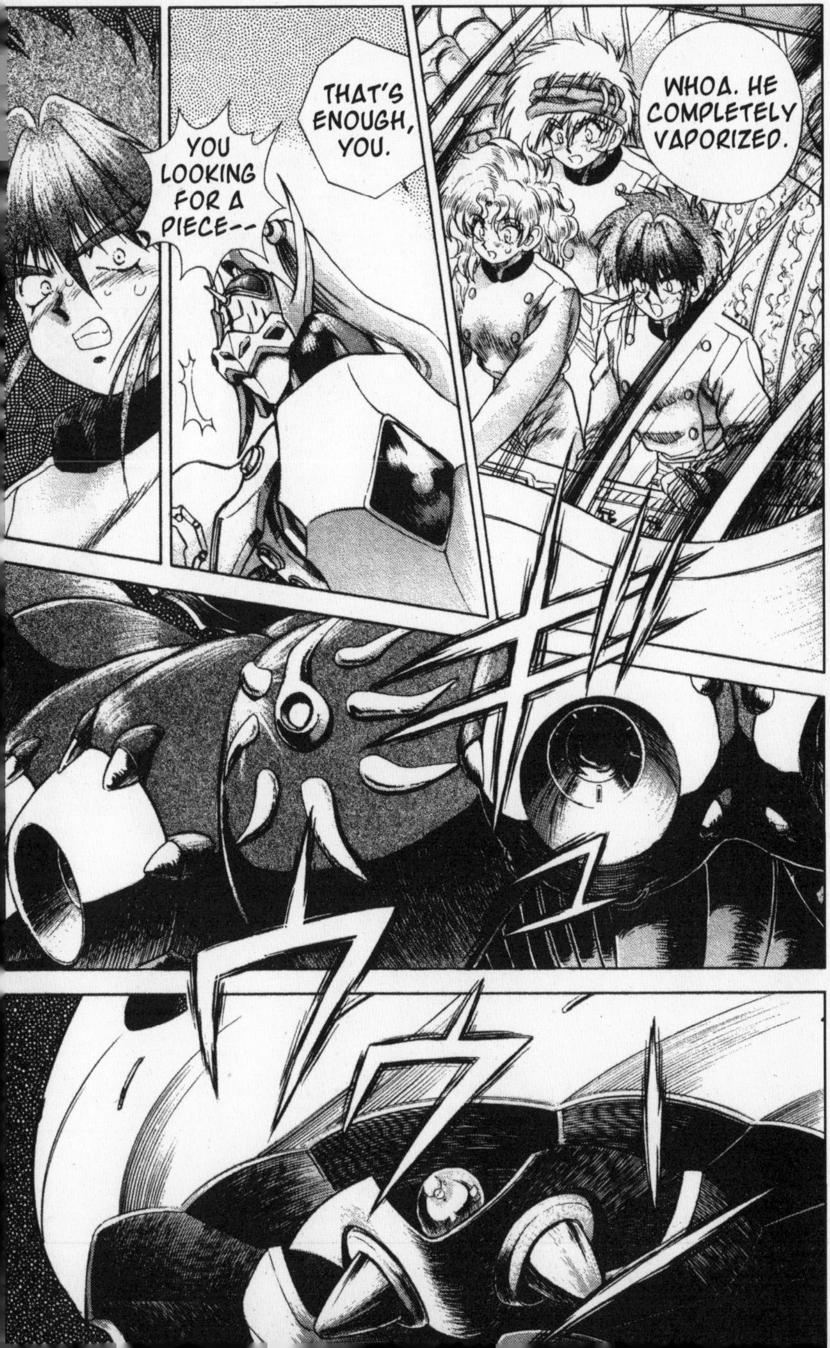
WHOA. HE COMPLETELY VAPORIZED.
THAT'S ENOUGH, YOU.
YOU LOOKING FOR A PIECE--

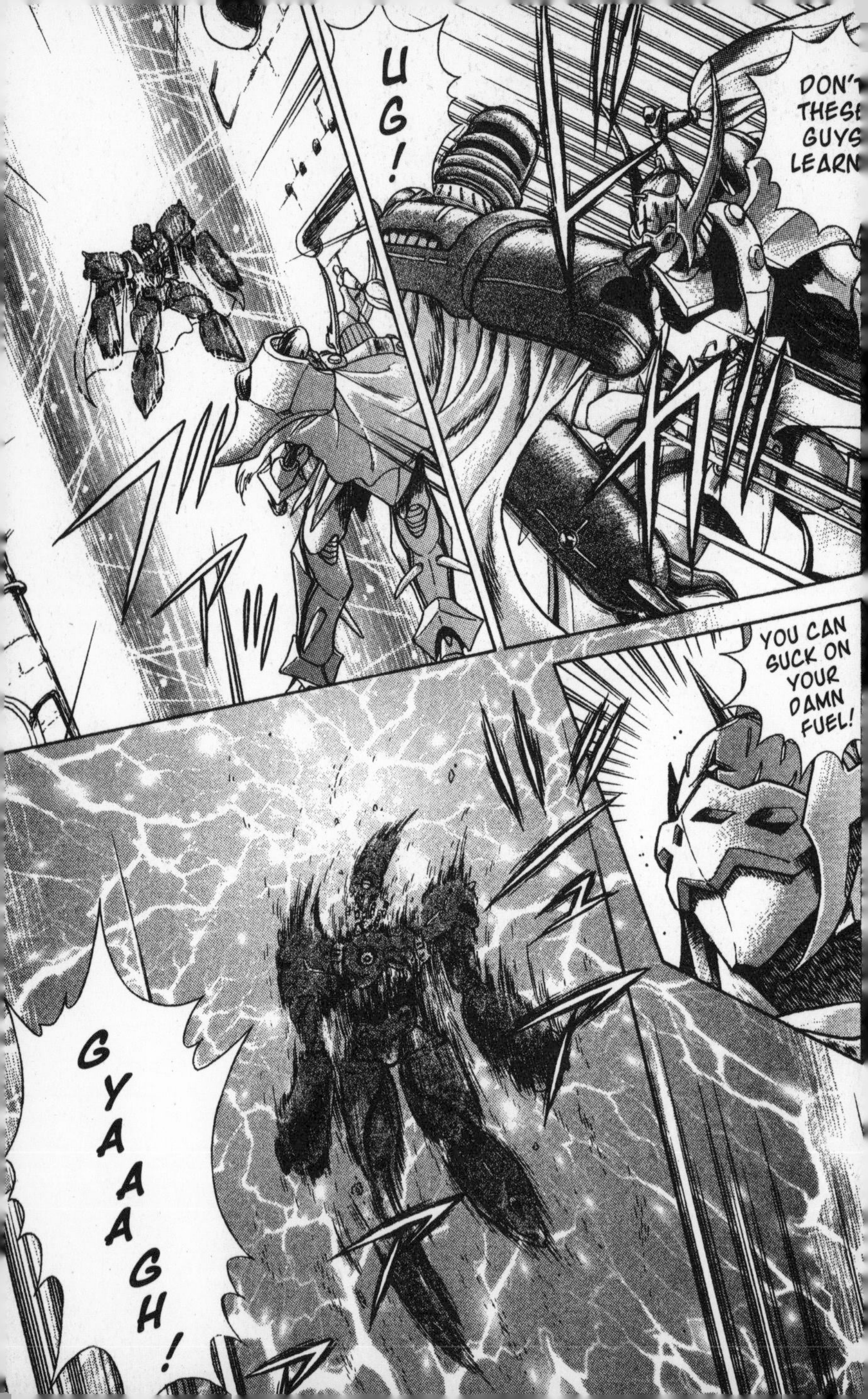

DON'T THESE GUYS LEARN
UG!
YOU CAN SUCK ON YOUR DAMN FUEL!
GYAAAGH!

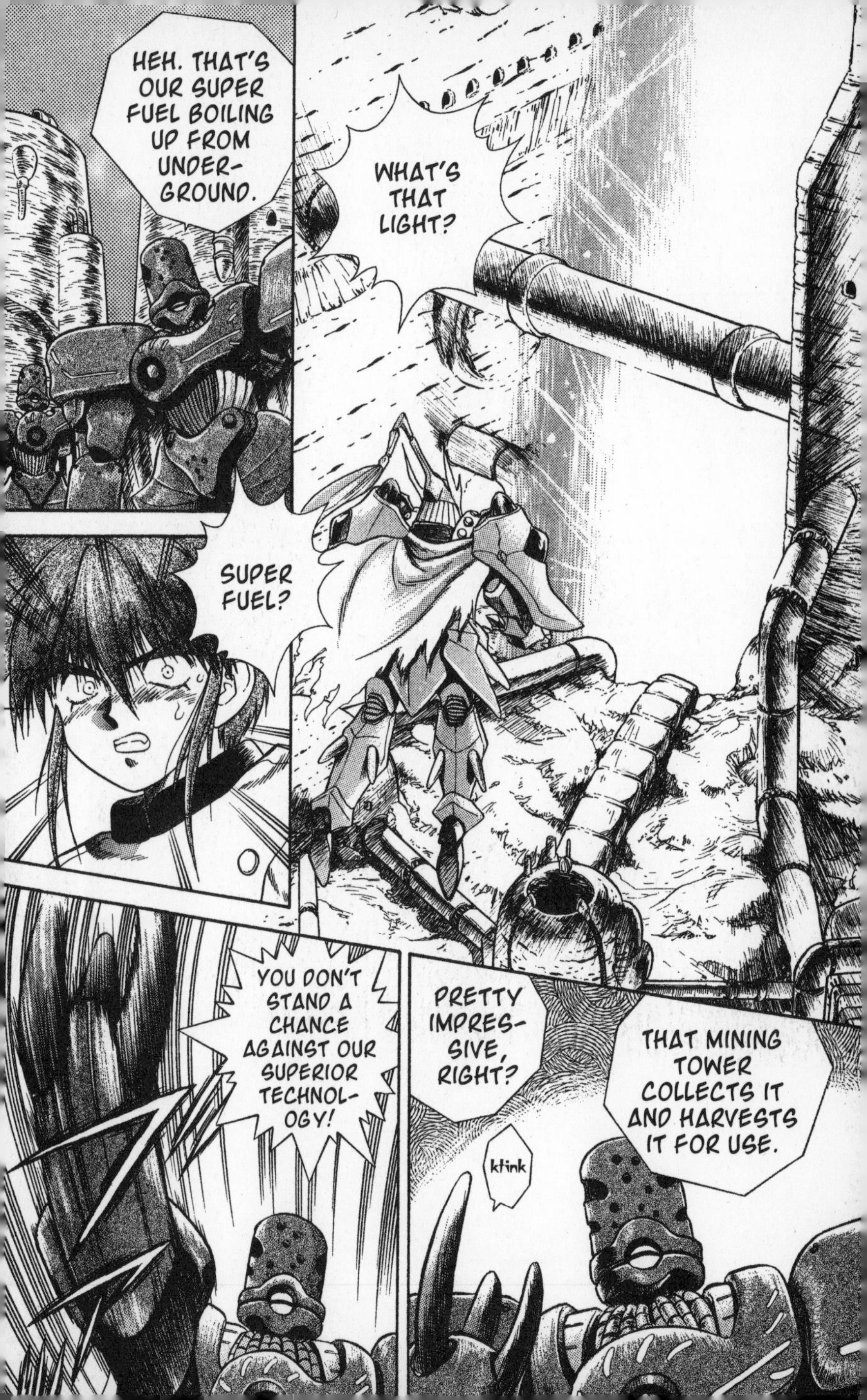
WHAT'S THAT LIGHT?
HEH. THAT'S OUR SUPER FUEL BOILING UP FROM UNDER-GROUND.
SUPER FUEL?
THAT MINING TOWER COLLECTS IT AND HARVESTS IT FOR USE.
PRETTY IMPRES-SIVE, RIGHT?
ktink
YOU DON'T STAND A CHANCE AGAINST OUR SUPERIOR TECHNOL-OGY!

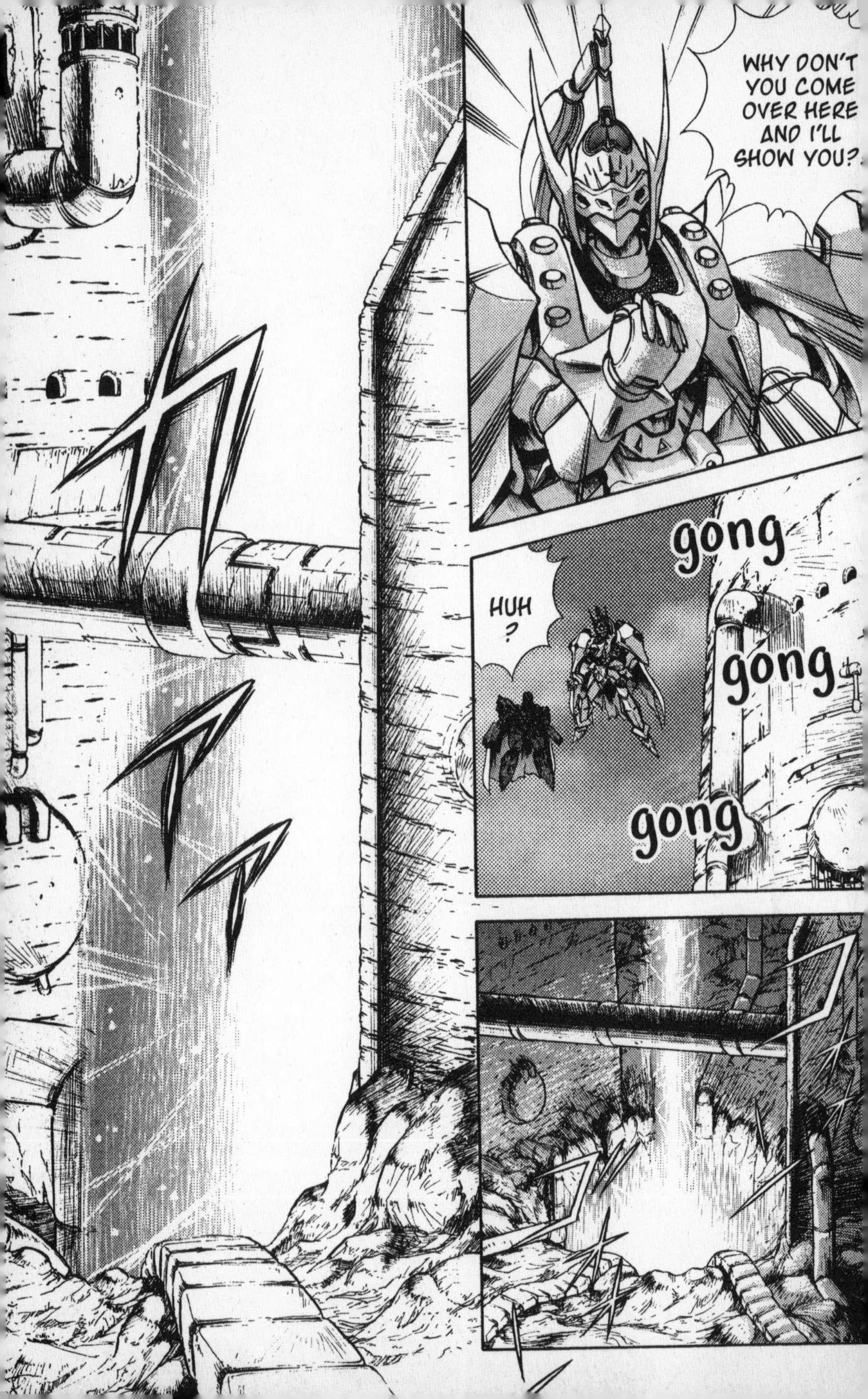
WHY DON'T YOU COME OVER HERE AND I'LL SHOW YOU?
gong
gong
gong
HUH ?

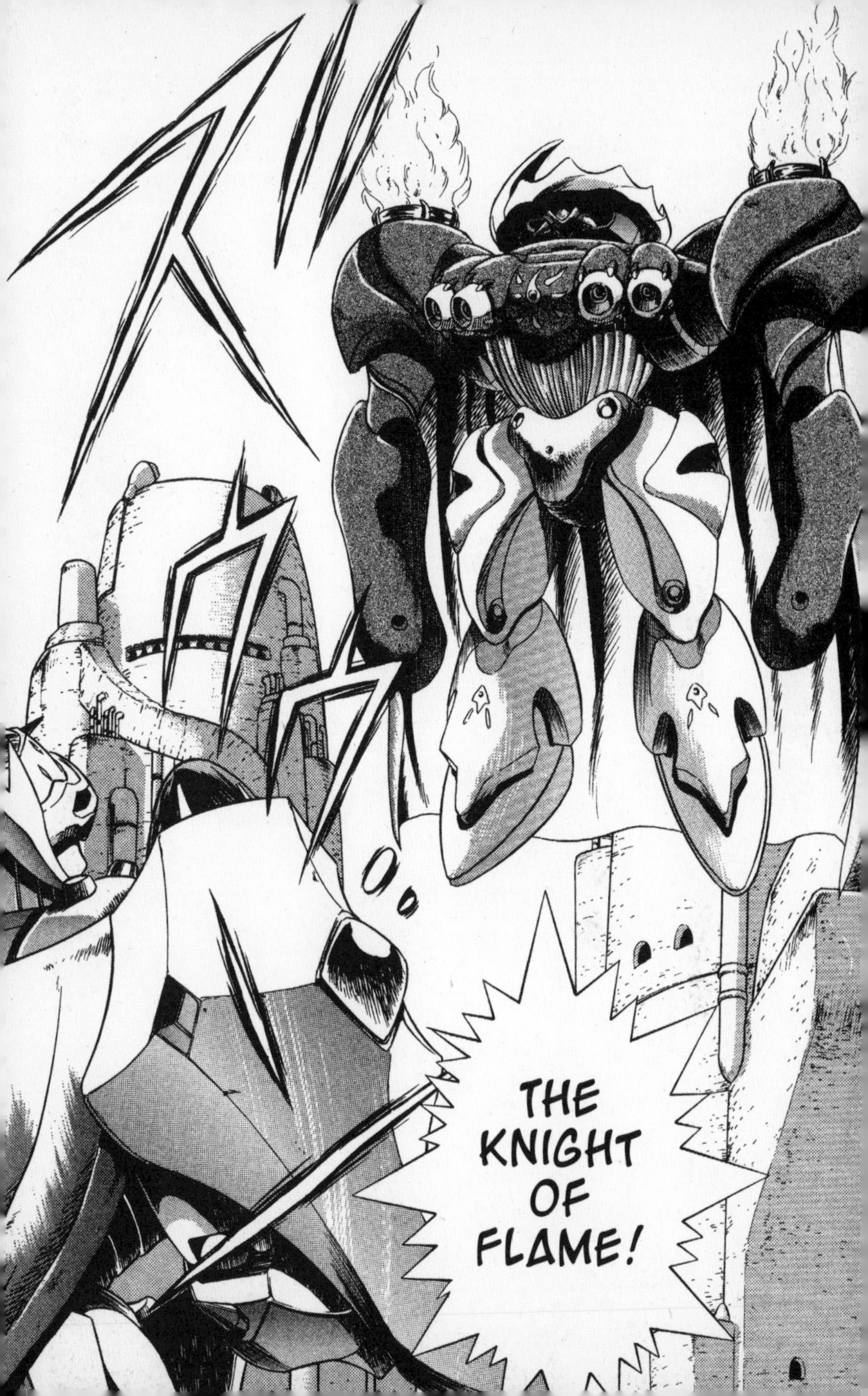
THE KNIGHT OF FLAME!

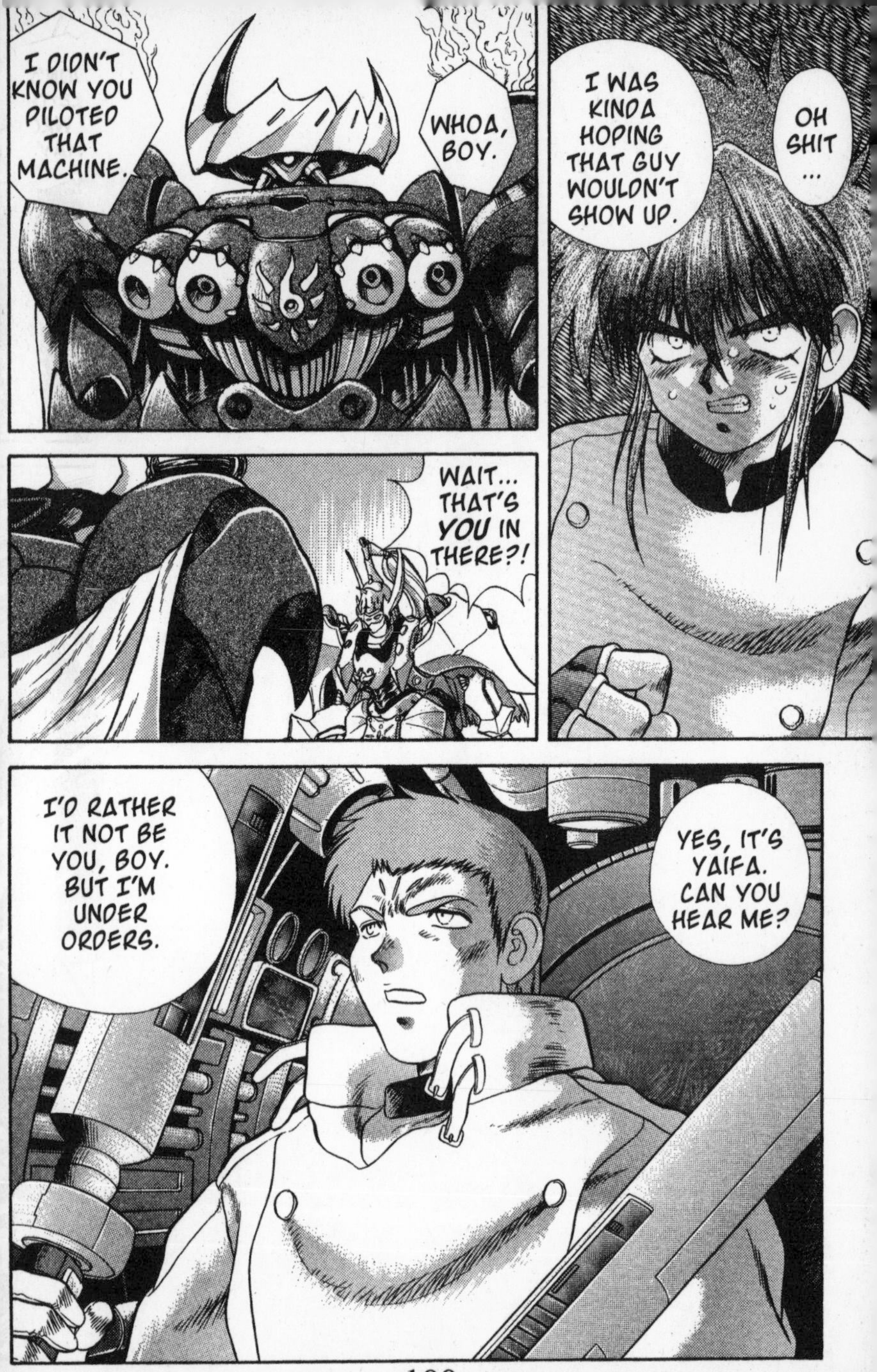
OH SHIT ...
I WAS KINDA HOPING THAT GUY WOULDN'T SHOW UP.
WHOA, BOY.
I DIDN'T KNOW YOU PILOTED THAT MACHINE.
WAIT... THAT'S *YOU* IN THERE?!
YES, IT'S YAIFA. CAN YOU HEAR ME?
I'D RATHER IT NOT BE YOU, BOY. BUT I'M UNDER ORDERS.

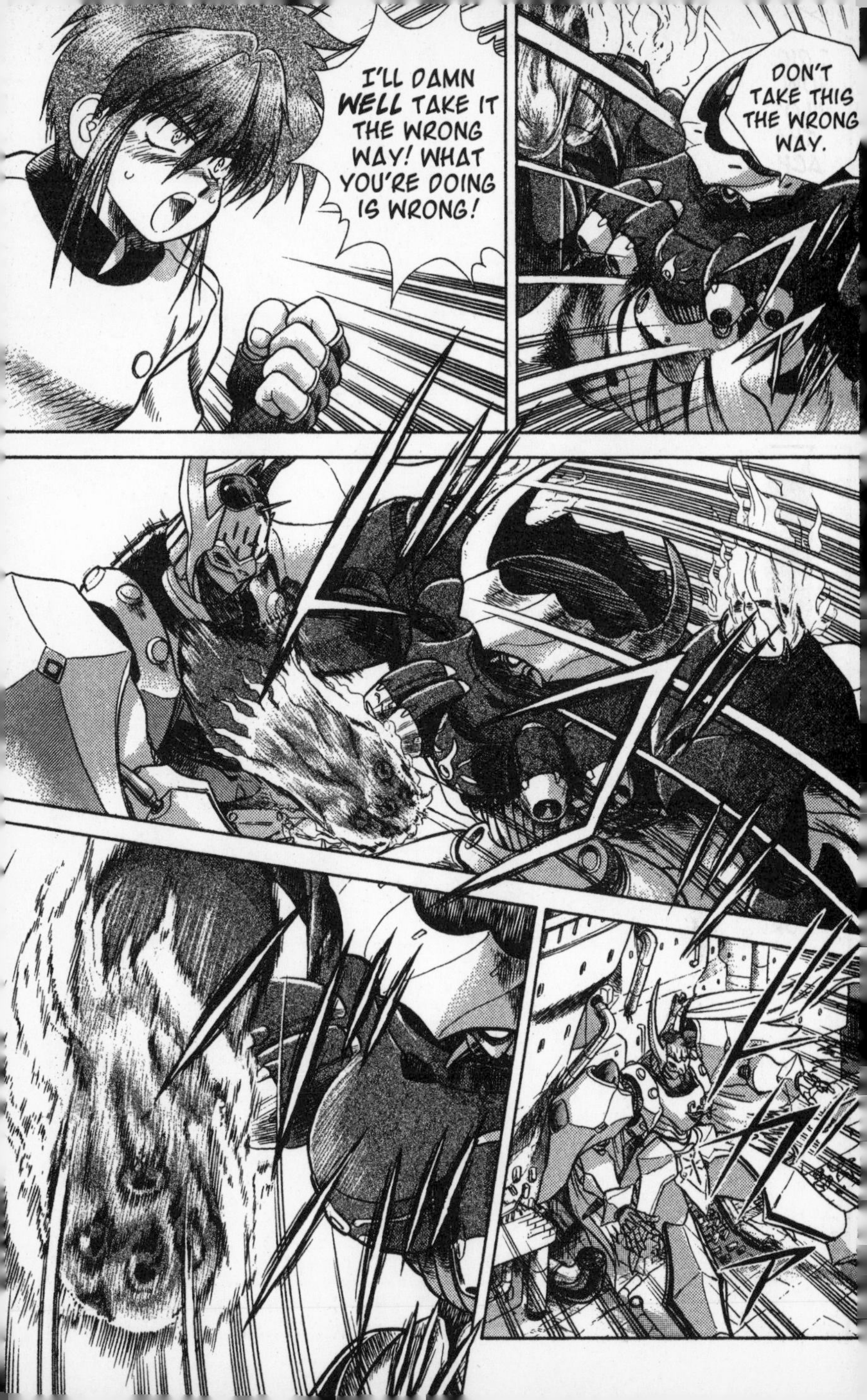
DON'T TAKE THIS THE WRONG WAY.
I'LL DAMN WELL TAKE IT THE WRONG WAY! WHAT YOU'RE DOING IS WRONG!

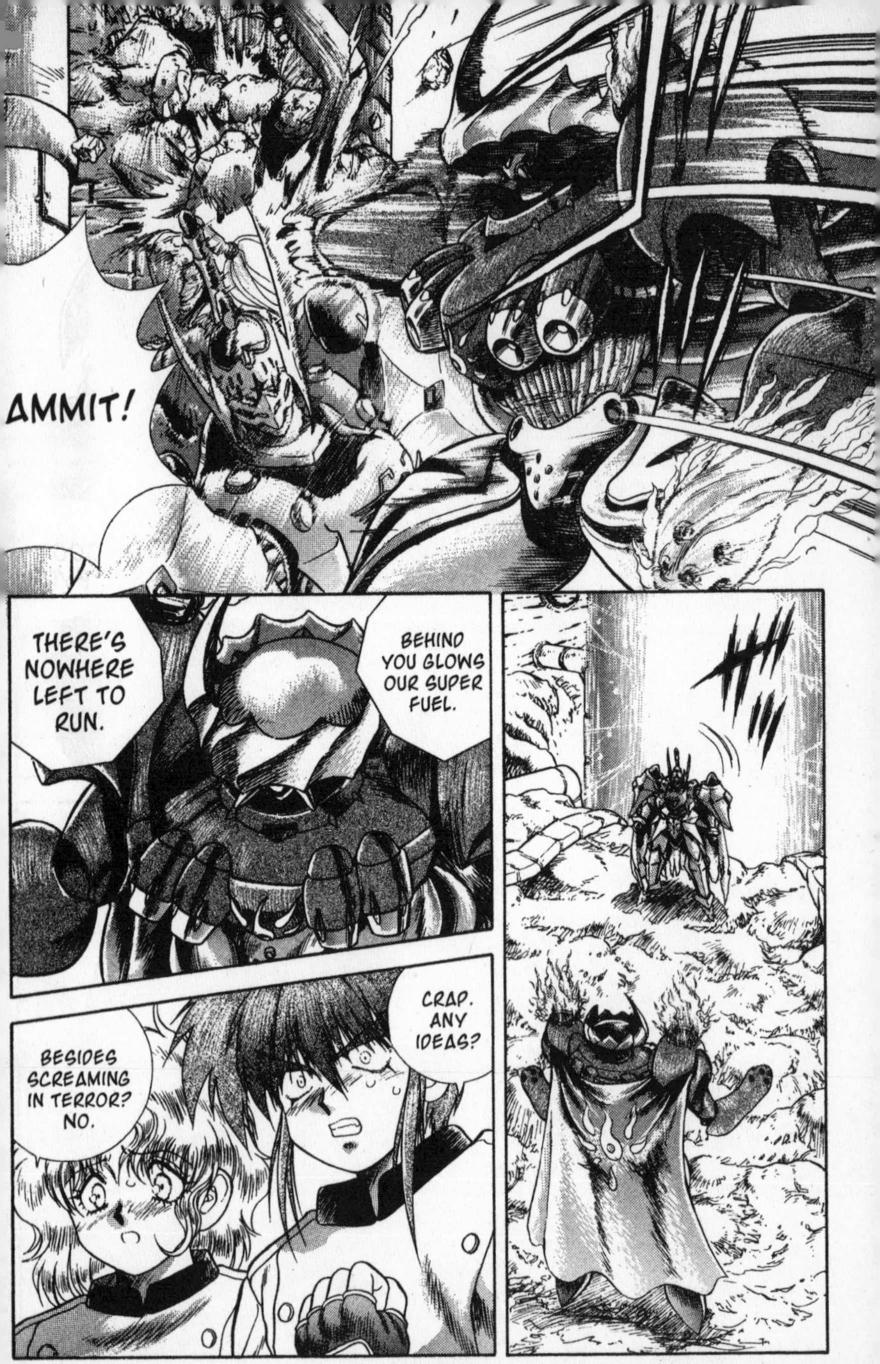
AMMIT!
BEHIND YOU GLOWS OUR SUPER FUEL.
THERE'S NOWHERE LEFT TO RUN.
CRAP. ANY IDEAS?
BESIDES SCREAMING IN TERROR? NO.

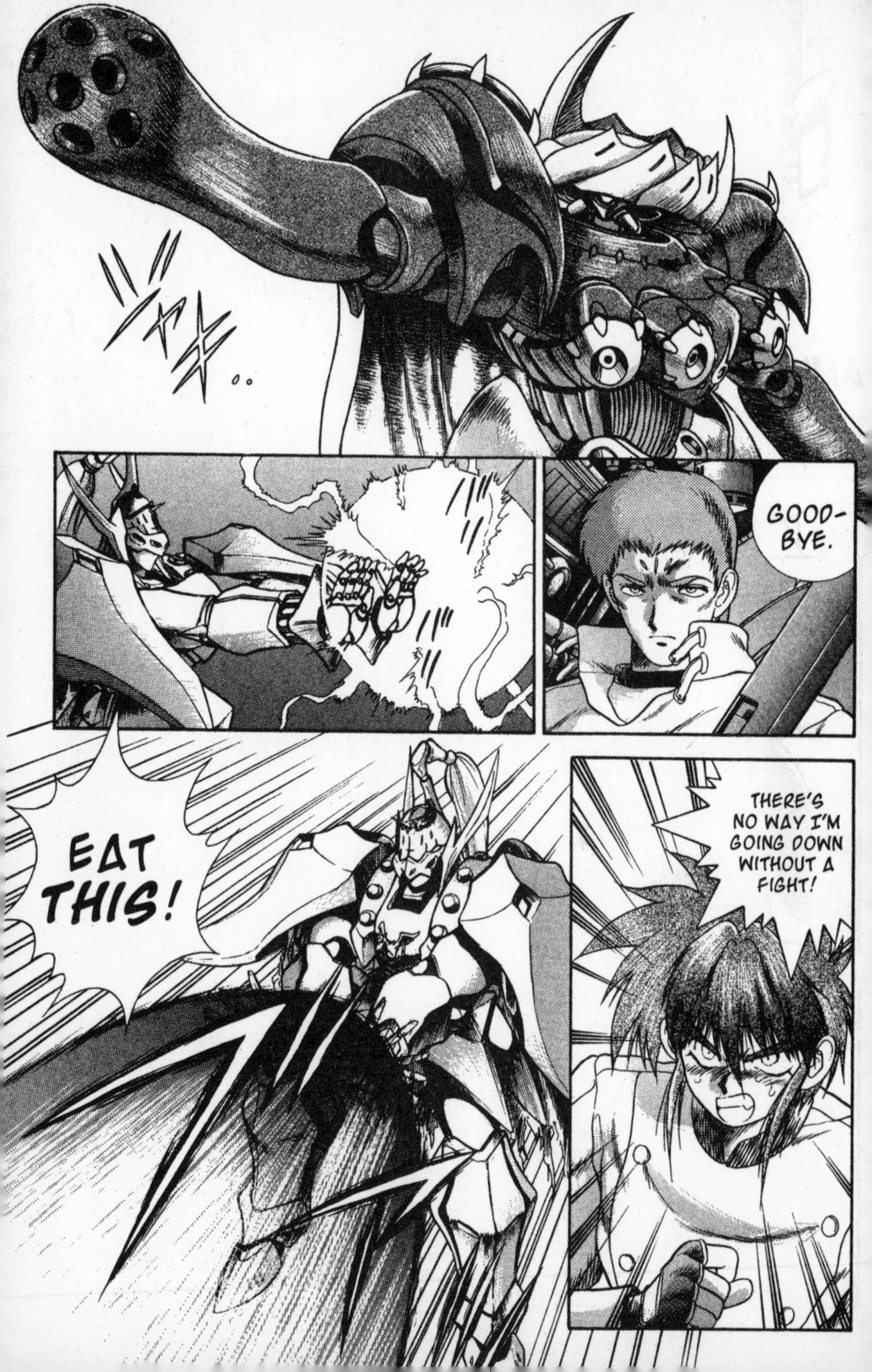
GOOD-BYE.
THERE'S NO WAY I'M GOING DOWN WITHOUT A FIGHT!
EAT THIS!

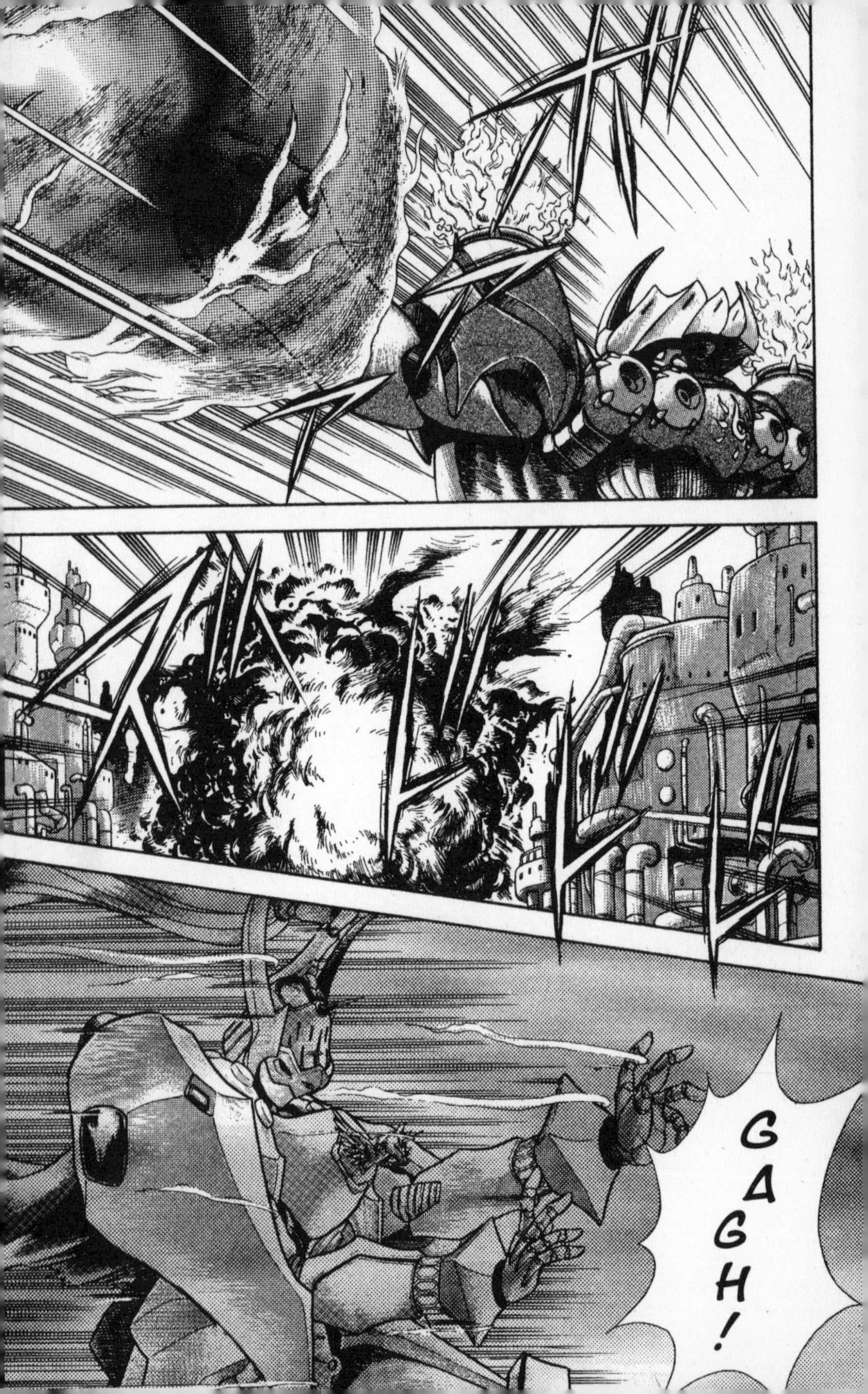
GAGH!

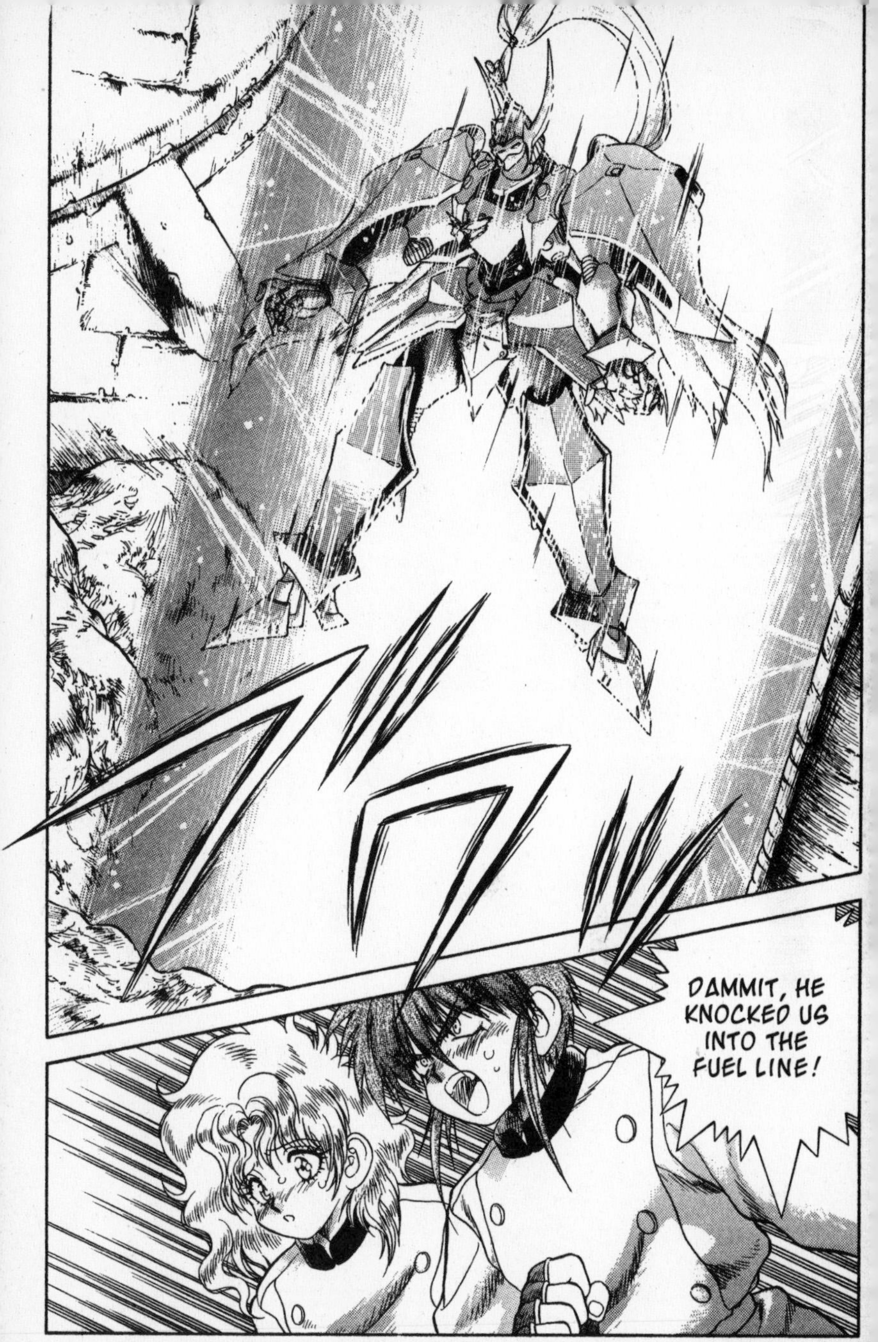
DAMMIT, HE KNOCKED US INTO THE FUEL LINE!

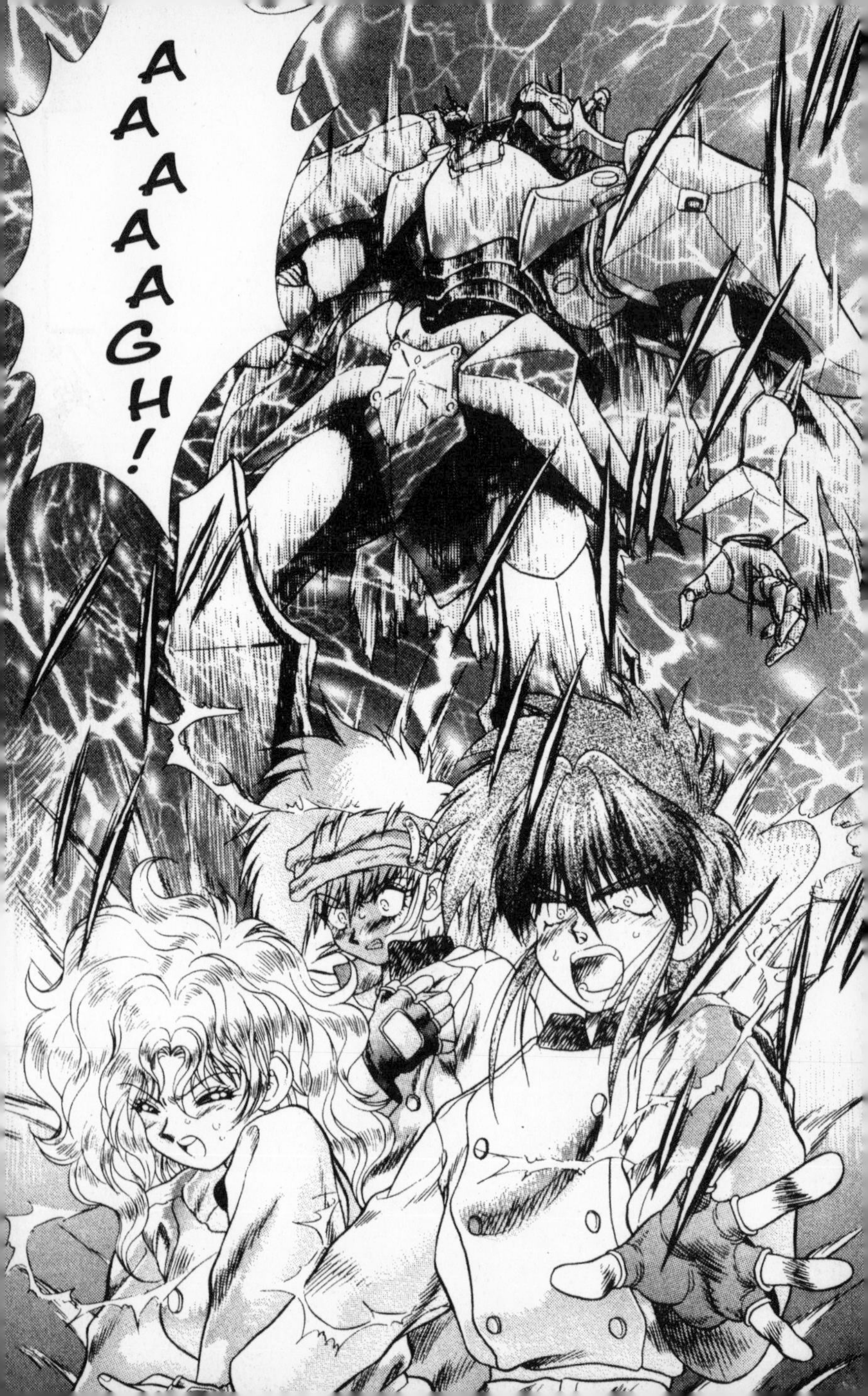
AAAAAAGH!

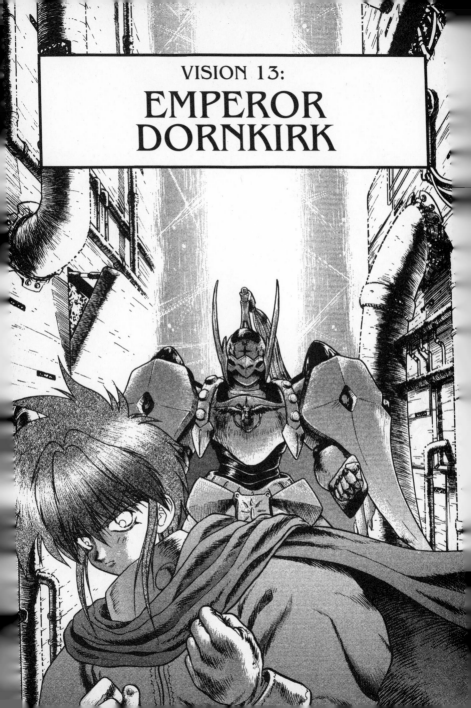

VISION 13:
EMPEROR DORNKIRK

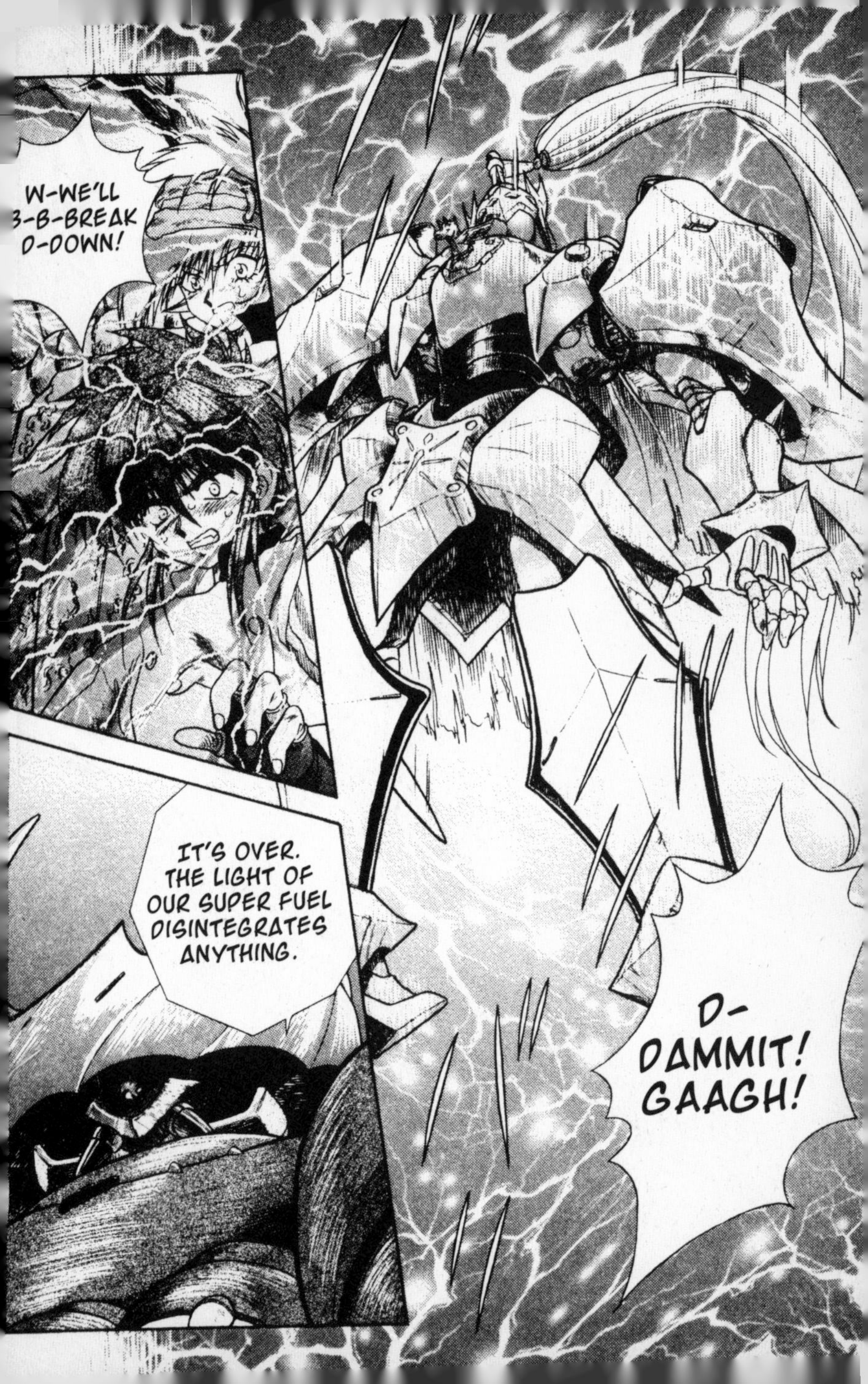
D-DAMMIT! GAAGH!
W-WE'LL B-B-BREAK D-DOWN!
IT'S OVER. THE LIGHT OF OUR SUPER FUEL DISINTEGRATES ANYTHING.

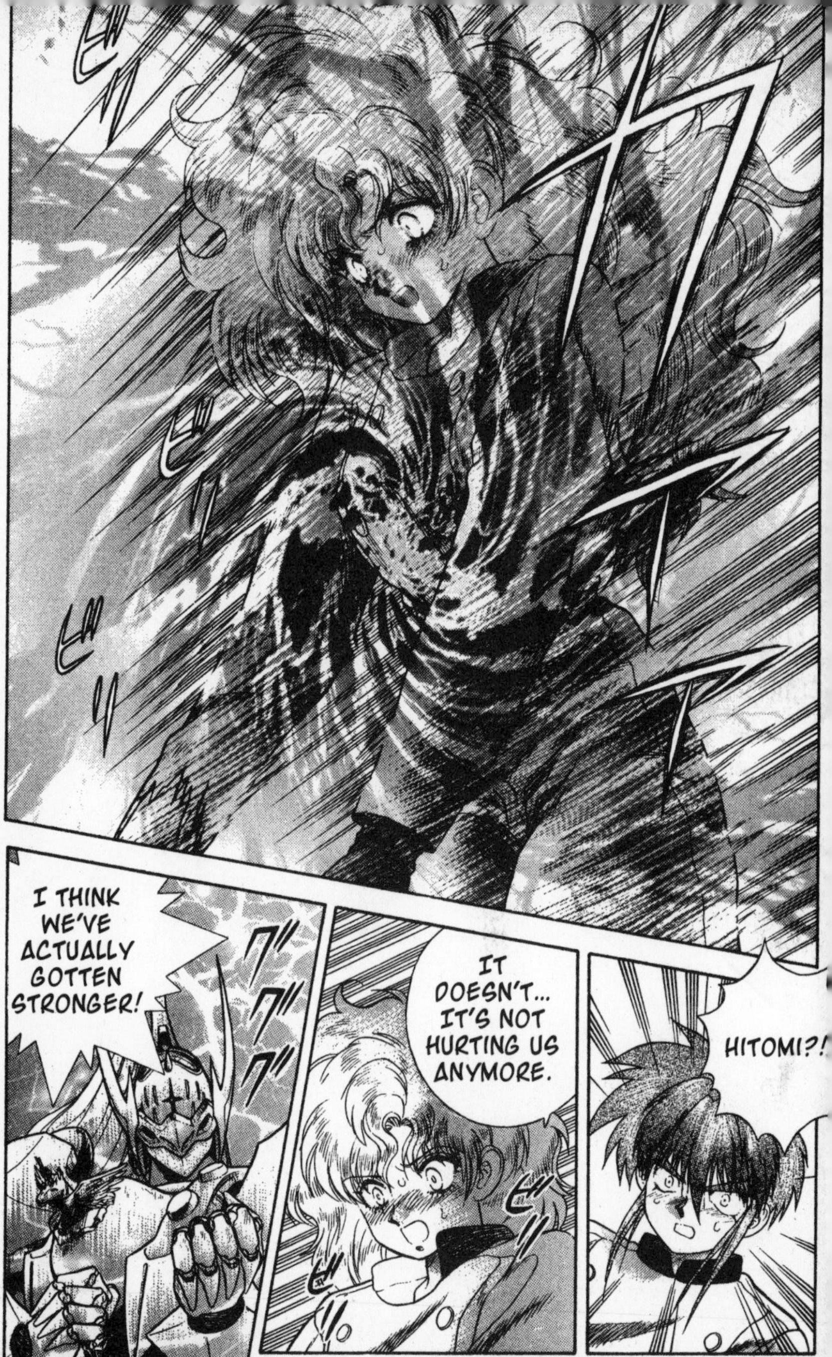
HITOMI?!
IT DOESN'T... IT'S NOT HURTING US ANYMORE.
I THINK WE'VE ACTUALLY GOTTEN STRONGER!

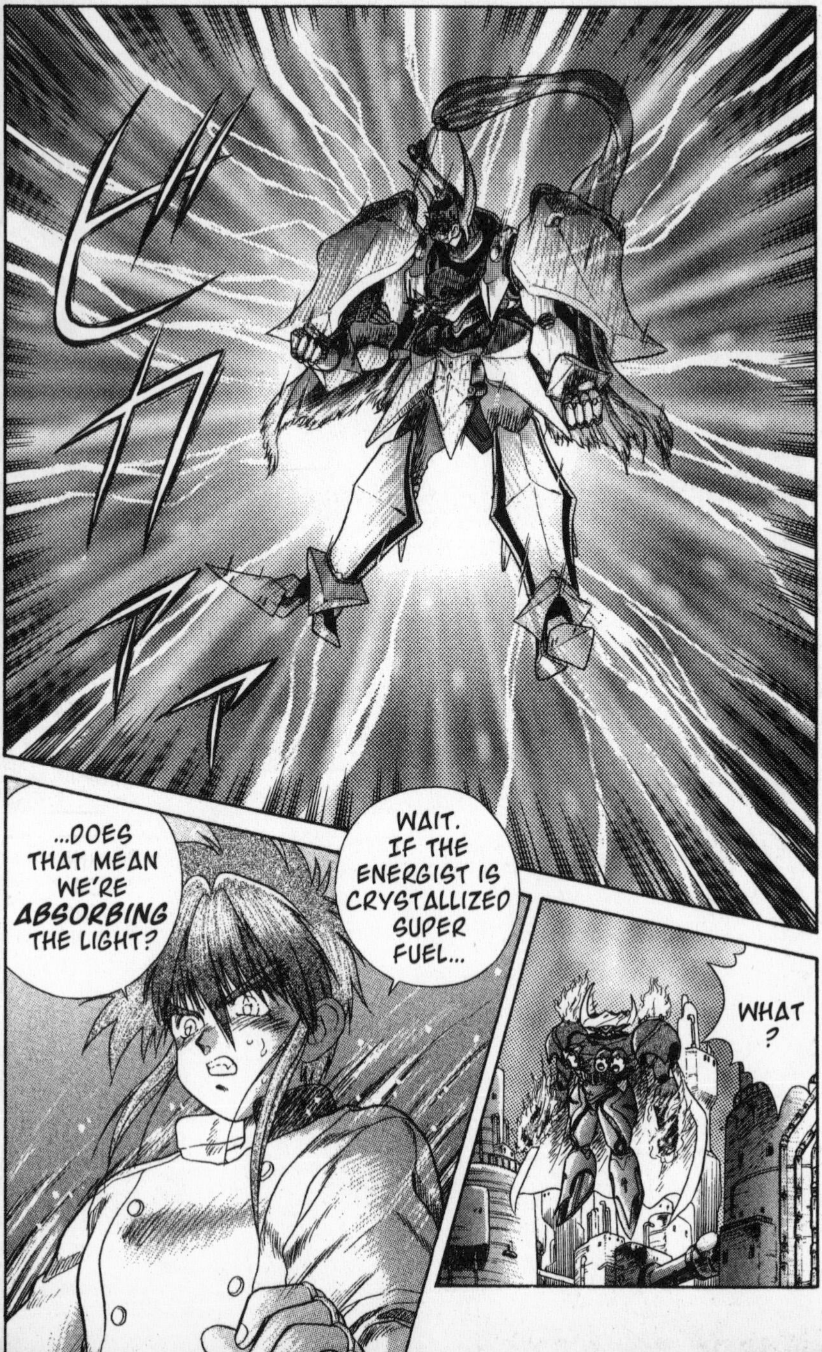
WAIT. IF THE ENERGIST IS CRYSTALLIZED SUPER FUEL...
...DOES THAT MEAN WE'RE **ABSORBING** THE LIGHT?
WHAT?

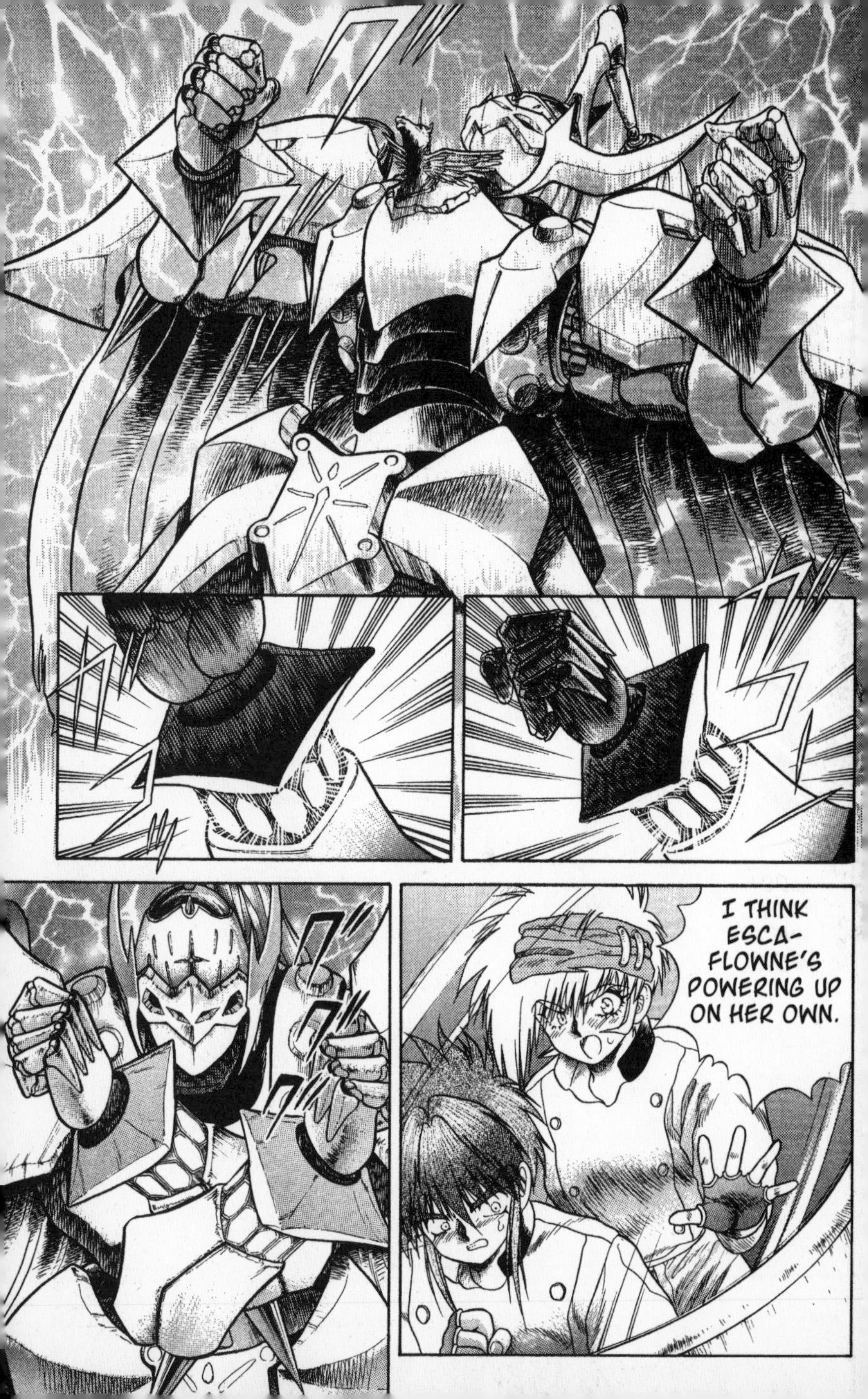
I THINK ESCA-FLOWNE'S POWERING UP ON HER OWN.

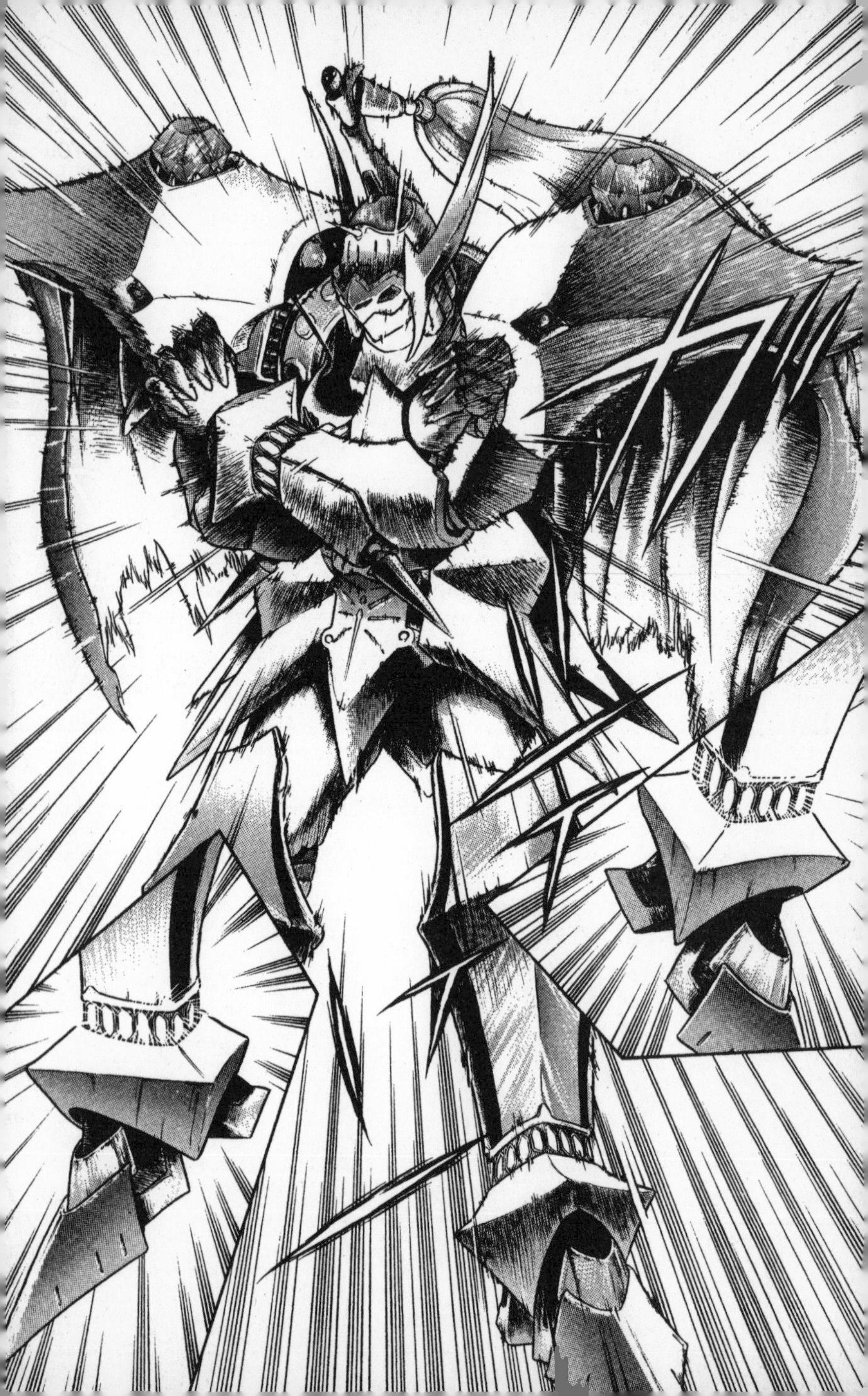

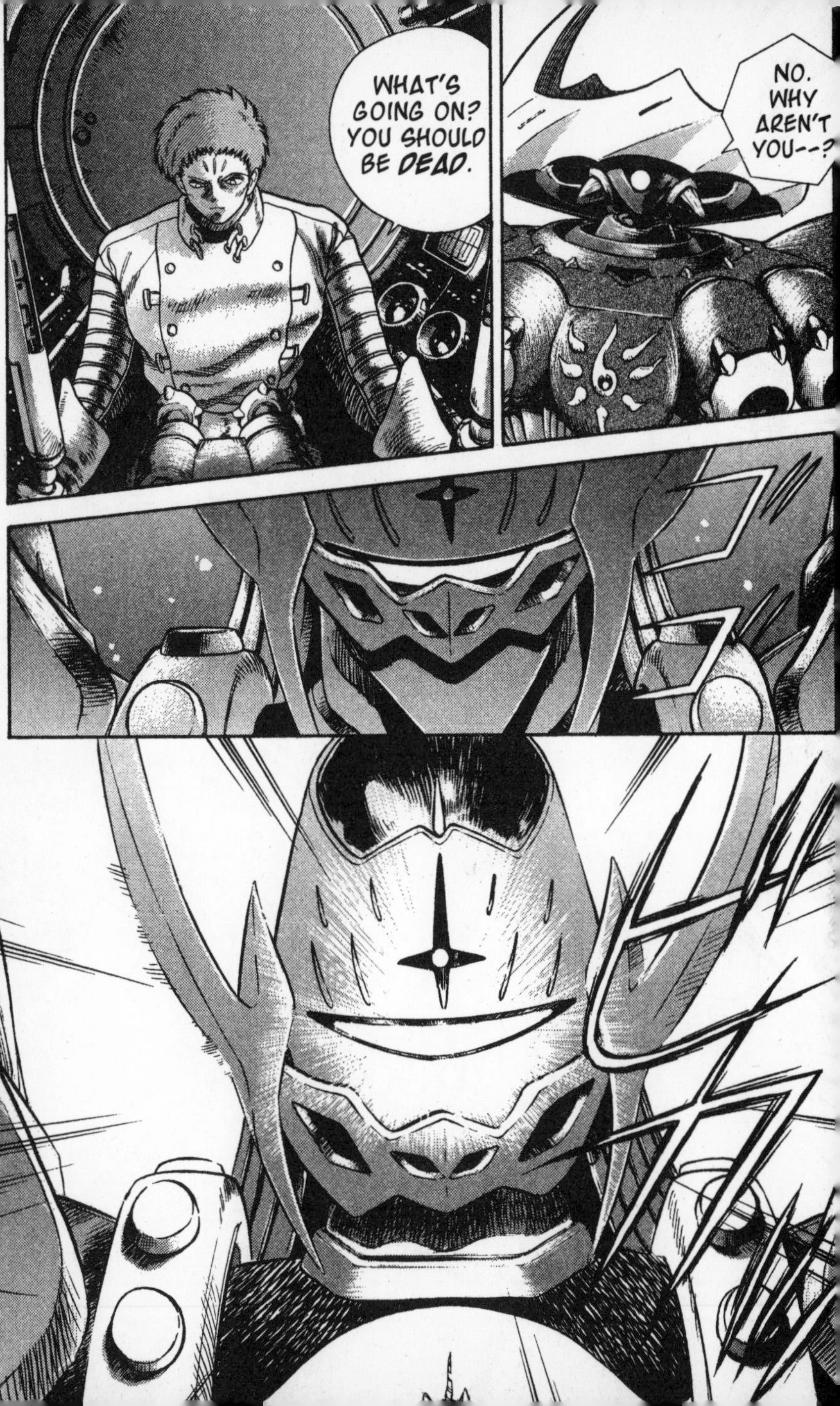
NO. WHY AREN'T YOU--?
WHAT'S GOING ON? YOU SHOULD BE *DEAD*.

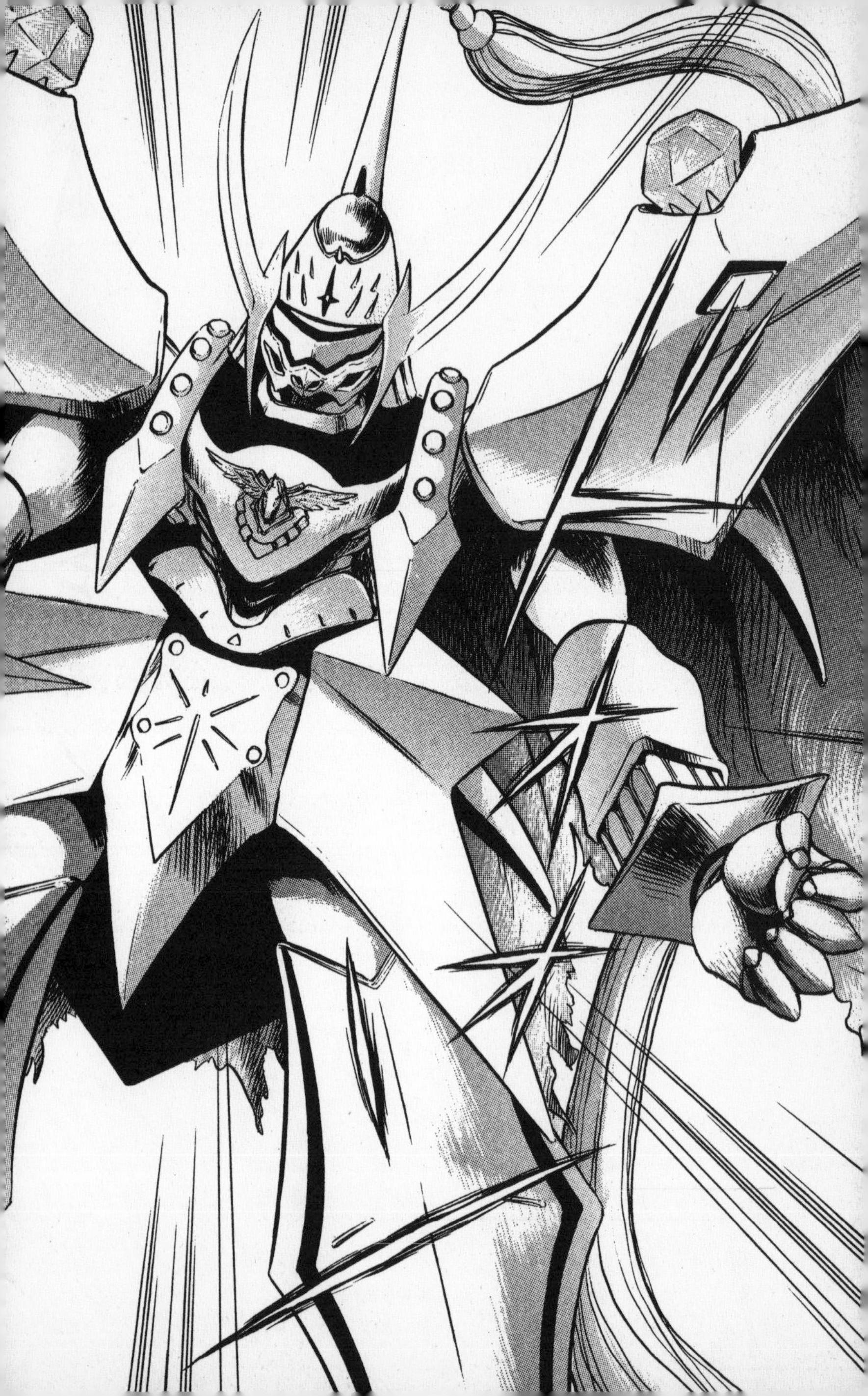

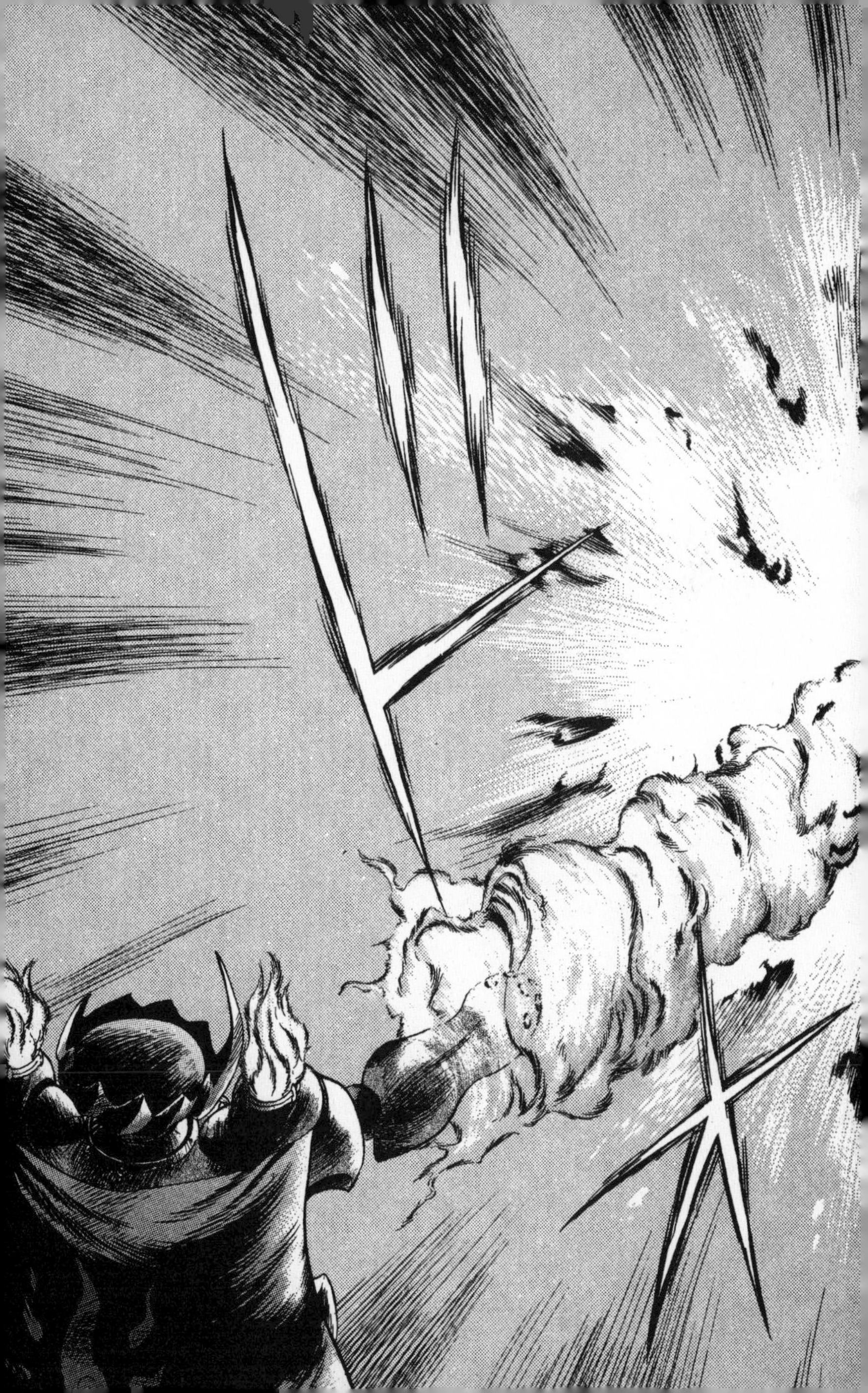

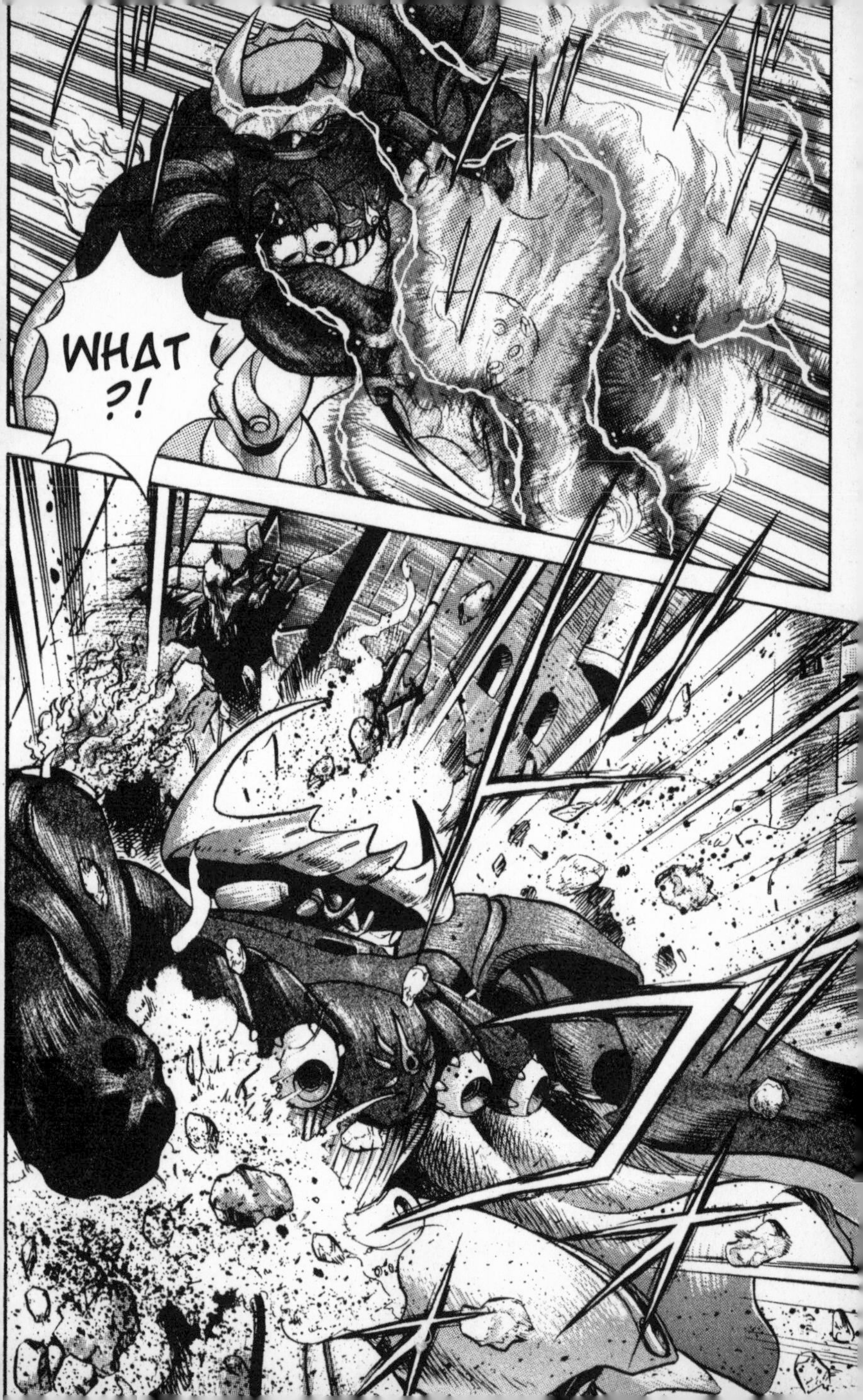
WHAT ?!

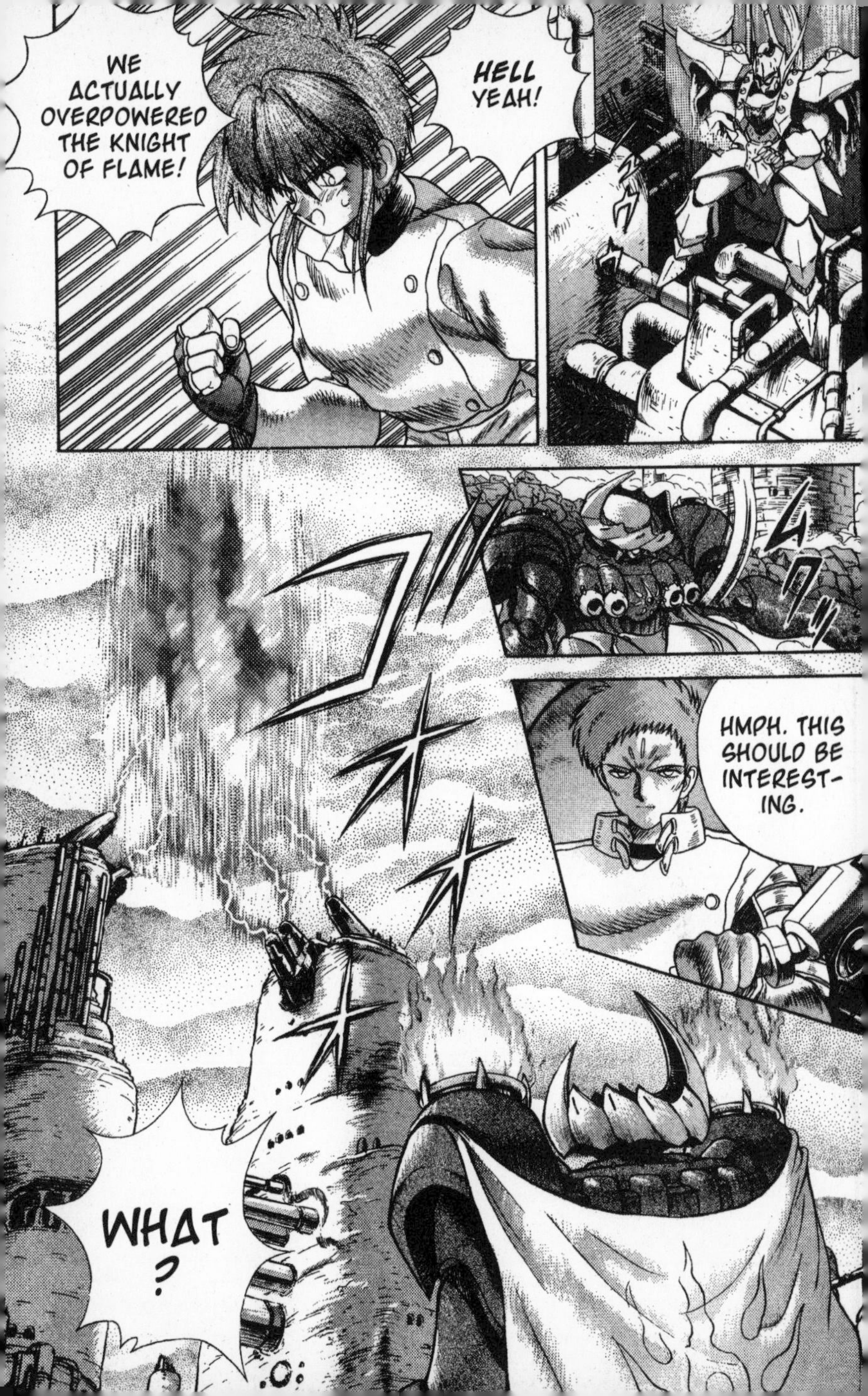
HELL YEAH!
WE ACTUALLY OVERPOWERED THE KNIGHT OF FLAME!
HMPH. THIS SHOULD BE INTEREST-ING.
WHAT ?

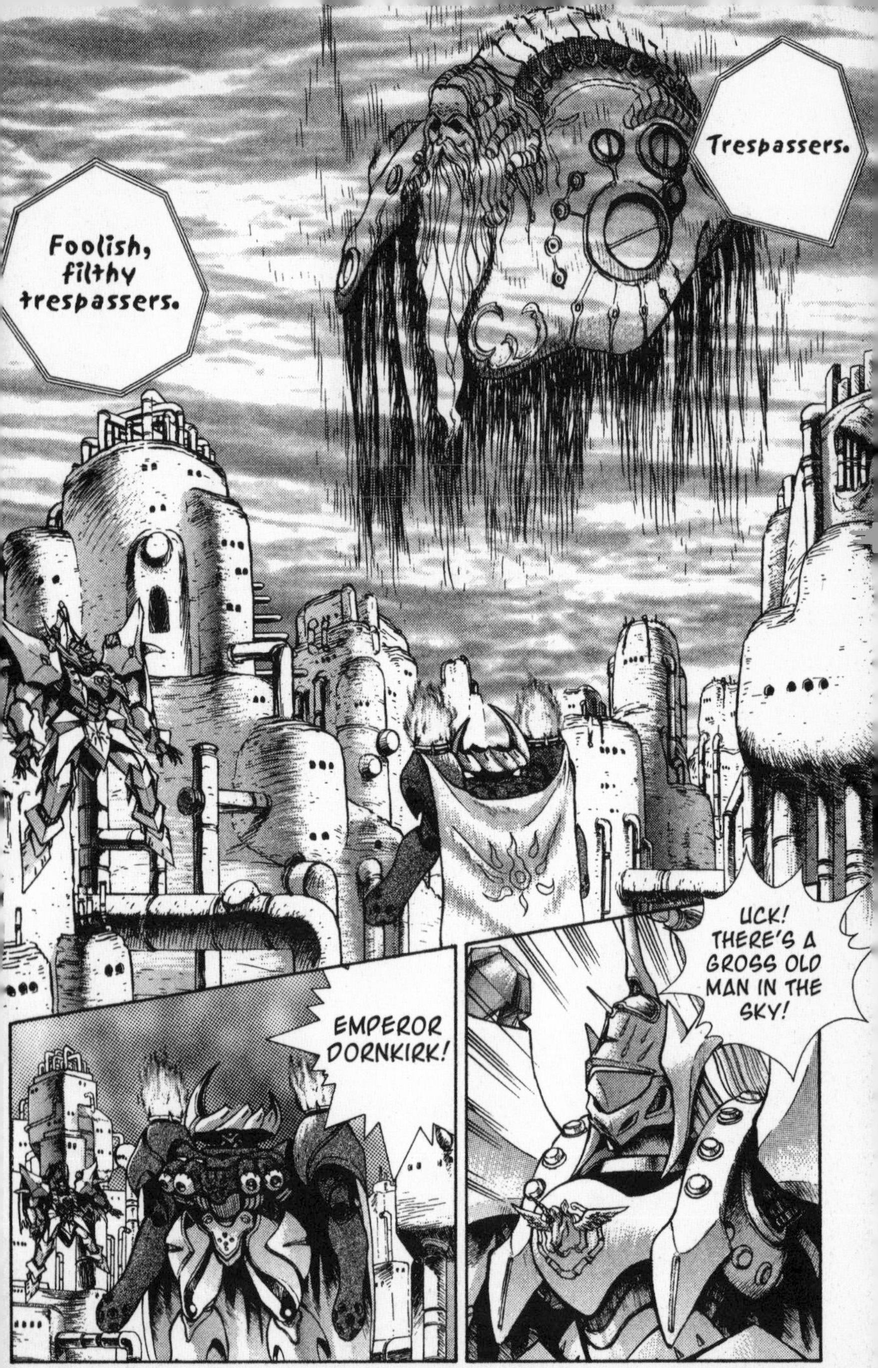
Trespassers.
Foolish, filthy trespassers.
UCK! THERE'S A GROSS OLD MAN IN THE SKY!
EMPEROR DORNKIRK!

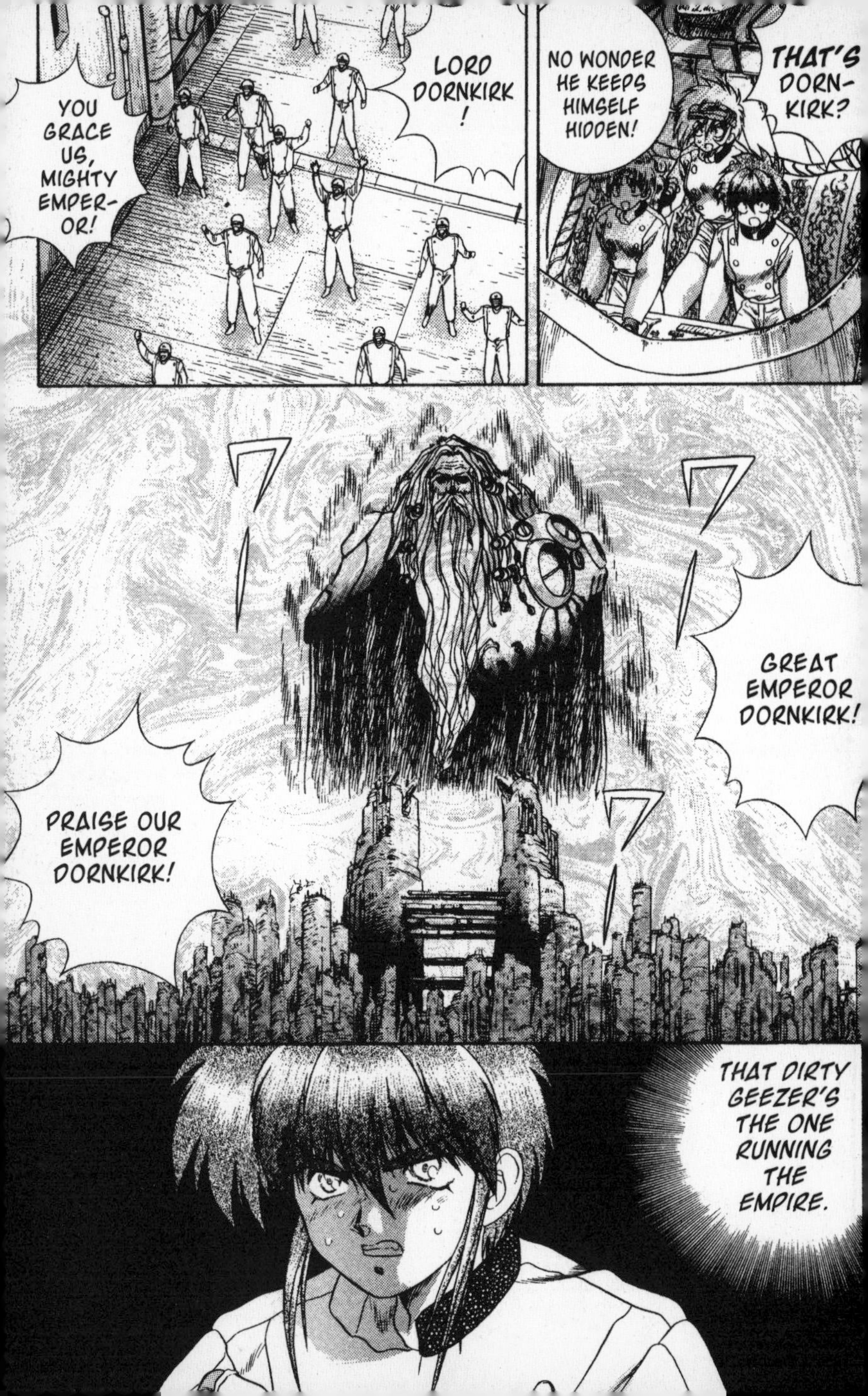
THAT'S DORNKIRK?
NO WONDER HE KEEPS HIMSELF HIDDEN!
LORD DORNKIRK!
YOU GRACE US, MIGHTY EMPEROR!
GREAT EMPEROR DORNKIRK!
PRAISE OUR EMPEROR DORNKIRK!
THAT DIRTY GEEZER'S THE ONE RUNNING THE EMPIRE.

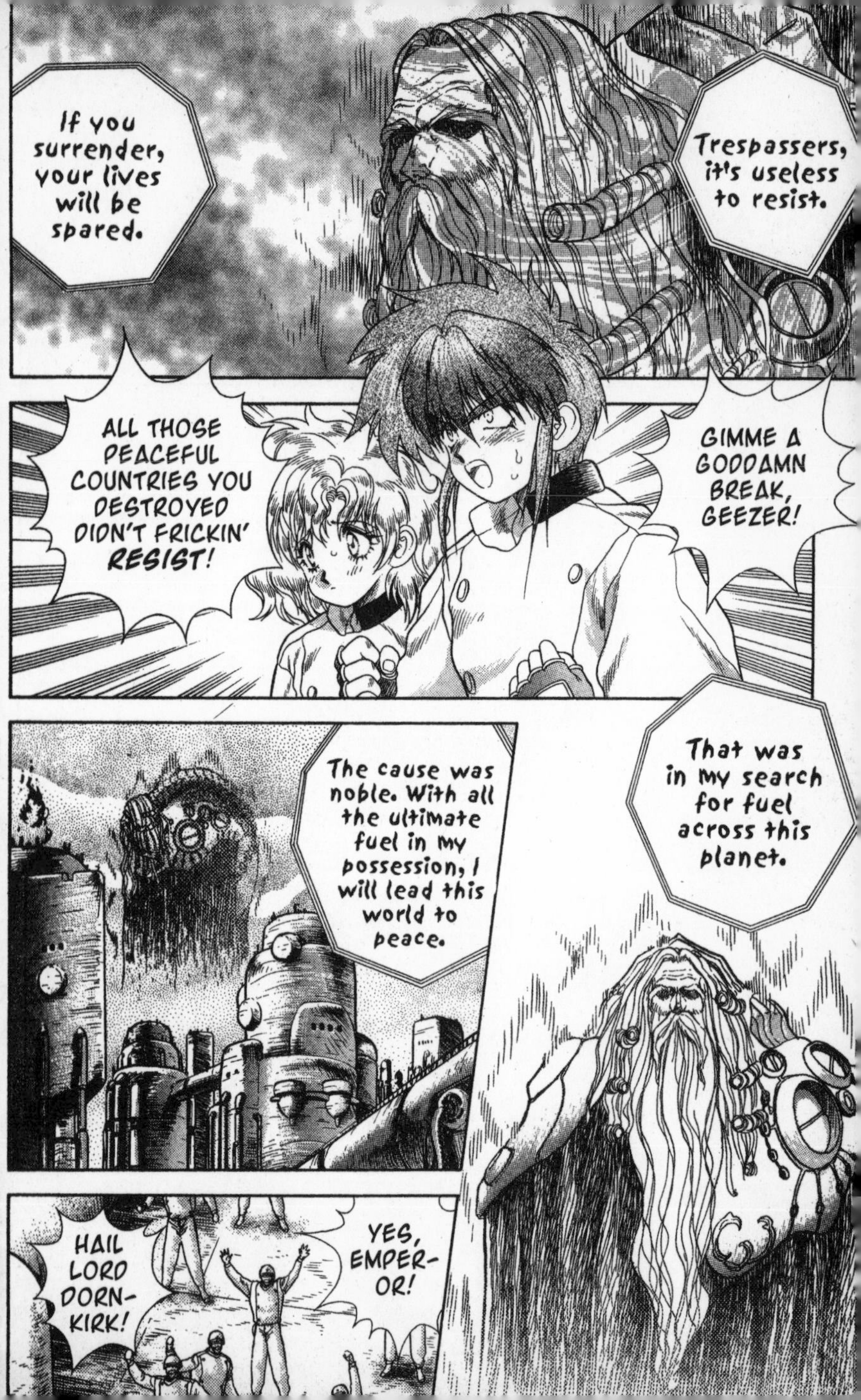
Trespassers, it's useless to resist.
If you surrender, your lives will be spared.
GIMME A GODDAMN BREAK, GEEZER!
ALL THOSE PEACEFUL COUNTRIES YOU DESTROYED DIDN'T FRICKIN' RESIST!
That was in my search for fuel across this planet.
The cause was noble. With all the ultimate fuel in my possession, I will lead this world to peace.
YES, EMPEROR!
HAIL LORD DORNKIRK!

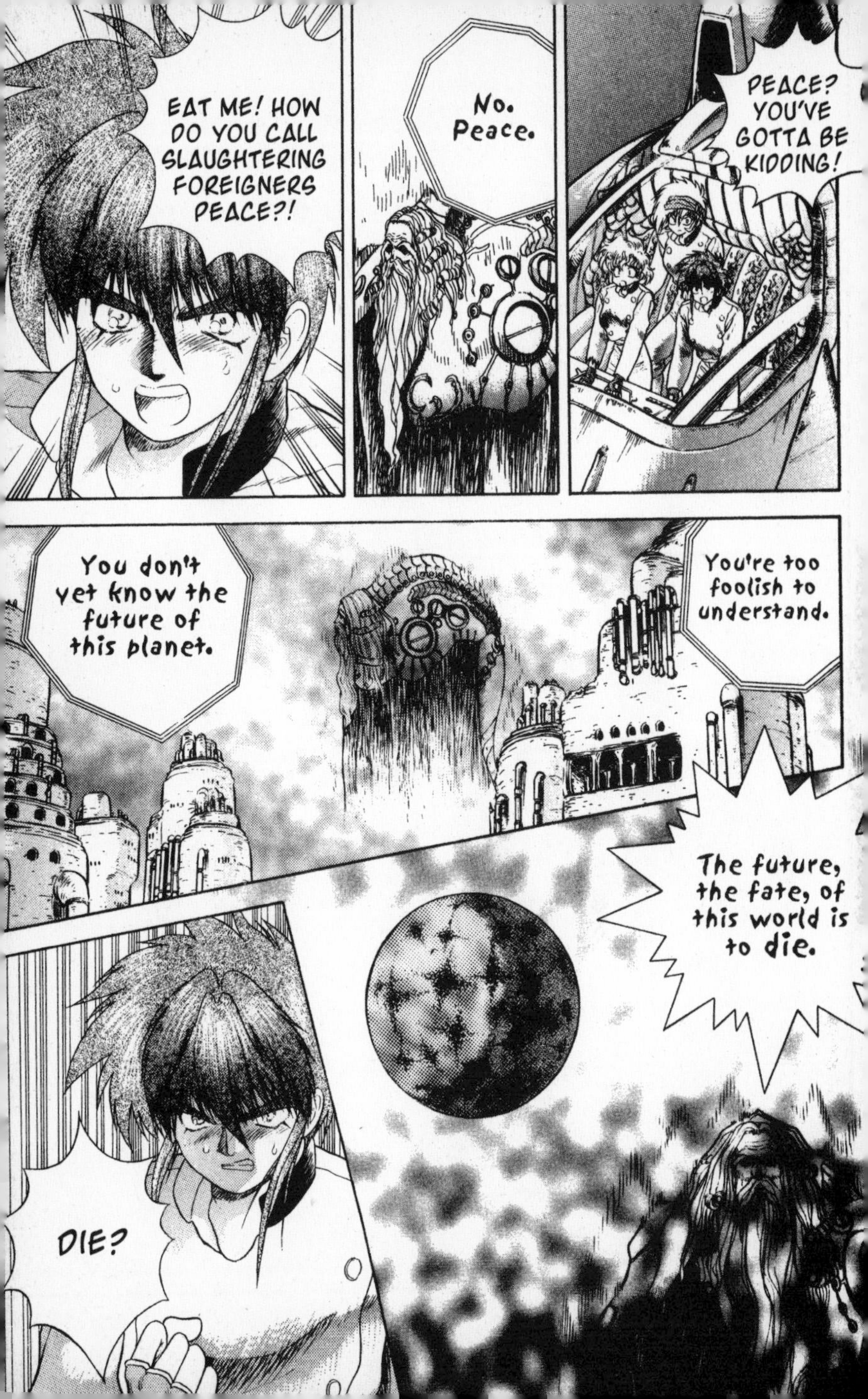
PEACE? YOU'VE GOTTA BE KIDDING!
No. Peace.
EAT ME! HOW DO YOU CALL SLAUGHTERING FOREIGNERS PEACE?!
You're too foolish to understand.
You don't yet know the future of this planet.
The future, the fate, of this world is to die.
DIE?

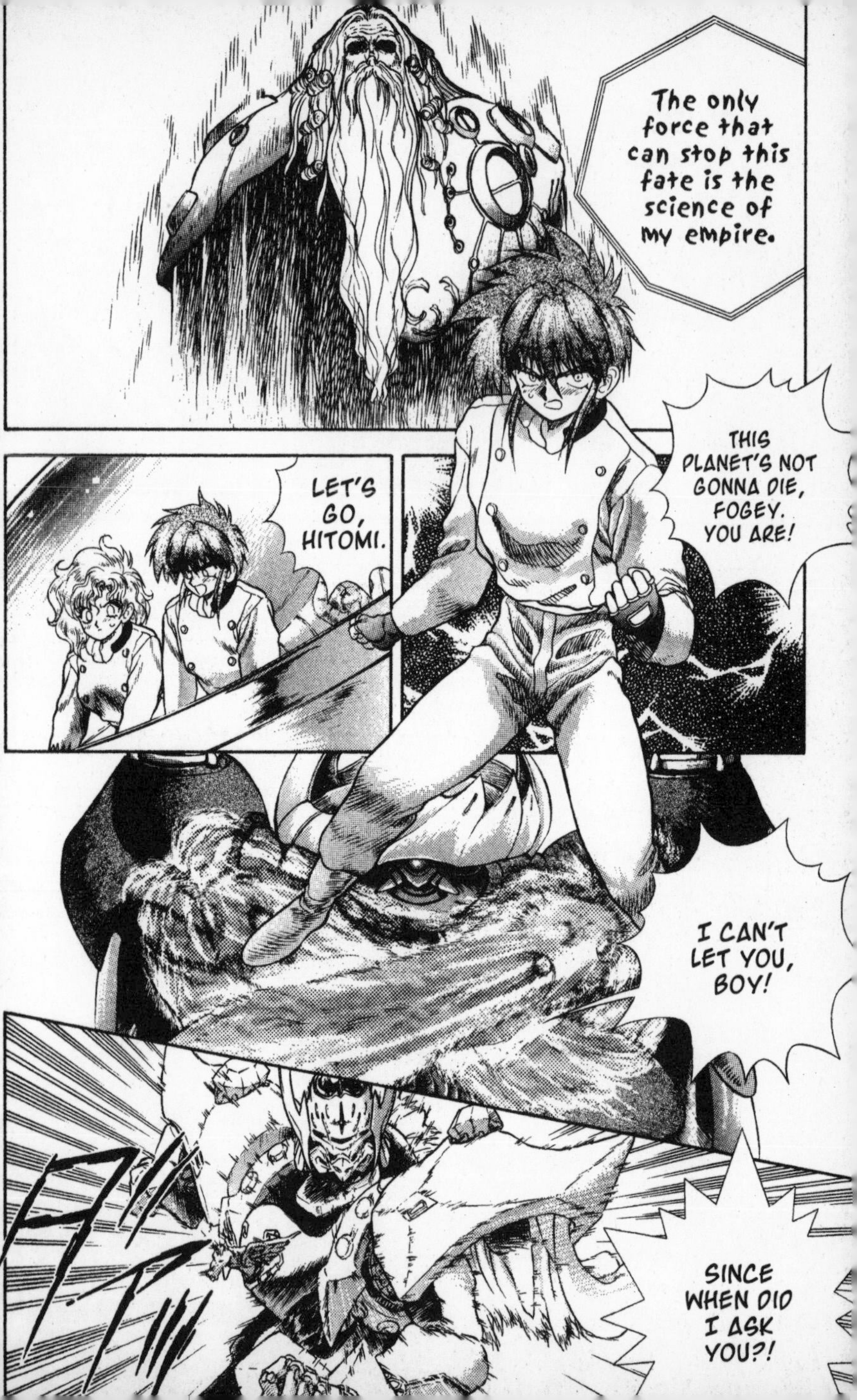
The only force that can stop this fate is the science of my empire.
THIS PLANET'S NOT GONNA DIE, FOGEY. YOU ARE!
LET'S GO, HITOMI.
I CAN'T LET YOU, BOY!
SINCE WHEN DID I ASK YOU?!

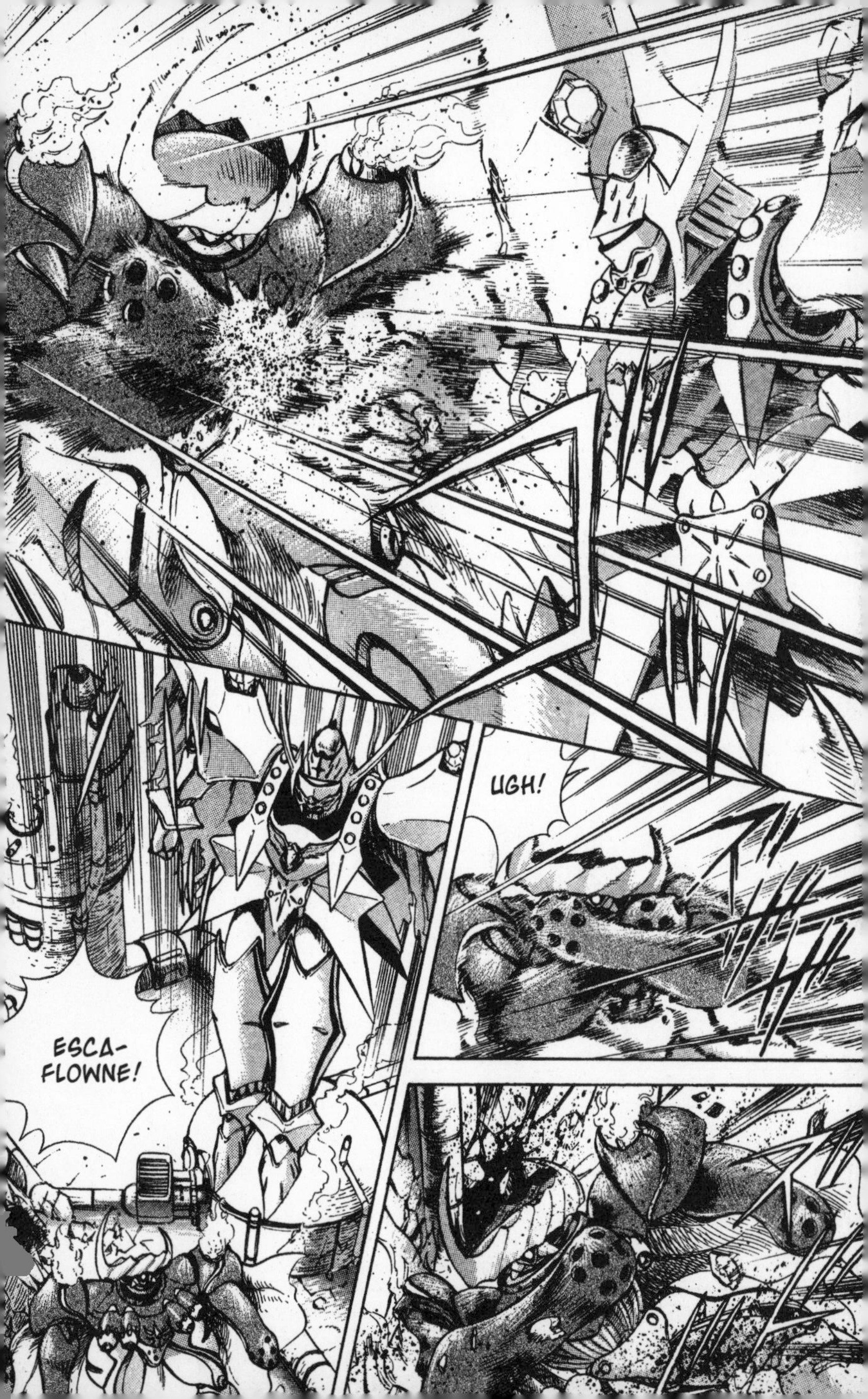
UGH!
ESCA-
FLOWNE!

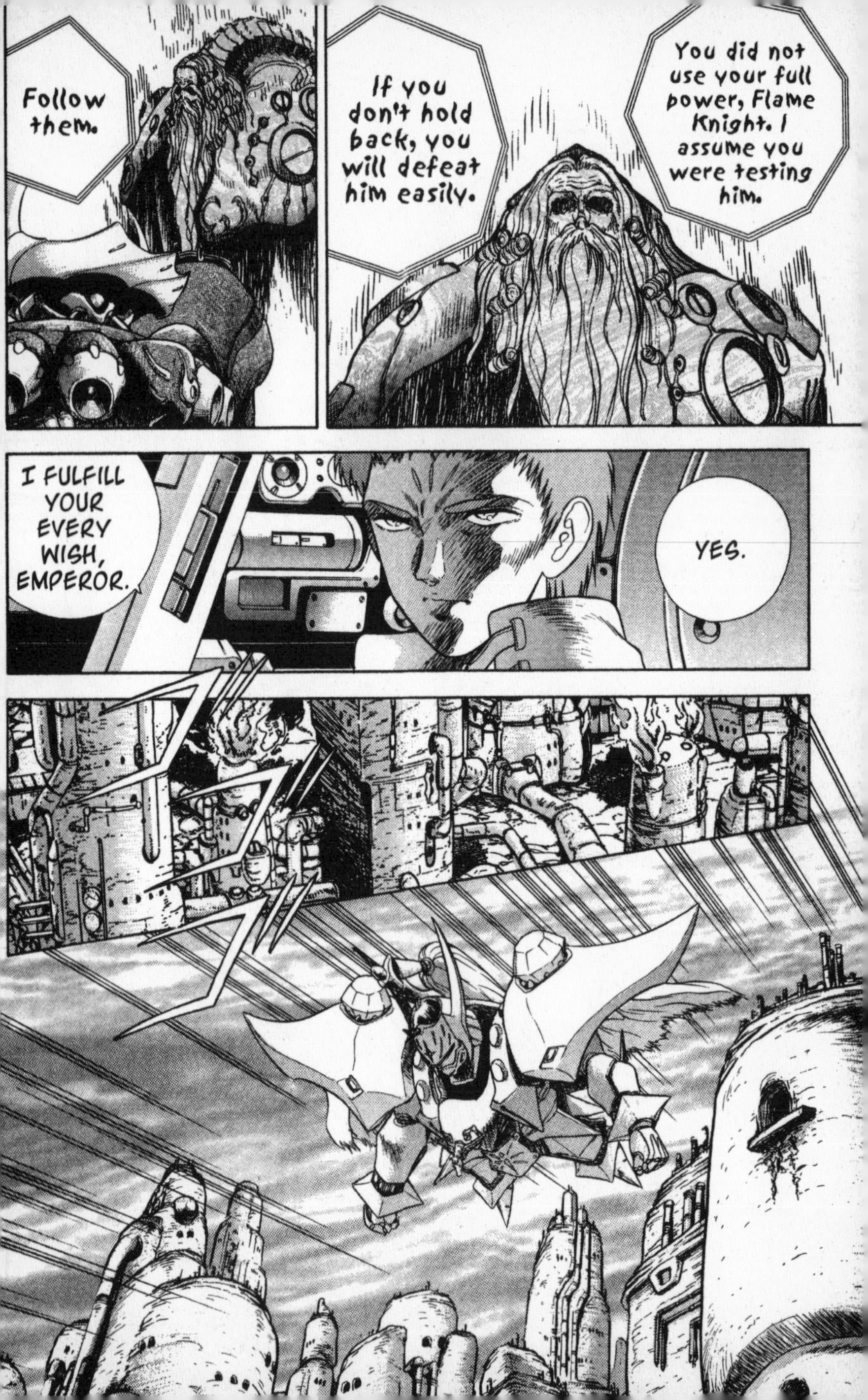
You did not use your full power, Flame Knight. I assume you were testing him.
If you don't hold back, you will defeat him easily.
Follow them.
YES.
I FULFILL YOUR EVERY WISH, EMPEROR.

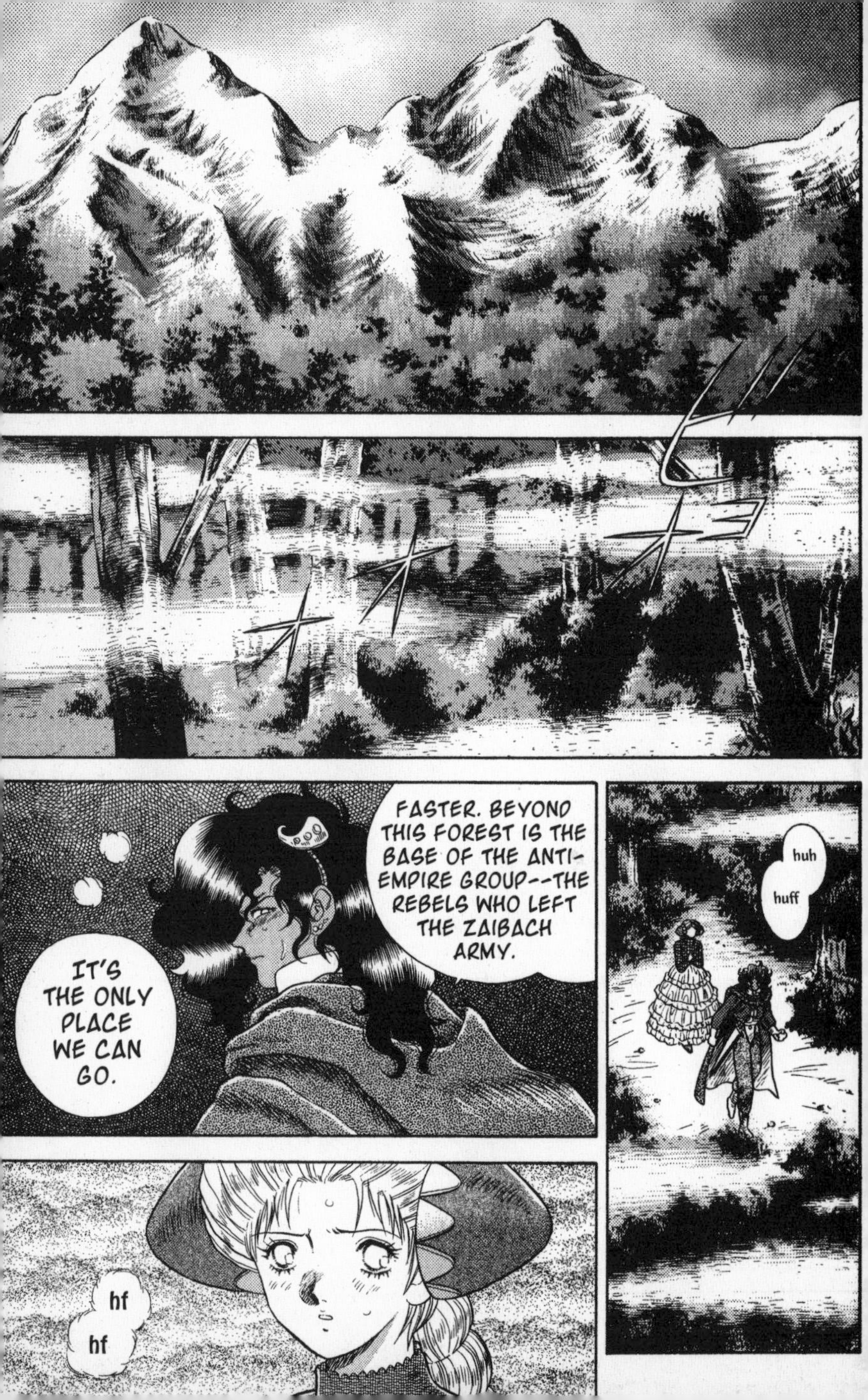
huh
huff
FASTER. BEYOND THIS FOREST IS THE BASE OF THE ANTI-EMPIRE GROUP--THE REBELS WHO LEFT THE ZAIBACH ARMY.
IT'S THE ONLY PLACE WE CAN GO.
hf
hf

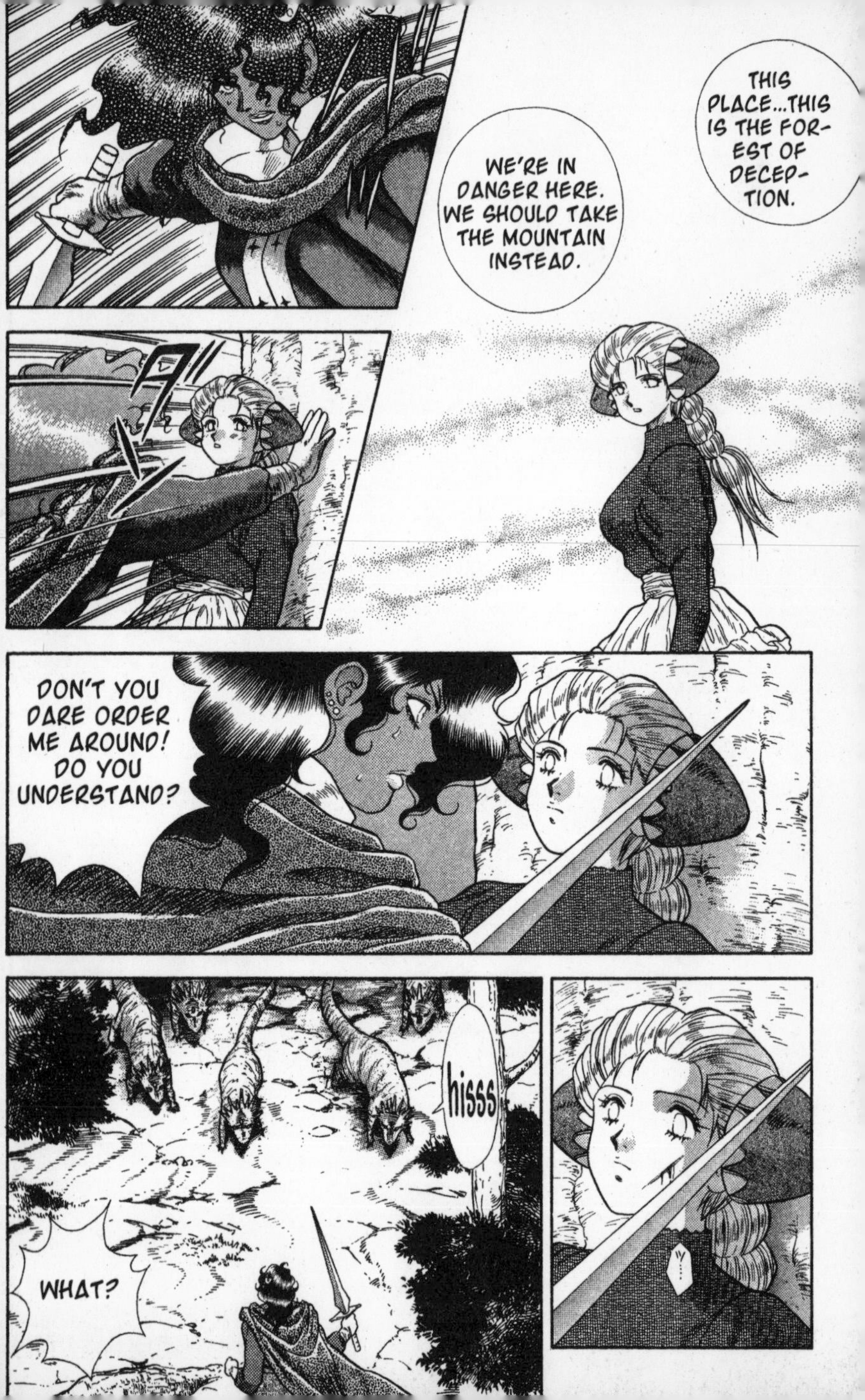
THIS PLACE...THIS IS THE FOREST OF DECEPTION.
WE'RE IN DANGER HERE. WE SHOULD TAKE THE MOUNTAIN INSTEAD.
DON'T YOU DARE ORDER ME AROUND! DO YOU UNDERSTAND?
hisss
WHAT?

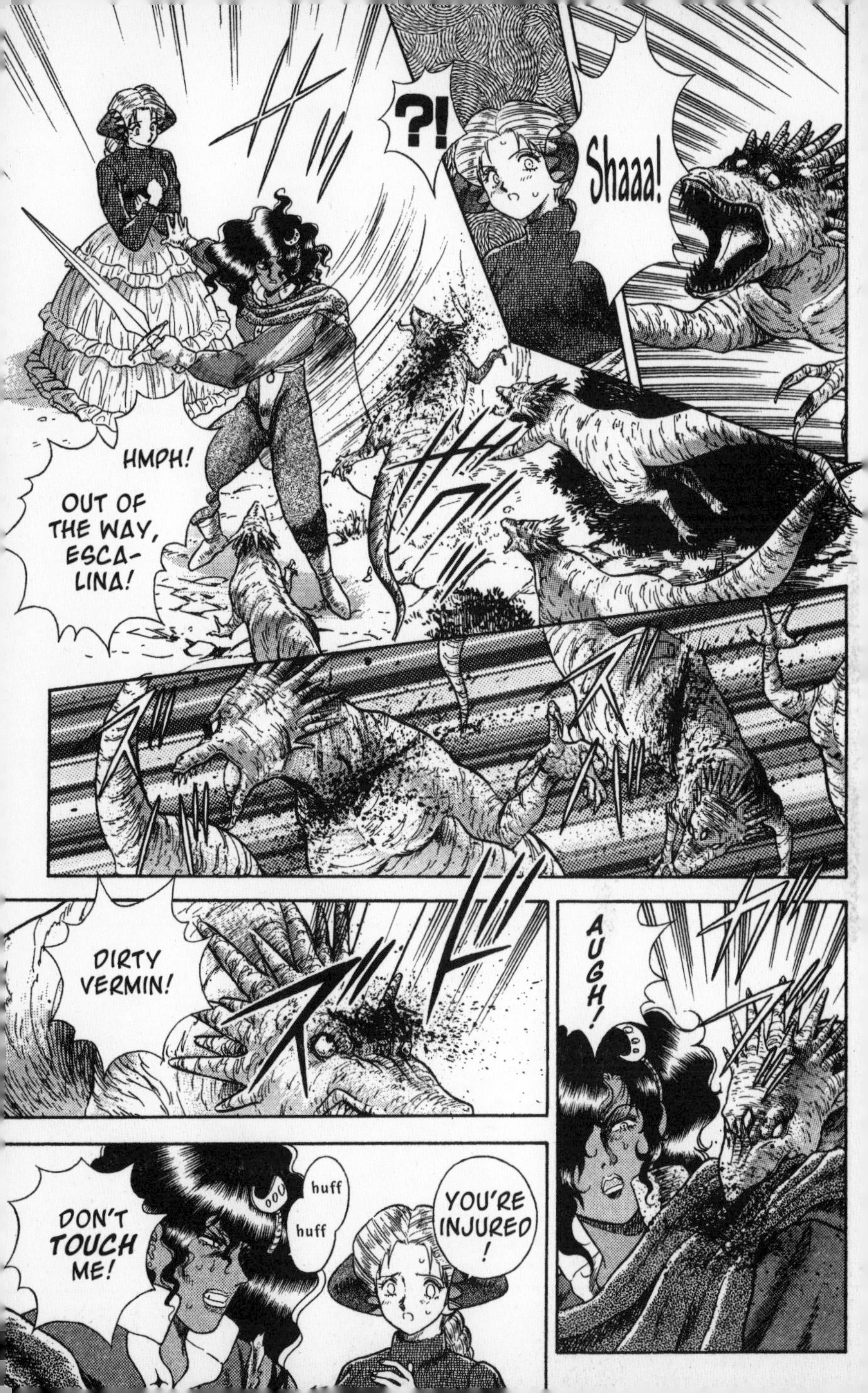
Shaaa!
?!
HMPH!
OUT OF THE WAY, ESCA-LINA!
AUGH!
DIRTY VERMIN!
YOU'RE INJURED!
huff
huff
DON'T TOUCH ME!

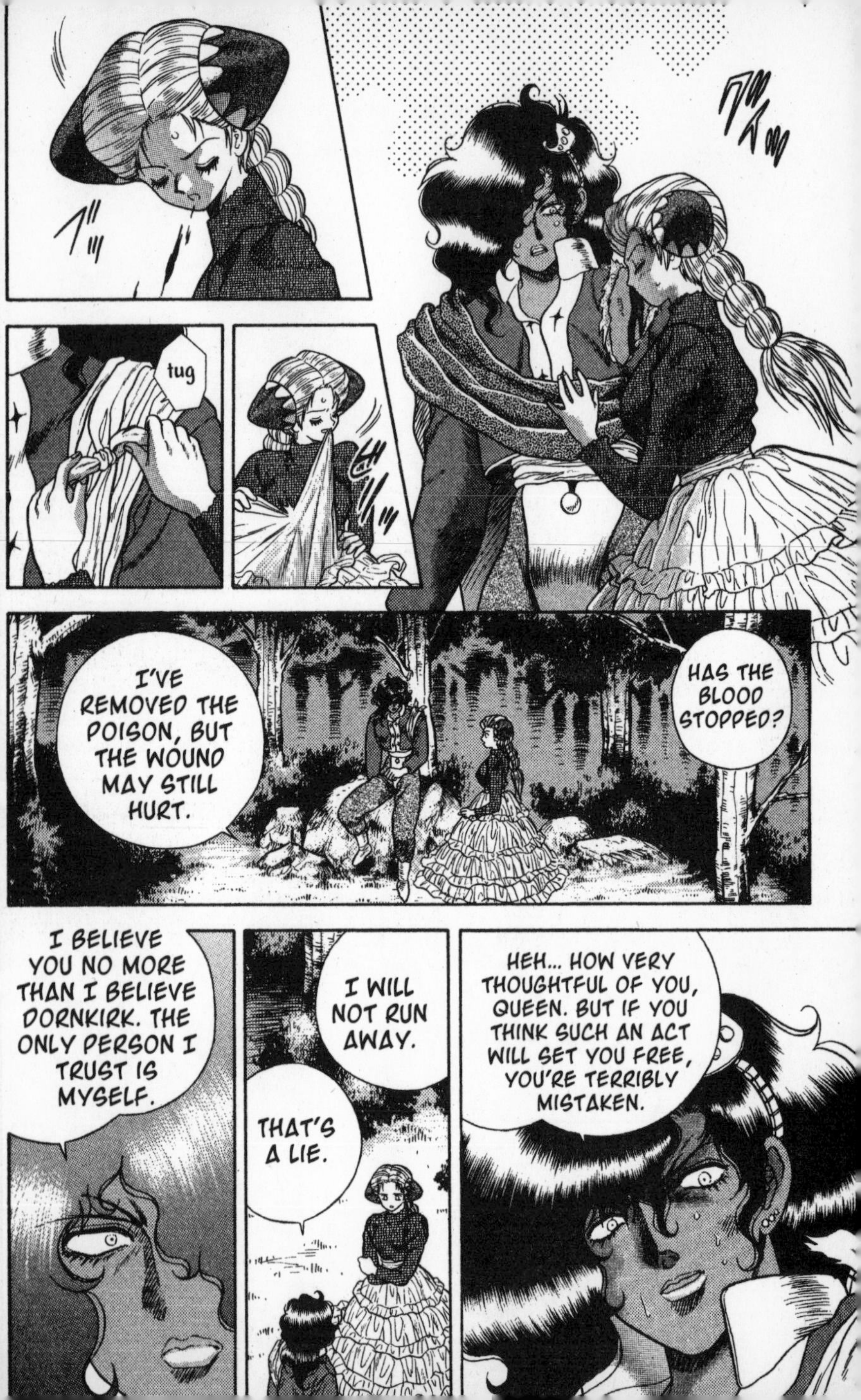
tug
HAS THE BLOOD STOPPED?
I'VE REMOVED THE POISON, BUT THE WOUND MAY STILL HURT.
HEH... HOW VERY THOUGHTFUL OF YOU, QUEEN. BUT IF YOU THINK SUCH AN ACT WILL SET YOU FREE, YOU'RE TERRIBLY MISTAKEN.
I WILL NOT RUN AWAY.
THAT'S A LIE.
I BELIEVE YOU NO MORE THAN I BELIEVE DORNKIRK. THE ONLY PERSON I TRUST IS MYSELF.

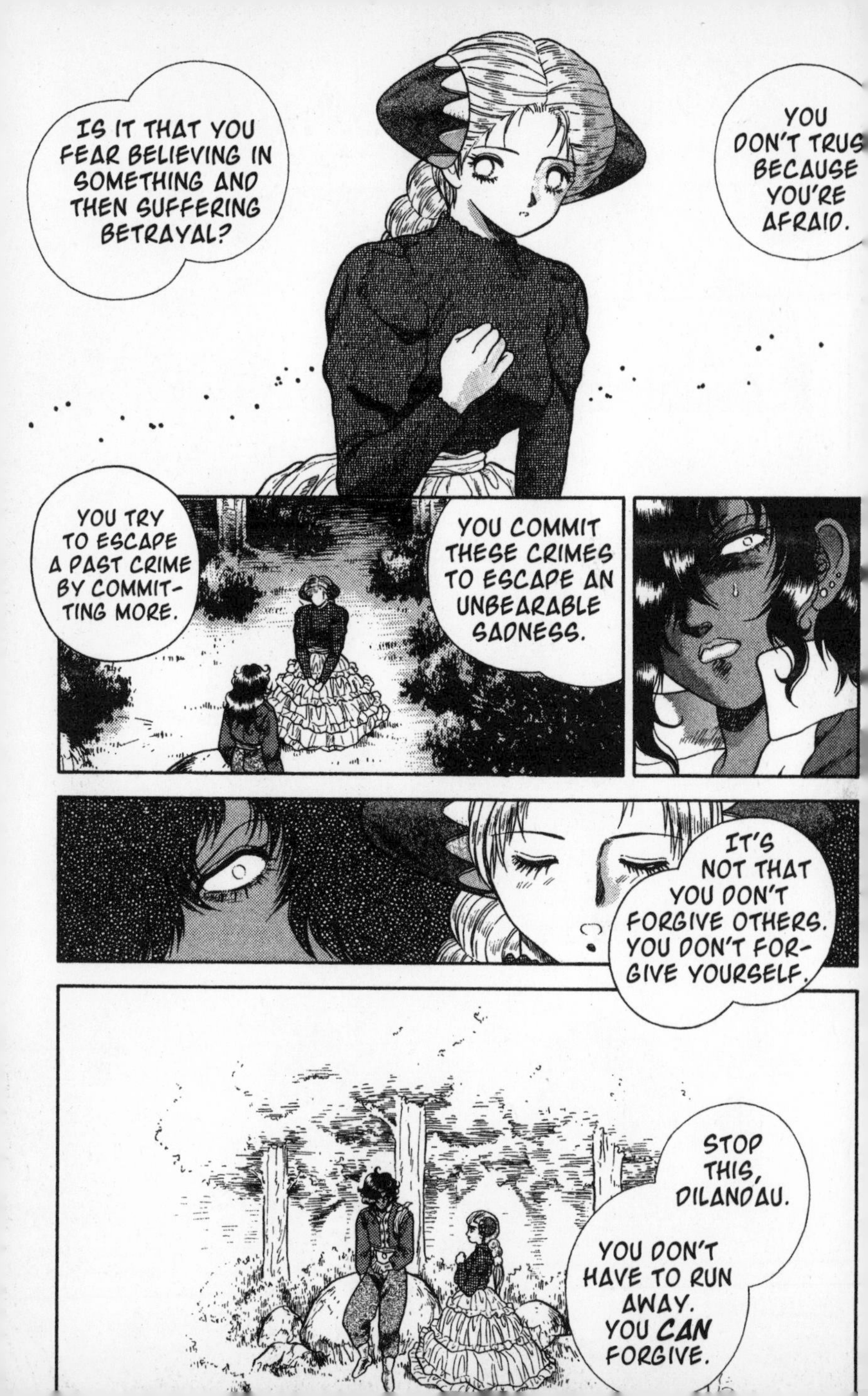
YOU DON'T TRUS BECAUSE YOU'RE AFRAID.
IS IT THAT YOU FEAR BELIEVING IN SOMETHING AND THEN SUFFERING BETRAYAL?
YOU COMMIT THESE CRIMES TO ESCAPE AN UNBEARABLE SADNESS.
YOU TRY TO ESCAPE A PAST CRIME BY COMMIT-TING MORE.
IT'S NOT THAT YOU DON'T FORGIVE OTHERS. YOU DON'T FOR-GIVE YOURSELF.
STOP THIS, DILANDAU.
YOU DON'T HAVE TO RUN AWAY. YOU *CAN* FORGIVE.

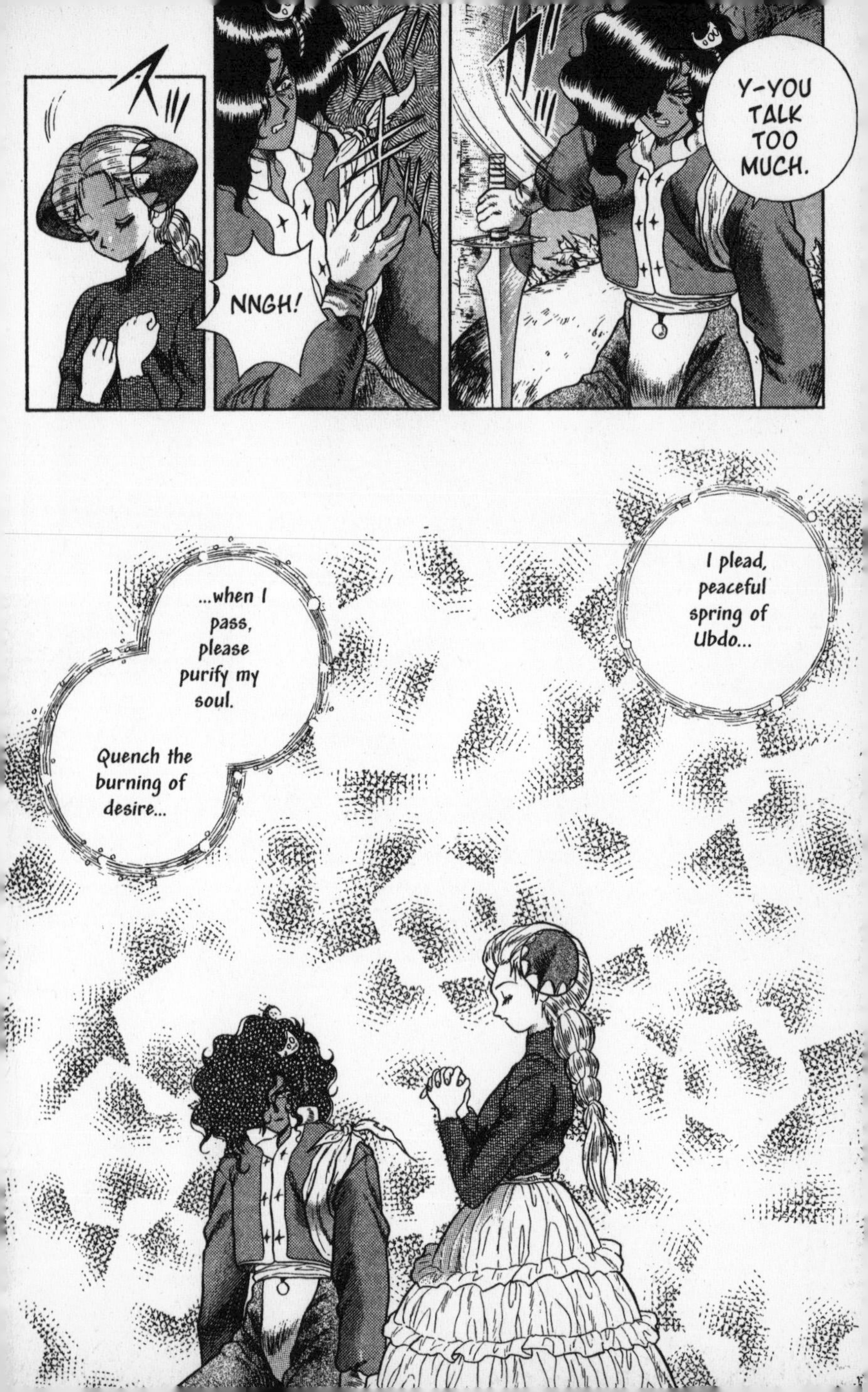
Y-YOU TALK TOO MUCH.
NNGH!
I plead, peaceful spring of Ubdo...
...when I pass, please purify my soul.
Quench the burning of desire...

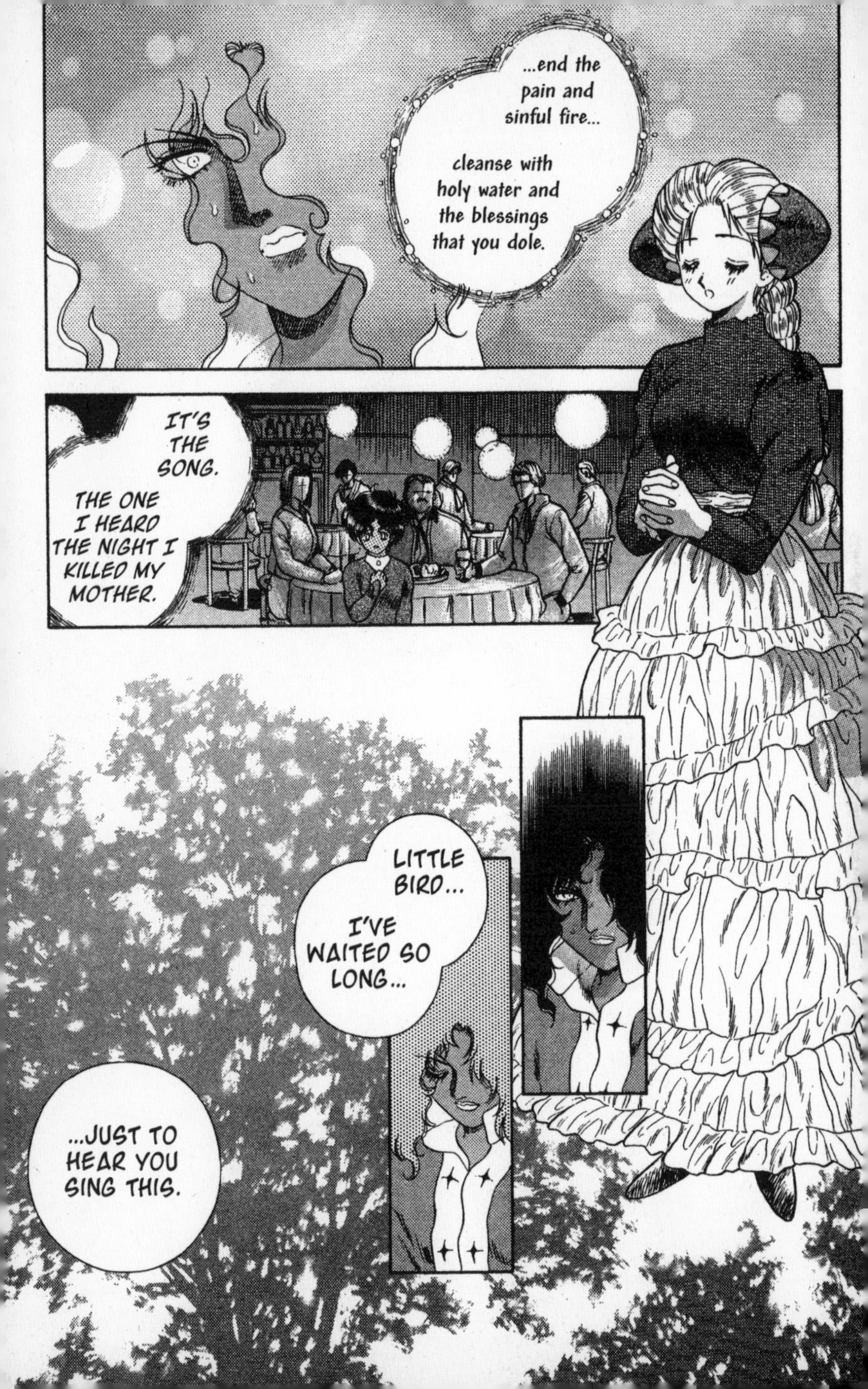
...end the pain and sinful fire...
cleanse with holy water and the blessings that you dole.
IT'S THE SONG.
THE ONE I HEARD THE NIGHT I KILLED MY MOTHER.
LITTLE BIRD...
I'VE WAITED SO LONG...
...JUST TO HEAR YOU SING THIS.

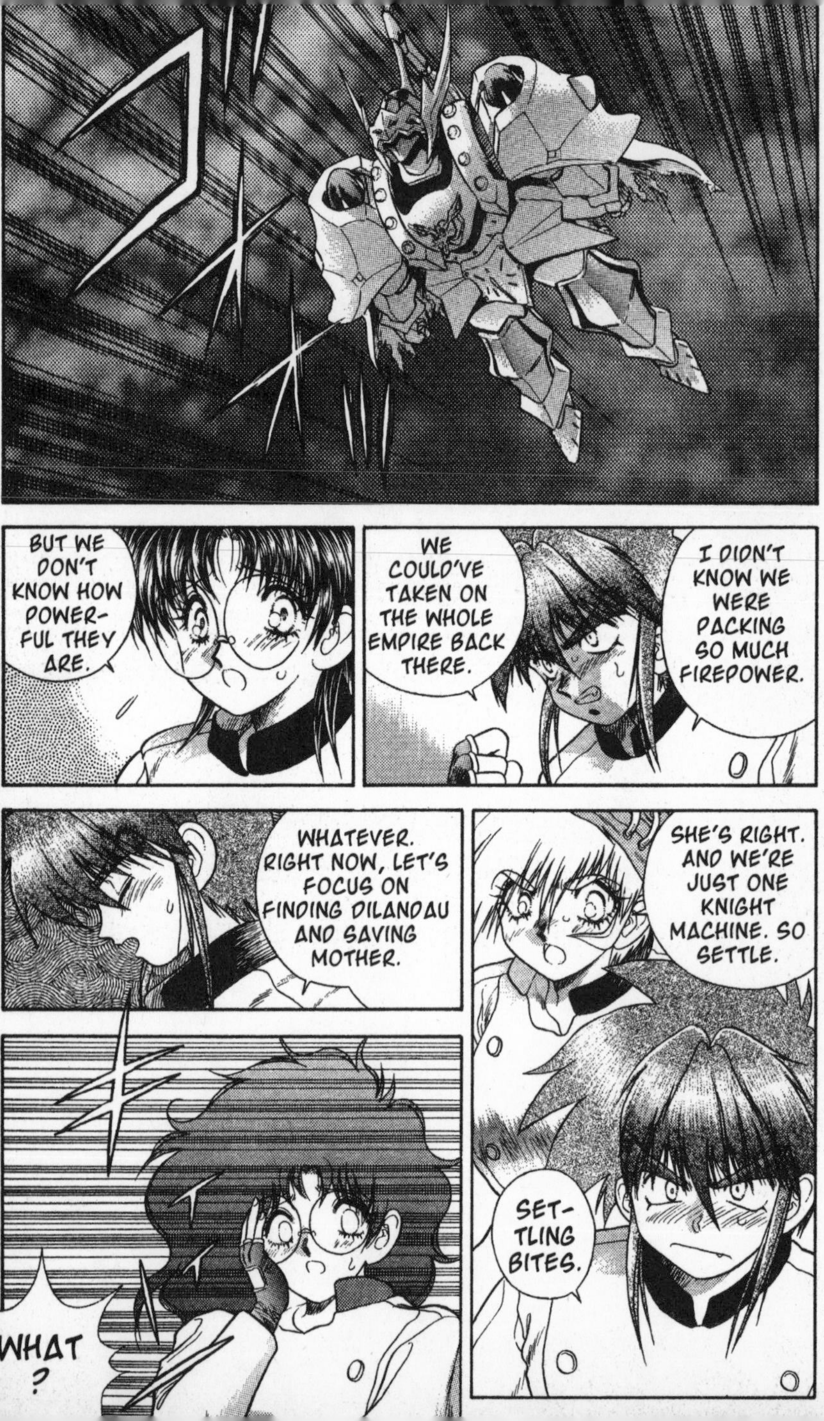
I DIDN'T KNOW WE WERE PACKING SO MUCH FIREPOWER.
WE COULD'VE TAKEN ON THE WHOLE EMPIRE BACK THERE.
BUT WE DON'T KNOW HOW POWER-FUL THEY ARE.
SHE'S RIGHT. AND WE'RE JUST ONE KNIGHT MACHINE. SO SETTLE.
SET-TLING BITES.
WHATEVER. RIGHT NOW, LET'S FOCUS ON FINDING DILANDAU AND SAVING MOTHER.
WHAT?

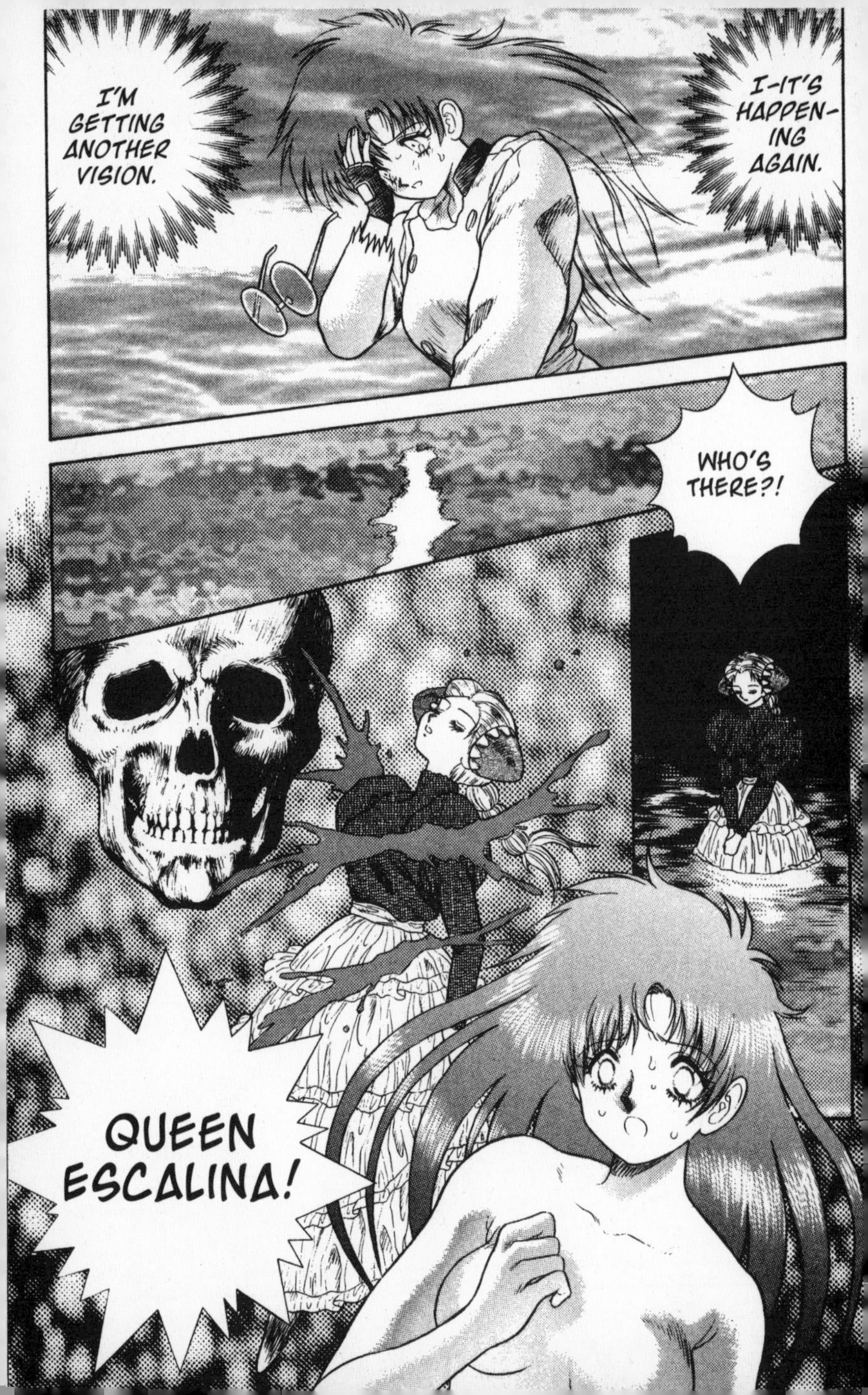
I-IT'S HAPPENING AGAIN.
I'M GETTING ANOTHER VISION.
WHO'S THERE?!
QUEEN ESCALINA!

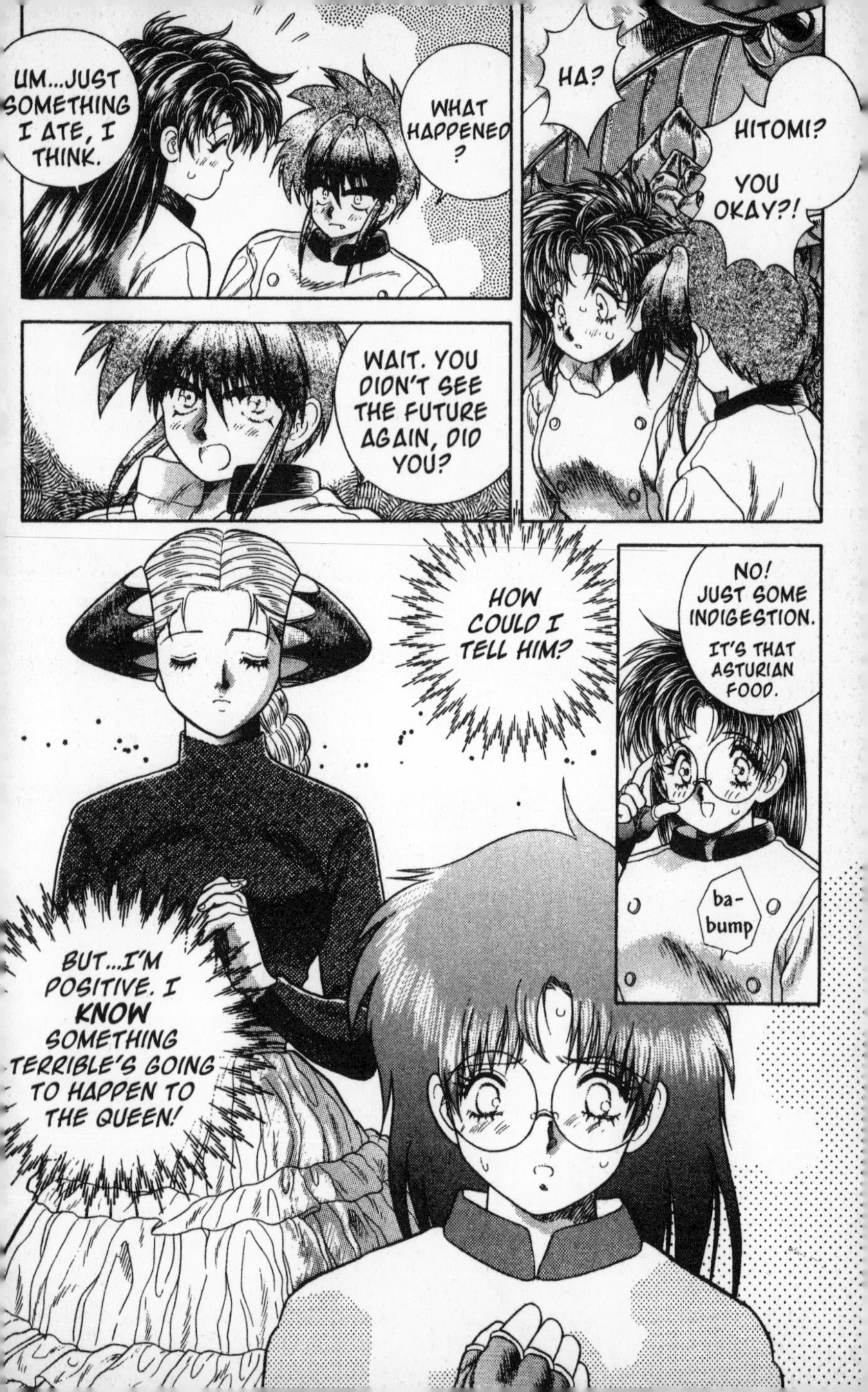
HITOMI?
YOU OKAY?!
HA?
WHAT HAPPENED?
UM...JUST SOMETHING I ATE, I THINK.
WAIT. YOU DIDN'T SEE THE FUTURE AGAIN, DID YOU?
NO! JUST SOME INDIGESTION.
IT'S THAT ASTURIAN FOOD.
ba-bump
HOW COULD I TELL HIM?
BUT...I'M POSITIVE. I **KNOW** SOMETHING TERRIBLE'S GOING TO HAPPEN TO THE QUEEN!

VISION 14:

THE FOREST OF DECEPTION

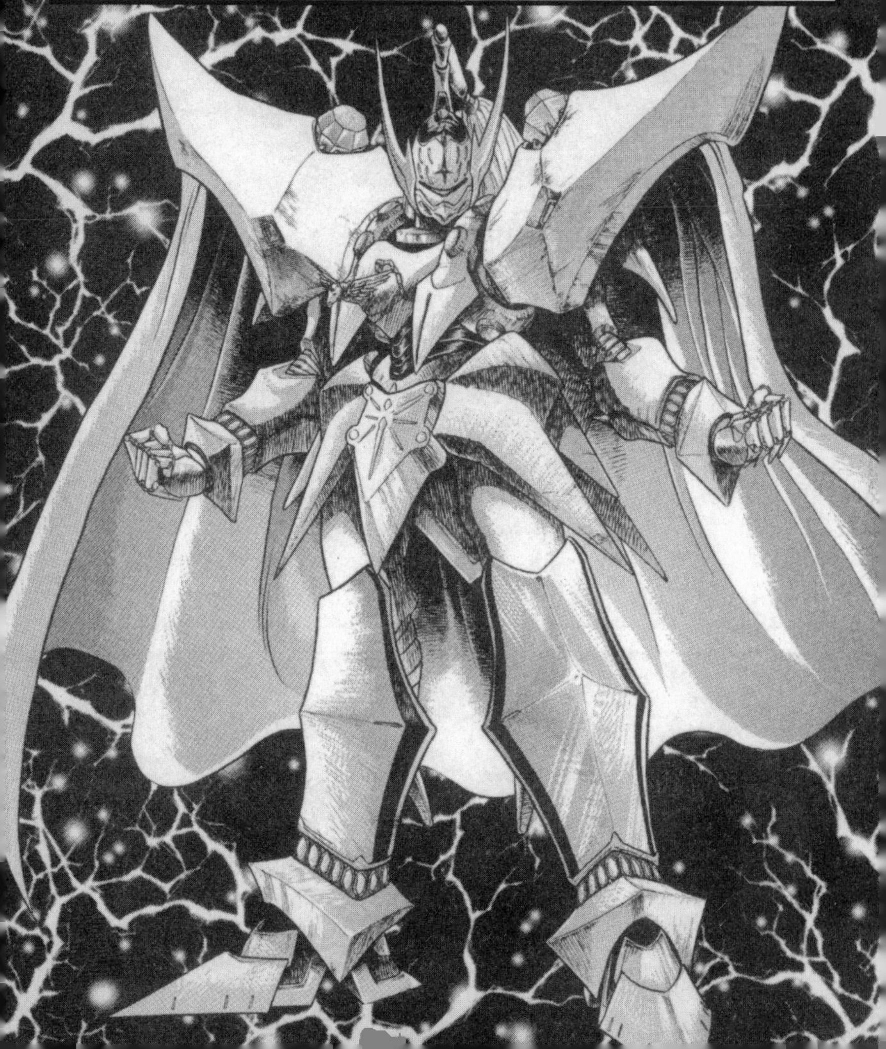

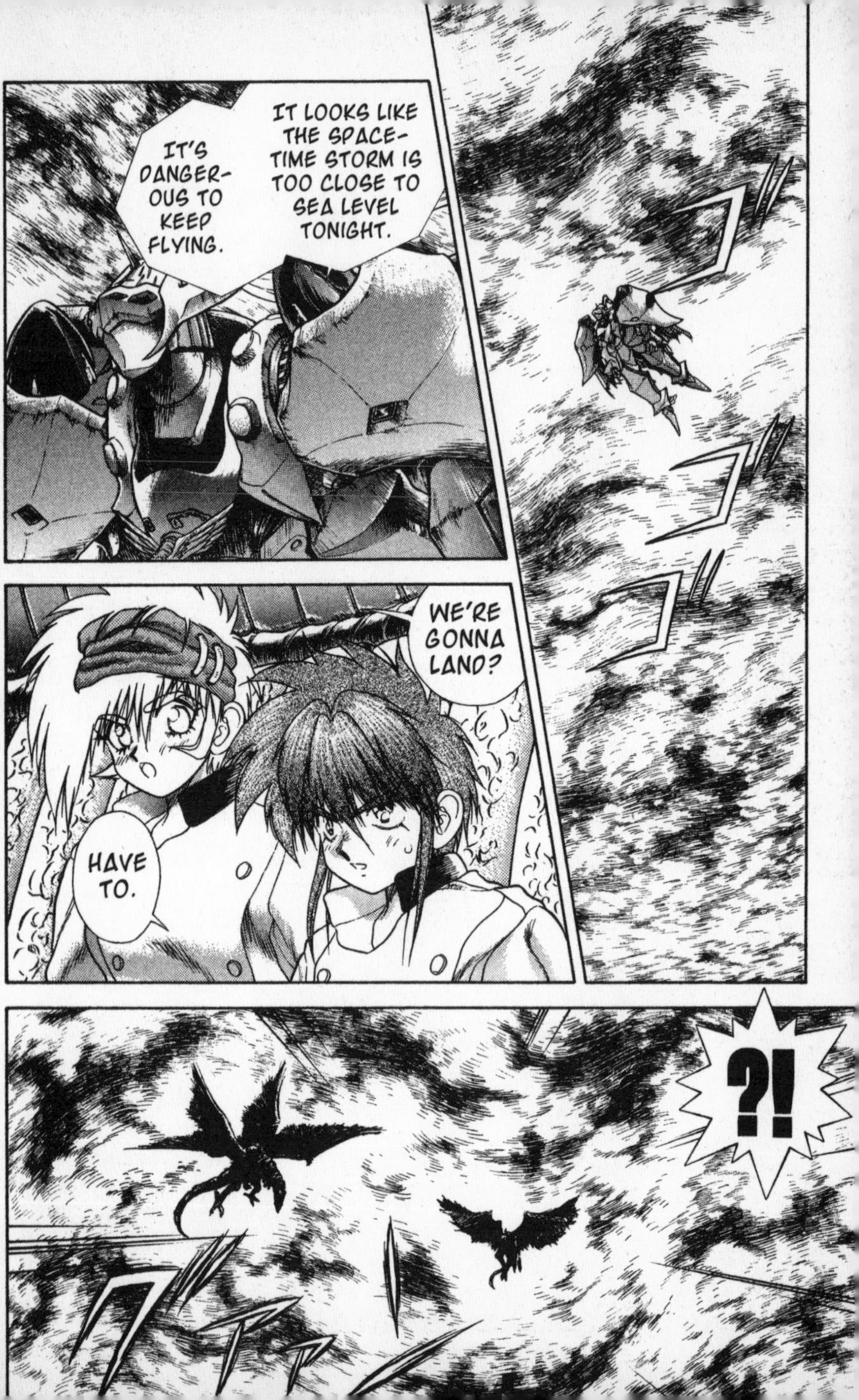
IT LOOKS LIKE THE SPACE-TIME STORM IS TOO CLOSE TO SEA LEVEL TONIGHT.
IT'S DANGER-OUS TO KEEP FLYING.
WE'RE GONNA LAND?
HAVE TO.
?!

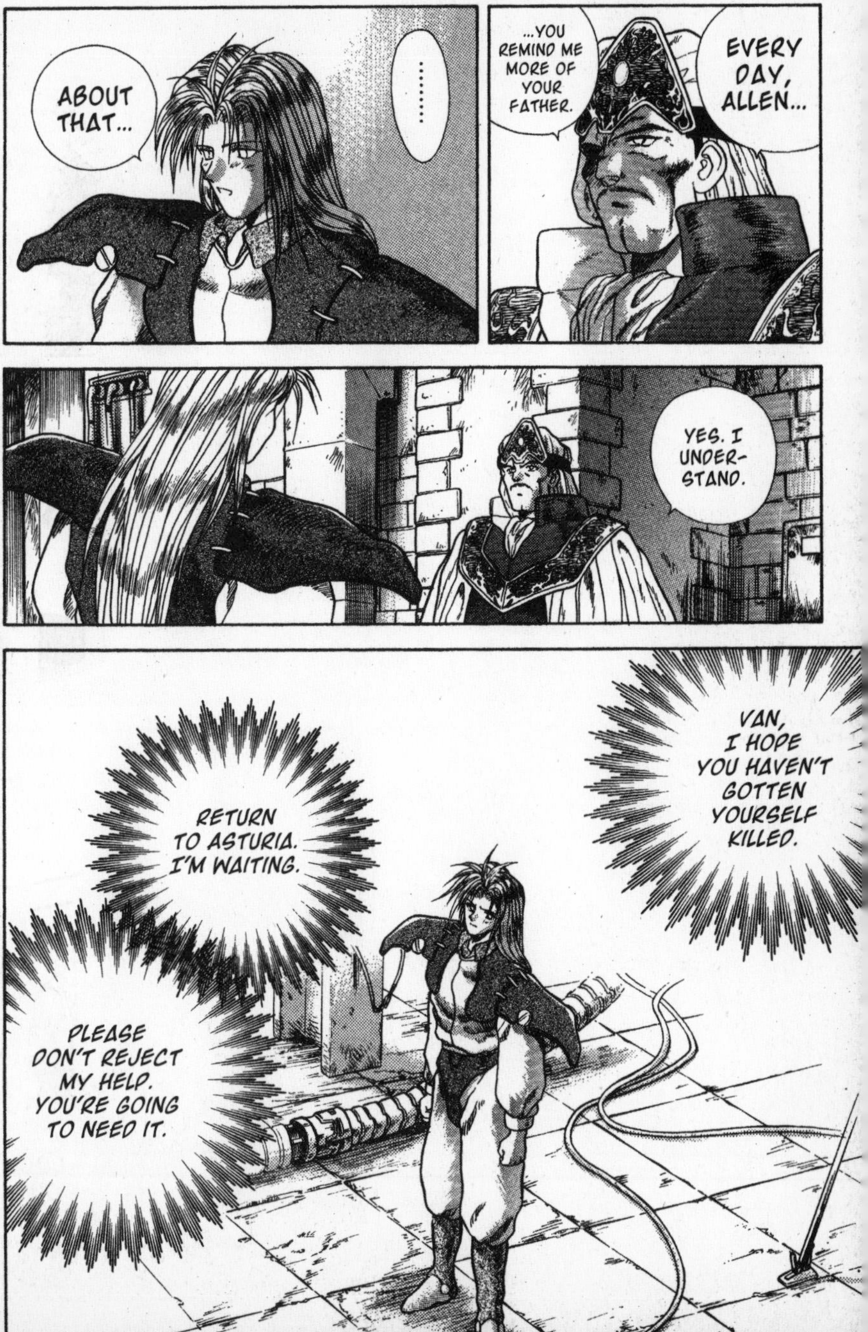
EVERY DAY, ALLEN...
...YOU REMIND ME MORE OF YOUR FATHER.
......
ABOUT THAT...
YES. I UNDERSTAND.
VAN, I HOPE YOU HAVEN'T GOTTEN YOURSELF KILLED.
RETURN TO ASTURIA. I'M WAITING.
PLEASE DON'T REJECT MY HELP. YOU'RE GOING TO NEED IT.

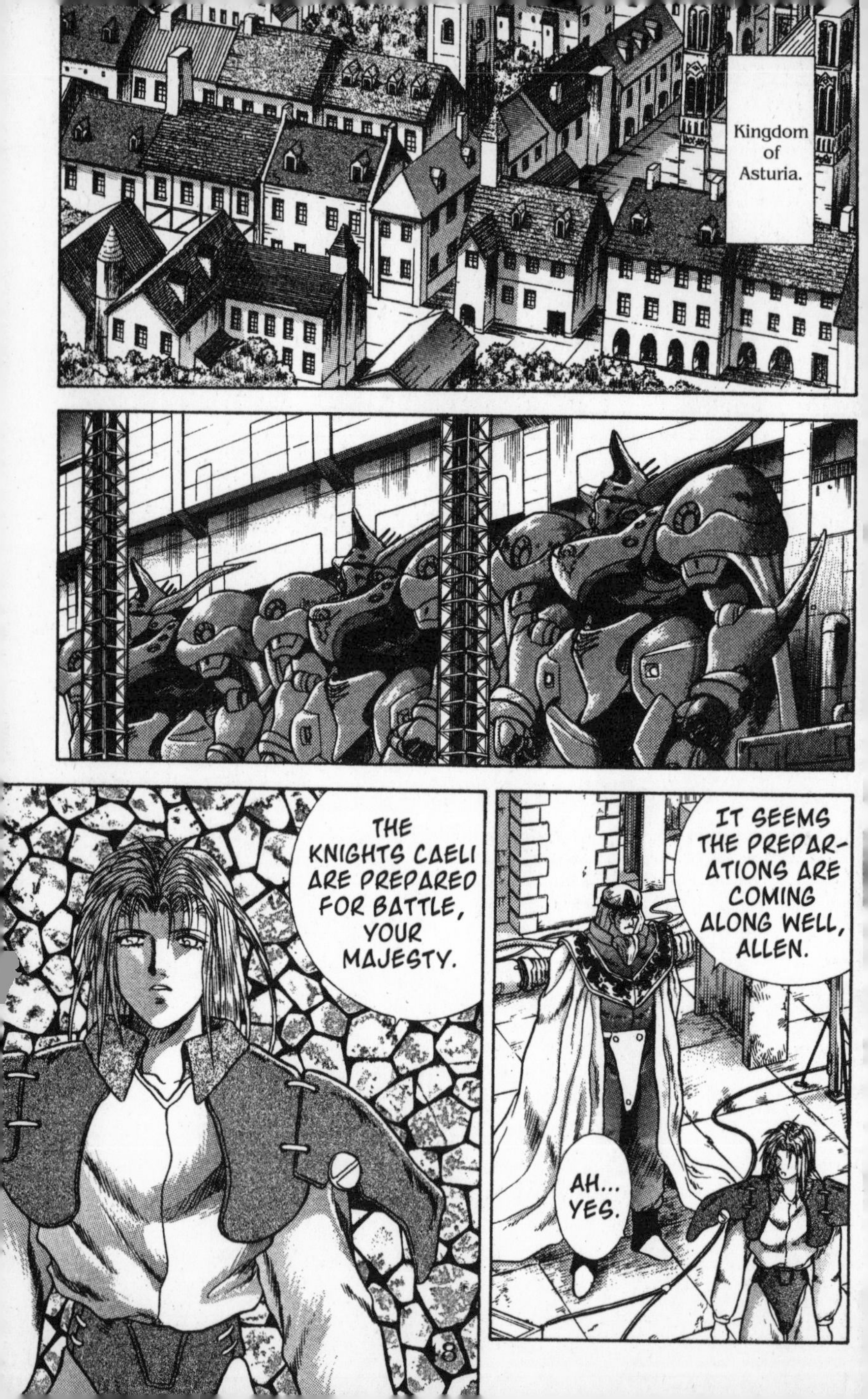
Kingdom of Asturia.
IT SEEMS THE PREPARATIONS ARE COMING ALONG WELL, ALLEN.
AH... YES.
THE KNIGHTS CAELI ARE PREPARED FOR BATTLE, YOUR MAJESTY.

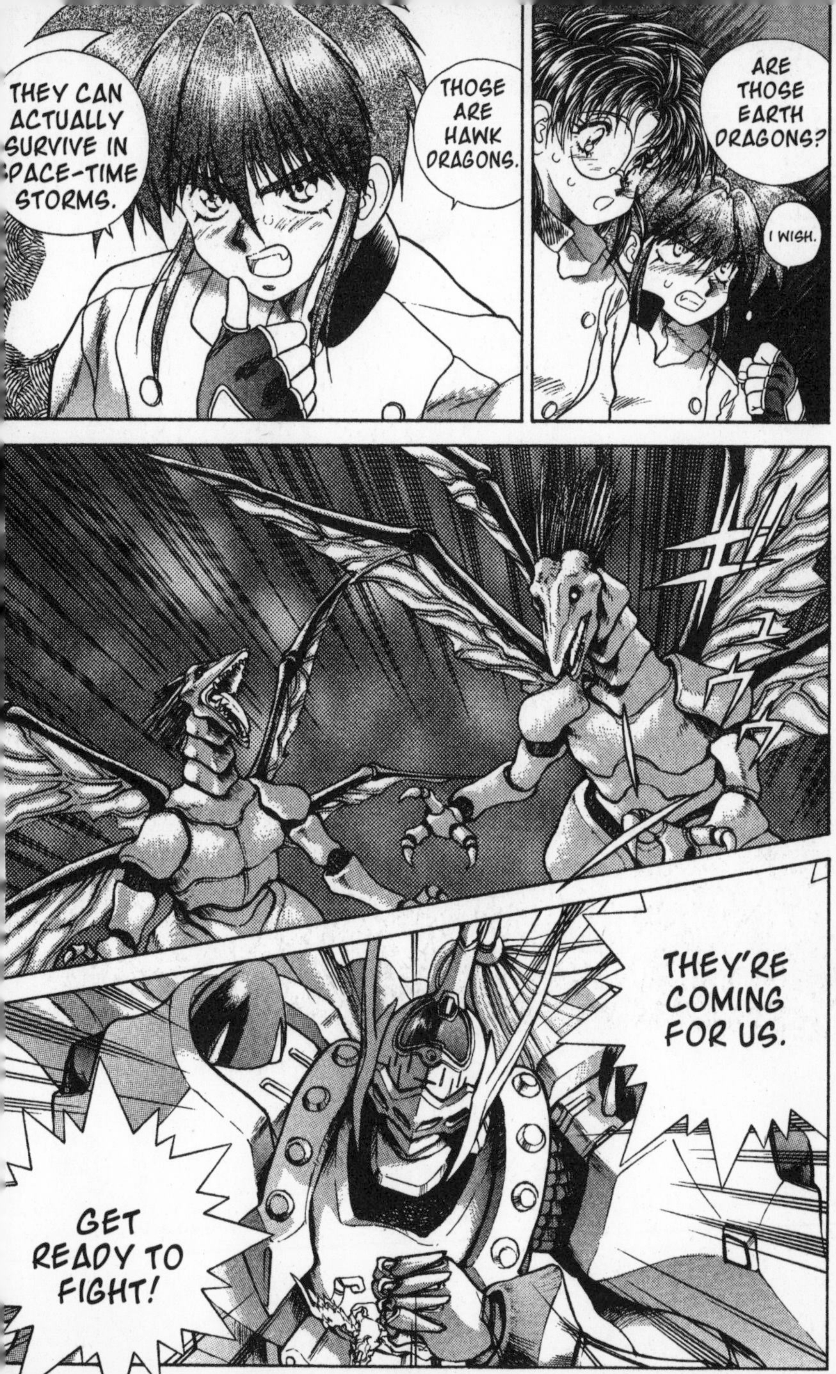
ARE THOSE EARTH DRAGONS?
I WISH.
THOSE ARE HAWK DRAGONS.
THEY CAN ACTUALLY SURVIVE IN SPACE-TIME STORMS.
THEY'RE COMING FOR US.
GET READY TO FIGHT!

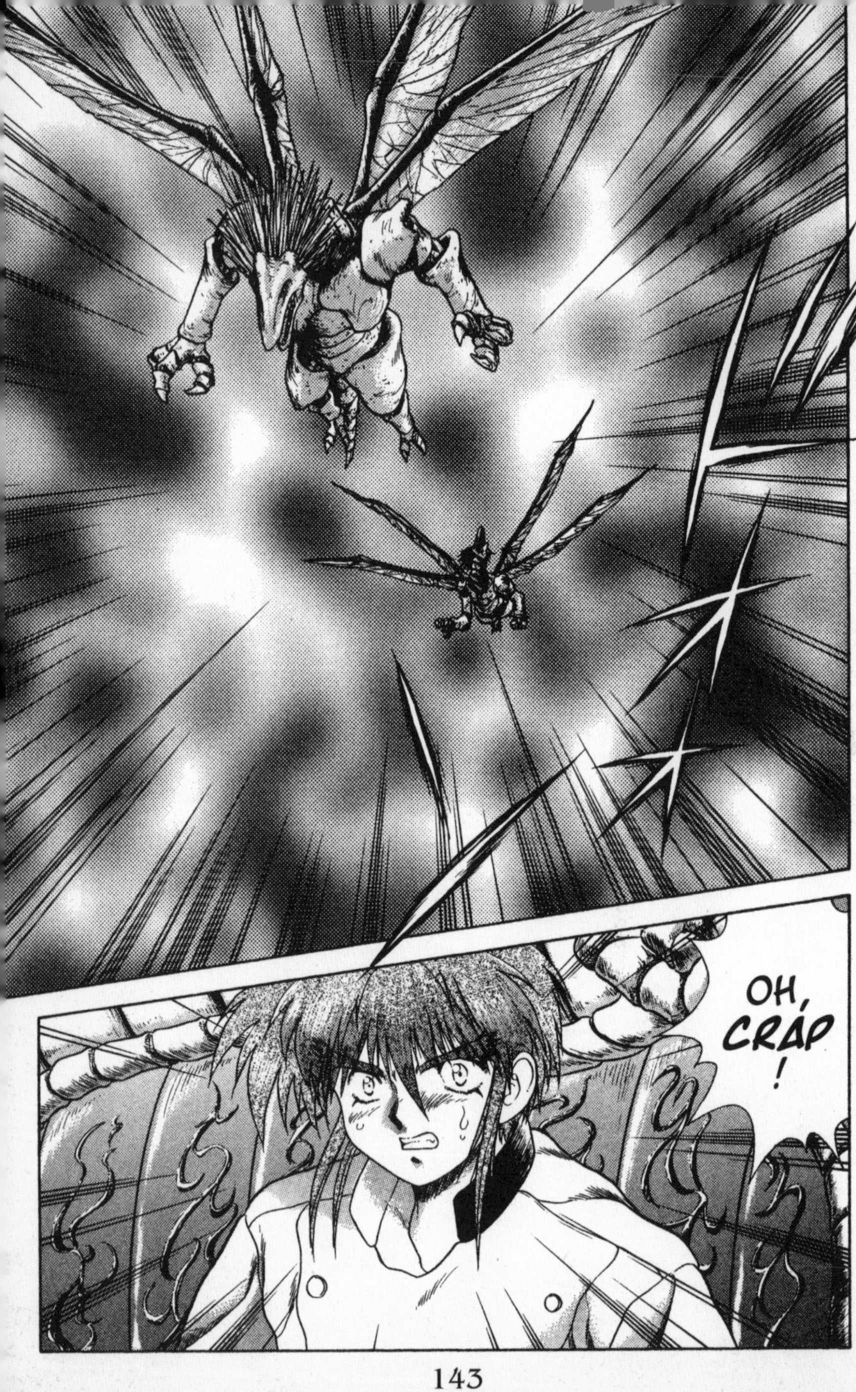
OH, CRAP!

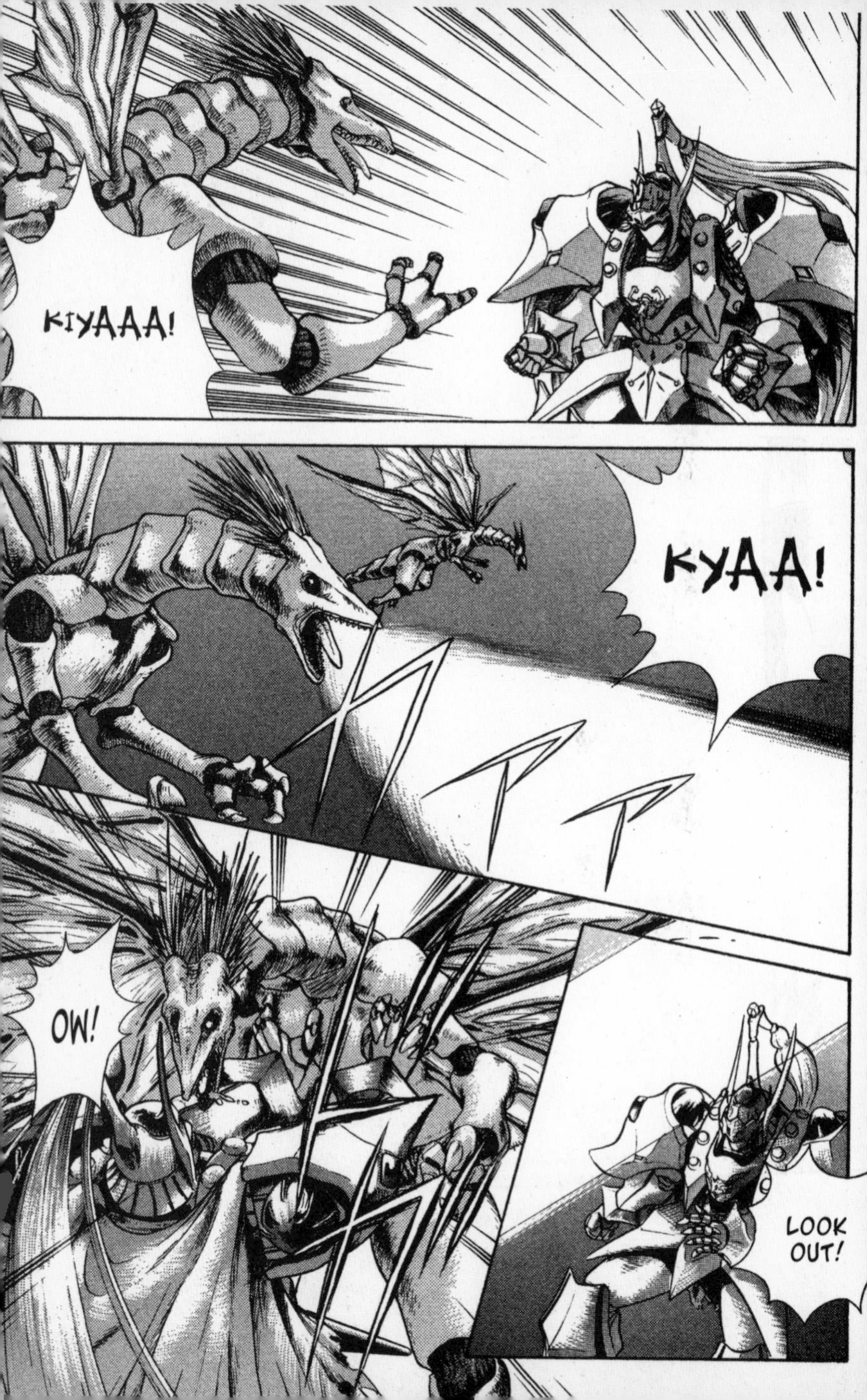
KIYAAA!
KYAA!
LOOK OUT!
OW!

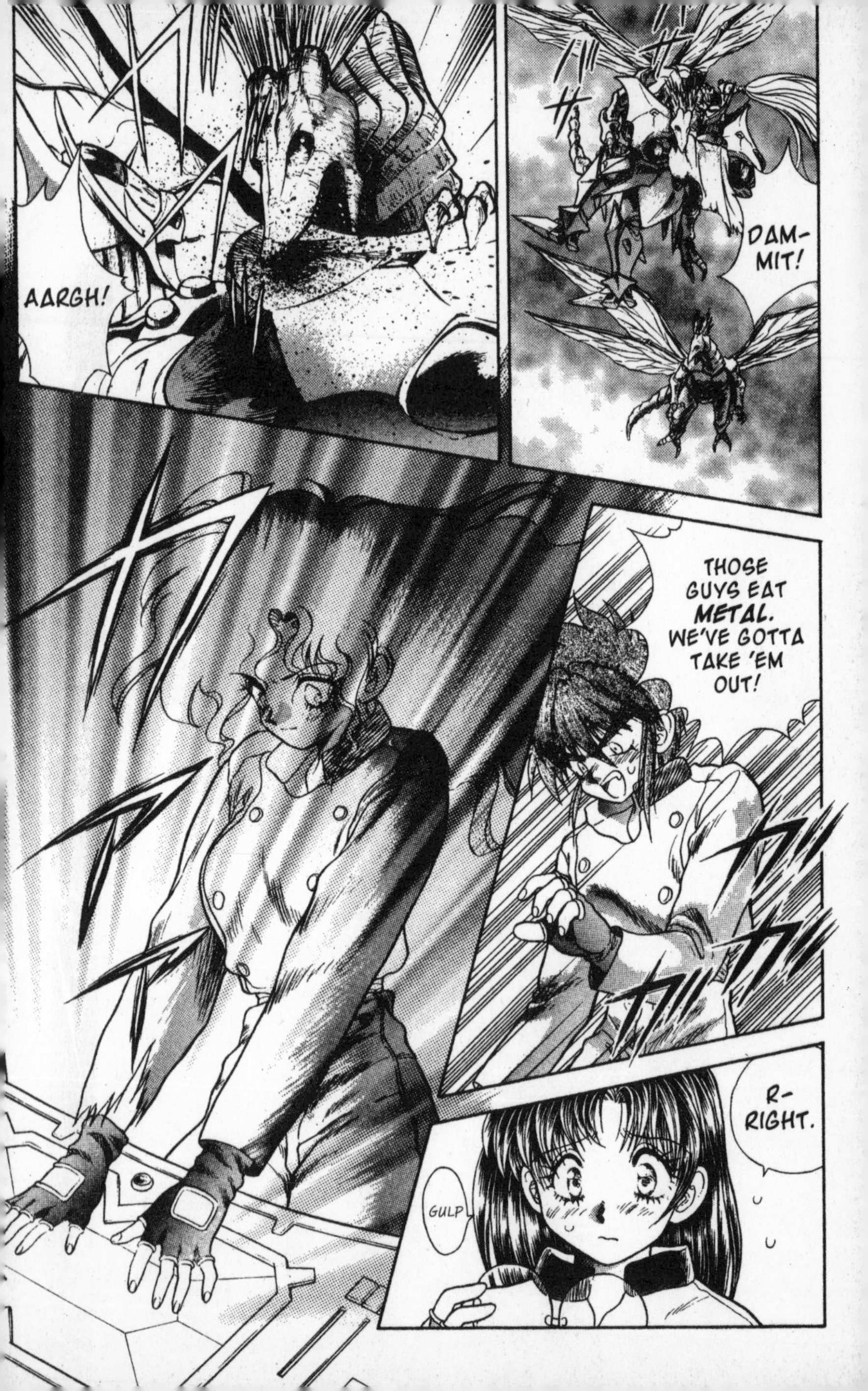
DAM-
MIT!
AARGH!
THOSE GUYS EAT **METAL.** WE'VE GOTTA TAKE 'EM OUT!
R-RIGHT.
GULP

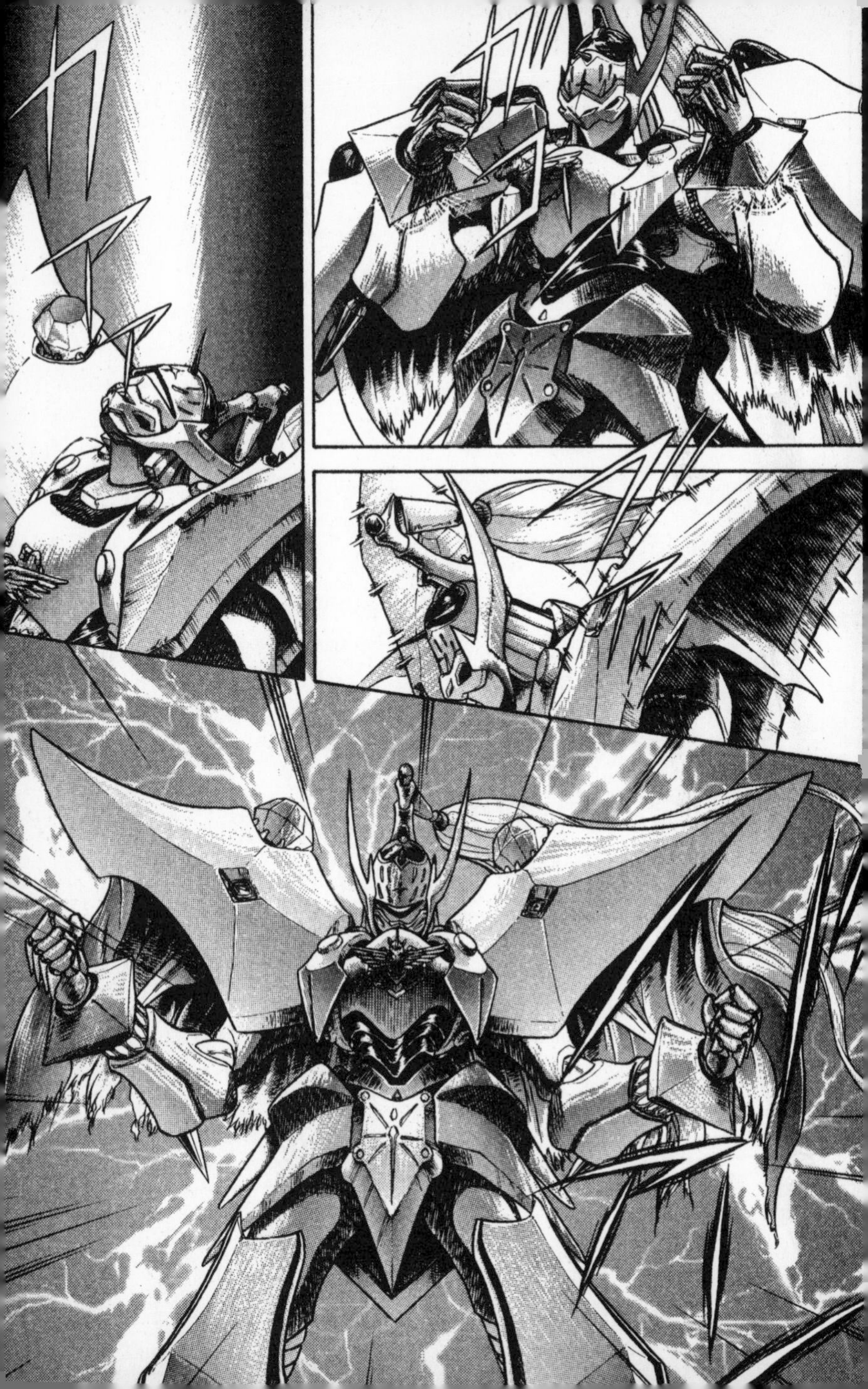

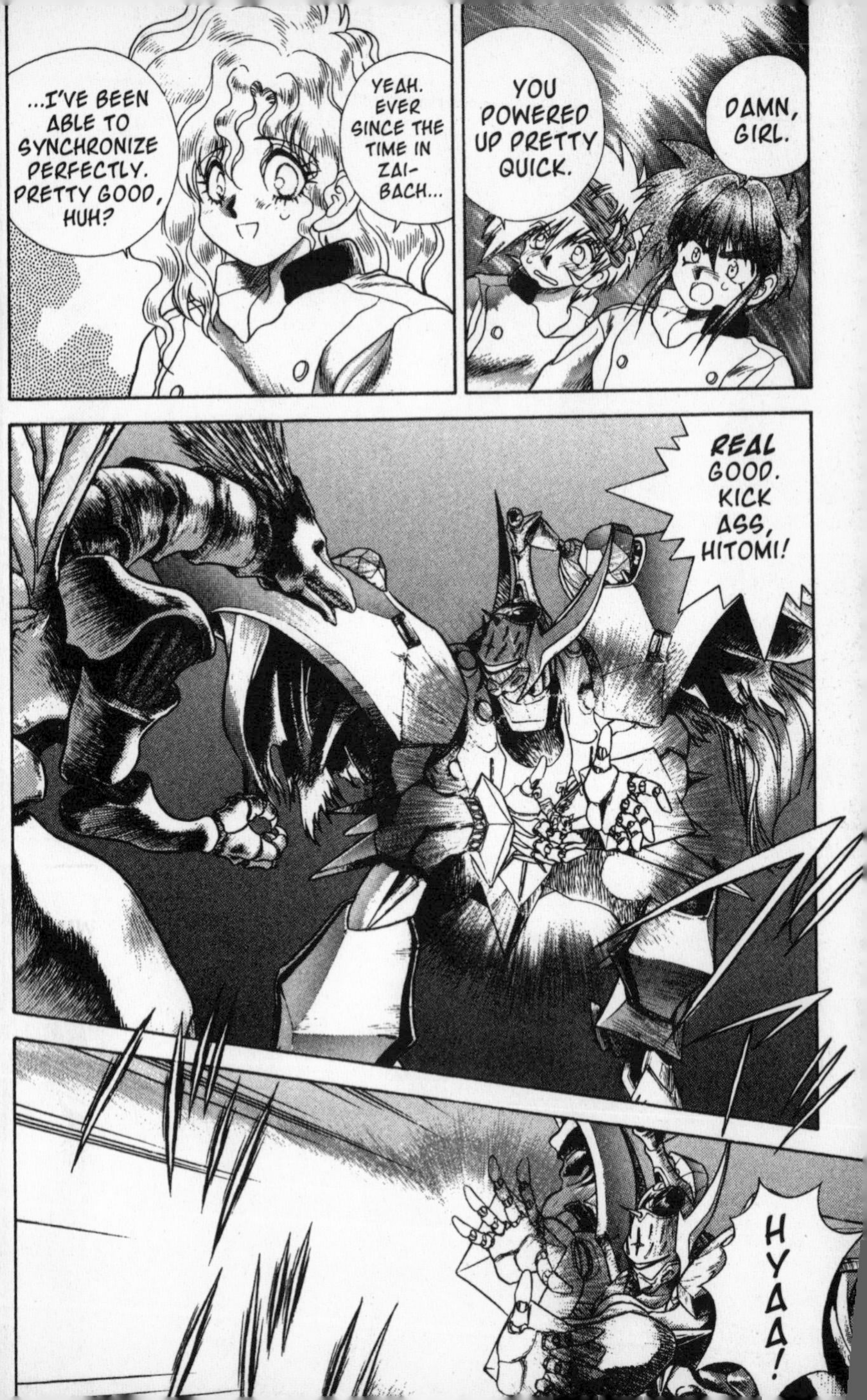
DAMN, GIRL.
YOU POWERED UP PRETTY QUICK.
YEAH. EVER SINCE THE TIME IN ZAI-BACH...
...I'VE BEEN ABLE TO SYNCHRONIZE PERFECTLY. PRETTY GOOD, HUH?
REAL GOOD. KICK ASS, HITOMI!
HYAA!

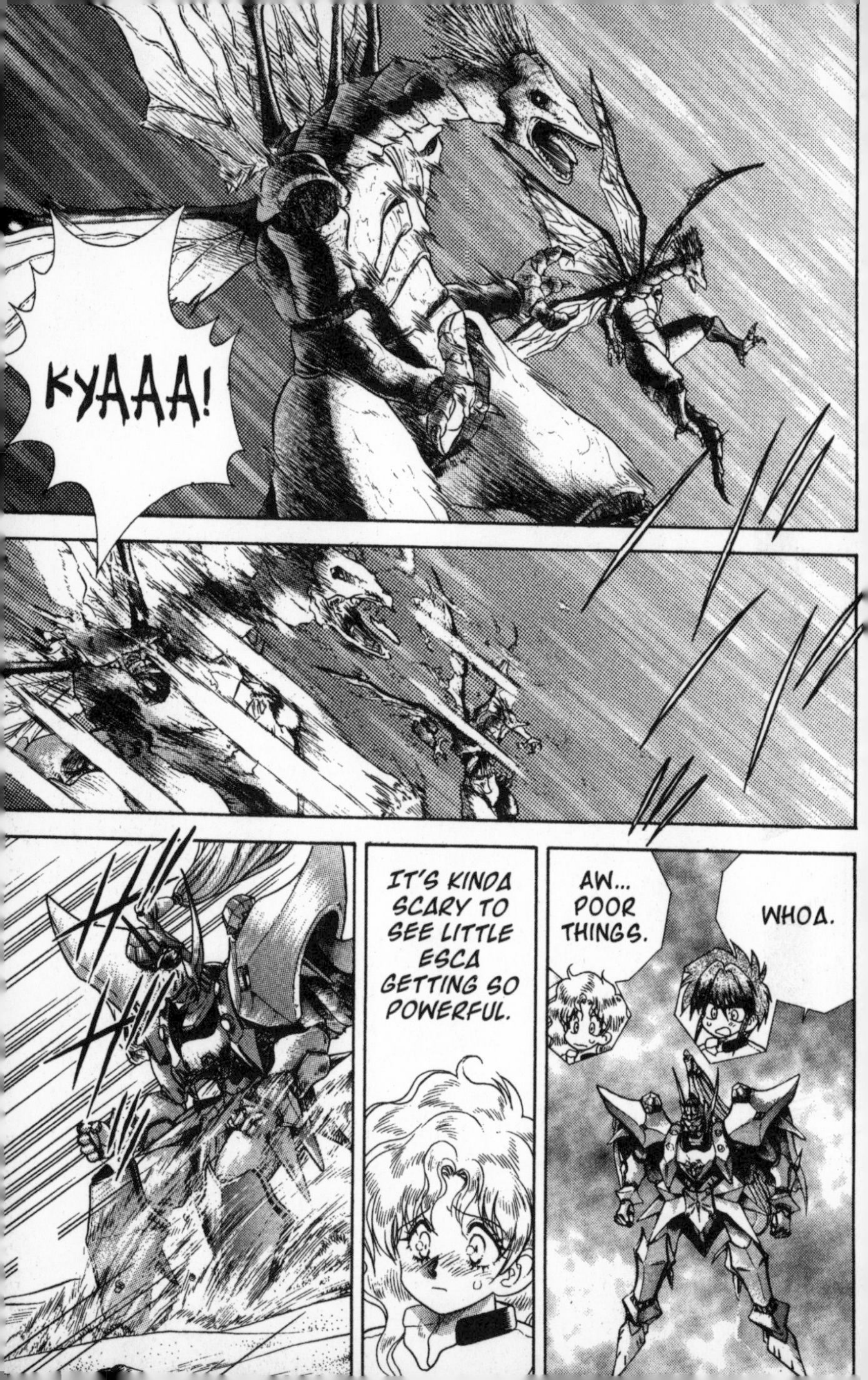
KYAAA!
WHOA.
AW... POOR THINGS.
IT'S KINDA SCARY TO SEE LITTLE ESCA GETTING SO POWERFUL.

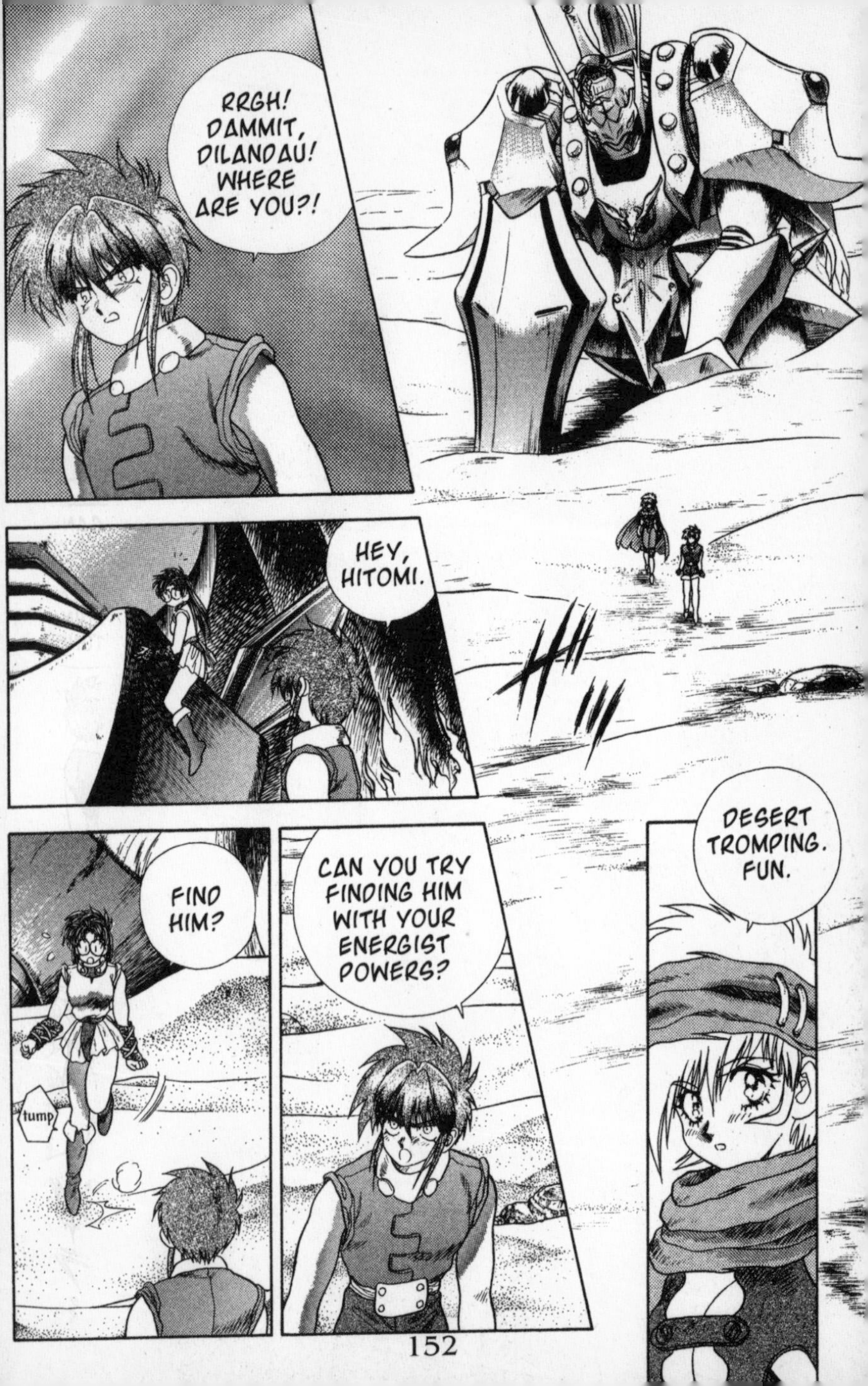
RRGH! DAMMIT, DILANDAU! WHERE ARE YOU?!
HEY, HITOMI.
DESERT TROMPING. FUN.
CAN YOU TRY FINDING HIM WITH YOUR ENERGIST POWERS?
FIND HIM?
tump

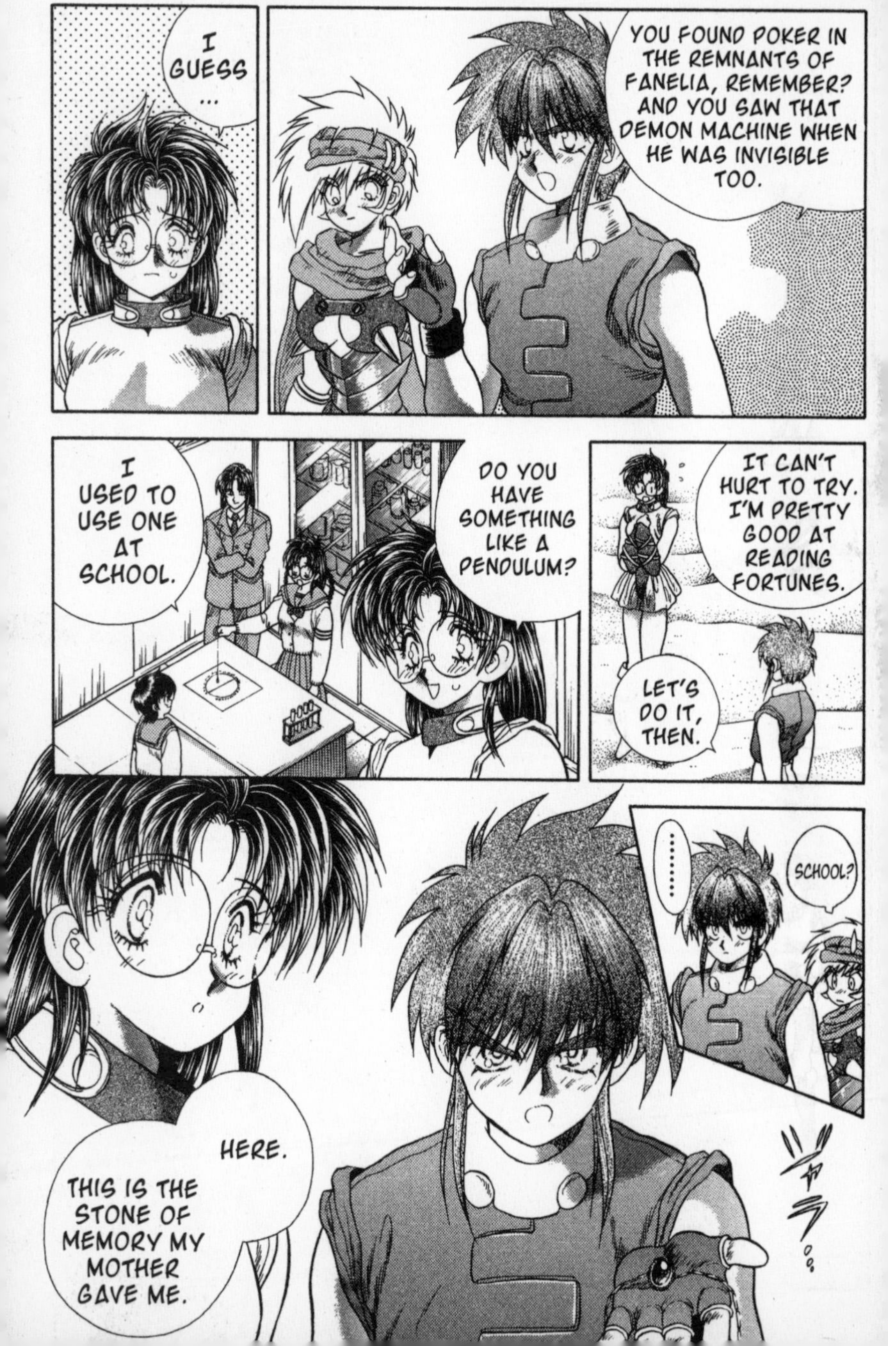
YOU FOUND POKER IN THE REMNANTS OF FANELIA, REMEMBER? AND YOU SAW THAT DEMON MACHINE WHEN HE WAS INVISIBLE TOO.
I GUESS ...
IT CAN'T HURT TO TRY. I'M PRETTY GOOD AT READING FORTUNES.
LET'S DO IT, THEN.
DO YOU HAVE SOMETHING LIKE A PENDULUM?
I USED TO USE ONE AT SCHOOL.
SCHOOL?
......
ジャラ
HERE.
THIS IS THE STONE OF MEMORY MY MOTHER GAVE ME.

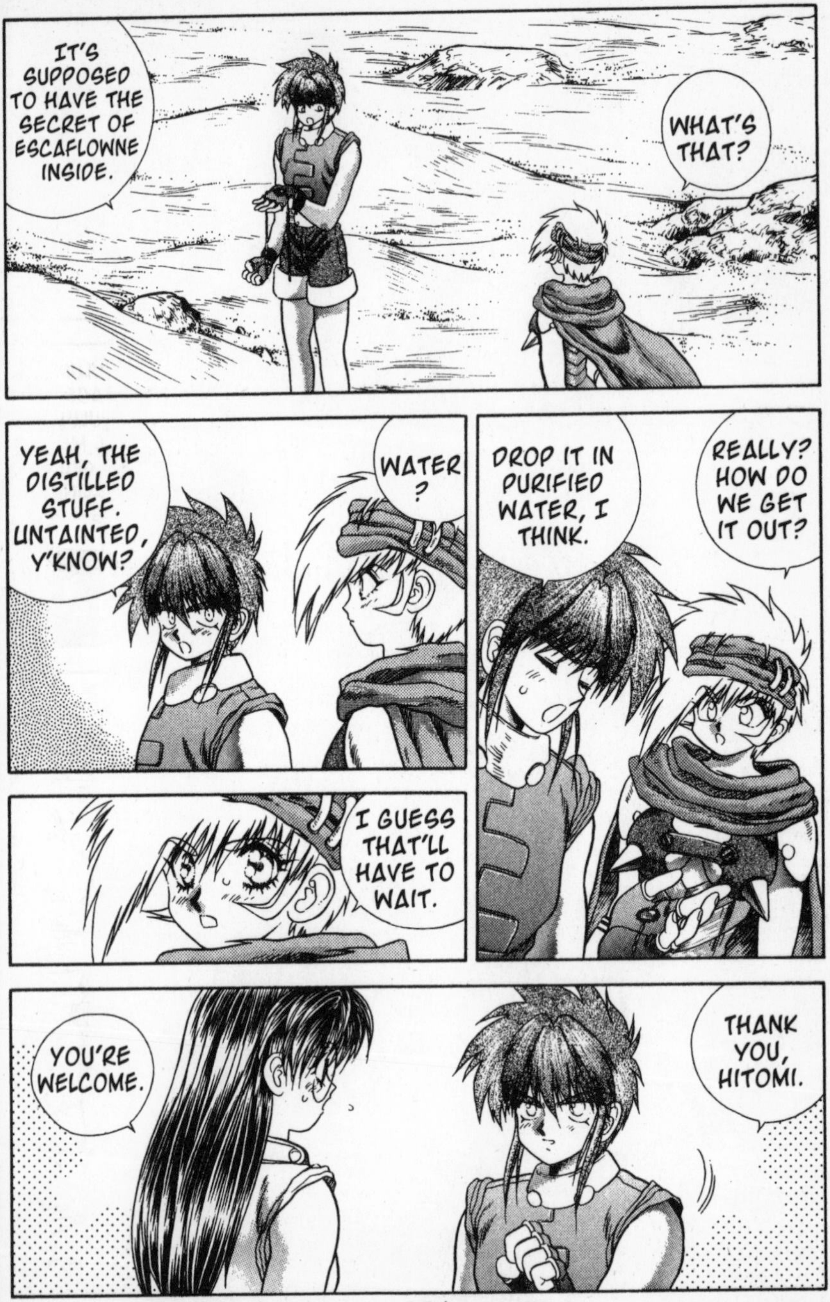
WHAT'S THAT?
IT'S SUPPOSED TO HAVE THE SECRET OF ESCAFLOWNE INSIDE.
REALLY? HOW DO WE GET IT OUT?
DROP IT IN PURIFIED WATER, I THINK.
WATER?
YEAH, THE DISTILLED STUFF. UNTAINTED, Y'KNOW?
I GUESS THAT'LL HAVE TO WAIT.
THANK YOU, HITOMI.
YOU'RE WELCOME.

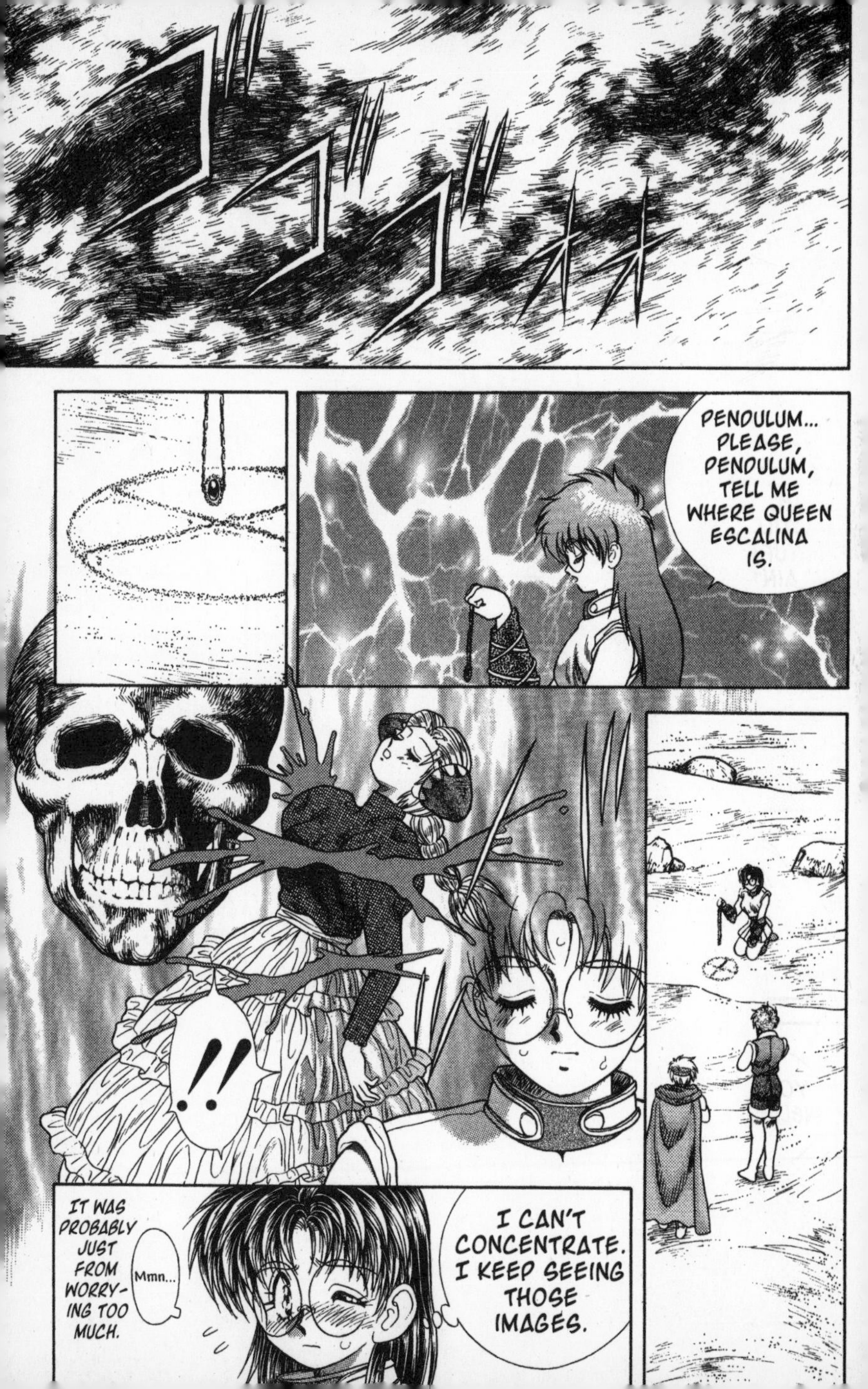
PENDULUM... PLEASE, PENDULUM, TELL ME WHERE QUEEN ESCALINA IS.
!!
I CAN'T CONCENTRATE. I KEEP SEEING THOSE IMAGES.
Mmn...
IT WAS PROBABLY JUST FROM WORRYING TOO MUCH.

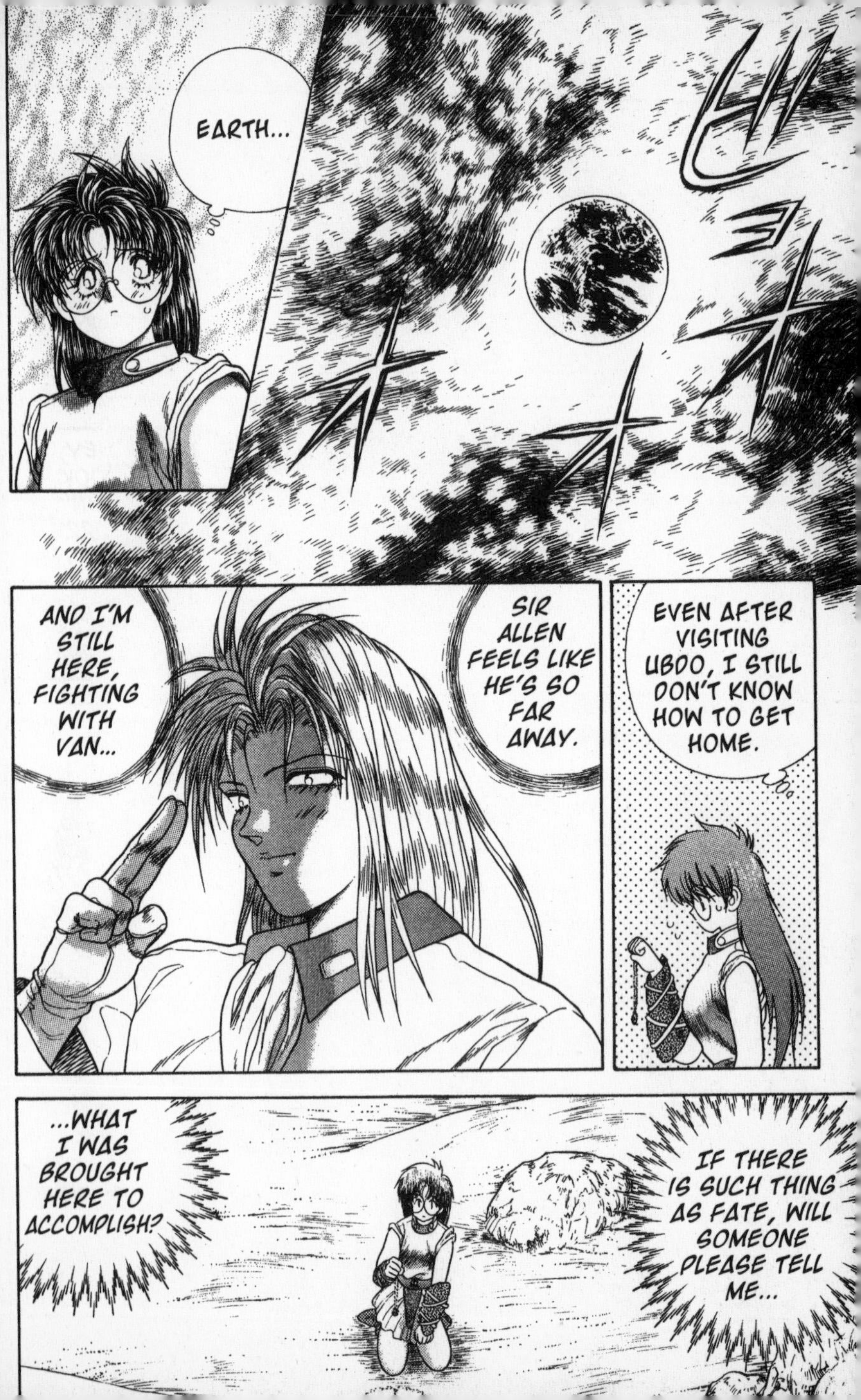
EARTH...
EVEN AFTER VISITING UBOO, I STILL DON'T KNOW HOW TO GET HOME.
SIR ALLEN FEELS LIKE HE'S SO FAR AWAY.
AND I'M STILL HERE, FIGHTING WITH VAN...
IF THERE IS SUCH THING AS FATE, WILL SOMEONE PLEASE TELL ME...
...WHAT I WAS BROUGHT HERE TO ACCOMPLISH?

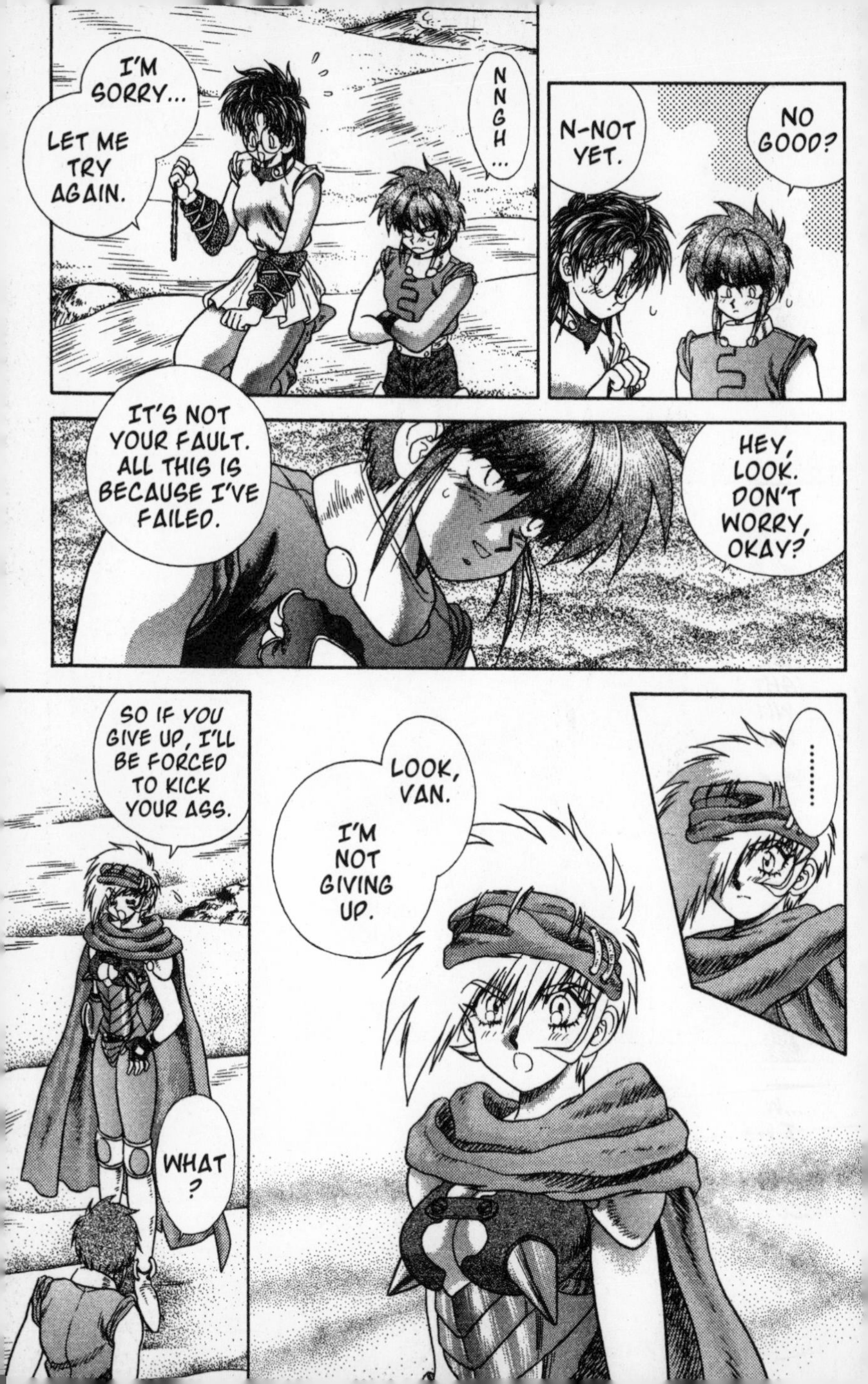
NO GOOD?
N-NOT YET.
NNGH...
I'M SORRY...
LET ME TRY AGAIN.
HEY, LOOK. DON'T WORRY, OKAY?
IT'S NOT YOUR FAULT. ALL THIS IS BECAUSE I'VE FAILED.
....
LOOK, VAN.
I'M NOT GIVING UP.
SO IF YOU GIVE UP, I'LL BE FORCED TO KICK YOUR ASS.
WHAT?

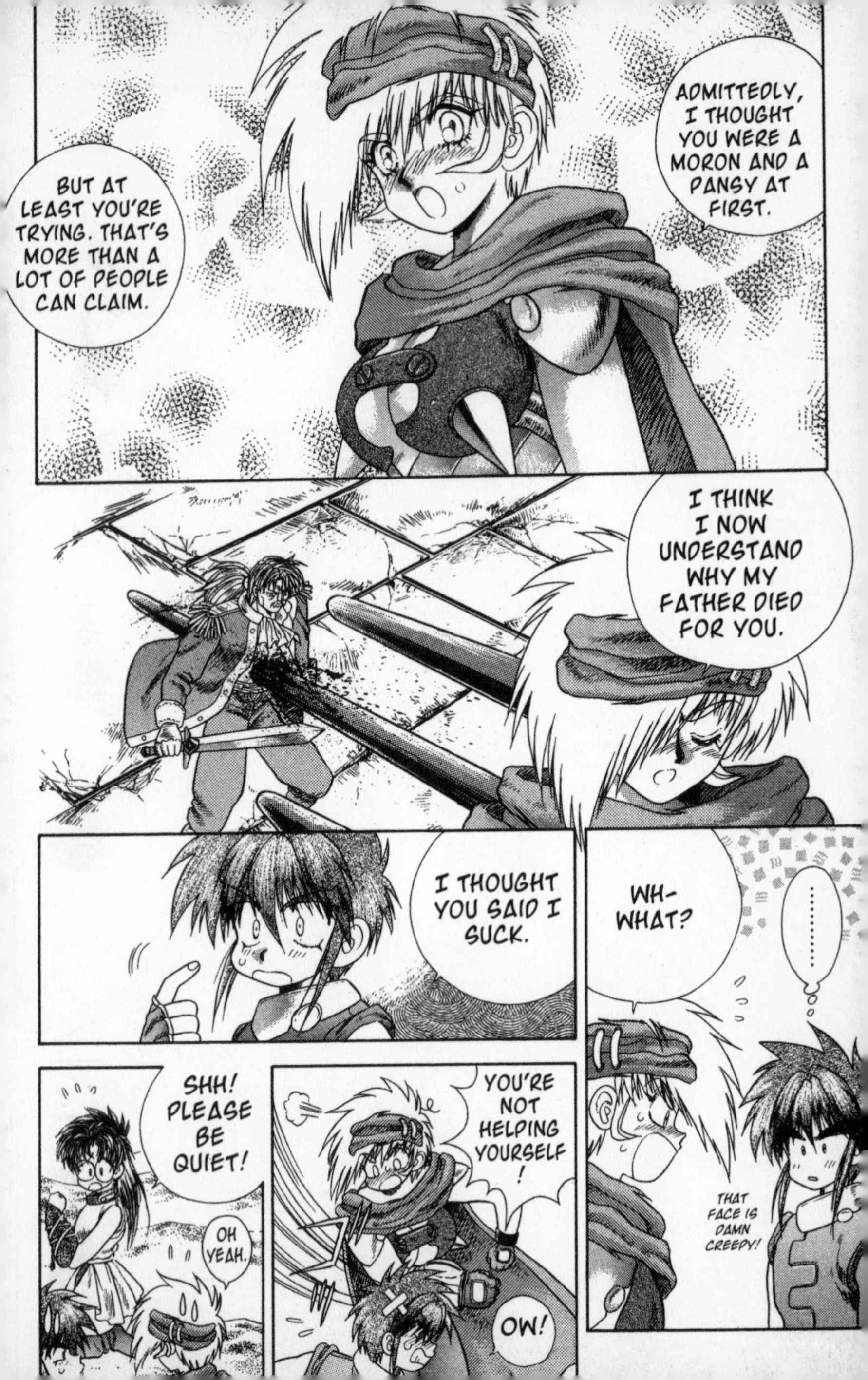
ADMITTEDLY, I THOUGHT YOU WERE A MORON AND A PANSY AT FIRST.
BUT AT LEAST YOU'RE TRYING. THAT'S MORE THAN A LOT OF PEOPLE CAN CLAIM.
I THINK I NOW UNDERSTAND WHY MY FATHER DIED FOR YOU.
......
WH- WHAT?
THAT FACE IS DAMN CREEPY!
I THOUGHT YOU SAID I SUCK.
YOU'RE NOT HELPING YOURSELF!
OW!
SHH! PLEASE BE QUIET!
OH YEAH.

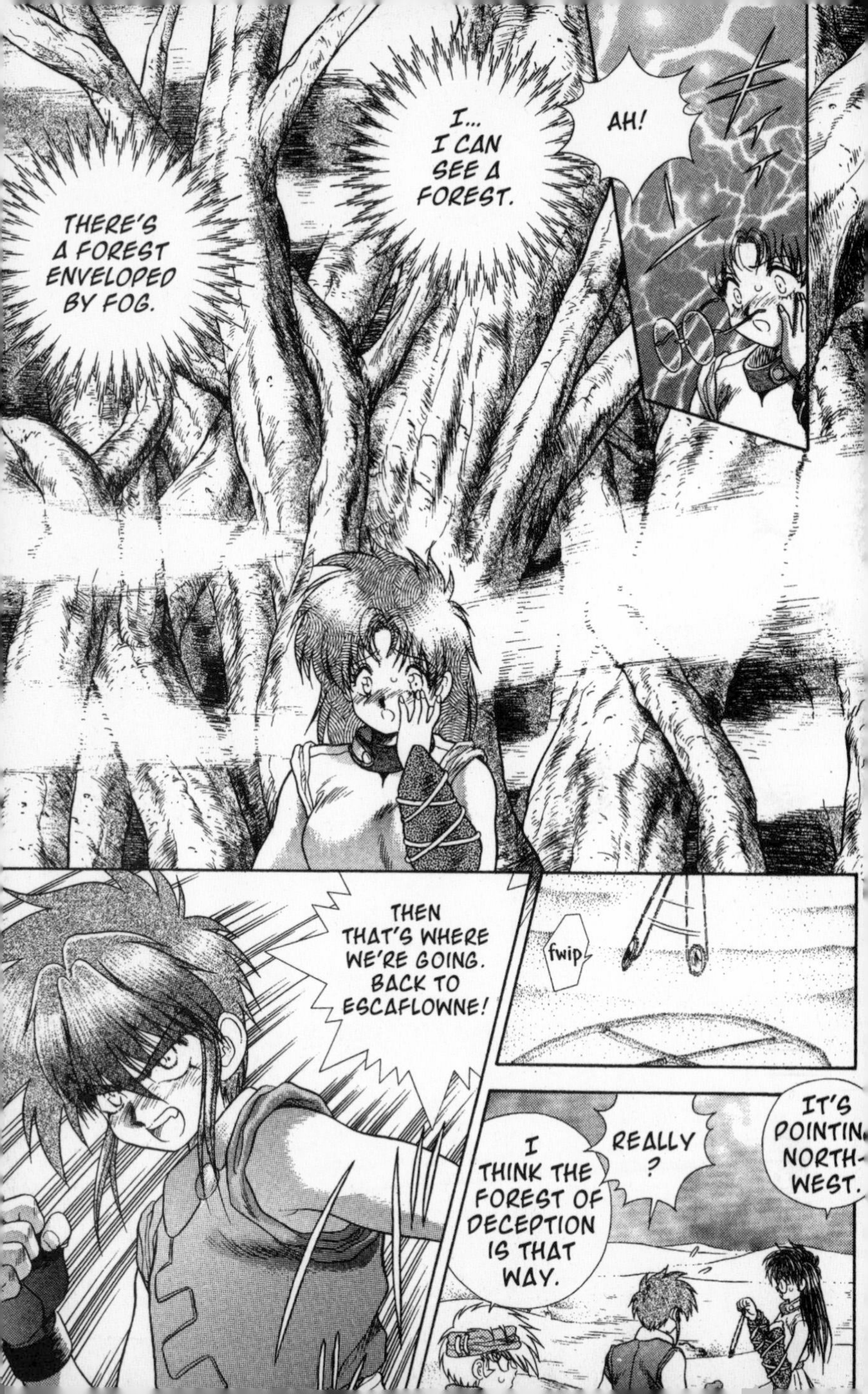
AH!
I... I CAN SEE A FOREST.
THERE'S A FOREST ENVELOPED BY FOG.
fwip
IT'S POINTIN NORTH-WEST.
REALLY?
I THINK THE FOREST OF DECEPTION IS THAT WAY.
THEN THAT'S WHERE WE'RE GOING. BACK TO ESCAFLOWNE!

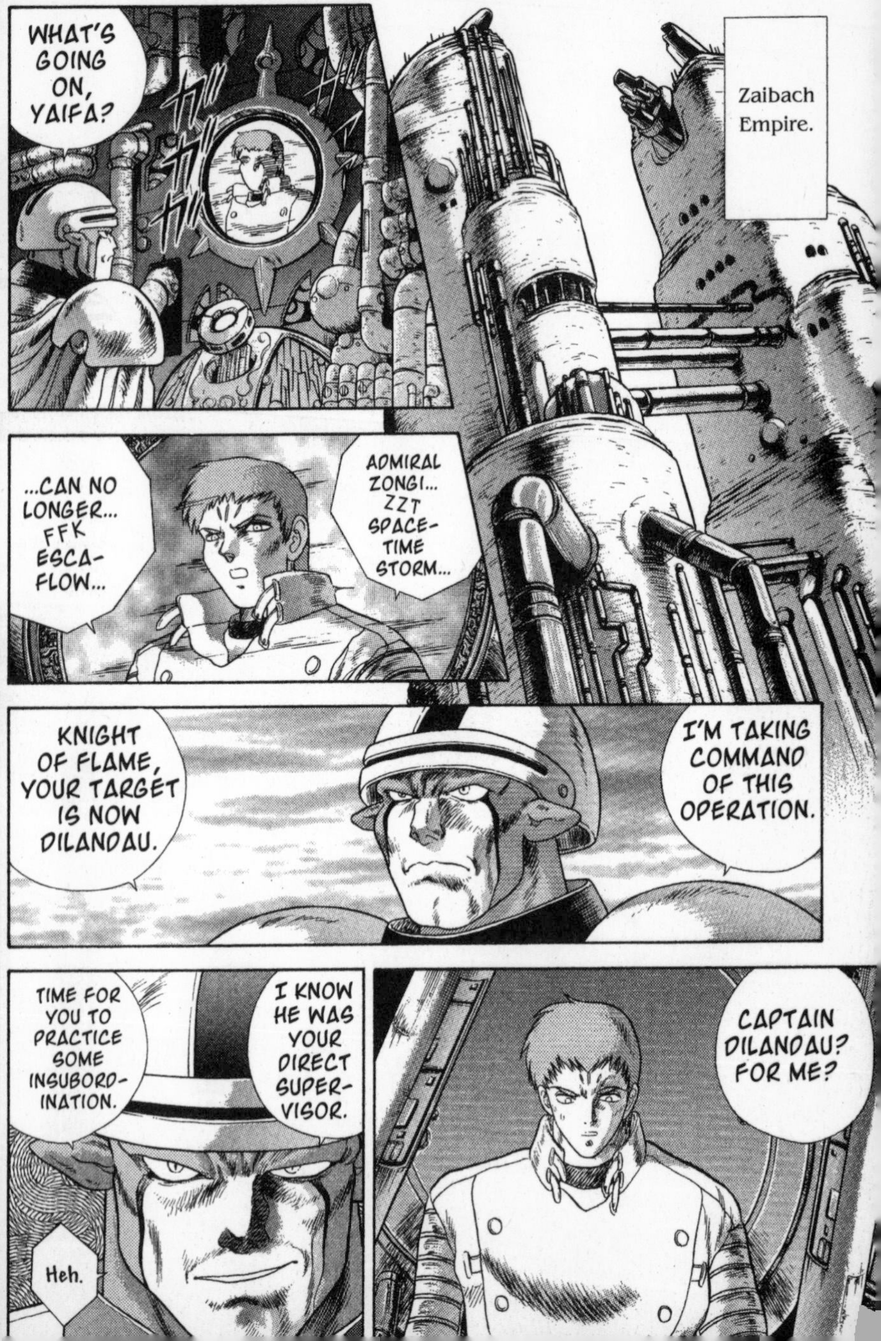
Zaibach Empire.
WHAT'S GOING ON, YAIFA?
ADMIRAL ZONGI... ZZT SPACE-TIME STORM...
...CAN NO LONGER... FFK ESCAFLOW...
I'M TAKING COMMAND OF THIS OPERATION.
KNIGHT OF FLAME, YOUR TARGET IS NOW DILANDAU.
CAPTAIN DILANDAU? FOR ME?
I KNOW HE WAS YOUR DIRECT SUPERVISOR.
TIME FOR YOU TO PRACTICE SOME INSUBORDINATION.
Heh.

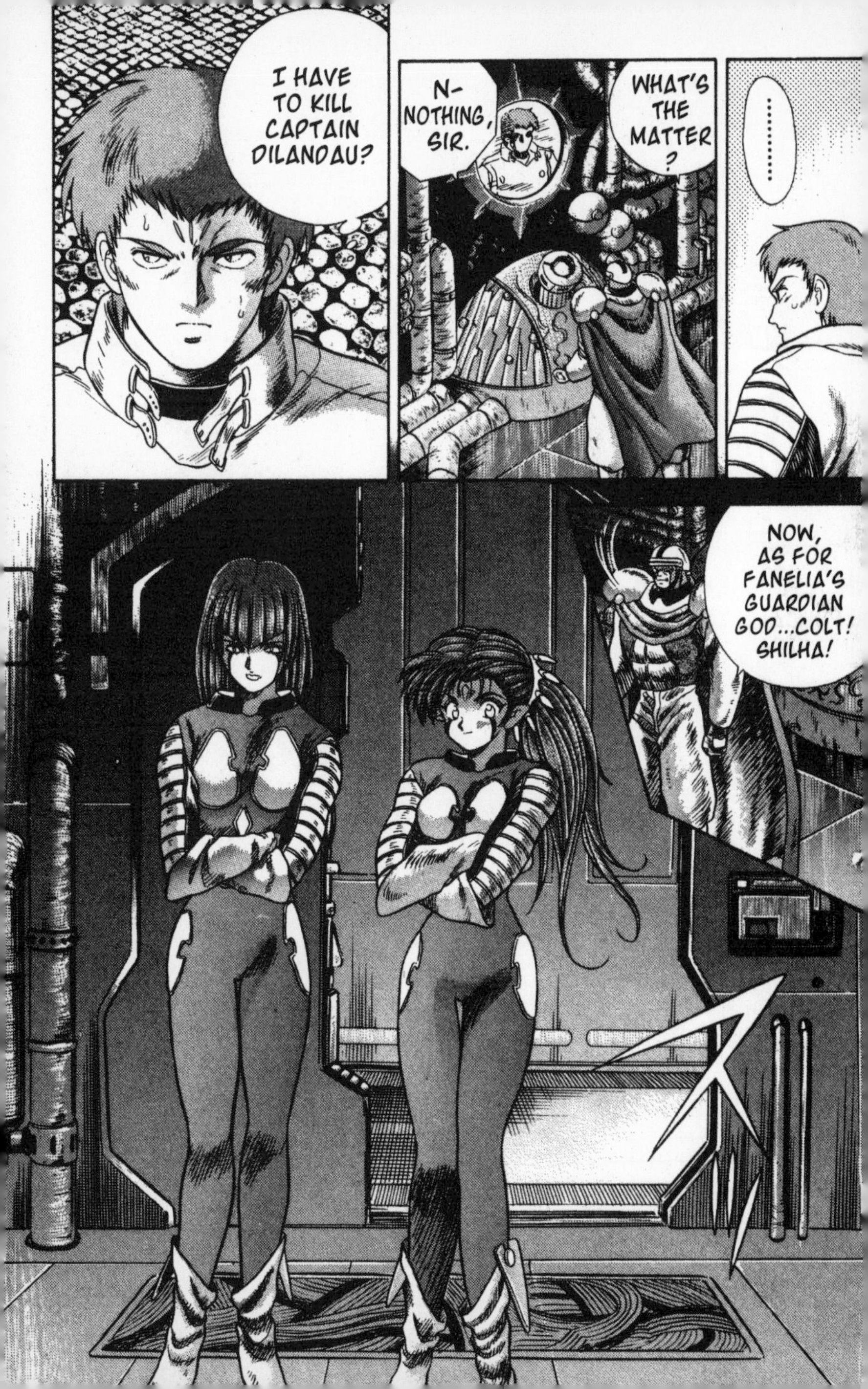
......
WHAT'S THE MATTER?
N-NOTHING, SIR.
I HAVE TO KILL CAPTAIN DILANDAU?
NOW, AS FOR FANELIA'S GUARDIAN GOD...COLT! SHILHA!

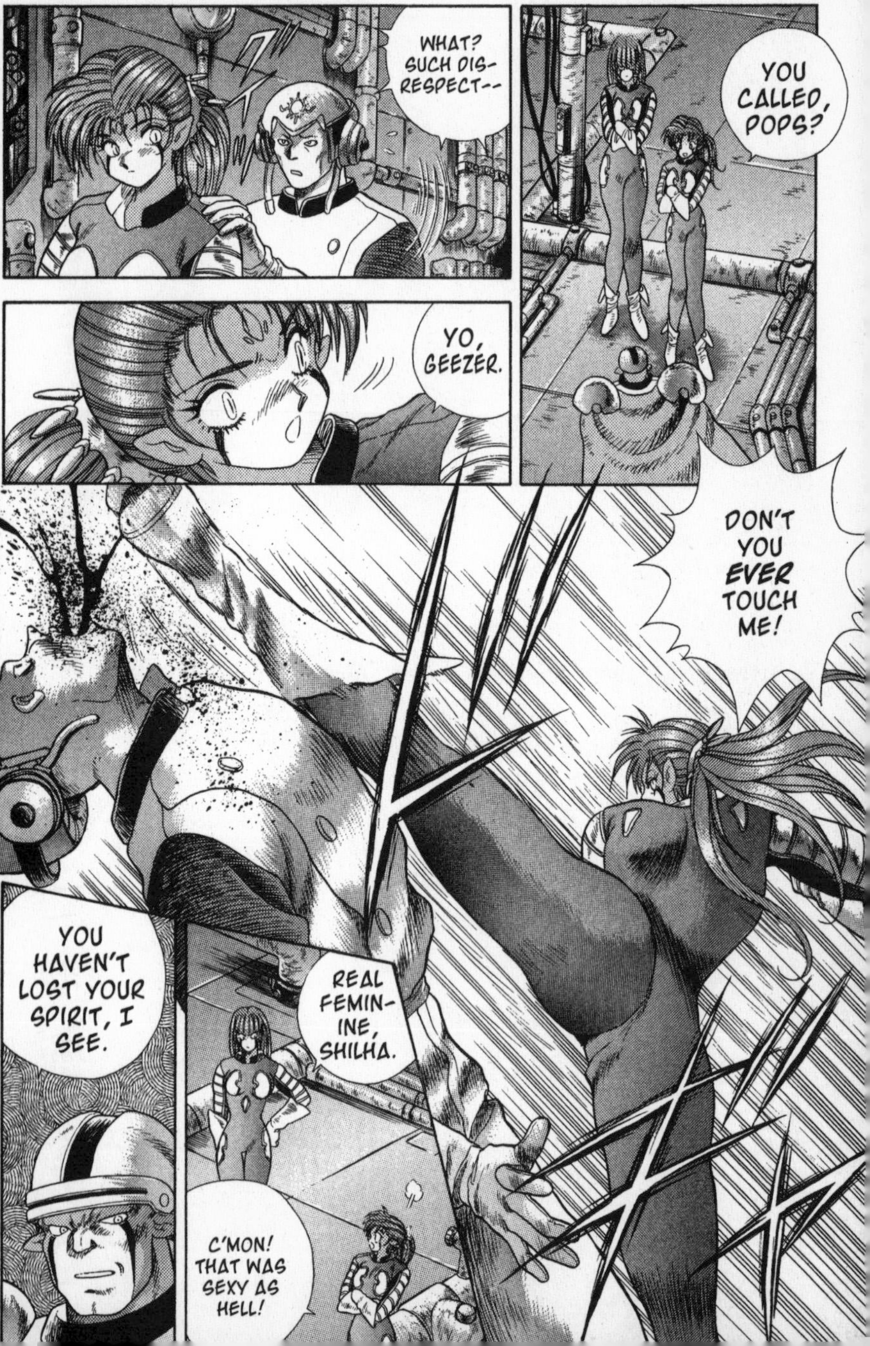
YOU CALLED, POPS?
WHAT? SUCH DIS-RESPECT--
YO, GEEZER.
DON'T YOU *EVER* TOUCH ME!
REAL FEMIN-INE, SHILHA.
C'MON! THAT WAS SEXY AS HELL!
YOU HAVEN'T LOST YOUR SPIRIT, I SEE.

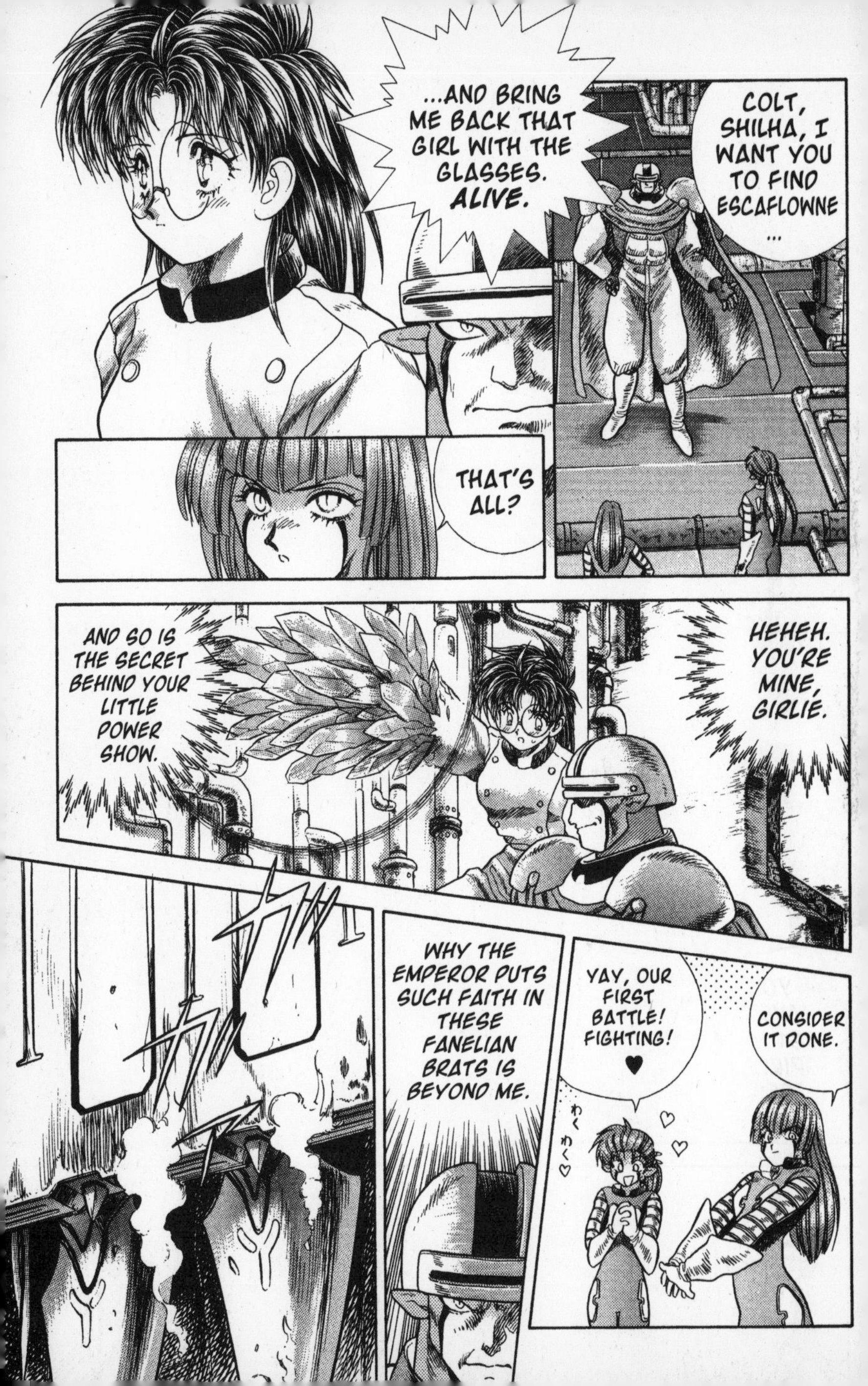
COLT, SHILHA, I WANT YOU TO FIND ESCAFLOWNE ...
...AND BRING ME BACK THAT GIRL WITH THE GLASSES. ALIVE.
THAT'S ALL?
HEHEH. YOU'RE MINE, GIRLIE.
AND SO IS THE SECRET BEHIND YOUR LITTLE POWER SHOW.
CONSIDER IT DONE.
YAY, OUR FIRST BATTLE! FIGHTING! ♥
わくわく♡
WHY THE EMPEROR PUTS SUCH FAITH IN THESE FANELIAN BRATS IS BEYOND ME.

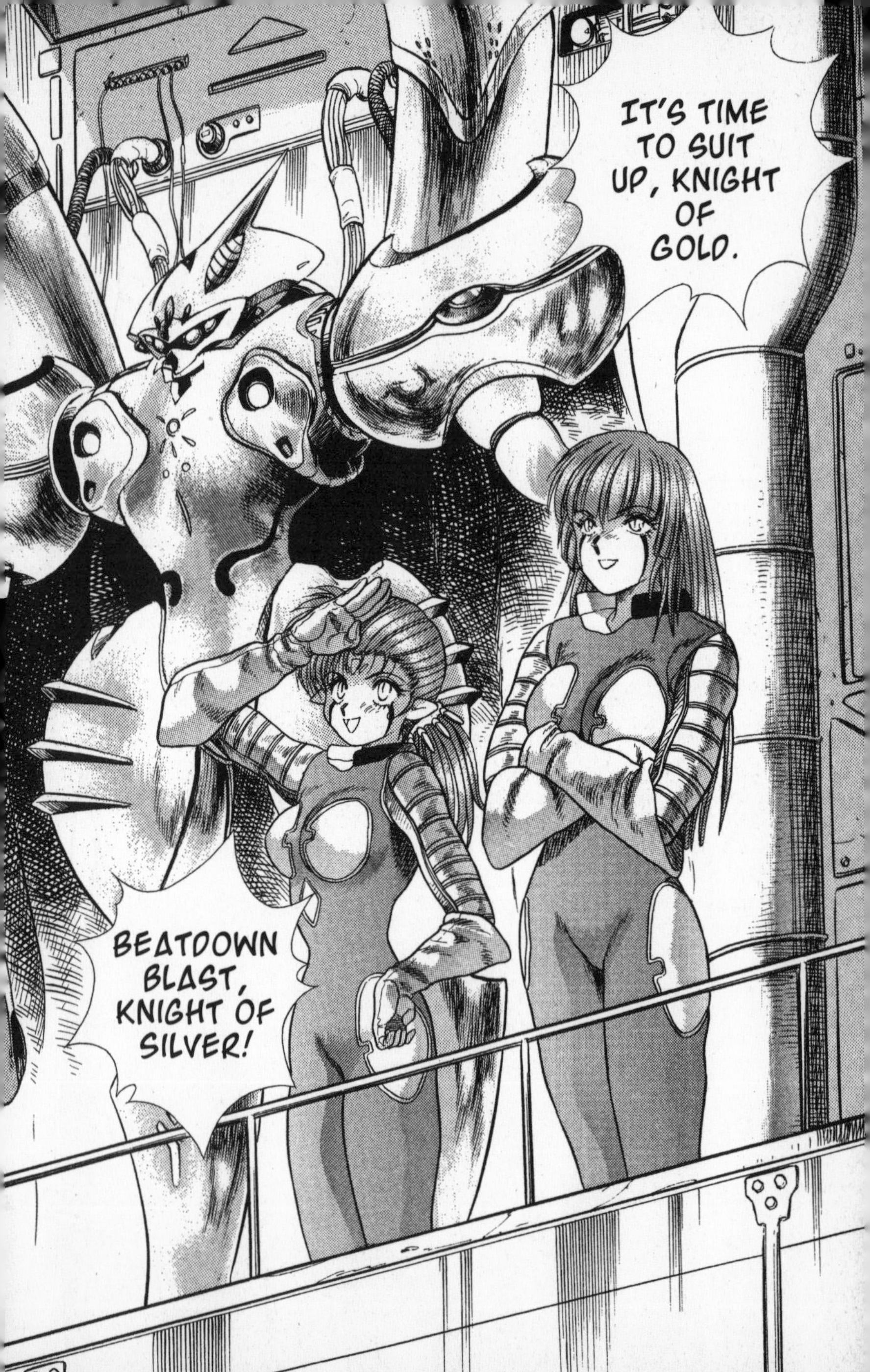
IT'S TIME TO SUIT UP, KNIGHT OF GOLD.
BEATDOWN BLAST, KNIGHT OF SILVER!

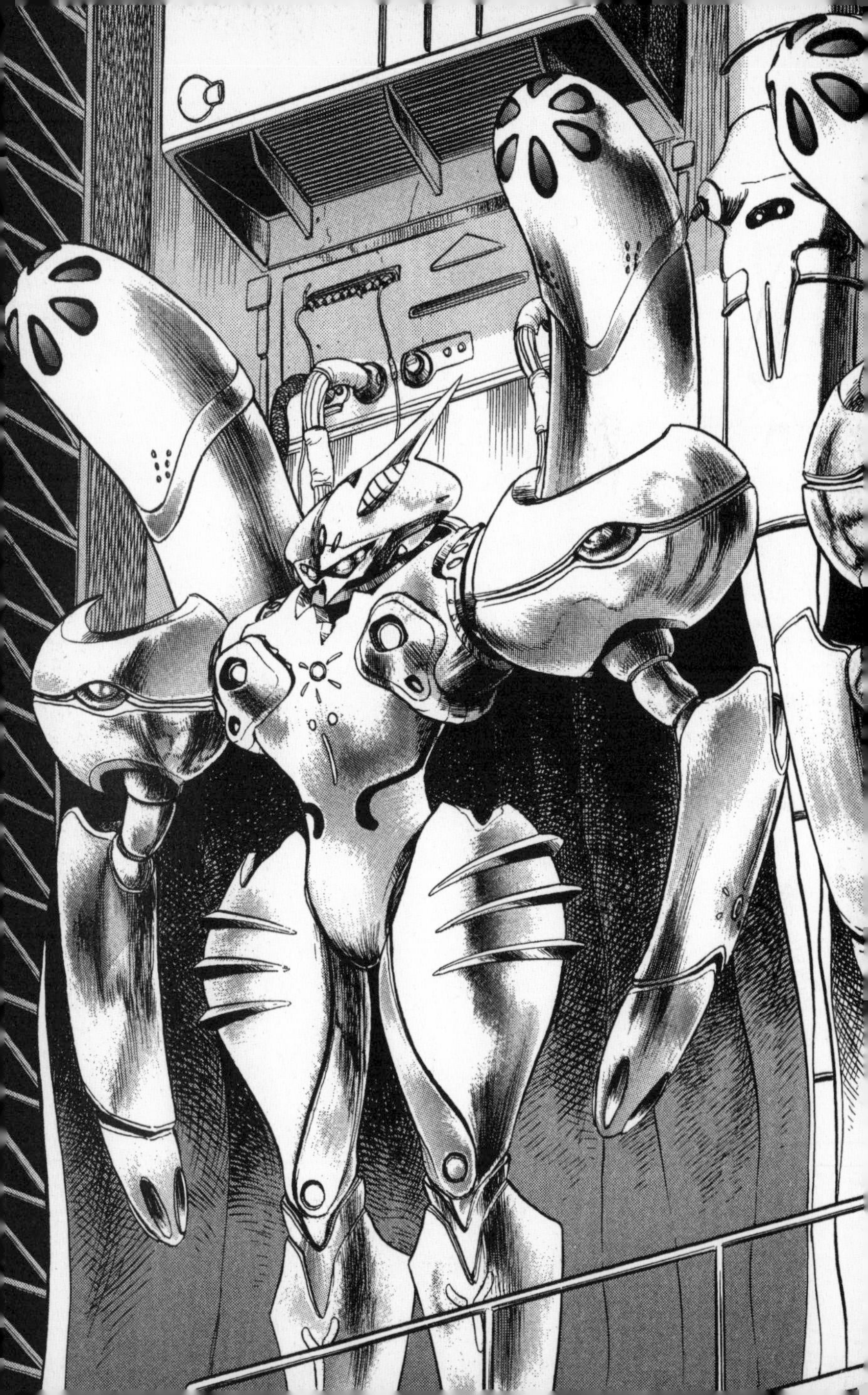

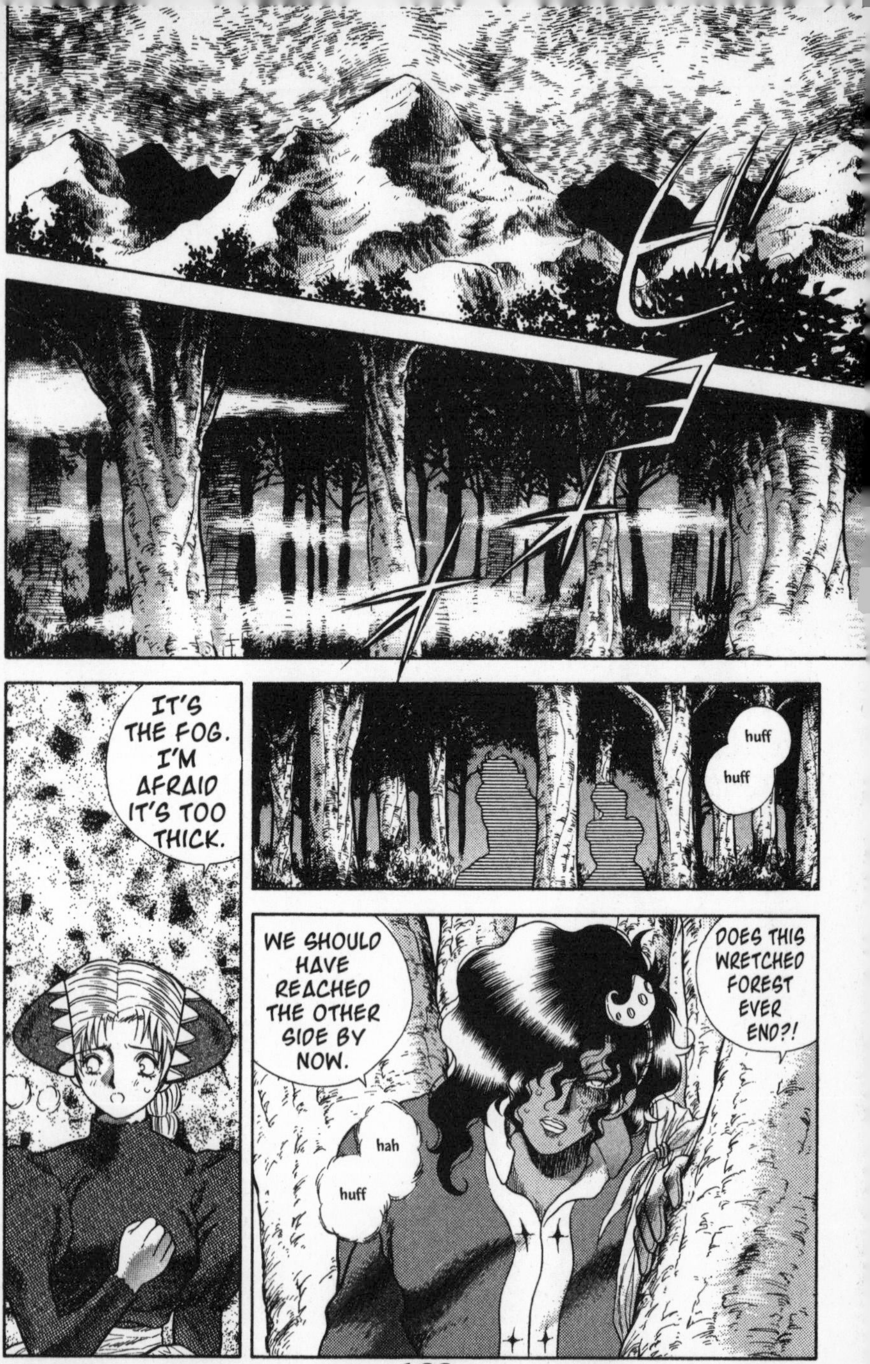
huff
huff
DOES THIS WRETCHED FOREST EVER END?!
WE SHOULD HAVE REACHED THE OTHER SIDE BY NOW.
hah
huff
IT'S THE FOG. I'M AFRAID IT'S TOO THICK.

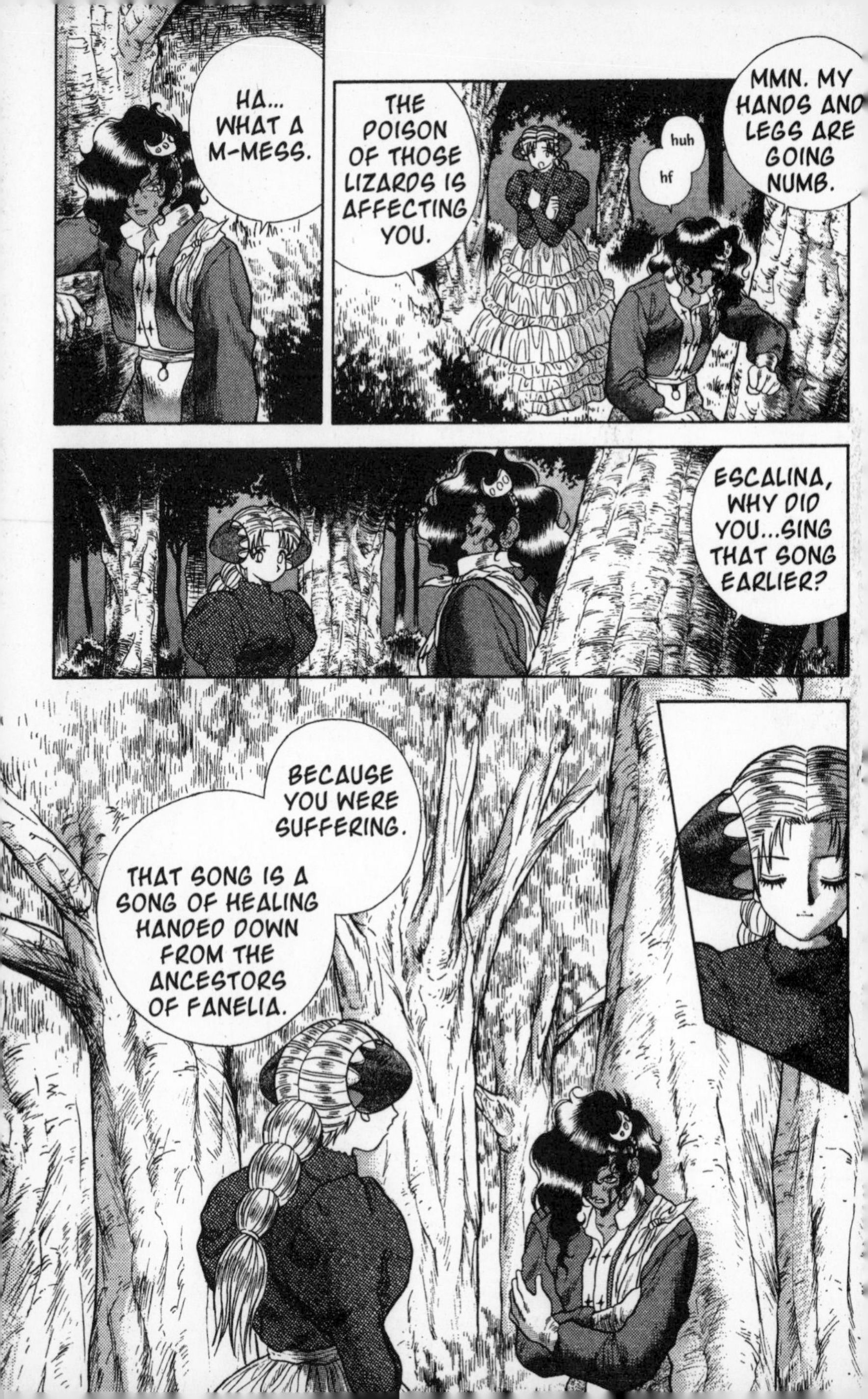
MMN. MY HANDS AND LEGS ARE GOING NUMB.
huh
hf
THE POISON OF THOSE LIZARDS IS AFFECTING YOU.
HA... WHAT A M-MESS.
ESCALINA, WHY DID YOU...SING THAT SONG EARLIER?
BECAUSE YOU WERE SUFFERING.
THAT SONG IS A SONG OF HEALING HANDED DOWN FROM THE ANCESTORS OF FANELIA.

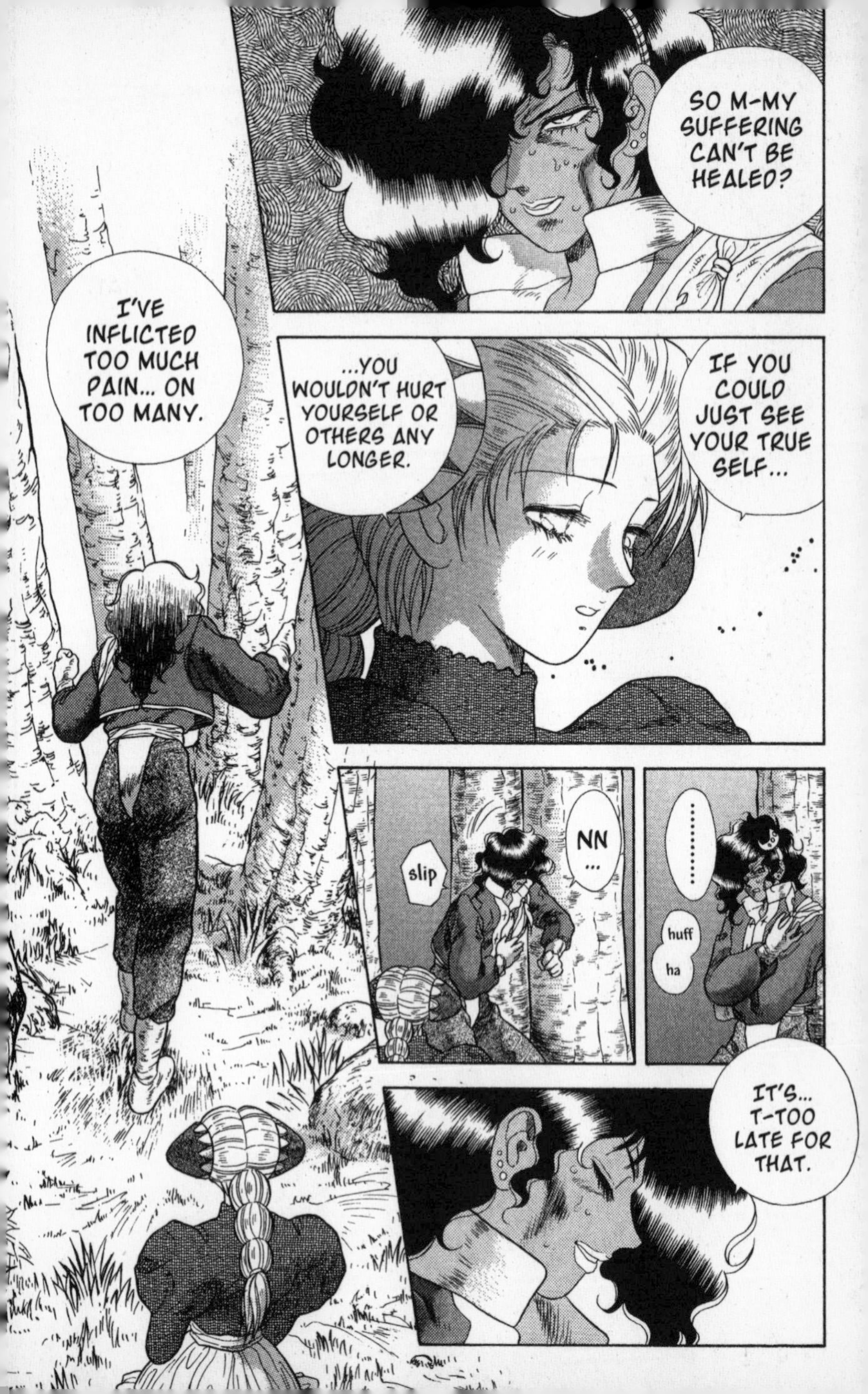
SO M-MY SUFFERING CAN'T BE HEALED?
IF YOU COULD JUST SEE YOUR TRUE SELF...
...YOU WOULDN'T HURT YOURSELF OR OTHERS ANY LONGER.
....
huff
ha
NN...
slip
IT'S... T-TOO LATE FOR THAT.
I'VE INFLICTED TOO MUCH PAIN... ON TOO MANY.

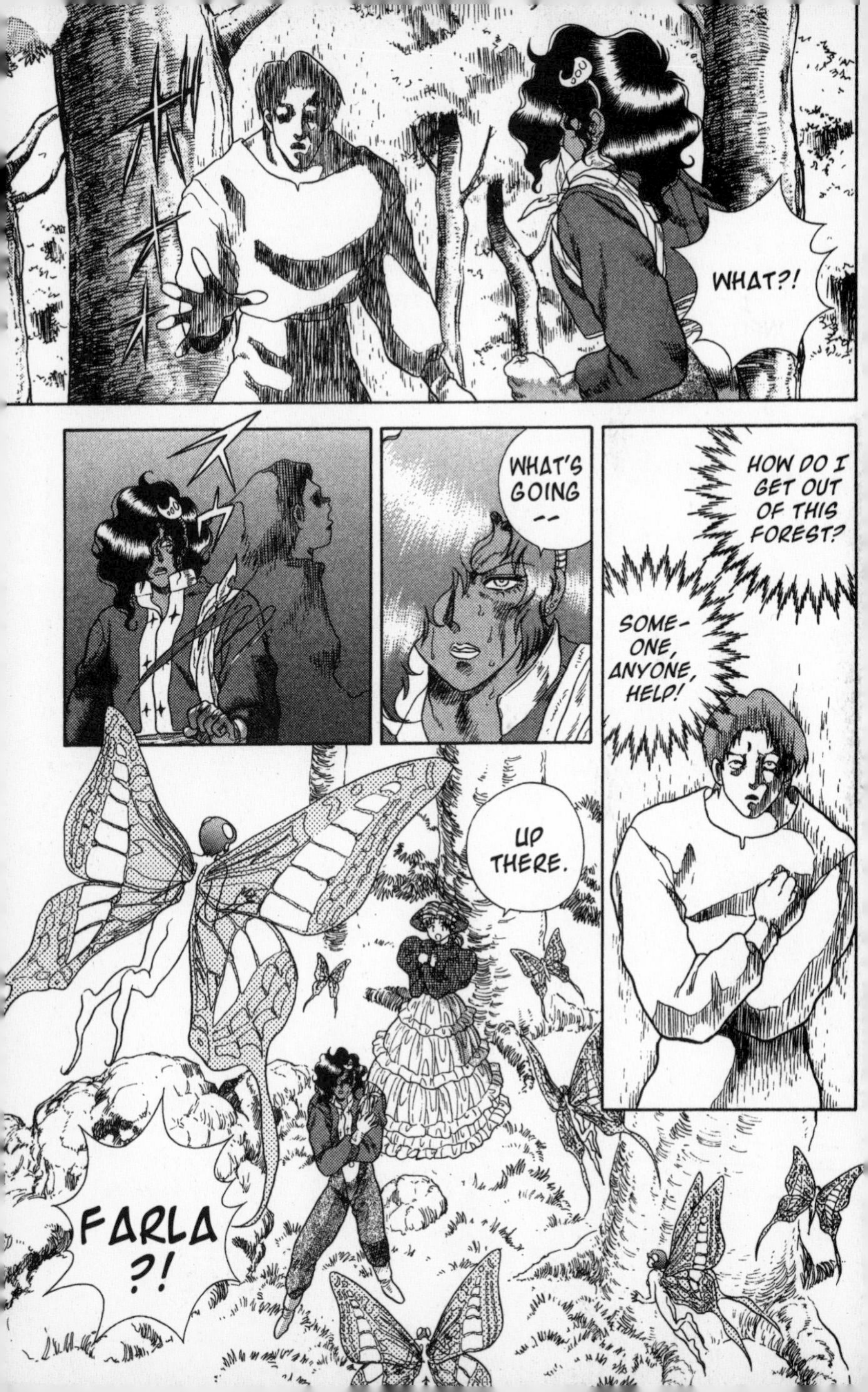
WHAT?!
HOW DO I GET OUT OF THIS FOREST?
SOME-ONE, ANYONE, HELP!
WHAT'S GOING --
UP THERE.
FARLA ?!

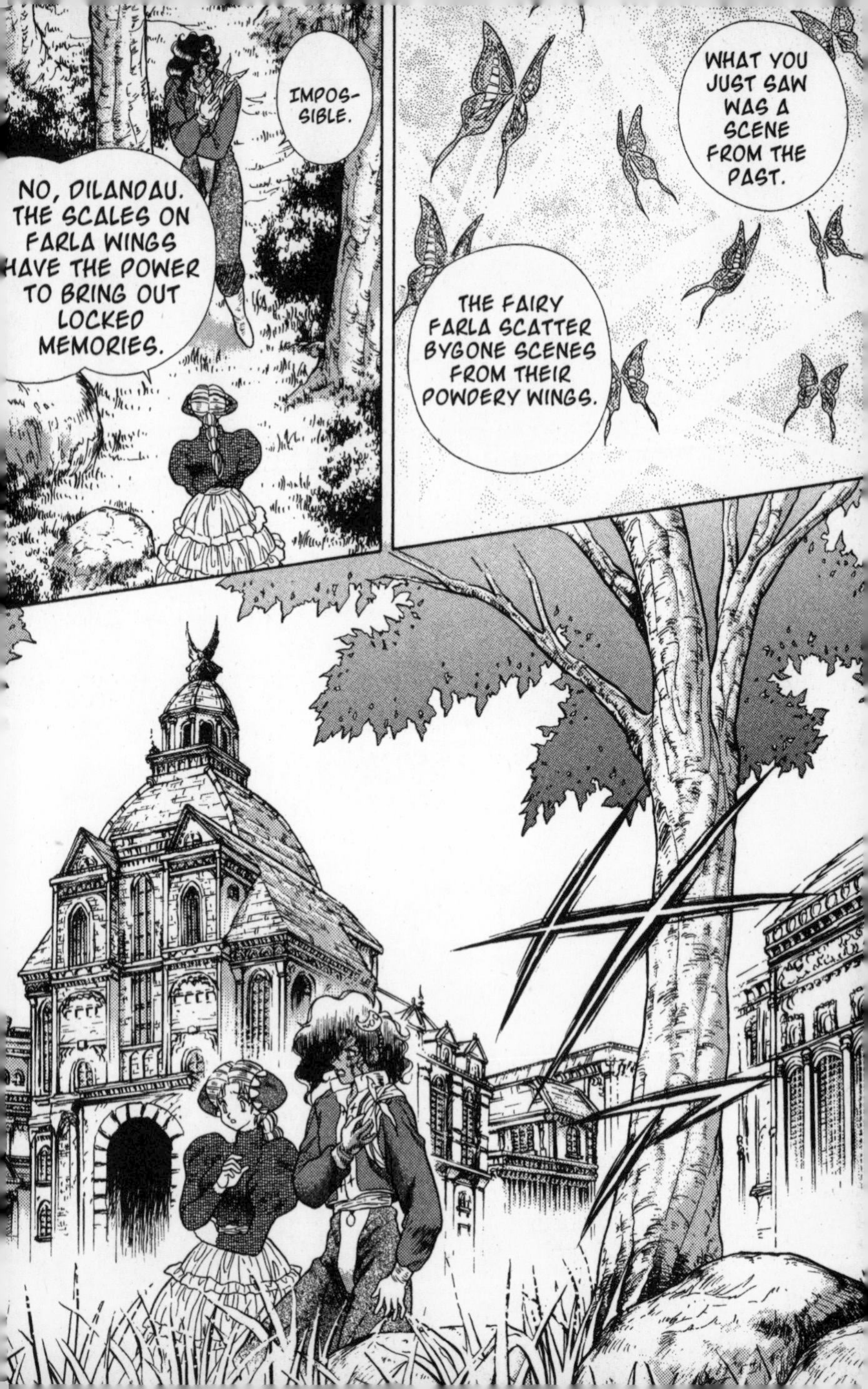
WHAT YOU JUST SAW WAS A SCENE FROM THE PAST.
THE FAIRY FARLA SCATTER BYGONE SCENES FROM THEIR POWDERY WINGS.
IMPOS-SIBLE.
NO, DILANDAU. THE SCALES ON FARLA WINGS HAVE THE POWER TO BRING OUT LOCKED MEMORIES.

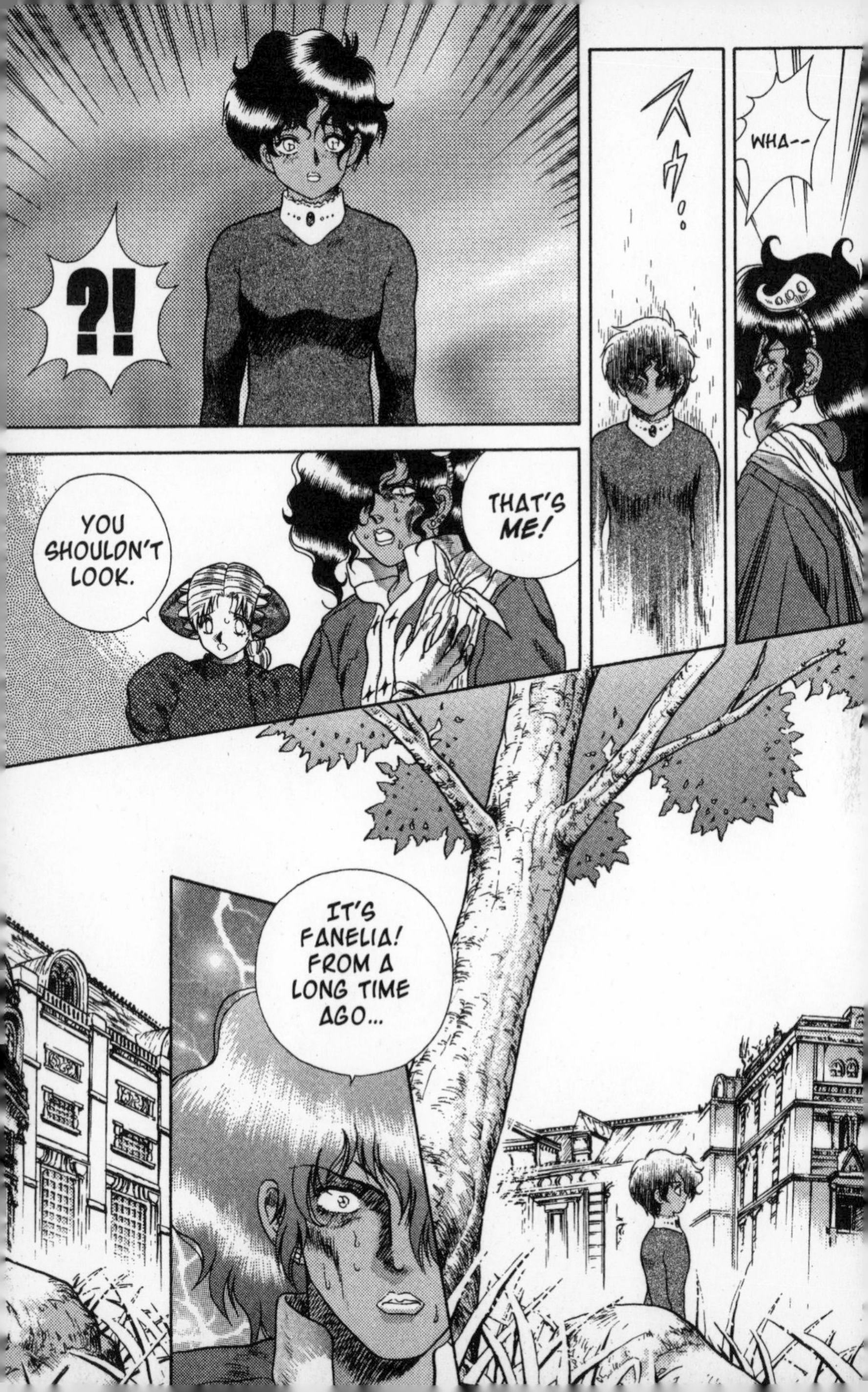
WHA--
スゥ
?!
THAT'S ME!
YOU SHOULDN'T LOOK.
IT'S FANELIA! FROM A LONG TIME AGO...

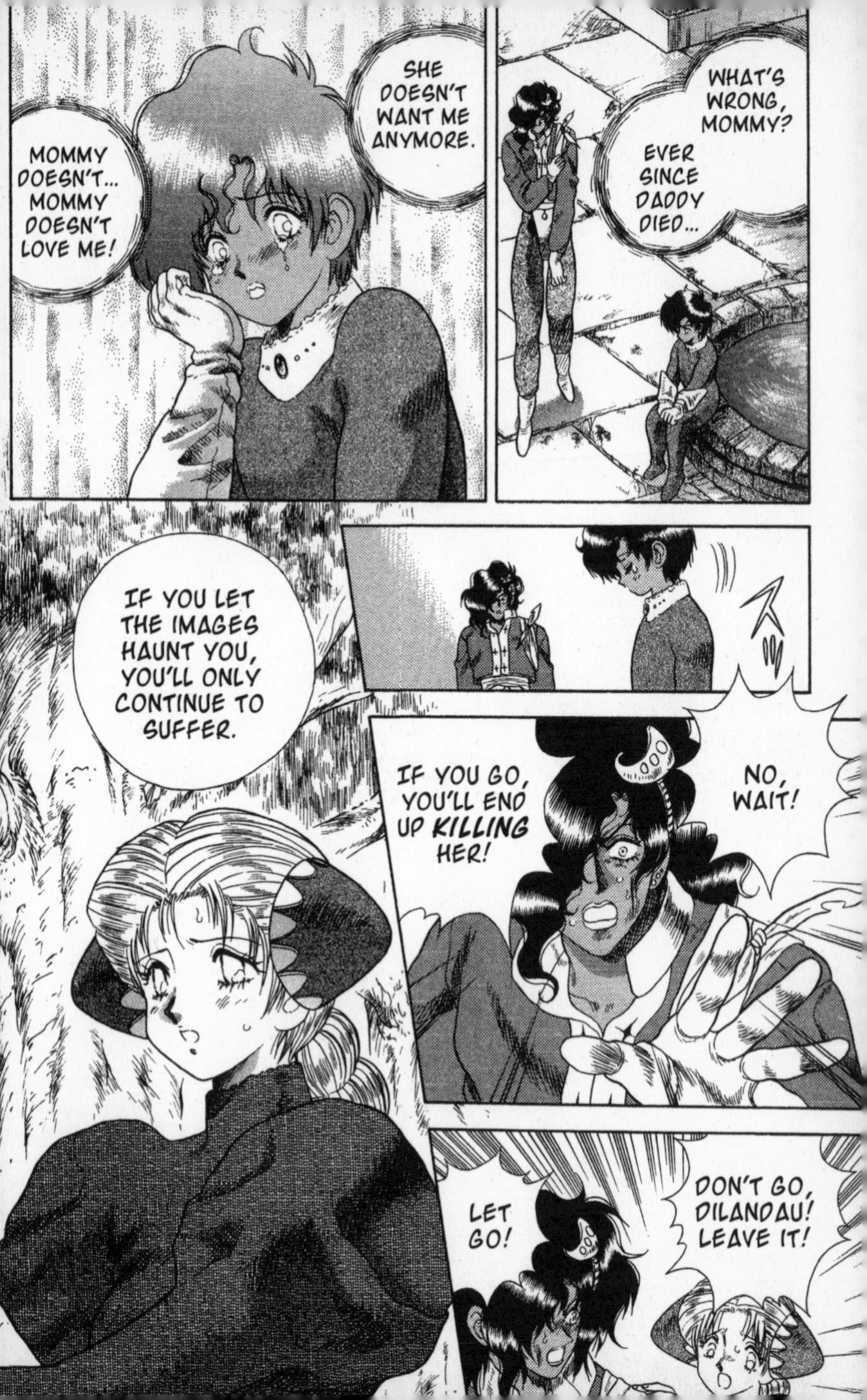
WHAT'S WRONG, MOMMY?
EVER SINCE DADDY DIED...
SHE DOESN'T WANT ME ANYMORE.
MOMMY DOESN'T... MOMMY DOESN'T LOVE ME!
ス
NO, WAIT!
IF YOU GO, YOU'LL END UP **KILLING** HER!
DON'T GO, DILANDAU! LEAVE IT!
LET GO!
IF YOU LET THE IMAGES HAUNT YOU, YOU'LL ONLY CONTINUE TO SUFFER.

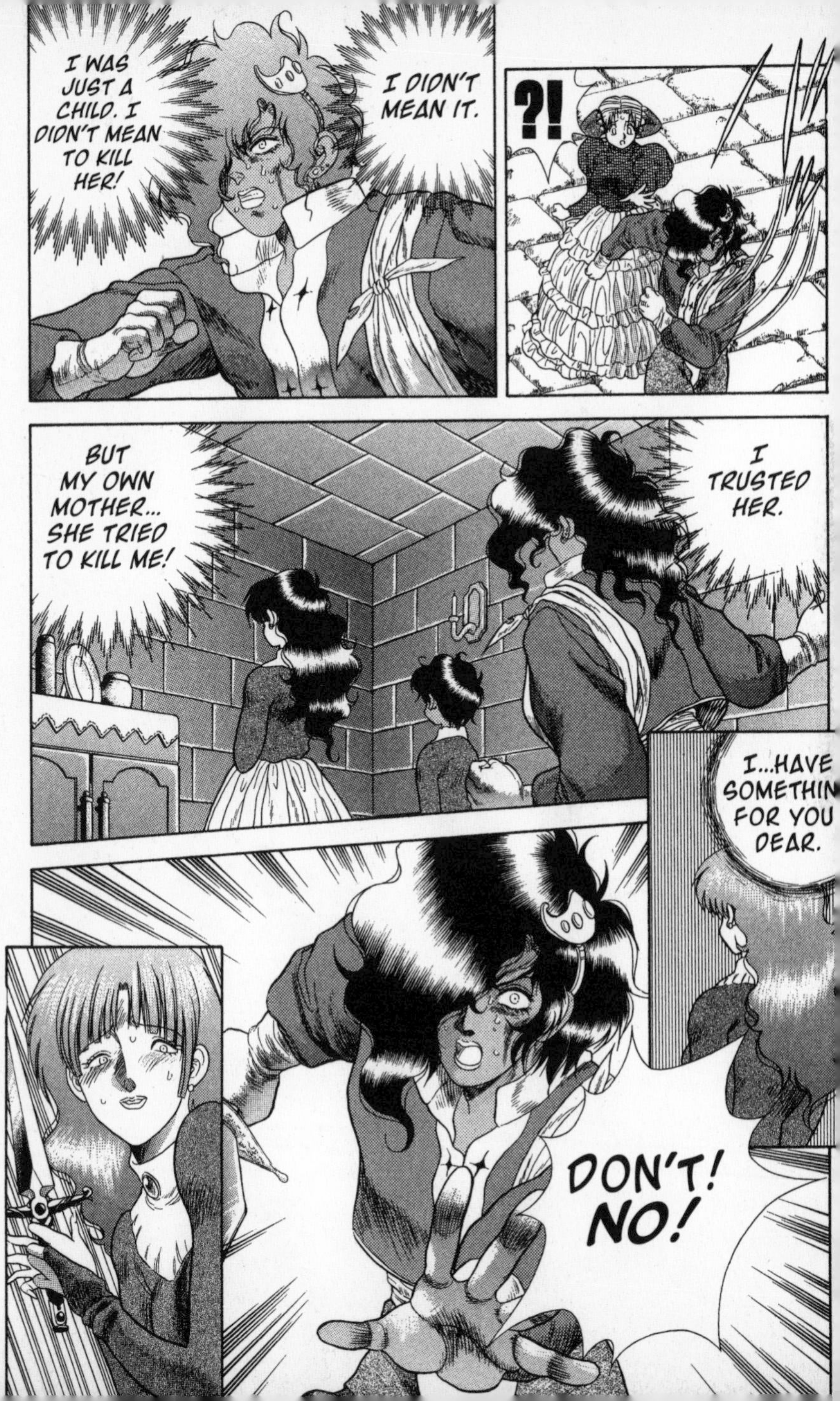
?!
I DIDN'T MEAN IT.
I WAS JUST A CHILD. I DIDN'T MEAN TO KILL HER!
I TRUSTED HER.
BUT MY OWN MOTHER... SHE TRIED TO KILL ME!
I...HAVE SOMETHIN FOR YOU DEAR.
DON'T! NO!

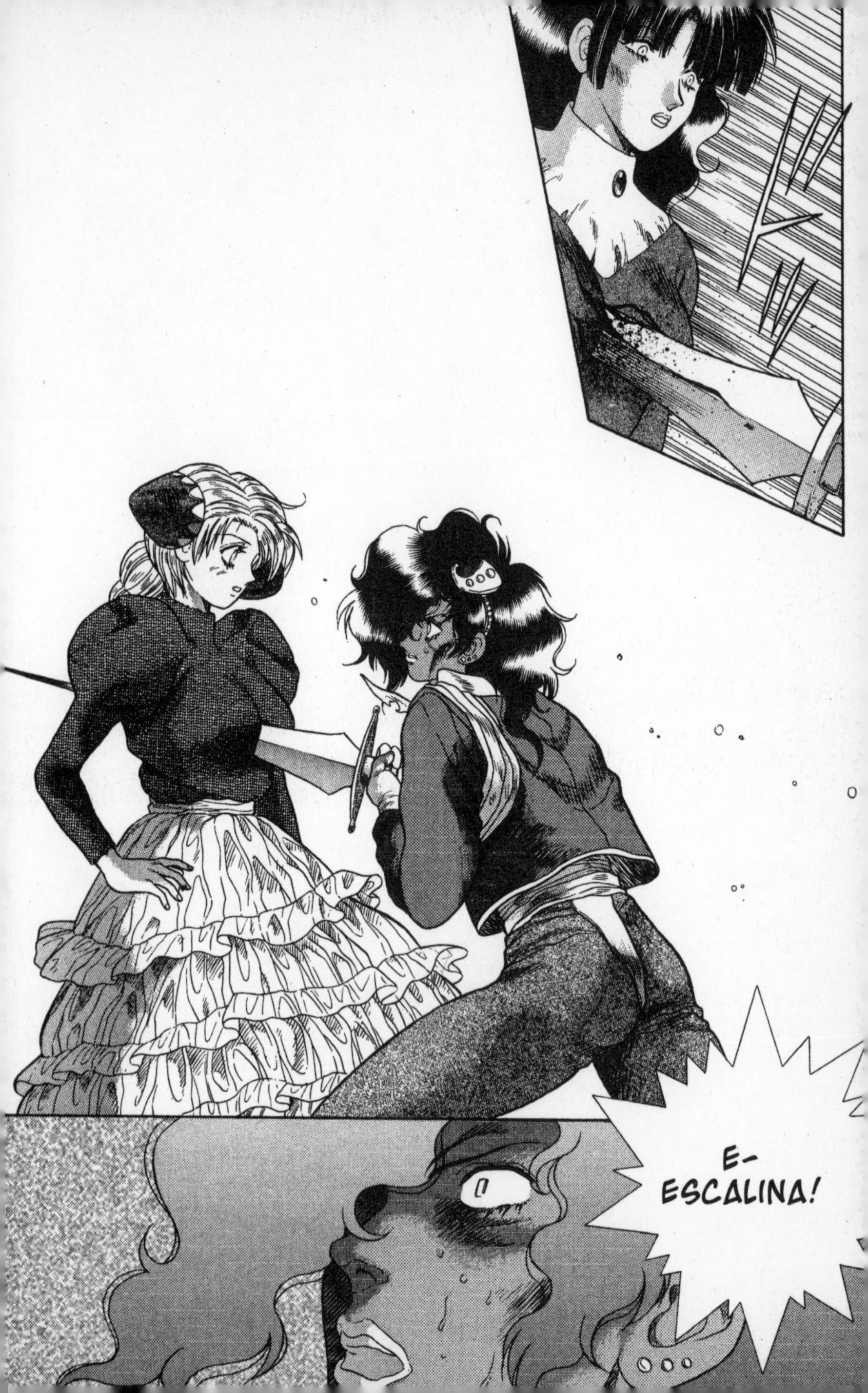
E- ESCALINA!

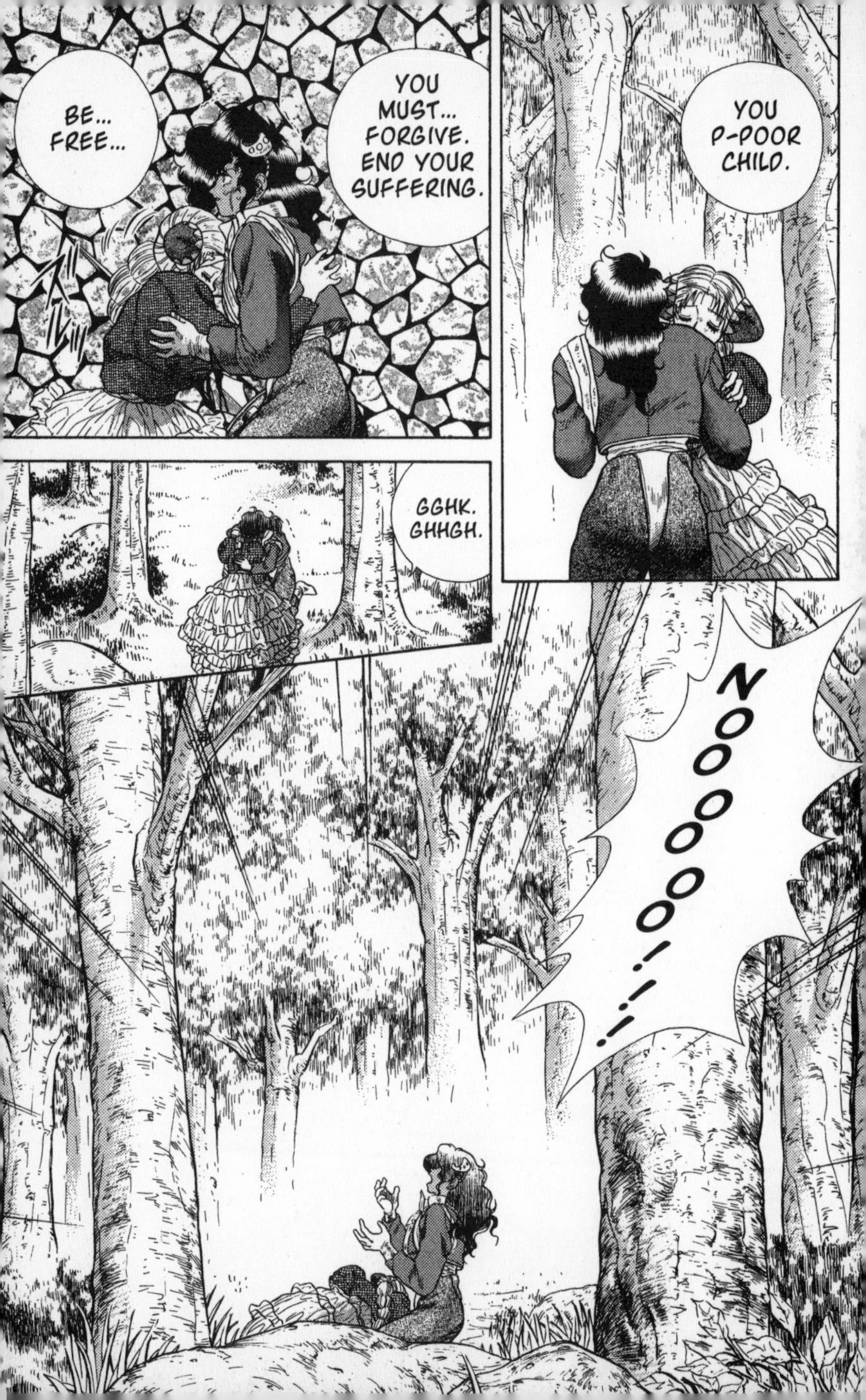
YOU P-POOR CHILD.
YOU MUST... FORGIVE. END YOUR SUFFERING.
BE... FREE...
GGHK. GHHGH.
NOOOOOOO!!!

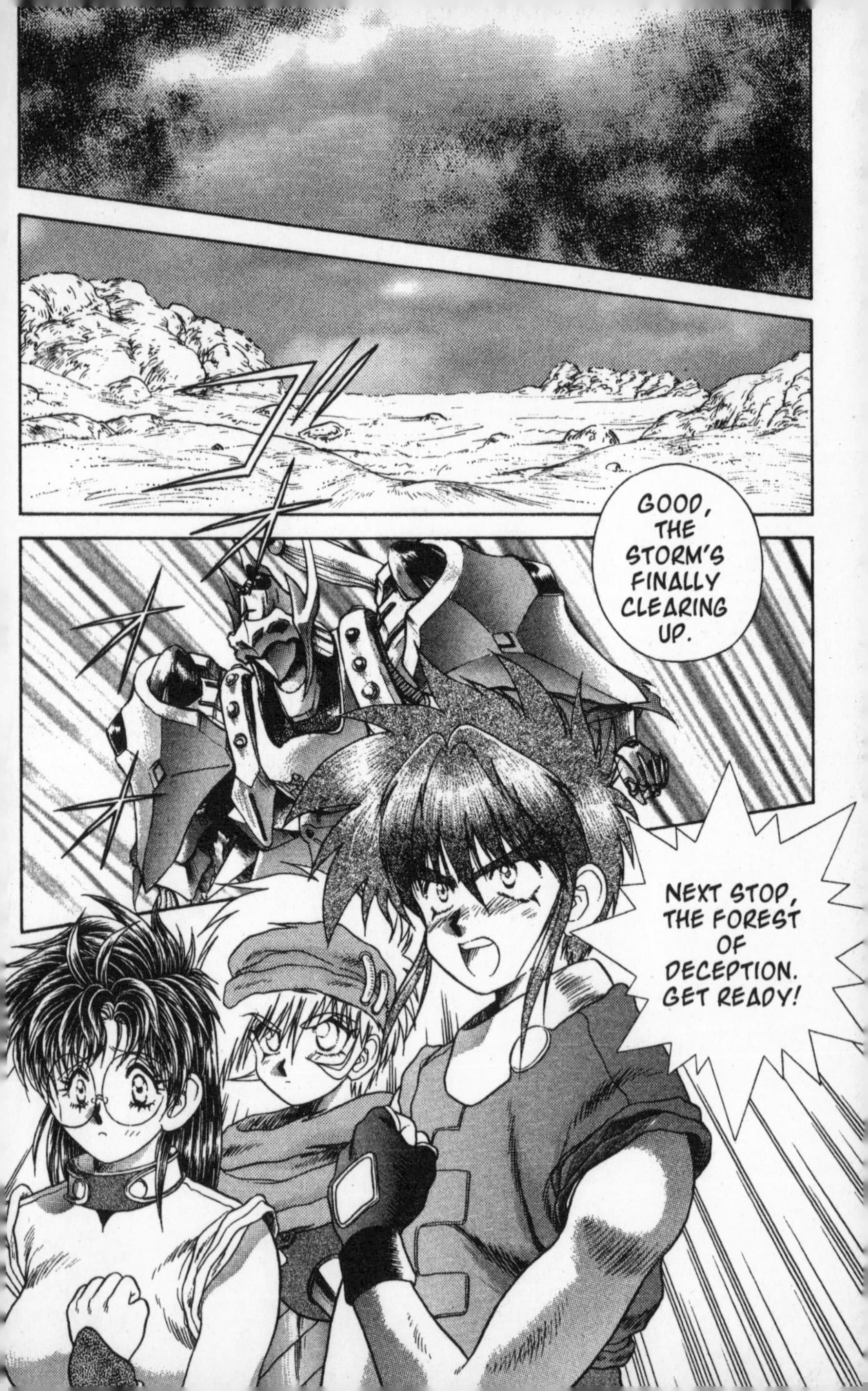
GOOD, THE STORM'S FINALLY CLEARING UP.
NEXT STOP, THE FOREST OF DECEPTION. GET READY!

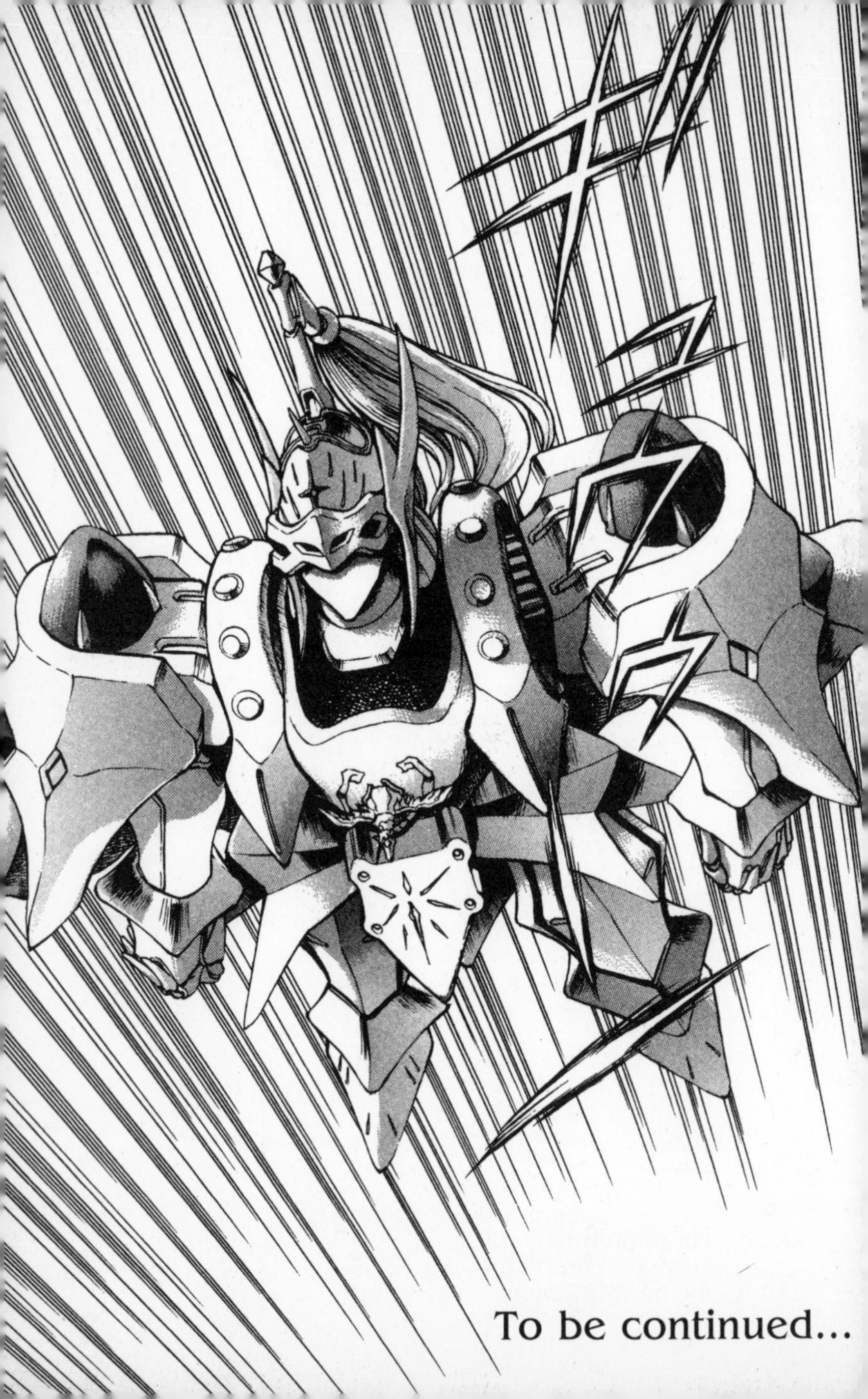
To be continued...

Author's Notes
Katsu Aki

Hey, Katsu Aki here!

To clarify things a bit, this manga of *The Vision of Escaflowne* is based on the original anime concepts by Shoji Kawamori. The anime version of *Escaflowne* (I'm sure some of you have seen it) is based on those same original concepts. Because this manga project started a year and a half before the anime production, we didn't create this manga with the same storyline as the anime version.

Due to the fact that this is being published in a different medium, there are scenes we intentionally changed from the original story. However, whenever we needed to make changes to characters or episodes, we always made sure not to destroy the original world of Mr. Kawamori. In addition, we tried to stay in tune with the animated *Escaflowne* by working closely with Mr. Kawamori-- especially when we introduced new characters. (It was some endeavor; we had to send faxes to Mr. Kawamori while he was staying in Italy, and we even had to track him down once and ended up finding him on an aircraft carrier. Oops, sorry, I'm digressing.)

My policy used to be that I only worked on originals pieces, but (perhaps because I'm older) I decided to take on this job in order to tackle a new challenge. So there you go.

From anime to manga. From manga to anime. There are many different approaches you can take, but please note and enjoy the differences between the

178

two types of media (as well as the differences in the story). It should come off as quite interesting, since these two versions stem from the same original concept.

Nonetheless, I hope you can enjoy both Mr. Kawamori's world, which provided the base and structure for everything, and my story, which I couldn't help giving a bit of my own flair. Very well then. I hope to continue to share *The Vision of Escaflowne* with you, and I hope you'll stay through the growth of Van and Hitomi with me.
April, 1996

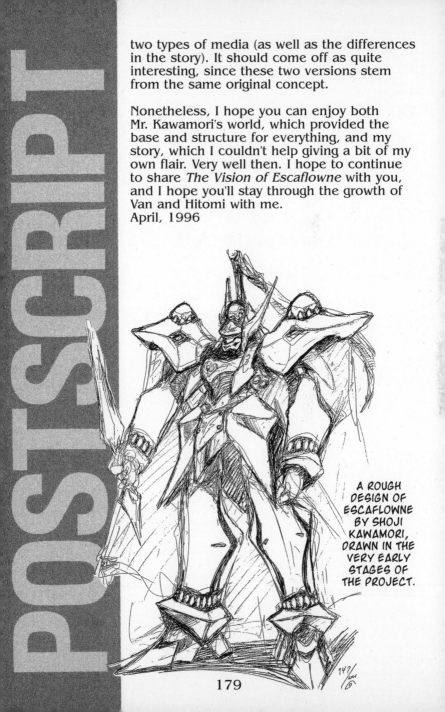

A ROUGH DESIGN OF ESCAFLOWNE BY SHOJI KAWAMORI, DRAWN IN THE VERY EARLY STAGES OF THE PROJECT.

179

In the next volume of

THE VISION OF ESCAFLOWNE

Unaware of Queen Escalina's fate, Hitomi, Van and Shian continue their quest for the missing monarch. The search leads them into the magical Forest of Deception where they must fight for their lives against Zaibach warriors while fighting for their sanity against the visions of the mad forest. Just when it seems things can't get any worse, Hitomi faces a terrible choice between giving up her life on Earth or sacrificing her newfound friends. What follows will take all of Van's ability, the strength of Hitomi's heart...and a miracle.

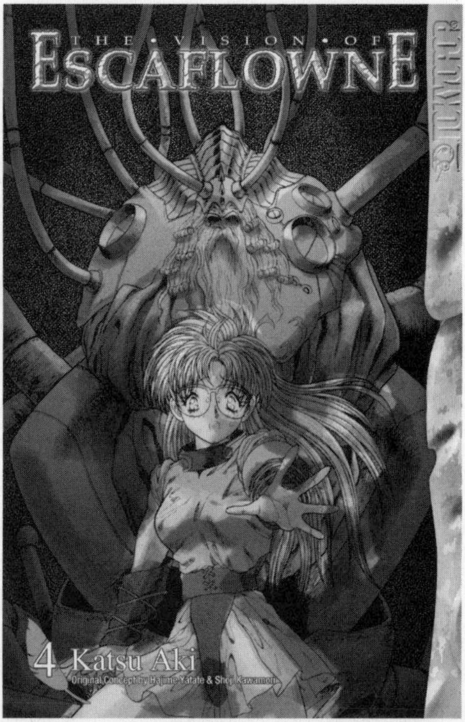
THE VISION OF ESCAFLOWNE
4 Katsu Aki
Original Concept by Hajime Yatate & Shoji Kawamori

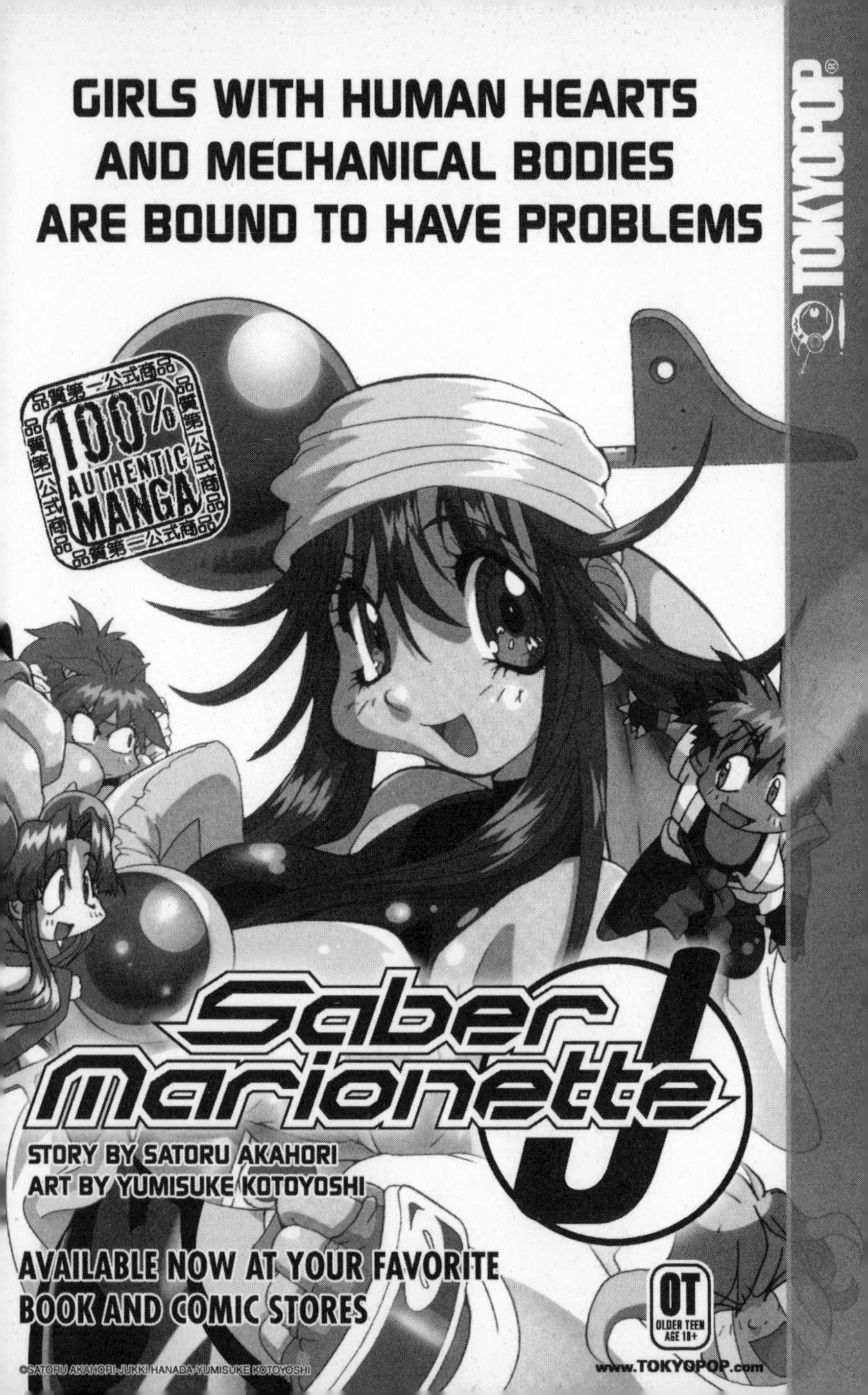
TOKYOPOP®
GIRLS WITH HUMAN HEARTS AND MECHANICAL BODIES ARE BOUND TO HAVE PROBLEMS
100% AUTHENTIC MANGA
Saber Marionette J
STORY BY SATORU AKAHORI
ART BY YUMISUKE KOTOYOSHI
AVAILABLE NOW AT YOUR FAVORITE BOOK AND COMIC STORES
OT OLDER TEEN AGE 16+
©SATORU AKAHORI·JUKKI HANADA·YUMISUKE KOTOYOSHI
www.TOKYOPOP.com

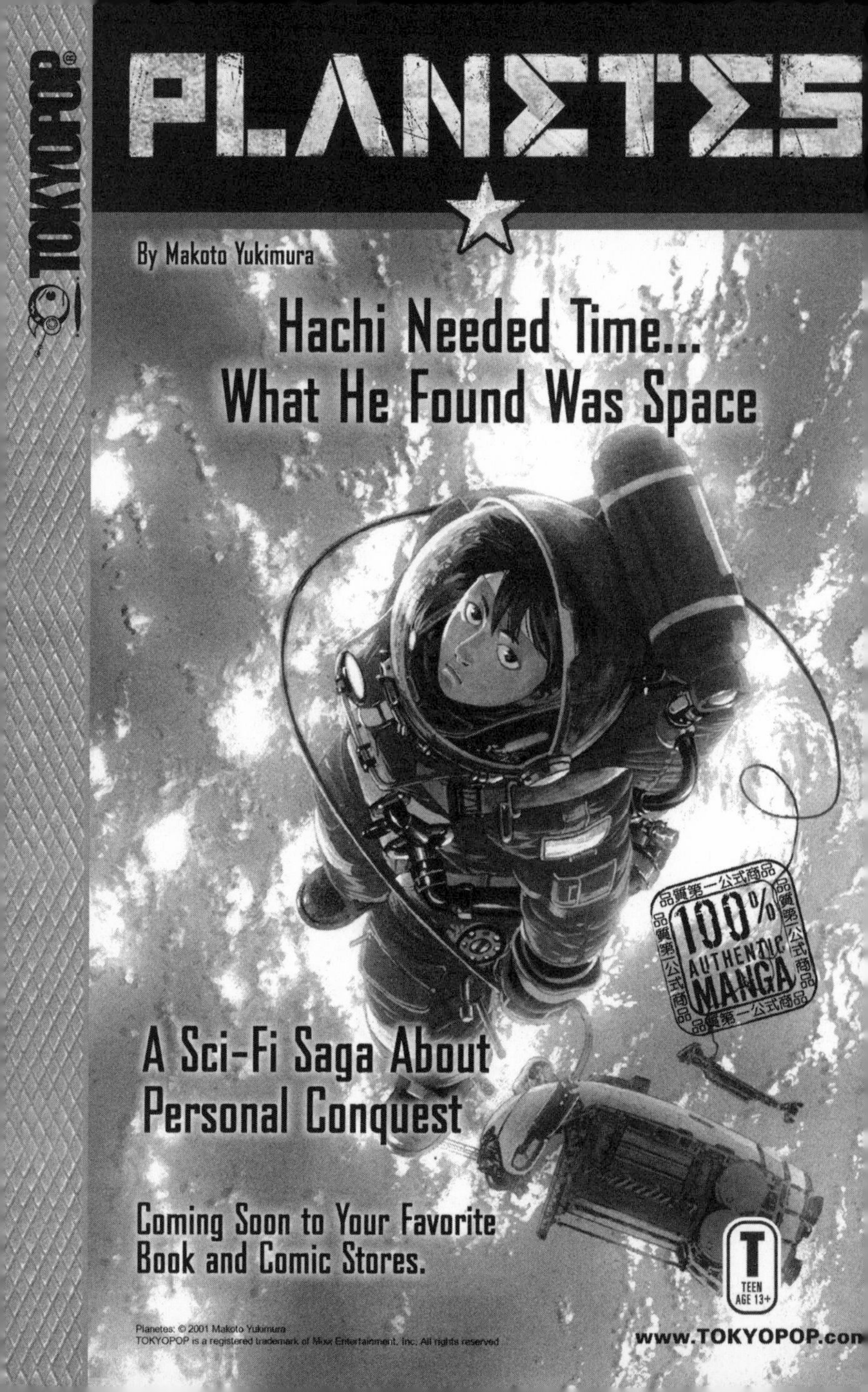
TOKYOPOP®
PLANETES
By Makoto Yukimura
Hachi Needed Time...
What He Found Was Space
品質第一公式商品
100% AUTHENTIC MANGA
A Sci-Fi Saga About
Personal Conquest
Coming Soon to Your Favorite
Book and Comic Stores.
T
TEEN
AGE 13+
Planetes: © 2001 Makoto Yukimura
TOKYOPOP is a registered trademark of Mixx Entertainment, Inc. All rights reserved
www.TOKYOPOP.com

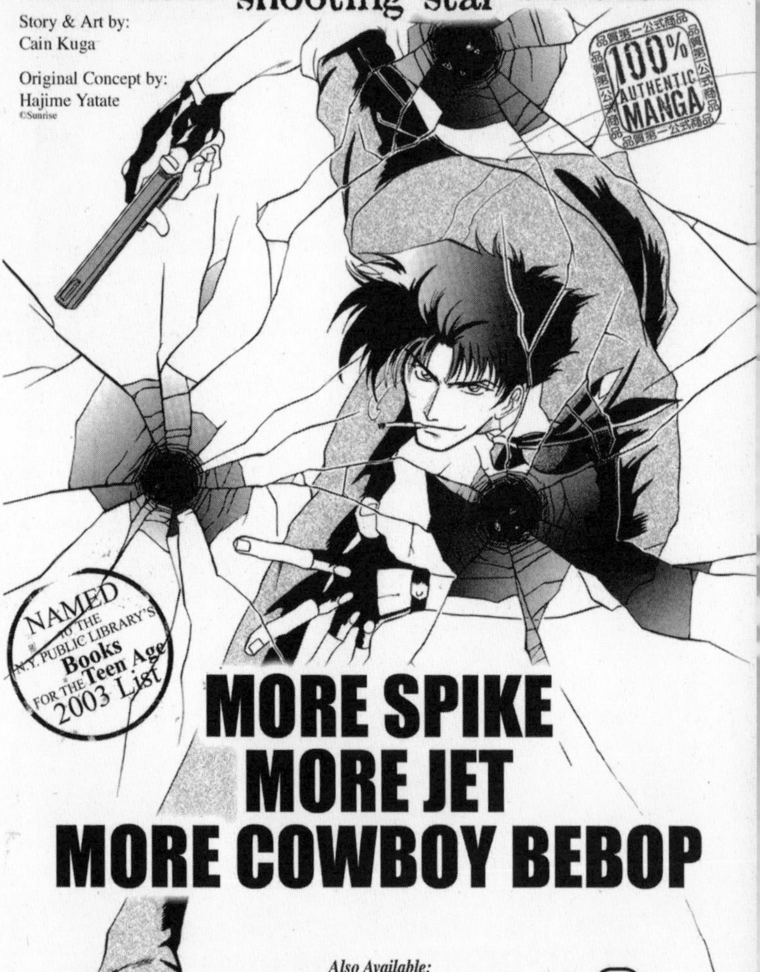

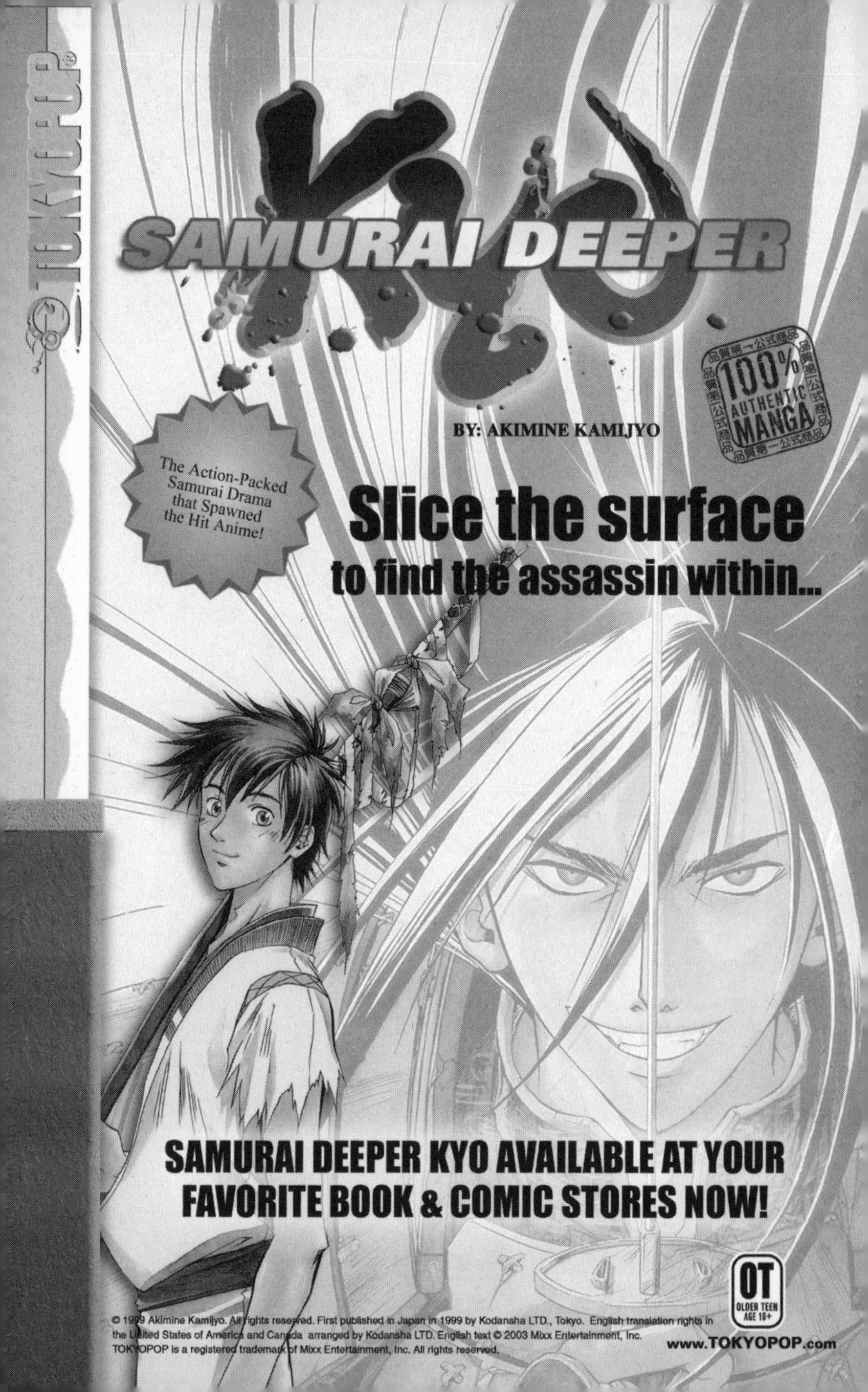
TOKYOPOP
SAMURAI DEEPER KYO
100% AUTHENTIC MANGA
BY: AKIMINE KAMIJYO
The Action-Packed Samurai Drama that Spawned the Hit Anime!
Slice the surface
to find the assassin within...
SAMURAI DEEPER KYO AVAILABLE AT YOUR FAVORITE BOOK & COMIC STORES NOW!
OT OLDER TEEN AGE 16+
© 1999 Akimine Kamijyo. All rights reserved. First published in Japan in 1999 by Kodansha LTD., Tokyo. English translation rights in the United States of America and Canada arranged by Kodansha LTD. English text © 2003 Mixx Entertainment, Inc. TOKYOPOP is a registered trademark of Mixx Entertainment, Inc. All rights reserved.
www.TOKYOPOP.com

CHRONICLES OF THE
CURSED
SWORD

BY YUY BEOP-RYONG

A living sword forged in darkness
A hero born outside the light
One can destroy the other
But both can save the world

TOKYOPOP®

Available Now At Your Favorite
Book And Comic Stores.

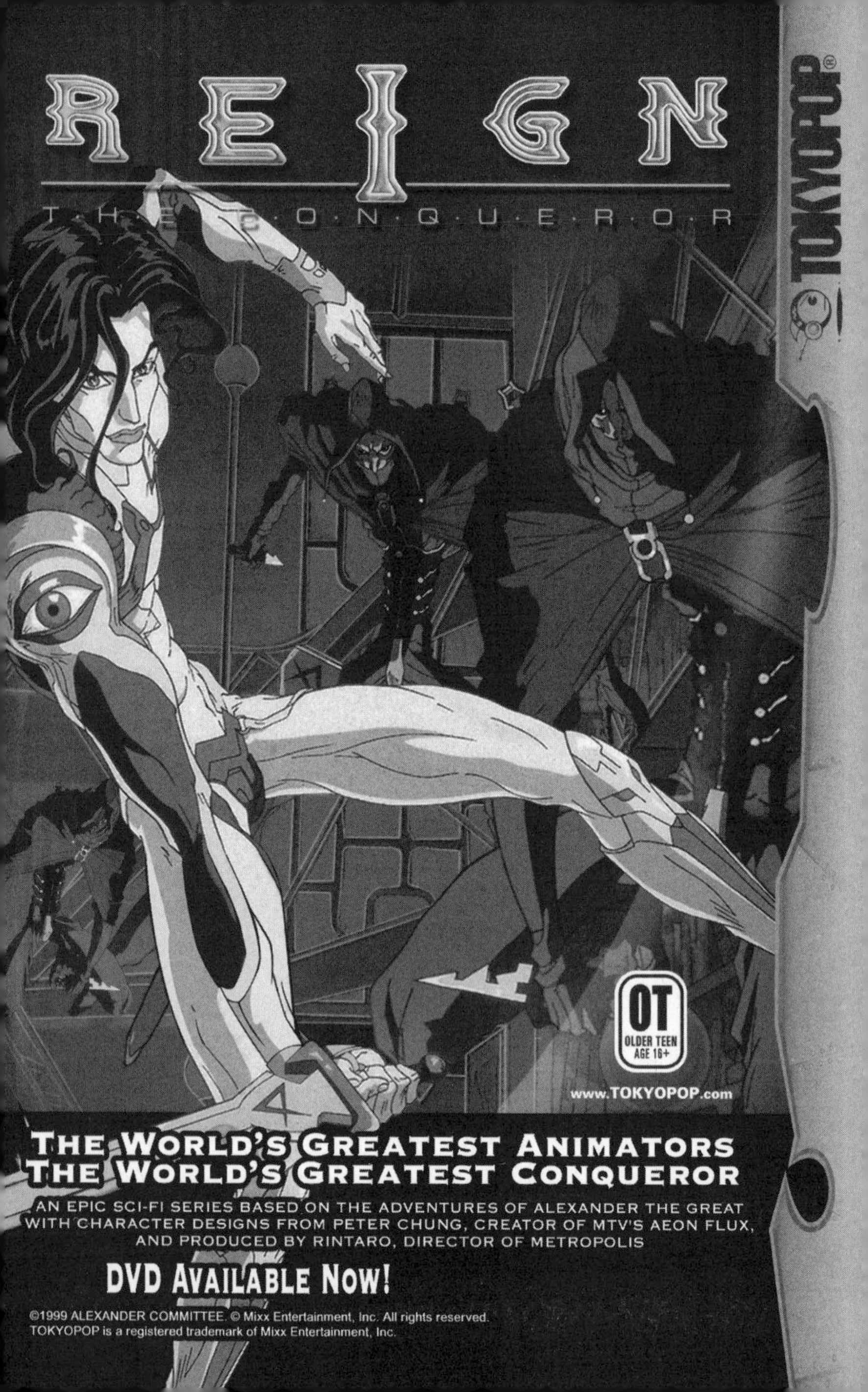
REIGN
THE CONQUEROR
TOKYOPOP®
OT
OLDER TEEN
AGE 16+
www.TOKYOPOP.com
THE WORLD'S GREATEST ANIMATORS
THE WORLD'S GREATEST CONQUEROR
AN EPIC SCI-FI SERIES BASED ON THE ADVENTURES OF ALEXANDER THE GREAT WITH CHARACTER DESIGNS FROM PETER CHUNG, CREATOR OF MTV'S AEON FLUX, AND PRODUCED BY RINTARO, DIRECTOR OF METROPOLIS
DVD AVAILABLE NOW!
©1999 ALEXANDER COMMITTEE. © Mixx Entertainment, Inc. All rights reserved.
TOKYOPOP is a registered trademark of Mixx Entertainment, Inc.